The Little School That Could

THE REMARKABLE STORY OF
THE CLASSICAL ACADEMY CHARTER SCHOOL
OF CLIFTON, NEW JERSEY, 1997-2016

Vincent DeRosa

The Little School That Could
The Remarkable Story of The Classical Academy Charter School of Clifton, New Jersey
(1997-2016)

Vincent DeRosa
vincentderosa44@gmail.com

ISBN: 979-8-9862174-0-6 (print)
979-8-9862174-1-3 (eBook)

Printed in the United States of America
Cover and Interior design: 1106 Design

To My Loving Wife Magda

Without Whom the Classical Academy Would Have Forever
Remained a Dream Unfulfilled

CONTENTS

ABOUT THE AUTHOR

Mr. Vincent DeRosa spent his professional career as a public-school teacher in several New Jersey middle and high schools. An award-winning classroom teacher ("Edna White Rome Prize," 1988, from the New Jersey Classical Association) for excellence in teaching Latin and Classics, he is credited with a number of "firsts" in New Jersey public education. He participated in the inaugural class (1984) of New Jersey's "Alternate Route to Teacher Certification" program and helped make that program the success it is today. He is also the state's only practicing classroom teacher to start (1997) and operate for 18 years a public Charter School, *The Classical Academy Charter School of Clifton* (New Jersey), Passaic County's first public charter school. As its singular creative, driving force—motivated by his revolutionary yet commonsense ideas on education reform and dedicated to expending Herculean efforts to implement them—he is responsible not only for founding *The Classical Academy Charter School of Clifton* but, as its long-time Lead Teacher/Principal (1997-2016), for making it one of New Jersey's most successful, earning in 2008, among other awards, the coveted National Blue Ribbon School of Excellence designation. Mr. DeRosa is also the author of: *An Act of War Unresolved: A Teacher Reveals What Is Wrong with New Jersey Public Education and How to Fix It* (to be published Winter, 2024). Mr. DeRosa resides with his wife, Magda, in Morris County, New Jersey, and spends his retirement researching and writing in the fields of education and New Jersey history, along with pursuing his landscaping and fly-fishing interests.

A NOTE TO THE READER

This work is best described as a *narrative memoir*. Like memoirs generally, this narrative does not pretend to be a work of scholarly endeavor relying on bibliographic sources and abounding in footnotes and evidentiary support of statements. This narrative emanates instead from the author's personal experiences, observations, and convictions as a lifelong New Jersey public-school teacher and principal, and his analytical conclusions based thereon.

All statistics cited in this memoir and upon which the author's comparison percentages are calculated, are from New Jersey Department of Education public information, or culled from other public sources. The views, statements, and opinions expressed in this narrative memoir are those solely of the author; they do not necessarily represent the views or beliefs of any organization, entity, or political ideology.

PREFACE

As a practicing public-school classroom teacher, I have enjoyed the rarest of opportunities and singular privilege of putting my education-reform ideas into actual practice by establishing a New Jersey public school, the Classical Academy Charter School of Clifton (New Jersey). The school was a showcase, a laboratory, if you will, which incorporated and exemplified those ideas, practices, and educational reforms I have come to believe after many years as a public-school classroom teacher, are the most critical for attaining remarkably higher student academic-learning outcomes, and at much lower costs, while fostering genuine adolescent character development.

For 18 years as the Classical Academy's chief administrator and lead teacher, those education reforms and practices guided my leadership as the paramount principles of both school operations and school philosophy. Over the course of nearly two decades, 1997-2016, of leading that public charter school, I demonstrated to supporters and critics alike that increasing less-advantaged, minority-student learning outcomes to comparatively lofty levels of student attainment—despite considerably lower school funding—is not an unattainable objective.

In a real sense, the middle school (grades 6-8) I founded and operated was a working demonstration for solving chronic problems of public education, epitomized by the "high costs-low results" phenomenon of New Jersey public education. The Classical Academy Charter School of Clifton, New Jersey, because of the transformative educational policies and practices I formulated and implemented, became an iconoclastic "high results-low costs" exemplary model public middle school. My narrative memoir explains how this remarkable and noteworthy accomplishment, so contrary to the accustomed pattern of public education, was achieved while overcoming formidable opponents and daunting obstacles.

Another persistent problem facing public education is the "learning gap" between children of more affluent parents and those reared in lower household-income families. As the reader will see, the Classical Academy Charter School of Clifton also solved this seemingly intractable dilemma, thus demonstrating that both these systemic defects of public education—high costs-low results, and the wide learning gap between advantaged and disadvantaged students—can be greatly reduced, if not eliminated, by following the educational reforms I designed and initiated.

The dedicated purpose of the Classical Academy's highly successful educational reforms was to increase, rather dramatically and consistently, the academic-achievement and scholastic-learning proficiencies of every one of its students, and to attain academic proficiencies well surpassing their Clifton Public School District peers. The Classical Academy would further demonstrate each year that its students, children of immigrant, lower-income families, could reach the same high levels of academic-excellence and scholastic-learning proficiencies, objectively measured, of New Jersey's most advantaged and accomplished middle-school students. The reforms and school practices to accomplish these near-unprecedented feats in New Jersey public education may be radical to some, but they are decidedly not theoretical. Their effectiveness has been proved for nearly two decades in the actual practice and operations of a high-performing, multi award-winning New Jersey public school and documented in this narrative.

My narrative memoir, therefore, advances a public-policy exhortation for specific educational reforms I advocate and have put into practice with extraordinary success. But apart from this public-policy advocacy, there is another reason I write this memoir: To document and chronicle the history and progress of the Classical Academy Charter School of Clifton, New Jersey, Passaic County's first public charter school. It would be an historical crime if the fierce struggles and savory victories, the "David and Goliath" battles and the monumental triumphs of this school were left untold and unrecorded. Who better to narrate this heroic story than I, the person whose ideas and determination gave birth to the school and who, as Principal and Lead Teacher, was its guiding force for nearly two decades.

Vincent and Magda DeRosa, Co-Founders,
The Classical Academy Charter School of Clifton, New Jersey

Chapter I

THE MAKING OF A RADICAL EDUCATION REFORMIST

That the reader may have a fuller and more insightful understanding of this narrative memoir, it behooves me to speak briefly about my own past and motivations. Having earned two undergraduate degrees, a BA in Philosophy and a BA in Classics, and a Master's degree in Classics, I, after several years' scholastic respite, undertook full-time Doctoral studies in Classics at Rutgers University, financially aided by an adjunct teaching post in "Introductory Latin" and "Etymology: Medical Terms from Latin and Greek." As with most in this field, I aspired toward a college teaching position in one of the traditional subsets of the classics discipline: classical languages, ancient Greek and Roman history, classical culture, philosophy, and archeology. My own interests led me to concentrate on classical philosophy, history, and the Latin language.

The prospects of securing at that time a full-time, tenure-track college teaching position in the classics field was, I had come to learn with disappointment, so extremely rare as to be virtually nonexistent. This sad reality was reinforced by the testimonies of numerous persons who, having had recently earned the doctorate in Classics, woefully related their disheartening job-search efforts. The best employment prospects a few recent doctorate recipients had reported was filling in for tenured professors' sabbatical leaves for a semester or two, and then having to search for other, temporary replacement positions every four to eight months in colleges and universities across the country, much like vagabond scholars—and these we esteemed the *fortunate* ones!

1

It was in the early 1980s that, soon after I had commenced a PhD in Classics at Rutgers University, public K-12 education became a top national issue. The 1983 publication of the Federal Government Commission on Education report, *A Nation at Risk: The Imperative for Educational Reform,*" had touched off a wave of education-improvement efforts. No state governor took action as quickly and energetically for substantial state education reform than the popular New Jersey Republican Governor Thomas Kean (1982-1990). Along with his appointed state Commissioner of Education, Saul Cooperman, the two boldly set out to confront New Jersey's K-12 public-education system, energized as they were by the ominously dire, often-quoted warnings the "A Nation at Risk" report proclaimed: "The educational foundations of our society are presently being eroded by a rising tide of mediocrity that threatens our very future as a Nation and a people"; and, "If an unfriendly foreign power had attempted to impose on America the mediocre educational performance that exists today, we might well have viewed it as an act of war."

Governor Kean and Education Commissioner Cooperman were attacked, reviled, impeded, and opposed at every stage of every proposed education reform they advanced by the state's teachers' union (NJEA), long New Jersey's most powerful educational special-interest group, together with its allies and elected state officials beholden to it. Despite the political obstacles and controversies, these two men were successful in many of the education reforms they promulgated, for which they were counted among the nation's most admired and productive education-reform team, and placing New Jersey in the forefront of education-reforming states.

Minimum starting salary for teachers of $18,500 (remember, we are speaking nearly 40 years ago), state takeover of failing ("academically bankrupt") school districts, mandated student testing for proficiency standards, mandated subject-matter tests for aspiring teachers, and Governor's Schools for Teacher Training were, among other initiatives, some of the more noteworthy Governor Kean-Commissioner Cooperman reforms.

Perhaps their most important, enduring education reform, and the one most duplicated across the country, was New Jersey's "Alternate Route to Teacher Certification" program. A prominent theme in the "A

Nation at Risk" report was how poorly trained America's teachers were and how relatively few had adequate subject-matter knowledge, especially in middle- and high-school academic subjects. Most of America's K-12 teachers came to the classrooms with loads of "education courses" in their collegiate histories, but they possessed shockingly insufficient training in or meager knowledge of the subjects they were hired to instruct students, particularly in science, mathematics, and English-language arts. The "A Nation at Risk" report criticized this long-standing practice, blaming it for populating our schools with subject-matter deficient teachers.

The objective of the "Alternate Route to Teacher Certification" was to open the doors to New Jersey classrooms for individuals well trained and well educated in their academic subject areas but lacking "education" or "pedagogy" courses. In New Jersey, as in other states, prospective teachers pursuing their career objectives in colleges or departments of education were required to devote a significant part of their undergraduate or graduate training to education courses. Traditionally, prospective teachers filled their schedules with courses in "education" or "methodologies," while taking few courses in or devoting much study to the academic subject in which they were intending to instruct students. Collegiate departments of education taught students *how* to teach, and if one knew *how* to teach, as education colleges insisted, one could teach any subject to anyone, notwithstanding one's poor knowledge of the subject itself.

Indeed, colleges and departments of education were the gatekeepers for the teaching profession and the authorities vested with teacher-credentialing powers. For the first time, the "Alternate Route to Teacher Certification" made it possible to become a teacher in New Jersey without graduating from a college of education, and without the requirement of taking a barrel-full of college courses in "education," which most subject-matter specialists lacked—and, frankly, abhorred.

Removing the bar of education courses would allow subject-matter, content-rich trained individuals to become classroom teachers. The "Alternate Route to Teacher Certification" would, therefore, permit public schools to select from a highly trained pool of state-licensed people hitherto excluded from New Jersey classrooms, and simultaneously increase statewide the cadre of desirable, well-prepared, subject-matter trained teacher candidates to benefit students.

The "Alternate Route to Teacher Certification" was hotly debated and fiercely opposed. The teachers' union and colleges of education, always collaborators in determining how public education is to be conducted in New Jersey, were drawn even closer in their mutual opposition. That people could be duly licensed to teach without submitting to what they had established as foundational knowledge and criteria for a professional teacher, was to them as bizarre as it was absurd. After all, could a person become a lawyer without attending law school? Could a person become a doctor without graduating medical school? It follows then that a person cannot become a teacher without attending or graduating from a "teacher college." (The telling retort was: "Under the existing teacher-certification rules, Albert Einstein—who never graduated from a "teachers" college and was not a "certified" teacher—would be deemed unqualified and thus barred from teaching mathematics to New Jersey students because he lacked "education" courses and thereby could not be teacher certified").

Feeling threatened to the point of becoming irrelevant, if not fearing pending extinction, the state's colleges of education, together with its allied teachers' union, undertook an intense, lengthy battle to defeat the Alternate Route plan. They hoped to convince legislators and the public that this program would welcome dangerously unqualified people into the classrooms, who were certain to damage students and create problems for the schools that would be seduced into hiring them.

Despite overwhelming opposition, the "Alternate Route to Teacher Certification" was scheduled to go into effect during the 1984-85 school year, precisely the time period when I was pondering my future: After already earning three degrees, should I toil for the next 3-5 years pursuing a doctorate in a field of study which I loved but in which winning a college teaching position was near impossible, or should I, perhaps, if not lower my sights, at least consider a different but perhaps satisfying pedagogical career path? A number of my peers in my same dilemma turned to law school. Knowing that our country was replete with lawyers, and confident that I would not enjoy dealing with peoples' legal or emotional problems every day, I eschewed this popular alternative to the professorate.

Reading about the problems in K-12 public education, which after the publication of the "A Nation at Risk" report was a frequent topic in the press and in national dialogue, I became informed of the education-reform initiatives Governor Thomas Kean proposed. One initiative was New Jersey's unique but controversial way of becoming a classroom teacher; I decided to make inquiries into the "Alternate Route to Teacher Certification" program. I completed the application and submitted my credentials for evaluation as the first required step for potential "Alternate Route" participants. The New Jersey Department of Education determined I was academically eligible, due to the subjects comprising my undergraduate and graduate degrees, for three subject-matter endorsements or licenses for public-school teaching: Latin, History (social studies), and English. (Since Philosophy and Classics are not disciplines recognized for teacher licensure or certification in K-12 education, it was the accepted convention in New Jersey that these college majors or concentrations, being highly literate fields of study, would equate to a middle- or high-school English certification).

Being accepted into the program's inaugural class, and suspending my doctoral studies in Classics, I, along with about 120 other aspirants statewide, composed the first group of Alternate Route teachers in New Jersey. Education Commissioner Cooperman told us, as we embarked on the program, that much depended on our success and that being in the vanguard of this fiercely opposed reform, the future of the entire "Alternate Route to Teacher Certification" initiative was in our hands. Opposition to the program was still at fever pitch; there were many hoping and working toward our individual and collective failure, anxious to spur calls for the program's early demise. With my academic credentials certified, having easily passed all subject-matter tests in my three teaching fields of teaching certification, and armed with the "CE" (certificate of eligibility), thus permitting me to seek public-school employment, I hastened my job search.

The "Alternate Route to Teacher Certification" was disparaged and feared, and some of the program's obligation on schools, such as that the hiring school must provide a "full-time" mentor for the first 20 days of employment, strongly discouraged schools from hiring anyone in the Alternate Route program. Most of the 120 aspirants in the program's inaugural class found securing employment difficult. No schools apart from those in the urban areas, which perennially had high turnover of teachers and usually always had teaching vacancies, would, for a moment, consider hiring teachers from the Alternate Route program's inaugural year.

My job search shared these difficulties. However, there were a few schools where Latin remained in their foreign-language curricula, and certified Latin teachers were scarce. This advantage did give me some employment opportunities, especially as I was certified in two other subjects and could serve two positions, thereby making my employment more appealing to school administrators and acquiring a full-time teaching post for myself more likely.

After some months of seeking employment, I was offered and took a position at an urban high school where 80% of students were African American. My assignment was to teach three classes of 11th- and 12th-grade English, and two classes of Latin to 8th graders who were in the school's "Gifted and Talented" program.

For Alternate Route teachers, the first year was rigorous and demanding. Teaching academic subjects for the first time to adolescents—planning lessons, scrutinizing learning materials, marking papers, creating tests, dealing with discipline issues—while having to attend a once-(sometimes twice)-a-week three-hour evening class, and sometimes all day on Saturdays to compensate for our lack of "education courses," and to perform the work associated with these seminars, could discourage even the most determined among us. At the completion of our year in the Alternate Route program (the program's inaugural year), the feedback and reports from supervisors, principals, parents, and students were quite heartening. Overall, the first group of Alternate Route teachers had proved themselves worthy by their high degree of subject-matter competence and knowledge, excellent pedagogical skills, indefatigable work habits, and fine classroom-management abilities.

Thanks to the talents and hard work of the first group of Alternate Route aspiring participants, among whom I am proud to count myself, the first year of New Jersey's "Alternate Route to Teacher Certification" was a success, justifying the program's continuance and expansion. To the immense benefit ever after of generations of New Jersey students, and vindicating Governor Kean and Commissioner Cooperman's teacher-education reform ideas, important elements of the original "Alternate Route to Teacher Certification" program are today common requirements for all people desiring to obtain a New Jersey teaching certificate and license.

After a year of teaching at my first school, an urban high school, receiving high supervisory evaluations, and upon successful completion of the "Alternate Route" program requirements, I earned my full (permanent) teaching licenses in English, social studies, and Latin (I am the first person in New Jersey to receive a Latin teaching certification via the "Alternate Route"). I remained teaching at this school for another year.

For the next fourteen or so years, I taught at three other schools—receiving tenure at all the schools in which I was employed for three years or more. Incidentally, I was an unenthusiastic, dues-paying member of the NJEA (teachers' union) at every school; peer pressure and the wish to get along with my colleagues would not allow otherwise. My choice of employment and schools sometimes had to do with commuting distances, but more often to gain the opportunity to see the operations and structures of a variety of schools. I was also eager to see how different, if at all, schools were in their functioning and school cultures. To do so on a more "scientific" basis, I selected schools with differing school demographics or socio-economic factors, and among high- or low-performing schools. During these years my classroom-teaching experiences took me from my initial urban high school, to an affluent middle school, to a large high school in a "middle-class" area, and, finally, to a combination middle school-high school in another affluent area.

Adding to my ever-diverse working experiences as a teacher, I was simultaneously and voraciously absorbing the growing literature on the issues of public K-12 education. Both in my firsthand experiences as a classroom teacher in various schools and in consuming writings and ideas on education reform, I secured an ever-increasing understanding and insight about public education: its problems, the alleged reasons for those problems, and a plethora of remedies and reforms to solve them.

My intimate, wide-ranging experiences at that time—and now reaffirmed after having amassed 34 years in New Jersey public education—convinced me that, if the purported goal of K-12 education is to provide, if not a serious academic education, with high standards for every student, then, at best, merely a universally mediocre or even a poor academic education by any standard, no better system for perpetuating the "high costs-low results" dilemma could be devised by man than that which I observed and lived daily as a public-school academic-subject classroom teacher. Indeed, if the New Jersey Department of Education, legislators, and the education establishment at all levels had deliberately conspired to contravene their constitutional obligation of a "thorough and efficient" educational system, and purposely intended to create a manifestly shallow and ineffective K-12 public-education system which inevitably and chronically produces low statewide student academic-learning outcomes at exorbitant taxpayer cost, they could not have constructed a better system than that which they have long imposed upon us.

When the results of standardized testing are revealed each year, or other revelatory indices of poor student performance if not outright failure are publicly released, everyone, from the individual school district, teachers' union, the New Jersey Department of Education, to elected officials and parents, all predictably lament the results and declare "More must be done," or confidently predict "We can and will do better."

The typical solutions to disappointing standardized test scores and other measures of systemic deficiencies are more resources, more programs, and more spending. A vociferous clamor, like a contagion, spreads, demanding smaller classes, expanding school breakfast/lunch programs, more counselors, more student-support services, more "Head Start," more "Pre-K," more technology, more teachers, better facilities, higher teacher pay, and similar popular nostrums. "It is despicably shameful to shortchange our kids and deprive them of a future they deserve, otherwise, we jeopardize the future of America," so the defenders of the existing and manifestly counterproductive system invariably proclaim. In truth, those who ignore or defend the true reasons for our deficient educational system are the loudest in decrying the system's inevitable mournful consequences.

They feign outrage by the terrible results they themselves cause or allow to continue!

My observations and firsthand experiences over a long period gave me a growing, intimate understanding of what was truly wrong with the public-education system—and why so many New Jersey students leave our schools academically poorly educated while the financial costs are so high. Having a practiced, intimate insight into these matters, I would often commiserate silently with myself or unburden my feelings to a sympathetic colleague when alone in the teachers' lounge. Concerned with employment repercussions and union-brotherhood solidarity, or displaying a "What's the use?" mentality reflecting the impossibility of changing or even improving a stratified, well-entrenched bureaucratic system over which they have no influence or authority, few other serious educators would openly challenge the true underlying reasons for New Jersey public-education's deficiencies and, in many schools, patent failures. Even those few educators recognizing the true causes of systemic academic mediocrity, could never be persuaded to raise their voices for the needed changes in an overarching system in which they are as insignificant as they are powerless. Acknowledging their impotency ever to improve student-learning academic outcomes, disenchanted but perceptive and ambitious classroom educators have only two pathways to eliminate frustrations and to improve their low status: desert the classroom and climb the school executive-administrative ladder, thus becoming part of the prevailing though feckless bureaucracy, or leave teaching in pursuit of other more satisfying career fields. A third option, that which I pursued, of creating oneself a public-school free from the endemic causes of education mediocrity and failure, is so extraordinary both in difficulty and rarity that it is not a conceivable option for those teachers dreaming of implementing their education reform convictions and ideas.

The reasons for public education's inadequacies and indeed failures, as I have concluded from long, direct experience and acquired understanding, are identified by the shocking misuse of school-day time and its large allocation to non-academic pursuits. The prevailing "anti-academic school culture," so inimical to academic learning, is also prevalent in every school in every community, and sustained by the emphasis, indeed priority, of "extra/co-curricular" pursuits and "interscholastic sports." Teachers' union contract terms and conditions suppressing teacher initiative and motivation are yet another cause of educational failure. New Jersey's state-imposed non-academic curricular demands which every school district must follow contributes strongly to poor academic learning outcomes, and compels the misuse of school-day time. Public education's virulently counterproductive, systemically perverse teacher incentives and the purposeful denial of the attributes of the real professions to the work of teaching, is too a factor in poor student learning. Deficient academic student learning outcomes are also a result of state education laws and regulations, often enacted at the behest of the teacher's union and intended to legalize and perpetuate its preferred practices and policies--thus ensuring its dominant influence in public education while making it near impossible to implement critically needed changes to the educational system. Lastly, the monopoly status of every public school in every New Jersey community prevents both meaningful competition and parental choice in education. All these, I have come to learn, account for the chronically disappointing student academic-learning outcomes that still undergrids the ominous "A Nation at Risk" assessment of 40 years ago.

After many years of being a public-education classroom teacher and intimately observing schools' habitually ingrained, counterproductive practices and policies precluding high scholastic proficiency universally attained, I became convinced of what reforms would be effective to increase student academic-learning outcomes, and to do so at lower costs. (For a full account of my analysis on the egregious, endemic defects of New Jersey public education, I invite the reader to consult my companion work: *An Act of War Unresolved: A Teacher Reveals What Is Wrong with New Jersey Public Education and How to Fix It,* to be published in winter, 2024.)

My diverse experiences also convinced me that all New Jersey public schools are fundamentally the same and operate according to the same systemic rules and dynamics. The reason some schools, invariably the ones in more affluent communities, are praised as "models of excellence" and have higher student-learning outcomes, is not because of greater funding, or because of the presumptive superiority of its teachers or administrators. Nor do "model schools" achieve higher learning results because of assumed greater creativity, talent, and motivation of its faculty and "executive educators" (administrators). High-performing schools and their comparative success—admired as "lighthouse schools" (a foolishly vapid designation the state once used for them)—owe that success to one factor and one factor only: the higher affluence and educational backgrounds of the parents of the students attending the school.

Schools in affluent areas operate nearly identically to those in urban areas, and so do all schools in between, from high middle-class to low middle-class schools. In public education, demographics is everything. What few differences that exist among public schools in every New Jersey community are but superficial and inconsequential to student academic-learning outcomes. All New Jersey public schools operate with essentially the same practices and policies, with basically identical curricula, the same emphasis on "extra-curricular" and "co-curricular" activities; the same predominating presence of "non-academic" classes; the same state mandates and regulations; the same ill-use of school-day time; the same emphasis on interscholastic sports; the same costly bureaucratic structures; the same degree of teachers' union control and dominance; the same systemically "perverted teacher incentives"; the same "Club Med for Kids" school ethos, and all generating the same "anti-academic school culture."

So convinced that I had unquestionably identified the causes—policies and practices—for public-education failings, and confident that I could demonstrate how to improve educational outcomes and elevate student-learning outcomes of all students, that I left public-school employment to spend nearly two years developing a school free from all the causes I had come to learn were responsible for low student academic outcomes and high financial costs.

I moved to Burlington County, New Jersey, which, at that time, had the greatest population growth in the state but lacked non-public-school choices to serve the growing population, a large segment of which were young families. I developed brochures and a prospectus detailing the proposed curricula and other distinctive elements of a school I named "*The*

Classical Academy of New Jersey." Working with tax records and other public documents to secure names and addresses of potentially interested county residents, I sent informational prospectuses to families who might be persuaded to enroll children in a new school of the type I proposed. I held informational group meetings with interested parties, and I developed a classical humanities summer enrichment program as an introduction to the school. Having rented summer classroom space at a local public school and securing a student enrollment of 30 students spanning grades 8 to 10, in which I was the sole teacher, this summer enrichment program was successful and received high parent praise and approval.

Despite my assiduous efforts and client satisfaction, and since this was, by necessity, a private school, I inevitably faced all the insurmountable obstacles and roadblocks in starting, singlehandedly, a non-public institution. The primary problem was funding, for starting a private school required a financial investment in addition to tuition far more than I could ever afford or ever secure from external sources. I sadly came to accept that my dream and noble experiment was quixotic, an unobtainable ambition. But in creating the components and principles of this projected school, The Classical Academy of New Jersey, I would be, unbeknown to me at the time, developing the prototype for a school I actually did establish some years hence under New Jersey's newly adopted charter-school legislation (passed 1995, effective January 1996).

Chapter II

THE CLASSICAL ACADEMY CHARTER SCHOOL OF CLIFTON: INCIPIENT STIRRINGS

A Dream Revived

After nearly two years of strenuous effort, my hopes of starting a private school, The Classical Academy of New Jersey, were as hopelessly moribund as once were my forlorn hopes of becoming a college professor of classics. Happily, I was soon to take a wife, a most wonderful young lady whose Roman Catholic family had immigrated to Canada from the Middle East some years ago. Our love for each other greatly animated our passionate determination to create for ourselves a beautiful, loving, and happy life together. Both blessed with parents who reared us with boundless love, ever enriching us with their examples of virtue and character, we inherited models of familial bliss and joyful togetherness. A few months before our wedding in Canada, I secured a part-time, middle-school, Latin-teaching position in an affluent Bergen County school district. The following year, the position became full-time, as I was contracted to teach several English classes along with my assigned Latin instruction.

My new wife and I lived in a small, second-floor apartment in a Clifton, New Jersey, home owned by my family. My newlywed, who has degrees in accounting and business, and fluently speaks, in addition to English, French and Arabic, soon obtained work in a nearby bank. Our sole, mutual objective was to save enough money from our modest salaries to purchase our own home, an objective we single-mindedly pursued for several very joyful years.

Our satisfying lives were proceeding predictably and happily. The addition of Magda, my wife, to my immediate and extended family was greeted with the utmost warmth and affection. My father and mother, of blessed memory, would often say that Magda brought such happiness into our family and that they loved her as their own daughter. My teaching career was also advancing well; when hired, I was placed on the highest salary guideline (MA+30 credits) and given some consideration for my teaching experience. My school district paid among the higher teacher salaries in Bergen County. In three years, I earned tenure; my instructional competence and effectiveness were consistently evaluated high, and my overall contributions to students and the school were praiseworthy. For the most part, students in my Latin and English classes were eager and well-disciplined; their parents frequently possessed graduate and professional degrees. As for public-school teaching, I had reached something of the vocation's apogee, and I esteemed myself fortunate to enjoy many of teaching's more coveted attributes: comparatively good salary, respectful students, good working conditions, many paid vacation days, near-absolute job security with excellent healthcare benefits, and, in seven or eight years, I would be at the top of the district's relatively high pay scale for teachers. I possessed what many believe is the kind of teaching job for which most teachers strive, and once attained, are most contented to remain for the duration of their entire career. Adding to our contentment, Magda and I were making fine progress of saving money toward our home-buying goal.

Then, in 1996, something of an earthquake struck our placid lives, strong enough potentially to derail my (and my wife's) gratifyingly stable life and careers. In 1996, one year after the New Jersey legislature passed its charter-school legislation, permitting creation of this new type of free public school, 13 New Jersey charter school applications were competitively awarded charter approval. If successful in fulfilling their charter-application expectations for facility acquisition and demonstrating financial viability, among completing several other application prerequisites, these 13 charter schools, the first schools of this type in New Jersey, would open in September 1997.

Reading about the recently enacted charter-school legislation, the first charter-school applications to be approved, and the schools which would begin in less than a year, my dormant-yet-far-from-extinguished passion of starting "my own school" was ardently aroused. I remembered the time, effort, and deep commitment I had devoted to my quixotic dream of founding The Classical Academy of New Jersey, a dream never forgotten but buried in my consciousness as unobtainable, an ambition never consummated.

Forgetting momentarily the impossibility of this dream ever becoming manifest, and like a person captured by irrational passion, I ecstatically reviewed rapidly in my mind what policies and practices by which my charter school would be operated: What curricula would be required to assure increased academic student learning? What elements of a resurrected traditional classical curriculum would I employ? What practices would I utilize to create an "academics first" school and school culture? I breathlessly envisioned a school which would be free of all those endemic public-school attributes which I had ascribed responsible for preventing or retarding so many students from achieving a high-quality, life-enriching, serious academic education. I envisioned, too, how my charter school would differ from traditional public-school structures and operational methods compelling the inevitable outcomes of "high costs, low results" and, instead, create an institution of "low costs, high results."

My composure became more sober as I turned my thoughts away from the nature and composition of the school about which I fantasized, and toward the possibility, however arrogant and impertinent, of daring to elevate myself to the same caliber as those 13 trailblazing charter-school leaders who had secured state charter approval for their proposed schools. They were well-funded and well-connected, so I imagined, having influence and advantages of the kind that I, a humble Latin teacher, did not and never would possess. Yet the prospect of fulfilling my dream, however improbable and unlikely, persisted in my consciousness.

Is it remotely possible, I wistfully speculated, that, on the force of my convictions and reasoning, on the strength of my charter-school proposals, on the kind of innovations and radical school reforms I championed, on the sort of educative curricula I would propose, on the policies and practices by which the school would operate, and on my pledged tireless efforts to bring to reality and successfully manage a proposed charter school, I could conceivably dare to think of winning state approval for my proposed charter school? Gradually, over a period of weeks and after many conversations about the matter with my wife, Magda, and my family, I resolved, fortified by my wife's limitless support and loving encouragement, to request and to submit a New Jersey charter-school application.

The charter-school application had to be submitted by October 1, 1997, for a school to become fully operational in September 1998, a year after charter-school application submission. My wife and I began the application project in May 1997, toward the end of my school-employment year, with the intention of total commitment for writing and completing the application during the summer months. My first step was to gather and review all the materials I had written or utilized for the private school I once hoped to start, The Classical Academy of New Jersey. I decided that the charter school would be in Clifton, New Jersey, the city in which I and my wife resided and in which had every expectation to remain. As a concerned resident, I also acquired considerable knowledge and understanding of the Clifton community and its public schools.

Charter-school law required that the term "charter" appear in the title/name of all charter schools; we thus selected the name "The Classical Academy Charter School of Clifton," a variant appellation of my previous attempt at school creation. The name also reflects the proposed charter school's humanities/liberal arts orientation of academic studies, to include those of a traditional "classical" curriculum (Latin, ancient Greek and Roman mythology and history, and the epics of Homer and Virgil in English translations, for example).

Historically, Clifton, New Jersey, was and still is a city of immigrants. Its first European settlement by 12 Dutch families, led by the Vreeland brothers, was established in 1679, a few years after England took control from the Dutch of the New Netherland territories in the New World. These families "immigrated" 18 miles northwest from what is now Jersey City inland to the banks of the Passaic River to make a land acquisition from Native Americans, called the "Aquackanonk Purchase." That region today encompasses not only Clifton City but also the cities of Passaic and Paterson, and the boroughs of Woodlawn Park and Little Falls. For a century, it remained nearly all Dutch in language and custom until the Revolutionary War, and it remained rural and agricultural until early industrialization and the advent of the railroads, soon after the Civil War.

The old "Aquackanonk Purchase" region was among the first to be heavily industrialized in post-Civil War America. The ever-growing diversity of the area's extensive manufacturing attracted immigrants of the kind common to northeastern cities, Irish and German in the 19th century, and then, in the early 20th century, Italians, Eastern Europeans, and Poles. From about the 1970s, large numbers of Hispanics and smaller groups of Arabic people took up residence in Clifton, many buying modest homes for the first time. To these people, as to immigrants before them, Clifton was seen as their first modest step upward into the lower middle-class—but middle-class nonetheless.

By 1997, the year I undertook the charter-school application process, Clifton public schools had a mixed academic reputation. Its elementary schools performed adequately, but its two very large middle schools and its one 4,000-student high school produced quite poor learning outcomes, as evidenced on standardized testing. Student learning outcomes mirrored those of the rather low student academic achievement-levels typical of the socio-economic characteristics of "D/E" District Factor Group school districts, in which Clifton was categorized. After the 2000 national census, Clifton's DFG was lowered one step to "C/D." The biggest complaint from parents was not primarily the questionable academic education their students were receiving, but the large student-population sizes of the middle and high schools. Bullying, school bureaucratic inertia and unresponsiveness, gangs, student safety, undisciplined classrooms, and other problems ascribed to overcrowding and ineffective school management were common concerns among Clifton parents.

Clifton seemed a most fitting locality for a charter school and for the educational choice at the 6th- to 12th-grade levels (middle and high school) it would provide Clifton parents. In 1997, as today, Clifton Public School

District had nearly 10,000 students in K-12; its high school is the second largest in the state. There were, in 1997, several Catholic elementary schools still functioning in Clifton, while the one Clifton Catholic high school had recently become defunct. In the area, there are several private preparatory schools whose tuition is prohibitively expensive, such as Montclair Kimberly Academy, thus excluding most Clifton residents from this form of educational choice. The demographic profile of its students, high proportion of immigrant families and children, lower middle-class family incomes, low student academic-learning outcomes, and lack of educational choices for parents persuaded me that Clifton would be an ideal community for a charter school—and, indeed, the type of community charter schools were intended to benefit.

During this initial stage, I had interested a few Clifton residents, some of whom I knew personally and others unfamiliar to me, but all finding an alternative educational choice in Clifton public education intriguing and something worth exploring. Several of these persons consented to be recorded by name on the charter-school application as tentative Board of Trustees members. It was also important for the strength of the charter-school application that it be seen that this project was not the initiative or work of one individual—which, in fact, it truly was—but something of a community effort, which, at this early stage, it certainly was not.

With the conscious understanding that my efforts of starting a school would, as before, likely yield similarly disappointing results, and as I applied my energies to the charter-school application during the summer of 1997, I nonetheless found myself experiencing exuberant episodes of hope and expectation. Convinced of the worth of my proposals for school reform and for raising student academic learning, and for showcasing a way to overcome the "high costs, low results" intrinsic inevitability of our public schools, as well as demonstrating the profound benefits of a traditional classical curriculum supported by an "academics-first school culture," my confidence of success began to grow.

Still, attempting to restrain my optimism, I invited doubt to mingle liberally with confidence, and each day I wondered about those faceless people whom I would never know but who would judge my application and give or deny me the opportunity of putting into practice my long-held education-reform convictions, and greatly influence my and my wife's future. Would they ridicule the contents and nature of my educational proposals? Would they assess my views on education absurd? Would they mock the ways in which I wanted to improve education and student learning outcomes? Would they discern even a particle of merit in my plan? Would they view my education reforms as too radical? Would they believe a school with mandatory Latin and elements of a classical education laughably incompatible with the modern-education emphasis on science and technology? Would they reject outright a school proposing a "no-tracking policy" and a school where there would be no dedicated classes in art, gym, or music? Would any of my proposed school reforms be construed as violations of New Jersey's Constitutionally mandated "thorough and efficient" education imperatives, thereby dooming forthwith my prospects of charter approval? Despite disheartening thoughts like these daily entering my mind but somewhat neutralized by a welcome intermixing of fanciful shreds of confidence and hope, and with my wife's support, I pushed forward with determined alacrity.

I applied myself to the many-faceted charter-school application, devoting many hours each day during July and August 1997; my wife assisted every moment she could after returning from her work at the bank. The two window air conditioners in our small second-floor apartment provided scant relief during the very hot, humid summer days and months of 1997. The charter-school application work was performed on my old "floppy disk Leading Edge" computer; my printer was a nameless antique "dot matrix" type, which took about seven minutes to print one page of text; it would often suffer heat stroke and cease printing entirely. When this occurred—and it did with maddening frequency—I found it mechanically effective to strike a few hard slaps to the printer's side panels or simply wait for it to cool before printing continued. When it finally resumed printing, the page was often full of smudges which I rendered less conspicuous by old-fashioned hand erasing.

When the writing of the charter-school application, having begun in May 1997, was finally completed at the end of August 1997, we brought it to Staples to be copied. We made 20 copies. In order to save money—keep in mind we were ourselves paying all costs and expenses for this venture—we ourselves collated each copy and perforated the pages with a binding machine I had purchased some years before for my first venture in "school creating." My wife and I devised a unique method of collating and binding the 120 pages of each application: we placed on our apartment floor beginning at the kitchen entrance and proceeding up a hallway into the parlor area, 20 copies of each numbered page from the cover page to page 40. We then proceeded on our knees to move across our apartment floor from the cover page to page 40; then we brought each pile of collated pages to the hand-operated binding device, which we had placed on the kitchen table. Then we punched out the holes where the plastic rib binding would be attached as the final act in this process. We repeated the same process for pages 41 to page 80, and again from page 81 to the end page (120) of the application. After having thus collated all 120 pages of each of the 20 application copies, we then used the binding device to attach clear plastic covers and rib bindings to each of the 20 completed applications. At the end of this collating activity, which took the better part of a week, my wife and I understandably celebrated with our own kind of "collation."

As required, we sent copies of my charter-school application to the Passaic County Office of Education (to its dismay), to the Superintendent of Clifton Public School District (to his utter disgust), and to the New Jersey Department of Education, Office of Charter Schools (also known as the Office of Innovative Programs and Practices). I also gave copies to several residents of Clifton interested in my project. Now there was little to do but to wait as I prepared my teaching duties for the new school year. The state informed charter applicants that decisions on charter-school applications—approval or disapproval—for schools hoping to open in September 1998 would be made sometime in January or February 1998. In November 1997, the Office of Charter Schools notified me that, after a preliminary review of my submitted application, certain elaborations and addenda needed to be submitted. These pertained to budgetary forecasts and a few other matters. I duly submitted what I hoped would further enhance the chances for favorable review.

Half the school year had now elapsed since I had submitted my charter-school application, and I was well along in discharging my teaching and employment responsibilities. My and my wife's life continued to progress toward our goals of saving for a home, visiting her Canadian family members, perfecting my teaching skills, and digesting tracts on charter schools and education reform.

Often, in private moments, I thought about those unknown Trenton bureaucrats who were assigned the evaluation of my charter-school application. I wondered, with a sardonic smile, if they thought my proposals unacceptably foolish at best, radical at worst. I imagined their extreme reactions to some of my novel and, to them, perhaps outrageous proposals, namely: resurrecting an antiquated and useless classical curriculum; ruining kids' lives, indeed perhaps inciting adolescent depression by doubling the amount of class time each day spent on mathematics and English; giving students little respite from the unremitting, tedious grind of a rigorous, mandatory 7-academic-subject program of studies undiluted with school-day "fun" of art, music, the joys of making cookies, of shooting arrows into targets, or of interpretative dance. I envisaged them discussing with disdain among themselves how my school practices and policies would retard students' acquisition of the critical, life-enriching values of "virtue" and "strong character," of the vaunted "social-emotional adolescent development" purpose of schools, and of "team building" by depriving students the opportunity of performing in stage productions or competing in school athletic competitions. I imagined the evaluators sitting together, hilariously ridiculing the contents of my application, chuckling among themselves: "Does this odd jerk really expect to get from us state permission to start a charter school with these absurdly outlandish proposals?" Musings such as these challenged any optimism I contrived for success.

Charter-school law provides that the school district in which a proposed charter school is located may submit arguments why the state should not grant a charter to the applicant. I speculated how and to what degree the charter-school-application evaluators would weigh the Clifton Public Schools Superintendent's "Request for Denial of Charter School Application" petition. In that petition, the Superintendent explicated on why the Commissioner of Education should not grant the Classical Academy a charter, pleading that there simply is no need in Clifton for a charter school, especially of the type the application describes. He maintained that the proposed charter school offers nothing new or anything Clifton schools do not already possess and presently address—making a point that charter schools are supposed to be innovative in their approach to education; this school, in his opinion, does not do so. Although he informed the evaluators that there is Latin instruction at Clifton High School, he criticized the Classical Academy, with its Latin and classical-education mandate for all students, as not meeting the needs of the typical Clifton student; nor did the proposed school mirror the character of the community. In his view, the Classical Academy more resembled a "private school," but one that wanted public funding. Praising the "comprehensive" nature of Clifton schools as serving to the maximum degree all kinds of students and their diverse needs, which the charter school simply cannot equal or satisfy, he predicted that the diverse needs of many unfortunate Classical Academy students, if the school were approved, would go unmet, legally and morally.

Clifton's Superintendent of Schools disparaged my critical descriptions of the "carnival-like" school environments and the extraordinary amount of "extra" and "co-curricular" offerings and activities which greatly detract from academic learning, and which I greatly reduced or, in many cases, eliminated from the Classical Academy. He asserted the commonplace view of educators coming out of collegiate schools of education for generations, (as well as obeying teachers-union demands) that all the "extra" and the "co-curricular" aspects of education were necessary to serve and to respond to the needs of a diversity of (10,000) Clifton students. He proudly mentioned that Clifton has "over 50 athletic teams . . . with marching band, concert band, jazz band, and a string orchestra program." The Superintendent cited Clifton's academic extracurricular programs, such as "Academic Decathlon," "Mock Trial," and science teams . . . *But be assured,* I thought as I silently mused when reading his objections, *that for every student in one of these worthwhile academic extracurricular activities, there are 100 participating headlong in the plethora of non-academic "fun stuff."*

In a telling statement in his plea to deny a charter to the Classical Academy (October 9, 1997), the Clifton Schools Superintendent well encapsulated the thinking which perpetuates mediocre academic learning and, for many students, ensures scholastic deficiencies: "The diversity of student needs is well represented in the co-curricular programs provided by the Clifton Board of Education. A school truly meeting the needs of its student body must provide a proper balance of academic and co-curricular/athletic programs" [a balance which the proposed Classical Academy lacks and indeed denigrates].

Here he nicely summarized the thoroughly accepted notion that a curriculum and school program must include an abundance of extra and co-curricular activities and athletics, otherwise, it is educational malpractice, school-sanctioned student abuse, and taxpayer-funded child neglect. However, in my experience, this "proper balance" which the Superintendent extolls, has long been decidedly and grossly tilted in favor of the non-academic portion of public education.

The tacit declaration also expressed by the Superintendent, held by so many at all levels of education, is that a high-quality, high-expectations, serious academic education is simply beyond the attainment or interest of many students, and because of this "diversity," schools must cater to their "needs" by "tracking" the non-academically inclined into lower-level classes, reducing the rigor and amount of academic learning, and filling their school days with non-academic classes and extra/co-curricular activities and programs. It is this prevailing *anti-academic school culture* (disguised as the "proper balance between academics and co/extra-curricular activities and athletics") and the destructive educational philosophy that underlies it, that the Classical Academy aimed to disprove and to replace with a pronounced "academics-first" school culture for every child. His statement also reflects the widely held attitude which sustains the anti-academic school culture and promotes the ultimate failings of large "comprehensive" schools, where every alleged "need" is provided for every student, according to each student's propensities or purported incapacities, or according to a student's own immature wishes and adolescent inclinations.

The Superintendent of Clifton Public Schools was an influential and worthy person who had held for many years one of the highest education posts in Passaic County, and who was the head of one of the largest public-school districts in the state. In summarizing the major points of his and the Clifton Board of Education's arguments against Classical Academy charter approval, I here enumerate further their major objections: Clifton does not need a charter school; there is no community support for a charter school in Clifton; a charter school will hurt Clifton schools and students financially; the charter school's curriculum is non-compliant with the state's mandatory "core curriculum content standards" (it lacks, for example, dedicated classes in state-mandated areas of "Visual and Performing Arts" and "Physical and Health Education"); its program does not address the needs of a diversity of students, including "special education" students; technological instruction is barely mentioned in the application; the proposed charter has insufficient money for realistic start-up costs and to ensure viability; and, finally, it has specified no school-facility location in its application.

This last objection was seized on by other charter-school opponents in other communities. An apparent inconsistency in the charter-school legislation seemed to require the charter-school applicant to specify in the charter-school application a building address in which the school would be housed. Apart from real estate speculators or charter-school "network" companies and their facility-provider backers hoping for attractive dividends, few others would be willing or possess the finances to invest thousands, perhaps hundreds of thousands of dollars in a charter-school facility before knowing if its application is approved.

Insistence on having a school facility as a required element for initial charter-school application approval would be a desirable legality to quickly curtail any possible spread of charter schools, as charter-school opponents well knew. *No building, no school* was their motto. To them lacking a specific facility location in the initial application for a charter school should render the application incomplete, if not invalid. Others, however, contended no such requirement exists in the initial application process. Of course, an approved building must be procured before the school opens to receive students and funding, but not required before the state (Commissioner of Education) approves a charter-school application, that is, initial charter-school application approval does not depend on the applicant already having acquired an approved school facility. This last interpretation became the accepted understanding regarding a charter-school facility at time of application.

Recognizing Clifton's Superintendent's high stature in education matters in the state and in the region, his criticisms, however much I disagreed with them, might well, I thought, win the day and influence the evaluators and the Commissioner of Education to reject the Classical Academy's application for a charter. On balance, whatever flights of optimism I forced myself to contemplate, inwardly I felt the near certainty that reality would once again defeat my ambitions of school creation.

Chapter III

OPENING THE DOORS: THE DESPERATELY STRIDENT "DAVID AND GOLIATH" STRUGGLE TO START THE CLASSICAL ACADEMY CHARTER SCHOOL OF CLIFTON

Actualizing Dreams Is Not for the Phlegmatic and Trepidatious

It was just before my wife and I began supper when the phone rang one day during the second week of January 1998. A person was phoning from the New Jersey Office of Charter Schools, an official with whom we had become acquainted from our attendance at informational sessions in Trenton for persons contemplating completion of charter-school applications. I gathered my wife, Magda, close to the phone, for I had a sense this call would one way or another be most consequential for us and our future. He began by saying, "Vincent, I have good news for you" and that he was pleased to inform me that I had received charter approval for the Classical Academy to begin in September 1998. He mentioned that my charter application was the first one Trenton had received for the "second cohort" of charter schools and the first of that cohort to be approved. We were, therefore, the 14th approved New Jersey charter school. He further mentioned we would be receiving a "charter school approval letter" in a few days, but he wanted to tell us personally of the state's decision, for he knew how important it was for us.

Oh, those beautiful-faceless-wise-courageous-visionary-omniscient-brilliant-eminent-illustrious bureaucrats—they had, after all, found promise and merit in my proposed charter school; God bless them! My wife and I danced around the parlor ecstatically, blissfully ignorant of the ferocious battle to come.

For the next several weeks, all I could think about were the very many tasks I had to undertake and to complete successfully in order to make the school a true reality in just 8 months. Assembling community support, recruiting students, interviewing prospective teachers, reviewing and ordering textbooks, writing school curricula, purchasing school furniture and equipment, and, of course, finding a suitable school building were some of the critical steps for establishing the Classical Academy, and I enthusiastically embarked upon them.

All charter-school approvals are contingent on submission of additional data and information before the school can begin operations, including facility acquisition and municipal certificates for fire, sanitation, and certificates of occupancy and use, updated budgets, teacher credentials, and more. With all this in front of me, I nevertheless beamed with satisfaction when, at a regular faculty meeting at my school of employment, the principal, in announcing my good fortune, told my assembled colleagues: "As teachers, we all at one time or another dreamed of running our own school. Well, Vince has done it." It was a most proud moment for me.

My devoted wife, Magda, gave me her total commitment; my parents, on the other hand, were fearful and hesitant. My parents cautioned that I had a fine job, came to work wearing a jacket and tie (an important point of pride for my mother), had a good and increasing salary, near-absolute job security for the rest of my working life, enviable work hours, summers free, excellent health insurance, and a joyful, young marriage to a loving girl they adored, all of which I seemed callously willing to jeopardize.

My parents were children of immigrant parents and Depression-era adolescents. Like so many of their era, they needed to seek work at an early age, and had never completed high school. Today, they are honored as members of the *Greatest Generation* (my father, of blessed memory, was a medal-winning World War II Army combat medic). To them, their only son's hard-earned achievements in academia and in his career were much too precious to put at risk. They remembered, too, my prior failed efforts at starting a school, and the time, hope, and money I lost in that quixotic venture. I was unmarried then, with some savings to rely upon, the sanctuary of a family home if desperation required, and better disposed to risk all for a dream. Now, they reminded me, I had greater responsibilities to my wife and to providing for both of us (we have no children) a happy, secure, and prosperously satisfying life, which my present situation would amply supply.

The greatest benefit the NJEA (teachers' union) ever rendered to me, despite their hatefully successful efforts at preventing teaching from ever becoming a true profession—which, if it did, would ensure the end of its power, relevance, and financial abundance—was to lobby successfully for a certain provision in the 1995 New Jersey charter-school legislation. This provision stated that any public-school employee and NJEA member who leaves one's tenured position to start or work in a charter school has three years to return to the job one (temporarily) vacated for charter-school involvement. Even more generous, such NJEA members as I would continue to accrue seniority and pay raises at my former school employer while working at the charter school. Upon the employee's return, the district by law must reinstate the teacher with the accrued years and increased pay as if the person had never left the district, so that one's (foolishly traitorous) charter-school sojourn would not exact a cost or in any way risk the teacher's job security or salary. This, dear reader, is an example of the might the NJEA possesses over education legislation.

My parents were somewhat mollified and became a little less anxious when I informed them of this provision in the law. I told them that, if the prospect of success seemed remote or dismal, or if the school proved unsuccessful after a year or two, my school-district employer was legally obligated to return my teaching job to me any time during the next three years, beginning September 1998. However, when I notified the superintendent of the school district in which I was employed of my charter-school approval and involvement intentions, as well as about this "Three-Year Right of Return" provision, and after he detailed the school district attorney to confirm my correct citation of the provision, he was more distraught than mollified. Incidentally, I do not personally know of another teacher who relied upon or utilized this NJEA-initiated charter-school provision, certainly not for founding a New Jersey charter school. Needless to say, I never had need to invoke this charter-school "insurance" provision the NJEA so thoughtfully provided me.

Powerful Opponents Rapidly Emerge, Enraged and Fiercely Determined:

When I received my charter approval, the first 13 charter schools were midway into their first year of operation. Except for the Princeton Charter School, a unique charter school in many ways, nearly all of these first charter schools were started in the state-operated urban school districts of Newark and Jersey City. There was little organized, vocal opposition to establishing these first state-sanctioned charter schools in state-operated school districts. In reality, the controlling powers of New Jersey public education—NJEA (teachers' union), school administrators, Boards of Education, collegiate schools of education, elected local and state officials—were taken almost unawares, insensible to the "charter-school crime" that had been done to their compliantly subservient and reliably monopolistic public-education system by these first 13 charter schools. But now, as the second group of charter schools was being approved, and fearing the dreaded virulence of charter schools would spread beyond urban communities and unleash untold damage to their protected domains, large segments of the New Jersey public-education enterprise united to prepare for war.

Along with the Classical Academy, 22 other charter schools were approved to begin in September 1998, and several of these, like the Classical Academy, were to be located in non-state-operated school districts. That charter schools would be approved for suburban and non-state-operated school districts was an outrage to opponents of educational reform and school choice, and not what many inferred the 1995 charter school legislation intended to permit. The gathering coalescence of statewide charter-school opposition quickly took form.

Charter-school opponents galvanized local school districts and municipal governments in communities where a charter school received charter approval to oppose their presence strenuously and utilized all manner of legalities and municipal powers to make establishing a "suburban" charter school like the Classical Academy near impossible. Clifton school and municipal authorities were especially exhorted—not that they needed much exhortation in this matter—to take up the sword. The war cry echoed through many a Board of Education meeting in Clifton and beyond. It resounded in the luxuriant enclaves of NJEA office suites, collegiate schools of education, and in school administrators' luncheon conferences; all in unison, the same clarion call for militancy went forth: "Clifton must fight for us and all non-state-operated school districts." "Clifton must vigorously battle to defeat decisively this Classical Academy and its leading protagonist, otherwise, our non-urban communities may proliferate with repugnant versions of Classical Academies, an infection sure to threaten our own public schools and our accustomed (and hitherto protected) monopoly prerogatives."

Clifton municipal government, from the Mayor, City Council, all elected local officials, Clifton Public School District officials, and citizen groups all united in their hostility and made common cause to do whatever needed to be done to stop me and the Classical Academy. The Passaic County Office of Education and its superintendent at the time, never proponents of charter schools, offered no assistance in resources, advice, or expertise in helping me establish Passaic County's first public charter school. It showed no supportive interest in this struggle—except perhaps rooting covertly for anti-charter school forces. I soon came to understand its true sympathies were with my opponents in this struggle, hoping Clifton and all Passaic County would be—for as long as possible—charter-school free.

After receiving charter approval, I informed the few Clifton residents who had shown an interest in my project of the happy outcome. Some of them were identified in the charter application as on our "Board of Trustees." They seemed willing to assist in whatever small way, even if only publicly expressing support for a charter school in Clifton, and encouraged me forward. That Clifton would have a charter school quickly became a public question of considerable import. In the forthcoming weeks and months, I was compelled to engage in defensive actions I had never anticipated or envisioned but which were necessitated by Clifton Board of Education's determined, strategic efforts to prevent the Classical Academy from ever taking root.

Establishing the Classical Academy Charter School under the best of circumstances would be a challenge, but establishing it when so many powerful forces, possessed of unlimited funds and governmental authority and influence were actively arrayed in strident opposition to it was a daunting "David and Goliath" struggle. Necessarily assuming the entire defensive responsibility while holding outside full-time employment was truly a Herculean undertaking as I strove to bring the Classical Academy to fruition.

However overwhelming and onerous were my tasks, I was single-mindedly driven to prove my ideas of education reform valid and worthwhile. I was further determined, having been given the unprecedented opportunity to a teacher of creating a public school in which one's ideas and ideals were manifest, to exert every effort and sacrifice toward success. My resolve to fight for my dream was fortified further by my belief that, if the school became a reality, young students of lower middle-class status or children of immigrant parents would benefit from a high-quality, life-enhancing academic education, the sort of education they would not receive at Clifton Public Schools. A Classical Academy academic education, as I planned to structure and design, would give these students the skills, confidence, and desire for meaningful destinies and upward mobility. Like the multitude of immigrants before them, Clifton's immigrant parents left their ancestral countries for a better future for their children; the Classical Academy would be an important part in realizing that future for them.

For these reasons, and despite the incredible amount of toil and demands I and my wife were confronting, I did not feel it to be a burden. It was my dream on the threshold of becoming real, and I was most willing—indeed, eager—to expend all my capacious energies to keeping that threshold open and my dream alive, and to defeating my formidable opponents who strove to bury it.

Rumors and Litigation Intended to Abort the Classical Academy's Founding:

Fabricated by charter-school opponents, rumors soon were being circulated throughout Clifton that the Classical Academy Charter School of

Clifton would be full of Black Paterson kids who would come to Clifton for schooling and that, just as false, Clifton taxpayers would be paying for Paterson students to attend the Classical Academy. Another rumor alleged that those behind the charter school send their children to Catholic schools, and their charter-school advocacy was solely motivated by the avoidance of paying Catholic-school tuition when enrolling their children in the free charter school. Still other rumors found receptive ears: that if the Classical Academy started, it would raise property taxes in Clifton; and that the charter school would divert funding away from the public schools and thus deprive Clifton students of needed resources. These falsehoods and misapprehensions were repeated in public fora by citizens and elected officials, and published in the Clifton press. Anti-Classical Academy feeling pervaded the Clifton community, and hostility to the school's establishment was palpable and deep.

The local weekly newspaper published some articles for which I was interviewed and in which I attempted to disprove the rumors and argue my beliefs in the power of educational choice and the ways in which Clifton residents would benefit from the Classical Academy. The "Letters to the Editor" section in this local weekly newspaper regularly contained citizens' views on the charter school, usually in opposition to it. Although not winning the public-relations battle, at least I was not allowing the rumors, lies, and slander to pass without challenge and counterdiction. My arguments and presence in the area press and at public meetings helped a bit with providing the public with an accurate understanding of charter schools, but not nearly enough to assuage the ferocity and weaken the determination of the potent opposition, who, after all, were fighting for their protected monopoly.

By invitation, I attended and was asked to speak at several Clifton City Council meetings, and at Clifton Board of Education meetings. Again, I endeavored to counter the many false rumors. I also spoke on the importance of school choice in education as a fundamental right all parents should enjoy. I told the elected and appointed Clifton City officials why I started the Classical Academy, why I selected Clifton, and why I believed strongly it would benefit the Clifton community. I pointed out that my starting a charter school in Clifton did not imply that the Clifton Public Schools are defective and should be deserted by parents and students. I used Princeton Charter School as an example that, even in affluent, high-achieving school districts like Princeton, New Jersey, those well-educated, prosperous parents now have an educational charter-school choice; why should we deny such a choice to Clifton parents?

I emphasized, too, that, although the Classical Academy is approved for both middle school grades 6-8 and a 9-12 grade high school, the school would begin with only grades 6 and 7 and grow slightly each year by adding a grade. Even at the end of its growth, six or seven years from now, its student population at final development will be, at most, about 300-350 students. I appealed to their common sense: Could a school of this minute size realistically wreak havoc and financial ruin to a 10,000-student public-school district? In spite of my arguments, at one such meeting of Clifton city officials and residents, a former Mayor of Clifton and at that time a state legislator rose to declare that he voted for the charter-school legislation, but if he thought that, because of that legislation, we would have a charter school in Clifton, he never would have voted for it. His comments were greeted with much applause and approbation from the audience.

I well remember a particular meeting to which both I and the Clifton School District Attorney were invited to attend and each to give a "pro" and "con" account of the public question the Classical Academy Charter School represented. The meeting was held at Clifton's Senior Citizen Center. Clifton senior citizens are a large and politically influential group. Clifton Public Schools were known for seldom passing a school budget, and the large senior-citizen vote generally was the cause for school-budget defeats.

The meeting was during a weekday afternoon. The tireless and time-consuming work I was doing while still employed full time during the months of January to June 1998, to fulfill the charter-approval demands and timelines, and in order to launch successfully the Classical Academy, caused me to use and thus deplete all my accumulated sick and personal days. The superintendent of my school-district employer understood my plight and motives but said that if I took any more days off from work for any reason, district policy dictated that I would be denied henceforth pay for each day absent. My attendance at this meeting was the first of numerous "pay-less" days I and my wife endured to start the Classical Academy.

The cavernous senior-citizen hall was full. I glanced at the school district attorney, a fellow Italian American, a *pisano*, as we say, and, in my mind, I contrasted our positions. Here he was, being paid hundreds of dollars, perhaps a thousand or two, by the school district for his appearance and his arguments against me, and here I sat, losing my comparatively meager daily wage for my attendance and for my cause. It was a symbol of the imbalance in strength and inequality of resources of our two competing sides, yet, as is often said in such matters, I had the truth of a noble cause on my side.

The attorney presented his arguments first, and he admitted that some of the rumors, such as Clifton taxpayers would pay for Paterson resident students attending the Classical Academy, were not true. He recited the usual points that Clifton schools are excellent and provide a superior education; a charter school would only hurt taxpayers and students; charter schools were meant only for disadvantaged urban students, not for communities like Clifton, where there was no need or desire for a charter school. His remarks were sympathetically and civilly received by the aged audience.

Returning to his seat, I was then called to the podium, with barely a word escaping from my mouth, loud jeers and catcalls were hurled my way; elderly men rose unsteadily but angrily to their feet with the aid of their canes shouting: "We don't need this school," "We pay enough taxes," "Get out of town," "Who the hell do you think you are to stuff this school down our throats?" and comments of similar tone. The elderly moderator had to intervene and remind the audience that I was an invited guest and should not be treated disrespectfully.

The audience being now somewhat subdued, I continued my presentation, citing some facts about the nature of charter schools and how they are funded, emphasizing that there would be no increased taxes to pay for the charter school and extolling the value and parental right of educational choice. During my efforts of providing accurate information to my mature audience and explaining my educational views, quiet but persistent hissing and booing could be heard, and gestures of disdain unavoidably in my sight were expressed with weathered middle fingers and wrinkled grimaces. As the traumatic event ended and the attorney and I left the stage, he glanced my way, and, in his surprisingly compassionate eyes he conveyed to me this clear message: *It's going to be like this and worse for you, DeRosa, as long as you persist in this foolhardy, sure-to-fail endeavor; you don't stand a chance against us. Stop now and save yourself grief and anxiety.* Soon after this event, I received for the next month or two a spate of personally threatening, anonymous phone calls: "We don't want your f—ing school"; "Get the f—k out of town, or else."

Lawsuits and Appeals Against the Commissioner of Education and Classical Academy:

Clifton Board of Education urged the superintendent and its attorney to initiate any and all means possible to stop the charter school from taking root in Clifton; it also encouraged municipal authorities to do their part in this unified effort at opposing the charter school.

In February and March 1998, Clifton Board of Education quickly filed two lawsuits. The first was to appeal the Commissioner of Education's Classical Academy charter approval to the New Jersey State Board of Education. When the State Board upheld the Commissioner's decision, as Clifton expected, it appealed the Commissioner of Education's decision to the Superior Court of New Jersey Appellate Division. In its appellate brief, hoping to overturn the State Board of Education's affirmation of the Commissioner's Classical Academy charter grant, Clifton's attorney recited many of the same arguments the Clifton Superintendent used in his letter of October 9, 1997, attempting to persuade the Commissioner of Education to deny the Classical Academy's charter-school application for approval.

Considering the Classical Academy's subsequent nearly two-decade distinguished history under my leadership—its record of high academic achievement and financial success, its several national and state awards for excellence—it bemuses me now to review briefly those arguments and chief points the opposition advanced seeking to overturn the Commissioner's charter approval in Appellate Court. Some of these points [quoted statements are from Clifton attorney's brief] were: 1) " ... it [Classical Academy] does not offer a more diverse approach than that currently offered in the Clifton Public School system" [i.e., nothing proposed in the application is not already being offered or done in Clifton schools]; 2) "The curriculum proposed by the charter-school application fails to provide for the constitutionally required thorough and efficient education of its students" [because our curriculum deemphasized "visual and performing arts" and "physical and health education," and sought to satisfy state requirements in these subjects in non-traditional or "integrative" ways]. 3) "The applicant's budget proposals are entirely speculative, unsubstantiated, and fail to meet minimal statutory standards so as to assess, with any confidence, the sufficiencies of the charter school's financial plan." 4) "Clifton is a low-funded public-school district; it has a long history of school-budget defeats and is forced each year to operate on small budget surpluses." "The money given to the Classical Academy via the charter-school funding mechanism, amounting to $700,000 if all of its 100 first-year students come from Clifton, will impact severely Clifton students; programs now offered may be cut or reduced, and other programs planned may be removed from future implementation." 5) "The failure to identify a school facility in the initial charter application should have in itself been sufficient cause for the Commissioner of Education to deny the charter."

Furthermore, the attorney cited expert testimony declaring: "It will cost much more to renovate and make 'school ready' a potential school facility than that which the Classical Academy allows in its projected first-year budget, therefore, clearly, the Classical Academy does not have the finances to secure and renovate a building to be used for a school. This fact should have been obvious to the Commissioner and should have been sufficient for charter denial."

These legal proceedings were filed against the Commissioner of Education and the State Board of Education, but in actuality were against me and the proposed Classical Academy Charter School of Clifton. The attorneys representing the Commissioner and the State Board of Education were drawn from the New Jersey Attorney General's offices, and from a well-respected private law firm in New Jersey. In all these legal proceedings,

I and the Classical Academy were involved as a "respondent." I acted as my own attorney ("pro se" and "pro bono") and provided the state's attorneys with whatever written information and depositions they sought, a portion of which became part of the legal record, as indeed was my entire charter-school application. I also provided from my ancillary position in this matter whatever informal aid or commentary that would be helpful to our common cause.

The court denied the arguments of the Clifton Board of Education's attorney and ruled in favor of the Education Commissioner and the Classical Academy. All court rulings and findings to this point in our battle all affirmed and reaffirmed the validity of the Commissioner of Education's charter-school application approval for the Classical Academy Charter School of Clifton. The opponents to the Classical Academy were suffering legal defeats at every stage.

The Classical Academy was not the only newly chartered charter school that a local board of education was litigating to nullify the Commissioner of Education's charter-school application approval. Several other second-cohort charter schools, particularly in non-state-operated school districts, were being similarly litigated against and whose establishment was opposed by both their local boards of education and their municipal governments.

However, no other newly approved charter school was as hotly and with such determined bitterness opposed than was the Classical Academy. Far from being cowed by legal judgments against them, our opponents did not relinquish or abate the battle against the Classical Academy. They now devised a legal strategy which was nothing short of a constitutional challenge to the entire 1995 charter-school legislation, particularly its funding mechanism. This entailed an appeal to the "Council on Unfunded Local Mandates."

The Council on Unfunded Local Mandates and Saving the 1995 Charter-School Law:

In May 1998, I received at work a call from an attorney in the State Attorney General's office. She said that Clifton School District, using the Classical Academy's approved charter as the cause of grievance, had filed a complaint against the state's charter-school legislation. Clifton's complaint specifically alleges that the funding mechanism for charter schools is a violation of the "Unfunded Local Mandate Statute." The attorney informed me that, as the Classical Academy's founder, it was imperative that I be present at a hearing before the "Council on Local Mandates" and that the Classical Academy must be represented by an attorney. Her office, she bluntly informed me, is not my attorney in this matter, but is representing and defending the Commissioner of Education and the state's charter-school legislation. However, since I and the Classical Academy are parties to the litigation, I must provide my own professional legal representation (at my expense) for the Classical Academy. The entire charter-school funding mechanism—and, thus, the entire charter-school legislation—she asserted, was in jeopardy and may be deemed invalid if the "Council on Unfunded Local Mandates" finds in favor of Clifton Board of Education. After ending our phone conversation, I mused that this humble Latin teacher was now called upon to assist in the defense of New Jersey's entire charter-school law. With all my other responsibilities and toils in starting a charter school, this rather grand task was now further thrust upon me. I undertook it with zeal.

In 1996, the New Jersey legislature passed a statute that essentially held that, if the state mandated a program or regulation which would require a local government to expend funds or otherwise would burden the taxpayers of a local government to underwrite the state-mandated program financially, the state, under certain circumstances, must instead provide the funding for that program or regulation, as burden relief of the local taxpayer.

To Clifton public-school authorities, the way charter schools were funded—by diverting 90% of the per-pupil taxpayer-supplied funding for each student in a school district who attends a charter school—seemed like an "unfunded local mandate" and, therefore, a violation of the "Unfunded Local Mandate" statute. When, Clifton Board of Education further argued, there is a financial loss to a school district due to charter-school enrollment, that loss must be replaced by an increased local tax burden. Decreased funding to the school district due to charter-school enrollment causes harm to the district's students and taxpayers; thus, a state-mandated program, as is the charter-school legislation, necessitates a decrease in local school funding, which must then be made whole by increasing local taxes.

Because of these facts, New Jersey's funding mechanism for charter schools was an apparent violation of the "Unfunded Local Mandate" statute, or so argued Clifton Public School District. Additionally, the charter-school program is a state program; hence the state, according to the argument of Clifton school authorities, should pay for charter-school students, not the local taxpayer. Specifically, there should be no funding diversion or transference from the public-school district's budget to a charter school the Commissioner of Education has approved for that public-school district. Simply stated, Clifton maintained that the funding for students to attend a charter school violates the "Unfunded Local Mandate Statute," and, thus, funding should not come from local taxpayers or subtracted from public-school budgets, but entirely be subsidized by state funds.

I selected a Clifton attorney, who, after some discussion, agreed to appear on behalf of the Classical Academy at the "Council on Unfunded Local Mandates" hearing, which was scheduled in about a month at Seton Hall Law School in Newark. I provided him with background preparation and the documents he requested or which I thought would be helpful to develop arguments against Clifton's assertions regarding charter-school funding.

With several members of our tentative Board of Trustees, I arrived at the meeting (of course, once again, losing my day's wages, but this time also paying legal fees). Already arrived was my *pisano*, the Clifton Board's attorney, appearing confident with self-satisfaction that he ingeniously devised himself or formulated with others this hitherto novel and unused argument not only against the Classical Academy, but against all New Jersey charter schools. If he were successful, the state legislature would have to scramble to structure a different charter-school funding mechanism, delay newly chartered schools from opening, and possibly suspend operations of the original 13 charter schools after their first year. If the anti-charter school forces prevailed at the "Council on Unfunded Local Mandates," the state legislature likely would not reach a timely consensus on a new state-funding mechanism for charter schools and simply let die, at least for the foreseeable future, this most promising of all education reforms. The attorney who brought about this situation would surely achieve hero-like status for all New Jersey haters of charter schools.

The "Council on Unfunded Local Mandates" was composed of 6 highly respected New Jerseyans who had distinguished professional careers in various fields. Having heard the arguments and reviewed the documentation, their decision in part is quoted here: "Without expressing an opinion whether there would be a significant financial hardship to the Clifton Board, the Council denies injunctive relief because the Claimant [Clifton Board] has failed to show a substantial likelihood that the challenged acts of the Commissioner of Education [his ordering Clifton Board to fund the Classical Academy from its school budget, as per the Charter School Law] impose impermissible, unfunded mandates within the Council's jurisdiction"; and, "The Council concludes that it is the Charter School Act, at N.J.A.A. 18A:36-12, that is the alleged unfunded mandate to fund charter schools, not the [subsequent] implementing regulations or order [from the Commissioner of Education]." Furthermore, the Council adjudicated, "That [Charter School] Act was enacted and became effective on January 11, 1996, *before* the beginning date of this Council's jurisdiction. Hence, the Council is without jurisdiction to resolve the issue presented."

Clifton Board of Education failed again to stop by its legal maneuverings and harassing litigation this plucky little Classical Academy Charter School, which found itself fighting not only for its own survival but also for the future of all New Jersey charter schools!

The Search for a School Building

All the while I was consumingly engaged with Clifton Board of Education legal strategies to prevent me from establishing the Classical Academy, I was simultaneously engrossed, from February to August 1998, with finding a building that could be used as a home for the Classical Academy. A suitable if not ideal charter-school building is one which, if needing renovation or conversion for school use, would not be prohibitively costly and one that could meet the state charter-school facility requirements, namely, that the building earn municipal-code certifications for fire and sanitation, a "C/O" (certificate of occupancy), and possesses or could obtain from the municipality an "E" (educational)-use zoning designation.

Finding, securing, renovating, and financing a building for charter-school use is often the most difficult, daunting obstacle charter-school founders must overcome, even when they are not bitterly obstructed by the local school district with its legal resources and unlimited funding.

The Classical Academy's school facility had to be in Clifton, so my search was necessarily confined to that city. I engaged the services of a local commercial real estate agent to assist in my search. Week after week, I would go to various locations and assess a structure's school-use potential and the projected costs both for lease and renovations. We looked at numerous buildings, none of which were practical or acceptable, no matter how much hope I irrationally placed in a building's potential. A one-story, large open-space building filled with computers and cables was one potential site. Still another was a defunct funeral home, where, in the basement, were still stored unused caskets. This last facility was owned in part by a Clifton elected official. When it was learned that his property might be the location for the despised Clifton charter school, he was publicly rebuked in the local press as "unreliable" and one who was interested more in money than in keeping Clifton charter-school free. Few prospects of genuine potential resulted in my uninterrupted, 6-month-long, vain search for a school facility.

Charter-school opponents well know, even if they lose the legal and public-relation battles, a charter school cannot begin without a municipally approved school-use building. As the months quickly passed without any success in sight, and knowing that the process of securing the required facility certifications and municipal permissions, as well as the time needed for facility renovations, may well accomplish what all the might and enmity of Clifton School District could not accomplish. The terrifying prospect haunted me daily: *No building, no school.*

A Divine Rejection

In the midst of my demoralizingly fruitless facility search, I received a phone call whose message was tantamount to a divine call from heaven. (Incidentally, all during the first year, from charter approval until the school actually opened, my home address and personal phone number were the official location and phone contact for all Classical Academy matters). The person calling was a former Clifton councilwoman. She informed me that a Clifton Catholic school which had closed several years ago was currently under lease contract to Newark Public Schools. Newark would bus to Clifton some of its high-school students in "alternative" education ("alternative" education is code for students having emotional or behavioral problems). The Clifton urban neighbors of this Catholic school were undoubtedly unhappy with this disagreeable use of their neighborhood Catholic-school building. The former councilwoman informed me that the lease was soon to expire and unlikely to be renewed, and suggested that this former Catholic-school building may be a fine facility for my proposed Classical Academy. She indicated that she would contact the parish priest to arrange for a late-afternoon visit to the school and discuss with the priest the expiring lease and obtaining the building for Classical Academy occupancy. Several days later, she called to inform me of the date and time she had arranged for my visit with the priest and inspection of this soon-to-be-available former Catholic-school facility.

I was uncontrollably exuberant, and that's minimizing my reaction! That evening, I called my wife, who was visiting her parents in Ontario, Canada. I told her about this heaven-sent, divinely sanctioned intervention in our disappointing facility search, which might have been a response to her many prayers for success. I further inflamed her expectations by assuring her that, when she returned, we may well be on our way to opening the doors of the Classical Academy and beginning my dream, which, out of love for me, she had made her dream as well.

A former school is the ideal location for a charter school; it already has all the municipal-issued occupancy certificates of fire and sanitation, which merely needed to be re-issued upon inspection, and a "certificate of occupancy" ("C/O"). Most critical, it is already zoned for "educational use" ("E") and requires no zoning variance. It also has all the other elements for school use—classrooms, desks, lighting, bathrooms, and the rest. Perhaps only a bit of cleaning and minor renovation or rearrangement, if any, need be done before welcoming students. I asked my wife to hurry home so that we could savor our mutual and latest victory, and continue with our now certain-to-open preparations of recruiting students, hiring teachers, purchasing textbooks, school equipment, and much more.

During work on the day I was to meet with the priest, I rode a cloud of blissful anticipation and counted the hours before our 4:30 p.m. meeting. I arrived at the priest's home and office; directly across the street stood the former parish school. Looking at the structure, I imagined where to affix the *Classical Academy Charter School of Clifton* sign. The neighborhood around the school was decidedly "Clifton urban." The mostly two-family homes of old construction were set close together; most had very small backyards. Some houses were in a state of mild dilapidation, and parked cars crowded the surrounding streets. There were no trees or grass in sight; concrete and asphalt abounded. Still it was a rare facility discovery, and I was so grateful that this school, which had for generations educated the children of eastern European Catholic immigrants, would now find a rebirth of educational opportunities for children of more recent immigrants seeking the hopes America offered. It was assuredly the site for the final realization of my long-held dream of school creation, and of actualizing my ideas for education reform and an academics-first public school.

I was full of enthusiasm and giddy with every prospect for success as I knocked on the priest's door. Not receiving a reply, I continued knocking to signal my arrival. His office appeared dark, with no sign of interior life. I then walked to the school; it, too, was locked, and no one was present to respond to my presence. I crossed the street and again went to the office to knock on the priest's door. Receiving again no reply, I walked to my car, entered, and waited for a half hour. Then I repeated the entire process of attempting to have my presence acknowledged. Finally, giving up hope that I would speak to the priest that day, I drove home, thinking perhaps I misunderstood the appointed day or time. How could I make such an unforgivable mistake? I upbraided myself mercilessly for my stupidity.

Returning home, I noticed a phone message had been recorded on my phone-answering device. A voice recited a terse message which deflated all my hope: "Mr. DeRosa, this is the Diocese of Paterson. The school facility in which you are interested will not be available to you." No further details were provided, and, frankly, the depth of my disappointment would not have found solace in *any* proffered justification or reason. I soon realized that Catholic schools saw free-tuition charter schools as competition for their already rapidly declining enrollments, hence, they were not disposed to assist charter-school development in any way.

I was too upset to eat supper, lamenting this perhaps irretrievably fatal setback. That evening, I called my wife to inform her of this odious turn of events. I remember telling her: "My love, we have been through so much and have devoted an immense amount of work and emotion to this project for a full year, and I know you did so out of love for me and wanting to help me, without reservation or complaint, to achieve my dream. But the forces against us are so powerful in their determination to stop us. The Mayor and the Clifton City Council, all elected Clifton officials, the Clifton School District, and most of Clifton's citizens are all vehemently against us—now, even the Catholic Church is against us. How are we ever to overcome such potent opposition?" She commiserated with me and encouragingly reassured me calmly that "We'll find a way."

The Dollymount Nursing Home: Destiny Fulfilled

Not long after suffering this grave disappointment, I visited a ladies-clothing shop on Valley Road in Clifton, not far from our residence. This quaint shop was one of the oldest retail stores in Clifton, having opened in the 1930s. Its elderly proprietress, a daughter of the store's founder, lived above the store. She was known to me, as some of her family members had married mutual friends of my family. During our time living in the neighborhood, my wife had purchased some items from her ladies' apparel shop on previous occasions, and, while doing so, the two had engaged in convivial conversations and had become acquaintances.

The purpose of my visit was to purchase postage stamps, her shop being an approved vendor of postage stamps and related postal paraphernalia. While waiting to be served and meditating on my recent crushing defeat in finding a school facility, I vividly recalled the old mansion-type structure a few blocks down the street on Valley Road; for years, I passed this building every day to and from my work. I recollected how often while driving, I glanced up admiringly at that majestic structure with its high Greek columns and front portico redolent of classical Greco-Roman architecture. The mansion was elevated on a hill back from the road; its spacious rear and front lawns, and large, century-old oak, beech, and chestnut trees, including an ancient mulberry tree symbolic of Paterson's once great silk industry, graced the property, all of which seemed to encompass at least an acre or more of bucolic charm and antique gentility. When frequently passing this charming structure, I remembered, when glancing up at its echoes of past elegance, I often said to myself, "What a wonderful place for a classical school."

I inferred the building was some sort of healthcare facility, because I often saw ladies in white smocks entering and leaving the building, who I assumed were nurses. When purchasing the postage stamps and engaging in some congenial banter with the proprietress, I said offhandedly, "Mrs. A, do you know anything about that old, large white building down the street on a hill?" She said she knew it well and that she had neighbors and friends who once worked there; it was the Dollymount Nursing Home. I pursued questioning her, losing my breath with ineffable anticipation when she told me that the nursing home was moving out in a few weeks, and she presumed the building was going to be sold.

I immediately departed Mrs. A's shop and hastened to the Dollymount Nursing Home. I met with the director on site. She confirmed Mrs. A's account; the nursing home contained several remaining residents who would soon be transferred to other area nursing homes; after that, the director said, the owners would probably sell the building. I implored her to give me the owners' contact information, for I assured her that it was a matter of the greatest moment. Later that evening, I called the phone number she had provided me.

I learned from the person with whom I spoke that she was one of the owners of the building, along with her three middle-aged siblings. They were the children of the deceased owners and longtime (since the mid-1950s) operators of the Dollymount Nursing Home. She and her three siblings had their own careers and lives, and could no longer feasibly manage the business, especially with increasing, costly facility regulations continually being imposed for federally approved nursing homes, as was the Dollymount Nursing Home. At its height, the nursing home could serve a maximum of about 20 elderly residents at any one time. It was the owners' mutual intention that, once all the residents had moved to other nursing homes within the month, they would place the property on the real-estate market, planning to sell their ancestral property.

I related in some detail who I was, what my intentions were of opening a state-approved charter school, what obstacles I was facing, and my desperate need to acquire a building that could be utilized as a school facility. I indicated that I was very much interested in determining if the building could be adapted for school use, and if so, I should be most eager to secure the Dollymount building for my state-approved charter school.

She told me that she could not commit to any decisions about the building, and that whatever the manner of disposition of the property, it must be mutually agreed upon by all her siblings, each sharing equally in the building's ownership. She said that, in several weeks, the family was to gather for a family event and that she would bring the matter before them for discussion. She would call me with any questions they may have or with what their attitudes were regarding a leasing agreement for the property rather than selling it. I responded that I was at their disposal and would provide documentation as to my character and intentions, and confirmation or elaboration of any aspect of the Classical Academy project.

True to her word, the owner of the Dollymount contacted me to tell me her three siblings were warm to the idea of leasing the building to me to house the Classical Academy Charter School. She granted me permission to inspect the facility for my evaluation as to its suitability for my intended purpose and to estimate what renovations would be necessary both for obtaining the needed municipal occupancy certificates and for student instruction. Upon my inspection, my overall evaluation of the building for school use, despite some space limitations, was exceedingly high, far surpassing any building for school use I had examined during the last six months.

Not wishing to misrepresent myself, I informed her in a subsequent phone conversation a week later that I did not have the purchase funds, nor could I obtain a loan for the amount they would be asking for purchase of the property. But according to charter-school regulations, once students began attending the school, starting in September 1998, state funding would begin. If all things proceeded well in obtaining the facility, I beseeched her to consider a four-year lease arrangement, with its first monthly payment due in September 1998, and that the lease contract have an option allowing the school to buy the building at the end of the lease term.

Shortly thereafter, I personally met with all family members. We agreed to a lease arrangement which included four vital provisions. First, the lease would be void if, for whatever legal reasons, the New Jersey Department of Education or Clifton municipal authorities reject my acquisition of the building for educational use. Second, the lease would be nullified if, for any reason, the school did not open in September 1998. Third, if the lease were implemented, the Classical Academy had an option to buy the building upon expiration of the four-year lease term—and at market price—before the owners could sell it to any other prospective buyer. Fourth, monthly lease payments would begin when funding for Classical Academy students begins in September 1998.

Agreeing to these lease provisions, the owners also expressed a melancholy satisfaction that, having grown up in their parents' nursing-home business, they had always associated the building with being a place of somber, end-of-life sadness. Now the building would ring with the happy, youthful sounds of adolescents and the joyful anticipations of those beginning their lives. But much still had to be done before such sounds would be heard in the building and on its park-like property.

Before the lease was drawn and signed, I took several more inspection tours of the structure, estimating what renovations needed to be undertaken and how best to use its rooms for instructional purposes. Smaller in interior space than what would be ideal, it was nonetheless a superb Clifton discovery for the Classical Academy facility. The interior configuration and rooms of the building were conducive to classroom and instructional use, and required little renovation. The nursing home had a small kitchen, with a commercial gas stove, where meals for the residents were prepared. Knowing we would not prepare food for students, one of the first tasks was to remove the stove. Another task was to increase significantly ceiling lighting, for which the installation of several banks of fluorescent lamps would be necessary in each classroom (previously the rooms of residents). Some toilet fixtures in the building's 6 bathrooms would need replacing. There was a common room, which could be used as a classroom. Closets in rooms and in hallways could be used for miscellaneous supplies and textbooks. There was a very large cellar, containing two boilers and a large room with many metal shelves, in which was stored commercial food supplies for the nursing home's kitchen—this was well suited for school supplies and textbook storage.

In all, the 2-story, wood-frame building contained 6 rooms which could be used for classrooms, 2 classrooms for each of the 3 middle-school grades. The facility possessed 2 smaller rooms for small-class tutorials or computers, 1 medical room for a school nurse and infirmary, and a room which was the nursing home's reception office, which could easily be utilized as the school's main office. Next to the common room was a small, alcove-like room which could serve as "Lead Person/Principal's Office." A second-floor room too small for a classroom could nicely serve as a teachers' room. The basement contained a walled-off room used by the nursing home's director as her office and which could be employed as a workspace for my wife and co-founder, Magda, as the school's "business administrator/administrative assistant."

More than a century in age, several of the mansion's rooms contained handsome but long-disused fireplaces with imposing mantles; several others had original coffered chestnut wood ceilings and ornate wall moldings; some rooms had colored stained-glass windows, and still others had expertly crafted painted windows depicting scenes of Medieval life.

Although it had been a long time since it was the home to a prosperous and locally influential person (see Appendix B)—and after many years of various uses—the structure, which originally stood on 12 acres of specially selected shade trees and outbuildings adorned with formal gardens, still possessed distinct features of its former grandeur. The building exuded a warm, home-like presence rather than institutional coldness; the outside property would afford peaceful seclusion in a pastoral setting conducive to outdoor student activities and recreations.

Taking all factors into consideration, with September only 2 months away and preparation time quickly dwindling, and after 7 months of an ever-disheartening search for a school site, it was by far the best building I could ever find in Clifton to be home to the Classical Academy Charter School. The cost of renovations for conversion into classrooms and other preparatory needs to the building was not beyond consideration, and, with my wife's enthusiastic consent, I would pay for all required facility renovations that could be completed in a relatively short time.

The biggest disadvantage was the lack of more classrooms and their interior space. When I was completing the charter-school application, there was a degree of reasonable speculation and ideal projection, the absolute fulfillment of which is often contingent on the size of the school facility the applicant has yet to obtain. Because of the Dollymount's space limitations, there would be no high-school grades as envisioned and approved in the charter, so beginning with the 6th and 7th grades of middle school would not only be preferable but imperative educationally.

Conforming to the Dollymount's space constraints and facility limitations, my goal would be to create 2 classrooms for each middle-school grade of 6, 7, and 8, with 40 pupils in each grade (20 pupils per classroom), amounting to a school total of 120 students by full middle-school development. The goal of full development would be reached, hopefully, in the third or fourth year of the school. Unfortunately, this is less than half of the 300-350 total students in grades 6-12 as projected in the approved charter upon final school development. Such a large reduction of maximum student enrollment would necessitate a corresponding diminishment of funding projections and far fewer operating revenues. But these were secondary worries compared with the acquisition of a rare school facility that enabled the Classical Academy to begin according to schedule—and to do so against all odds.

Securing the Dollymount Nursing Home facility for the Classical Academy after the wrenching heartache of the Catholic-school debacle validated my wife's reassuring prediction of only weeks ago: "We *did* find a way." But now a new phase of the battle commenced: the Clifton Board of Education handed off its hostile offensive efforts to stop the Classical Academy to the equally unfriendly powers of the Clifton municipal government, exhorting it, as it seemed to me: "We tried all means without success to stop the charter school. Now it is your turn to use your powers to block this unwanted and threatening project. Do not fail us!"

I retained the attorney who represented the school at the "Council on Unfunded Local Mandates" hearing to help with the process of securing municipal occupancy certifications and for transferring the Dollymount Nursing Home facility to Classical Academy for educational use. We began this process in late July 1998, when we requested to be on the agenda at an upcoming Clifton City Council meeting to begin our goal of securing the required building certificates and, of course, the essential, highly coveted "E" (educational)-use zoning variance so that the building could be used to house the Classical Academy.

The City Council, upon which also sat the Mayor, indicated that we needed to attend several meetings and provide certain documents as the process for a facility "Change in Use" request could not be accomplished carelessly or in a rush. My attorney argued to the City Council, attempting to accelerate the process and ease some of the open hostility to the charter school, that the Classical Academy will be an asset to the city, and that the number of students to attend the Classical Academy had been reduced by more than half due to the space limitations of its chosen school building. It is inconceivable that a school of only 120 students at maximum growth would adversely affect, financially or programmatically in any way, a school district of 10,000 students. Still the council delayed and seemed most disinclined to issue the needed "C/O" (certificate of occupancy) and the "E"-use zoning variance, employing disingenuous reasons like traffic and parking concerns, and that a school in the Dollymount building would be disruptive to and incompatible with the essential residential nature of the neighborhood (despite there being a Clifton K-5 public school a mere 2 blocks away on Valley Road).

At one such contentious public meeting, a number of neighbors of the Dollymount Nursing Home appeared in organized opposition to voice their concerns to the City Council of having the Dollymount building used as a school. Placing credence in the rumor that the school would serve Paterson youth who were predominantly Black aroused neighbors' fear of crime, vandalism, and property-value decline. Assuring them of the falseness of this persistent rumor, they nonetheless complained of the likely noise, rowdiness, and general neighborhood disruptions attendant to a school. After all, they reminded the elected officials, they have been accustomed to environmental tranquility a small nursing home imparts to its surroundings. To quell residents' opposition and perhaps to induce them to reconsider their unreasonable objections, one owner of the Dollymount building, not in complete jest, suggested I tell the residents surrounding the Dollymount that, if the Classical Academy were not allowed to lease the building, the building owners would sell it to nearby St. Joseph Medical Center, to be used as an outpatient drug-rehabilitation center. Then, adjacent residents would *really* have something about which to worry and fret.

Precious weeks elapsed; the Clifton City Council took no action except to stall and raise objections against using the Dollymount structure as a school. We were informed that the municipal-issued certificates of fire, sanitation, and health were contingent on first obtaining the "Change of Use" permission to an ("E") educational use; and that this "E"-use designation required a zoning variance, which Clifton officials would not grant.

Mid-August had arrived, less than one month before, according to its charter approval, the Classical Academy was to begin. But our hopes, as ever, were being blocked by city elected officials. Despite our best efforts, securing municipal permission to use the Dollymount for the Classical Academy was at a standstill, and prospects were so dim that building renovations required for student occupancy were forestalled.

I and the few Classical Academy supporters considered using the New Jersey State Department of Education's "Planning Year" for charter schools. This permitted a charter school to take, if needed, an additional developmental year to plan and successfully implement its charter approval. In a few weeks, if no progress had been made obtaining the essential building certificates, and should we seek an additional planning year, I then intended to contact the superintendent of my school district and inform him that I would rescind my Leave of Absence and return to my job in September.

An Orthodox Rescue

One person who was interested in the Classical Academy's progress volunteered a suggestion which may, he said, help the immediate situation. He knew a parishioner of a Greek Orthodox church located 2 miles down on Valley Road in Clifton. In the church's basement, he believed, were classrooms with student desks used for "Greek School."

The next day, I pursued this suggestion and visited the church. There, indeed, were 7 basement classrooms, including an open cafeteria space, which were used only on certain evenings and weekends to instruct Greek-American youth of their ancestral language and heritage. This school space needed no renovations, no need to purchase student and teacher desks, boards, or other essential furnishings; all instructional necessities were present for the Greek School, which, during weekdays, was unused. As the space was used for instructional purposes, the facility possessed all the required and up-to-date municipal certificates for educational ("E") use, along with fire/health and sanitation certificates. The facility thereby afforded a desirable "move-in" simplicity, with only the Classical Academy and St. George Greek Orthodox church as parties to any facility rental agreement or contract. Clifton City authorities and Clifton School District could not legally impede or prevent such an agreement; only the Department of Education could prevent this arrangement.

I asked the Greek Church official with whom I spoke about renting the classrooms, providing him documents certifying the legitimacy of the

Classical Academy, my own role in the project, the number of expected students, teachers, anticipated time length of rental, and other details he would need to bring the matter before the church's Board of Trustees, which was largely composed of parishioners of the church.

The advantages a temporary location offered were obvious and potentially critical to the Classical Academy's founding—indeed, its very future. For instance, the Classical Academy could begin September 1998, as charter approval provided, without taking an additional planning year. Whatever benefits a planning year might provide, the Dollymount owners understandably would not or could not be expected to hold the building for us for such an extended period. They would withdraw from our lease contract and sell the property; we, losing the best facility we could have discovered for the Classical Academy, would have to begin anew our facility search. Temporary occupancy would also afford us time to continue our legal quest to obtain the required municipal certificates permitting the Dollymount building to be used for the Classical Academy. Temporary residence in the Greek Church would also give us time to conduct renovations to the building before we moved the school, if matters turned to our favor, from the Greek Church to the Dollymount building, finally becoming, after a strident "David and Goliath" struggle, the Classical Academy Charter School of Clifton.

Several weeks after my offer, the Greek Church official notified me that the church's Board of Trustees had consented to rent their Greek School basement classrooms to the Classical Academy on a month-to-month basis. We discussed details, contingencies, and provisions to the rental contract, namely: 1) that the New Jersey Department of Education agrees and permits the Classical Academy's temporary use of the St. George Greek Orthodox Church of Clifton; 2) rent to begin when student funding begins; 3) rental agreement terminates with 30-day notice of either party. The rental terms were agreed to, despite the church charging a substantial monthly rental fee, which would affect our originally estimated first-year expenditure-incoming revenue balance. Nevertheless, I and my wife believed strongly that, if we did not act decisively and rent the temporary school facilities, the Classical Academy's establishment may well be deferred permanently.

Optimistically, in about three weeks, if matters developed favorably, my wife and I would begin Passaic County's first public charter school in St. George Greek Orthodox Church at Valley Road, Clifton, New Jersey.

Recruiting Students and Hiring Teachers

Before describing further my ongoing effort to secure the Dollymount building, discovered by chance or by destiny after an unrelenting search for a Clifton facility to house the Classical Academy, and in addition to my critical participation in the legal battles initiated by the Clifton Board of Education, I was actively engaged in two other tasks vital to the Classical Academy's founding: First, recruiting students, and, second, hiring faculty.

As early as March 1998, I took out advertisements in the local papers for outreach and recruitment of students. I invited parents to send for further information, having developed an informational brochure detailing prime aspects of a Classical Academy education. My wife and I also spent many weekends going house-to-house, distributing flyers about the Classical Academy. I would choose a Clifton neighborhood, and we walked its streets, putting these informational flyers in mailboxes. When we were told by a postman that placing unsolicited, unstamped documents in mailboxes was illegal, we resorted to sliding the flyers in screen doors or under doormats. We also, with permission of the store, erected a folding "informational table" near the entrance of several Clifton food stores, such as Pathmark or Acme. Some people stopped and asked questions about the school. We placed informational brochures on the table and asked interested parties to take one. A few seemed interested, but others walked away, tearing up the brochures with disgust and then placing the torn pieces in nearby trash bins.

Responding to questions and concerns, I would also meet with parents at small gatherings, sometimes at their homes, or I would secure the premises of a small hall for a larger group informational meeting. Of course, without knowing the outcome of the legal battles and not having a school facility, all my remarks and enticements for parents to obtain for their children a high-quality academic education were tentative and, by necessity, uncertain. This uncertainty led to dissuasion of many otherwise-interested parents.

By mid-August 1998, our six-month student-recruitment efforts resulted in only 20 Clifton parents whose commitment to enroll their students was moderately strong, however, a final decision depended on school location, transportation, and other details parents needed to know before enrolling their children. Even at this late stage, there was still much left unknown and doubtful, militating against parent confidence in school opening. Some parents said that, in a week or two, they needed to pay Catholic-school tuition, which is non-refundable, hence they would not consider enrolling their child if the school's opening remained uncertain, maybe even doubtful, and when Classical Academy enrollment would mean monetary loss of their prepaid non-refundable Catholic-school tuition payment.

With all these factors hindering recruitment of students, the low number of prospective students after a six-month effort seemed to corroborate the opponents' adamant assertions that the Clifton community did not want or need a charter school. Difficulty in student recruitment was furthered by certain tactics of the opposition, deliberately employed or merely misguided. For example, I received unconfirmed information that some Clifton public elementary- and middle-school guidance counselors were recommending parents of difficult or behavioral-problem students to enroll their children in "Clifton's new alternative school," a tactic which, surprisingly, did not result in increased enrollment numbers. Another unconfirmed report told of a Clifton Public School low-level administrator who had expressed interest to me in enrolling his daughter in the Classical Academy. His superiors bluntly told him, the report alleged, that if he sent his daughter to the Classical Academy, he could expect to lose all opportunity of climbing the "executive-educator ladder" to higher administrative positions in the Clifton School District. Whether this was true or not, I never verified, but he did, without explanation, withdraw his daughter's Classical Academy enrollment application.

Yet another deterrent to Clifton parents enrolling students was the persistent rumor that most of the Classical Academy students would come from Paterson (the Dollymount building was only two blocks from the

Paterson border, a fact nurturing this rumor). Above all, only a smattering of parents was willing, despite whatever persuasive talents I may possess and the qualities of the school I proposed, to send their students to a new school without any record of client satisfaction, student learning results, testimonials from friends, or recommendations from neighbors.

As opening day approached, it was clear that we were far from our projected Clifton enrollment numbers of 80 students, 40 in the 6th grade and 40 in the 7th grade. The 80-student objective was based on the maximum-size limitations of the Dollymount building (our acquisition of which was still far from certain) and on the charter school's ultimate development of 120 students in grades 6, 7, and 8.

Charter-school rules allowed for enrollment of students outside the charter school's resident district if application numbers from the resident district were insufficient. Consequently, so that all our efforts to this point would at least yield a minimal inaugural-class student enrollment, and to begin without necessitating a planning year, or sacrificing the opportunity the Greek church offered as a temporary location, or losing entirely the Dollymount facility, we decided to enroll students from outside Clifton. Even with this strategy, only 48 students, half from outside of Clifton and far short of our target of 80 students, were enrolled on the Classical Academy's inaugural opening day in September 1998.

Regarding our first teachers, I adhered to my firm belief that a high degree of knowledge of the subject one teaches is paramount for instructing youth, thus, I sought out teachers with a master's degree in the subject they would be hired to teach, not an undergraduate or graduate degree in the field of "education." I sought persons who were duly state certified or were eligible for the Alternate Route certification program. My prime solicitation method was to place "Teacher Wanted" ads in the education-employment section of the *Star Ledger*, often referred to as New Jersey's "newspaper of record." Interviewing prospective teachers at various places of convenience for both parties, I invited some interested people to my home, to a mutually convenient restaurant, or even to the Clifton Public Library for teacher-interview locations. I provided interested teacher applicants with much the same printed information about the school that I would supply to parents. I believed it important that each knew about charter schools and specifically the Classical Academy, its mission, curricula, the "academics-first" culture, and what the school could pay for salaries and how tentative and uncertain were the Classical Academy's immediate prospects and the obstacles for its long-term success.

As much as we could, and despite the greatly reduced revenues from a very small first-year class, we would offer them all the benefits usually associated with public-school teaching: health coverage, paid school vacation days, and paid sick days, and enrollment in the state's public education employee pension system. Their salaries, however, would be similar to Catholic-school teachers, and not comparable to public-school teachers in adjacent school districts.

Several weeks before school opened, we had hired the school's first five faculty: Social Studies (history), English, Mathematics, and Science (biology). I myself would teach Latin; all held a master's degree in the teaching subject; the social studies teacher had earned a PhD in history. Of course, in my designed curricula, no non-academic subjects were offered, and, thus, no non-academic subject teachers were hired. I requested that each provide me with the information on textbooks or other instructional materials they had selected and wished the school to purchase, as well as to write a basic curriculum in their subjects for 6th and 7th grades.

The State Department of Education granted my petition to start the Classical Academy in the temporary quarters in the church's basement-classroom space, as it also granted permission to accept students from outside of Clifton, while I engaged in the ever-diminishing prospect of seeking municipal approval and permanent acquisition of the Dollymount building. I thereupon signed the rental contract with the Greek Church, which, not knowing the fate of the Dollymount building, was on a month-to-month basis. The rental cost was substantial, $6,000-$7,000 per month; but it was an expense—a short-term expense, we prayed—we had to bear if the Classical Academy was ever to begin.

A few days before school began, the Passaic County Superintendent of Education visited me at the Greek Church to see the facilities. My wife and father of blessed memory were present (for years my father would assist us in unpaid, voluntary janitorial work and be at my beck and call if I needed any item for the school or a task performed). The superintendent concluded that the school was a "family affair," a comment which, I think, was not meant to be a compliment but to which I assented proudly. She insisted that the children not use the main entrance when arriving to or departing from school because the main vestibule was adorned with images of "Greek Saints." The separation of church and state, she asserted, would forbid such obvious religious surroundings to be seen by or in close proximity to public-school students. Fortunately, there was a back entrance leading to the basement classrooms, which we used all during our Greek Church occupancy, and Classical Academy students' vision was never assaulted by images of saintly religious icons.

Chapter IV

OPENING DAY AND THE CLASSICAL ACADEMY'S
TUMULTUOUS FIRST YEAR

Because of the increasing need for her time and expertise in preparing documents for enrollment, funding, establishing the proper accounting systems that the state and county education offices required, and many other documentary processing tasks related to financial, budgetary, and student-reporting requirements, my wife Magda, in August 1998, resigned from her job to devote herself full time to the Classical Academy. Like myself, she did so without any compensation or salary.

We were very clear in all the papers we had signed and processed with the state regarding governance of the Classical Academy Charter School of Clifton, that my wife, Magda DeRosa, was a co-founder of the school and, like myself as Lead Person, would be employed by the school, when and if the school begins, as its "school business administrator," a position for which she was qualified by her degree in accountancy from a Canadian university and her background in finance. Her New Jersey "SBA" certification would be acquired through a state-approved "alternate route" program consisting of an on-site mentorship program provided by a retired New Jersey School Business Administrator. Our quickly appointed first Board of Trustees endorsed by resolution both our Classical Academy positions and job titles.

Using the Greek Church school facilities offered a temporary solution, but acquiring the Dollymount building as the school's chosen facility faced legal barriers that Clifton municipal government had erected; there was every likelihood of a protracted and uncertain struggle. The mantra of *"No Building, No School"* reverberated in my head, as it did in my opponents'.

Because of our greatly-reduced anticipated first-year school revenues, and our personal and increasingly precarious financial situation, worsened by the loss of my wife's income, and the specter that, after having resigned my teaching position in June 1998, we would have no family income whatsoever or health insurance, I forged an employment-contract agreement with my school-district employer Superintendent. I would rescind my "Leave of Absence" and continue for the 1998-1999 school year to teach 2 classes of Latin, with 1 "prep" period, amounting to three-fifths employment. He would schedule the 2 classes in the morning—8:00 a.m. to 11:30 a.m.—permitting me to leave after the third period, at 11:30 a.m. I could then return to the Classical Academy by noon each day to manage the school and teach 3 Latin classes, 2 for 6th-graders and 1 to the 7th-graders. In effect, during the Classical Academy's first year, I was teaching full-time while performing all administrative school function, a nearly impossible undertaking which could only be executed successfully with the indispensable and able assistance of my wife, Magda.

With the opening day of school at St. George Greek Orthodox Church, the Classical Academy, years in the making, against all odds, and in defiance of the most powerful forces coalesced against it, was finally established, tentatively and weakly, but established! Our first group of Classical Academy students consisted of a total of 48 students in 6th and 7th grades; 34 were 6th-graders, and 14 were 7th-graders. In total, only half were Clifton-resident students; the other half was composed of students from communities bordering Clifton: Paterson, Passaic City, Garfield, and Montclair. Located in temporary quarters, the Classical Academy began its life with far fewer students than expected, and nearly half the students resided outside Clifton; our budget and incoming revenues were, therefore, less than half of what was anticipated and what was projected in my charter-school application of 1997.

Notwithstanding enrollment numbers far less than hoped and acquisition of our school facility being blocked by municipal authorities, when Classical Academy students arrived at the Greek Church that first morning after Labor Day, September 1998, it was an exuberant event, long-dreamed and long in the making. Adorned in a Roman toga my wife had fashioned and crowned with a garland wreath, a Roman mark of triumph, I greeted our first students and families that first morning as they entered the parking lot and school.

My wife, Magda, each day would open the school and start the day as teachers and students arrived at the Greek Church. As the administrator on site, she managed all aspects of the school in my absence until I arrived at noon each day. Magda's unpaid job as School Business Administrator of a newly established charter school required her to deal with managerial situations and find solutions to countless pressing obligations and responsibilities: paying teacher salaries, purchasing supplies, setting aside funds for facility rent, finding ways to "scrimp and save" in order to meet a panoply of financial obligations with the most meager of finances, setting up accounting and budgetary procedures compliant with state requirements, school transportation, and dealing with teacher, parent, and student issues. Transacting with several school districts that did not have charter schools and were perplexed as to their funding responsibilities for their resident students enrolled in the Classical Academy was another of Magda's multitude of tasks (several of these districts refused for months to comply with their funding obligation, further rendering our cash flow even more constrained).

As an aside, let me mention that charter-school law prescribed that if an "out-of-resident" charter-school student's district had a higher per-pupil cost, as indeed all our non-Clifton students had, the tuition to the charter school was 90% of the lower resident district, that is, of Clifton's per-pupil cost—not 90% of the considerably higher Paterson, Passaic City, and Montclair districts. For example, in 1998, Paterson enjoyed an approximately $10,000 per-pupil cost (largely at state taxpayers' expense), and Clifton's was $6,000 (nearly entirely from Clifton taxpayers). The Classical Academy received 90% of Clifton's lower per-pupil cost, not 90% of the higher Paterson per-pupil cost, or, for that matter, the higher per-pupil cost of all our other non-Clifton enrollees. This represented a tuition loss of about $4,000 for every non-Clifton student, a monetary sum the Classical Academy desperately needed but by law never received for each Paterson, Garfield, Montclair, and Passaic City student attending the Classical Academy.

I worked at my Bergen County School District in the mornings teaching 2 Latin classes, after which I would return to the Greek Church just before school lunchtime. With Magda's indispensable help, I managed all aspects of the school, and taught as well several afternoon Latin classes to Classical Academy students. Financially, we lived off our savings and our greatly reduced one-income household; our saving for a home of our own became a deferred life goal, as our mutually committed zeal was entirely dedicated to working for Classical Academy success.

Each day we would confront the challenges with varying degrees of success: teacher problems with certain students, low funding and allocation of resources, parent and student issues, developing ways to create and implement an "Academics-First School Culture." Our first teachers were willing to assist in diverse ways in launching the fledgling school and allied themselves in the common effort for school survival, if not success. Each day brought its problems; when I arrived just before school lunchtime, Magda would recite to me the list of situations, challenges, and daunting financial issues that arose or were ongoing. Whenever I despaired, she would arouse my flagging resoluteness with: "We'll find a way."

On the Brink of Demise

All this time, the attorney and I were working toward acquisition of the Dollymount building for the Classical Academy's permanent home. Despite our efforts, the city council and its zoning board continued to refuse us the legal permission to use the facility for the school, particularly rejecting our application for the "E" educational-use certificate, which required a "zoning variance" and the "C/O" (certificate of occupancy), itself contingent on "E"-use certification. Both documents, along with fire/health-sanitation certificates, were required by the city and by the State Department of Education before the Classical Academy could occupy the Dollymount building for a school.

The zoning (planning) board, composed of the mayor and members of the Clifton City Council, was most conscious of the *"No Building, No School"* strategic tactic, and were complicit in this struggle against the charter school. It also knew that they were the last defensive wall against the Classical Academy, the charter school which, despite the severe imbalance of forces and resources, had nonetheless emerged victorious in all its battles to this point. Clifton municipal authorities and I knew that this was the last and most determinative battle in the entire struggle to establish Passaic County's first public charter school.

The Clifton City Council employed various arguments to deny an "E"-use zoning variance for the Dollymount building. They recited again their feigned and false concerns: a school is out of character with the neighborhood; nearby residents' vocal opposition; building is not suitable for a school; parking and traffic concerns; noise complaints; safety concerns, and so forth. Of course, we could appeal the zoning board's rejection, as was commonly done. But, as the City Council, zoning board, and Clifton public school authorities well and smugly knew, an appeal would entail a long and costly legal battle, for which the Classical Academy was in no position to engage. Furthermore, as I was paying the lawyer, and considering the sum Magda and I had already expended on the Classical Academy cause, I was most reluctant—indeed, unable—financially to undertake such litigation, and there was no outside entity, governmental or private, willing to come to our aid.

We were quite alone in this struggle; no assistance, legal or financial, and no advocacy on our behalf were forthcoming or offered by any governmental agency, including the Passaic County Office of Education or the State Department of Education. Although I did not expect but would have welcomed powerful allies in this struggle, I found it something of a betrayal as it was I and the Classical Academy that had helped save the New Jersey charter-school program. The battle to acquire the Dollymount Nursing Home building was strictly a struggle between me and Clifton municipal government; no state education office or department felt it had the authority, legal or persuasive, to involve themselves.

Just as disheartening, it was most unlikely that the owners of the Dollymount, who were sympathetic supporters of me and the school, would be willing to retain ownership of the building and keep it off the commercial real estate market for months or longer while lengthy litigation against Clifton municipal authorities was underway, and a favorable decision an uncertain outcome. Since Clifton's zoning board stood adamant in denying the Dollymount building a zoning variance for "E"—educational use, it was most reasonable and understandable for the building's owners to decide in the next several months to void the tentative lease contract with the Classical Academy and return to their original intention of selling the Dollymount property. To compound our acute troubles, I was told by a church official that, after the new year, in about two months, the church's board of trustees was planning to terminate our monthly rental arrangement.

No Greek Church, no Dollymount, no feasible alternative facility—all were distinct and imminent probabilities; my despair even surpassed that produced by the Catholic-school building rejection. The inevitable consequence would be to dissolve the school, pay existing bills and satisfy, if we could, all remaining financial obligations, terminate contracts, and after a 4-month aborted, ignominious beginning, initiate all other unhappy transactions enforced liquidation demanded. Perhaps, I thought in my more optimistic moments, the state would consent to grant a "planning or developmental year" so we could regroup, continue to search for another facility, and essentially to start over. Returning to reality, I confessed it would be highly improbable that the state would consent to a "second chance" after so egregious a failure and after such an unpromising beginning. Having come so far and so close to fulfilling my dream, desperate and near hopeless, I was grasping at the most meager irrational hope of survival, while the voice of my wife's reassuring words echoed in my mind as they comforted my anxious thoughts: "We'll find a way."

The Dollymount "Miracle"

I tried to appear confident, especially to Magda, during these most dismal times for me and the embryonic Classical Academy. Contemplating the near certainty that the Classical Academy would succumb in utter failure just a few months after its most difficult and unlikely birth, I felt that I had "met my Waterloo." I even likened myself to the unfortunate characters of classical mythology, where the gods smote them down mightily because their hubris extended beyond human bounds, becoming too offensive to the rulers of Mt. Olympus for thinking themselves divine-like in their extravagant aspirations.

I then recalled that, about the first week in September, as we took occupancy of the Greek Church, the owners of the Dollymount building had given me a trove of Dollymount Nursing Home documents. I now took the time to review these dusty, yellowing papers one evening at home in early November 1998. Upon inspection, I saw that most of the documents were meaningless old medical records or long-ago nursing-home operations documents. Then I took up from the pile a one-page certificate-appearing issuance from Clifton Zoning (Planning) Board. As I read the document, my heartbeat increased, and I became alternately perplexed and euphoric. It seems that the Dollymount Nursing Home, decades ago, had applied for and had been granted by Clifton authorities an "E" (educational)-use zoning permission. *Could it be that the Dollymount building had, for many years, unbeknown to all, already possessed the golden "E" (educational)-use facility-code endorsement? Could I be holding in my hands the very "E"-use building-code endorsement, the very same municipal permission which the Clifton zoning board denied me but upon which the entire future of the Classical Academy depended? If so, it literally would be the salvation of the school!*

I must have reread this document 50 times, believing it could not be true or that I was delusional in comprehending what I was reading. I fantasized that, as soon as I should collect my wits, the words would rearrange themselves to become nothing more than an old, meaningless bill or utility statement. But no, each time I read it, the words remained: *"The Clifton Zoning Board Hereby Grants to the Dollymount Nursing Home, 20 Valley Road, Clifton, NJ, an Educational ("E") Facility-Use Designation."* I then called my attorney and read to him every word, verbatim, from the certificate. I asked him incredulously, "Does this mean what I think it means?" He replied, "It sounds like it does."

We made an immediate request to the zoning board to be placed on their agenda for their next meeting, at which time I and the attorney presented them with the Dollymount's "E" (educational)-use certificate.

It had no expiration date, and, as far as we could determine, it was never rescinded. We presented it to the City Council and zoning board, and each shocked member passed it around for their colleagues' inspection. The precious document finally arrived in the hands of the city attorney, who attended the meeting. City Council and zoning-board members looked at each other, confessing in their frowned expressions that *"this was a problem."* The attorney assured the Council and board members that he would research the document and announce his assessment next week at a special City Council meeting.

That meeting with the Clifton City Council and the zoning board took place the third week of November 1998. Everyone was anxious for the board attorney's report. All eyes focused on him as he, with forlorn visage and in an apologetically somber tone, informed the assembled dignitaries that the 20 Valley Road building, known as the Dollymount Nursing Home, indeed possessed a valid "E" educational-zoning designation and that, therefore, the building's proposed use as a school does not require a zoning variance or special-use request from the city's zoning board. We were as elated at this unimaginable—need I say *miraculous*—turn of events as the Clifton municipal authorities and Clifton Public School officials were sullen and distraught. As we left the meeting, I euphorically embraced my wife Magda, her words yet again resounding in my consciousness: *We'll find a way.* Well, my love, you were right! We *did* find a way, and we had won! David had beaten Goliath, yet again!

Incidentally, the owners of the Dollymount knew nothing of this "E"-use designation. We can only surmise that, years ago, their parents or their parents' attorney thought it prudent to petition Clifton municipal authorities to be granted an "E" (educational)-use zoning designation because, in the building's "Common Room," there were periodic instructional classes in crafts or other activities the elderly residents enjoyed in the sunset of their lives. If these long-departed blessed souls had not found pleasure learning about the making of mosaics, crocheted doilies, macramé, Christmas decorations, or genealogical charts, then the Classical Academy Charter School of Clifton would have certainly died in early infancy, collapsing after only four months of life. To these angelic spirits, I owe, in no small measure, the fruitfulness of all my efforts and the fulfillment of my dream.

The Move to the Dollymount: From the Somber Silence of the Aged to the Vivacious Sounds of the Young

Notifying the Greek Church that we would terminate our tenancy at the end of December 1998 and signing the Dollymount building four-year lease, which was to begin January 2, 1999, we had but six weeks to prepare the new school facility and transform the Dollymount Nursing Home into the Classical Academy Charter School of Clifton.

Our priorities for renovation were determined by supplying the very basic physical necessities of a school. One of a number of appealing features of the building was that conversion to a school did not require exorbitant costs and time-consuming alterations. An immediate necessity was to install in all classrooms—which, just weeks ago, had served as bedrooms for nursing-home residents—and in the several adjunct rooms, banks of overhead fluorescent lighting units. Since we used student desks of St. George Greek School, we now had to purchase our own. The simplest and least-expensive solution was to purchase about 25 6-foot- and 8-foot-long folding tables, along with 50 metal folding chairs. This would satisfy our current needs, and adding some more folding chairs would suffice for our anticipated needs for our second year's increased enrollment, or so we hoped.

Large "whiteboards" with dry-erase markers were placed in each class-room; determined by a room's configuration, some were placed on movable easels, while others were attached directly to the wall. For teacher desks, we used a few that belonged to the nursing home; two were donated, and two were purchased, which required assembly, as did several purchased bookcases (a task my father of blessed memory gladly took in hand, as he would do without hesitation in countless other occasions in the years ahead to help his son and adored daughter-in-law manage the Classical Academy). Ceiling lights, desks (table and chairs), instructional whiteboards, textbooks—the most fundamental of instructional accoutrements—were acquired used or inexpensively purchased, mindful that the ancients had produced some of mankind's greatest learning and eternal works of mind and spirit in schools held under olive trees or in open porticos.

Before beginning classes in the Greek Church, our founding faculty had selected textbooks for their respective subjects, which we transported to the Classical Academy facility. I added to these by scouring my employer school district's textbook closets for disused and discarded schoolbooks marked for disposal, but which I salvaged with the principal's permission for supplemental use in "my school." Some very fine, out-of-publication books for English, literature, and Latin subjects were thus appropriated and given a second life for Classical Academy students' benefit, and without cost.

We had valuable and much-appreciated parent involvement in making the move from the Greek Church to the Classical Academy building. Some parents seemed to sense the importance the Classical Academy would mean for their own child's education and what it represented to public-education reform. Others, too, wanted to acknowledge with gratitude both my vision and the self-sacrificing doggedness Magda and I had expended to establish the Classical Academy, thereby providing to parents a degree of educational choice. Recognizing our efforts, they wanted to contribute generously their welcomed assistance. We had purchased, for example, student lockers, an amenity many parents expressed a desire that their students have. The lockers were placed in hallways and in some classrooms offering sufficient space. At less cost, one could purchase the lockers in an unassembled condition, an option we chose. On several weekends in December 1998, groups of parent volunteers spent many hours spread over several days to assemble the lockers—no simple task—and fasten them in rows to the walls in certain hallways and classrooms so that their students would have these when they began school in January 1999.

Since the Classical Academy did not prepare food for students, we disposed of the commercial 8-range gas stove/oven, affording a bit more kitchen-area space. As in the Greek Church, students brought their lunches from home; retaining the two commercial refrigerators would allow us to place lunch bags in refrigerators for food needing refrigeration. We also placed in the kitchen several newly purchased microwave ovens for student use during lunchtime.

In addition to preparing the building for school use and student occupancy, our simultaneous task was to obtain the sanitation and fire-safety certificates required by the City and the Department of Education. These certifications had to be obtained prior to the issuance of a "Certificate of Occupancy" for school-facility use. Before students occupied the facility, the owners had the building thoroughly cleaned, just after we signed the four-year lease.

To comply with federal and Medicare rules, the nursing home some years ago—and at much expense—had installed an extensive sprinkler system throughout the building, including the attic, basement, and even in closets. The Classical Academy building (the former Dollymount building) is a 2½-story-high wooden structure. It may well be that the Classical Academy was the only New Jersey public school housed in a wood-frame building (yet again, just one of the Classical Academy's many distinguishing attributes). It was because of the existing and twice-yearly tested full sprinkler system that a school, despite the valid "E"-use designation, could exist in a wood-frame structure and remain compliant with state fire-safety regulations. The structure contained a full attic, with 8-foot ceilings, which we believe was once used in the 1950s as a rental apartment and, during its original owner's time, maid quarters. The city fire marshal instructed me that, despite the existence of "sprinkler heads" in the attic and its ample space, no one was to occupy it, and no items of any sort could be stored therein. It was a matter having to do with fire-truck ladder-extension size and wooden buildings. This quickly ended any plans for future renovation of this 3rd-level attic space for student or school use.

Upon inspections by the relevant Clifton municipal offices, The Classical Academy received both Sanitation and Fire Safety Certificates, to be renewed each year. Because the building already possessed the "miraculously bestowed" "E" (educational)-use zoning designation, the culminating "C/O" (certificate of occupancy) was the final state and local facility requirement allowing the Classical Academy to be housed in the former Dollymount Nursing Home facility (I shall no longer use the name "Dollymount"; from this point forward, the building was, in every sense, the Classical Academy Charter School of Clifton's home).

Clifton Public School District complied with charter-school transportation rules and supplied to us one school bus, whose route and student qualification for school-bus transportation its own office of transportation determined. All the non-Clifton students had to supply their own private transportation to and from school; non-resident districts were not legally mandated to provide any of their resident students with school transportation to an "out-of-district" charter school.

It was a day of victory and vindication when our first-year students arrived to the Classical Academy that first morning after New Year's Day, January 2, 1999. I was there to savor the momentous event (but without my toga) for which my wife and I had long struggled. The same arrangement for school management and operations practiced at the Greek Church was continued for the entire Classical Academy first school year (1998-1999). Magda would be in charge of the school until I arrived at lunchtime to be both the Lead Person and the teacher of 3 Latin classes (2 for 6th-graders and 1 for the 7th-graders).

The students seemed to develop a fondness for their unique school facility: its home-like atmosphere; its antiquity; its intimate or "human-size" interior space; learning in rooms with ornate fireplaces and chestnut moldings and paneling; windows adorned with majestic stained glass or colorfully painted scenes of Medieval Europe; taking outside recess under huge trees, on spacious lawns, and where an imposing Magnolia, with its spring-bloom profusion of purple flowers gave particular pleasure. Some students asked, "Mr. D, is our school building haunted?" and I would reply, "Yes, with the ghost of learning."

Our pastoral, campus-like school property was a treat for the majority of our students who lived in highly urbanized neighborhoods, where trees and lawns were a rarity. Occasionally deer and wild turkey would roam down from Garret Mountain Reservation, to which the school abutted, and grazed on school property, affording special delight to all. I speculated that these physical features, along with a small student-body size, would contribute to an *esprit de corps*, a common-purpose ethos providing a conducive foundation upon which to build and solidify as we went forward, the school's "academics-first school culture."

By taking advantage of some nearby amenities, we began several activities which would become not only enduring Classical Academy programmatic staples, but endearing traditions. Several times yearly we took hikes to and along Garret Mountain Reservation, a 568-acre county-owned "forever wild" nature sanctuary, to see the resident deer and other wildlife, and in the autumn, to enjoy the colorful foliage. Some blocks away, reached by a 20-minute walk, was a large Clifton Municipal park with several baseball diamonds, tennis courts, and large, open grass fields. Here we began to have "Friday Afternoon Field Days" in fall and spring months, weather permitting, while satisfying—in our unique way—state physical-education requirements.

Even before we left the Greek Church, we began our student recruitment for our second school year, 1999-2000. Charter School regulations, acquiescing to public-school district complaints that they needed to know by mid-January of each year not only the number of resident students who would attend the charter school, but also their names and addresses. This ostensibly so the school districts and citizens would know the budgetary impact of charter-school costs before citizens voted on school budgets in April. Not even the most exclusive private schools have secured their next year's student enrollment so early and so long before September classes begin. But any hardship a public-school district can perpetrate on a public charter school is deemed worthwhile policy; too often, the New Jersey Department of Education succumbs to their wishes, oblivious to the difficulties certain state-imposed rules and regulations inflict on the charter-school operations.

In securing our second-year enrollment, we held a number of "Open House Informational Sessions" for parents and students, both on Saturday afternoons and several evening sessions, at the Classical Academy building. By law, non-Clifton-resident enrolled students are permitted to continue their Classical Academy matriculation each year until graduation. The Classical Academy is, by design and charter, a Clifton district charter school, but it is allowed, as stated earlier, to accept non-Clifton students only after all Clifton students wishing to do so have enrolled by January 15, and student vacancies still exist. Our outreach never was overtly extended to non-Clifton students, and we made it clear to non-Clifton parents seeking admissions of their children that the admissions priority, by law, must be given to Clifton residents. But non-Clifton students did provide the school, in those early years, a lifeline for financial survival at a time when most Clifton residents shunned the school, believing the slanders against it, or were not attracted to the Classical Academy, whose record for excellence was not yet established or recognized.

Striving for a second-year recruitment of 40 new 6th-grade students, 20 students in each of our 2 6th-grade classrooms, our final 6th-grade enrollment, however, numbered a disappointing 26 students, 7 of who were non-Clifton residents. Fourteen students advanced to our first 8th-grade class (this would be the school's first 8th-grade graduating class, in 2000), and last year's group of 6th-graders advanced to our second year's 7th grade, yielding a total of 29 7th-graders (several new students were admitted to this 7th grade). As we approached the Classical Academy's second year, 1999-2000, our total enrollment was 69 students, short of our target of an 80-pupil student body. We nevertheless hoped, if our school could achieve its mission of academic excellence and operational success, to reach 120 students and full school enrollment in grades 6-8 in several years.

Regarding student enrollment and community acceptance of the Classical Academy, it must be said that, in the early years of the Classical Academy, the school had strong support from parents and families belonging to the religious denomination called "The Unification Church," founded by the late Reverend Sun Myung Moon of South Korea. Magda and I, both practicing Roman Catholics, found members of this religious group—disparagingly referred to as "Moonies"—who enrolled their children in the Classical Academy to be trustworthy, intelligent, family-oriented parents who cared about their children's education; they were also strong supporters of the charter-school movement. Members of this religious group residing in Clifton became a valuable part of the small Classical Academy family, and several were early members of our Board of Trustees. Having confidence in Magda and me, they supported us as we navigated through some of the most difficult times of the Classical Academy's inchoate years. Satisfied with the way the school was managed, the high-quality education their children were receiving, and the disciplined school environment, they recommended the Classical Academy to parents both inside and outside their religious community. Members of The Unification Church thus became assets to the school when it had few supporters or allies.

As we advanced through the winter and spring months of the Classical Academy's fledgling first year, I reflected on our progress to date. I recall that, after submitting my charter-school application (about nineteen months prior) and the pointed arguments that the Clifton Public School Superintendent made against charter approval, most presumed the Classical Academy would never be granted a charter. When, shocking everyone, it received charter approval, the feeling was strong that the newly chartered school would not survive the several legal challenges against the Education Commissioner's approval. When it did survive, the popular belief was that Clifton's challenge to New Jersey's charter-school legislation's funding mechanism before the "Council on Unfunded Local Mandates" may well deliver a fatal blow to the Classical Academy and, indeed, to all charter schools. When the Classical Academy prevailed before this Council, the firm and certain conviction took root that the Clifton city government, now taking up its potent sword against the weak and war-weary charter school, would at last vanquish the Classical Academy and never grant to it the legally required municipal certificates, especially an "E"-designated zoning variance for school use, thereby denying occupation of its chosen school facility. Again, their strategy was simple: *No Building, No School.* When yet again the Classical Academy miraculously prevailed against Clifton municipal powers, the opponents' final hope of defeating the Classical Academy ultimately focused on its less-than-half projected first-year enrollment (and much-reduced funding level), relishing the expectation that the school would never successfully complete its first year due to lack of sufficient funds and parental interest.

Still, as our first winter turned to early spring, and as our second-year student enrollment was finalizing, we would begin our second year with about 69 students, slightly more than half our 120 projected maximum number of students at final development. Although this was disappointing, it was yet 20 students more than our tumultuous first year. We could therefore contemplate a more confident future, one less threatened with the sort of problems and opposing forces any one of which could have easily prevented the school from beginning—or have destroyed it during its first-year infancy. But as we were to discover, our first-year struggles were not yet finished, against which Magda and I had to gather yet more unyielding fortitude to battle forward. Two circumstances seriously threatened the Classical Academy's fragile first-year survival and gave our opponents, who had endured so many defeats, renewed hope that yet an ultimate victory over the Classical Academy was very much still possible, if not likely.

Emotionally Disturbed Parent Threatens School

One source of our opponents' hope for our failure was the turbulent repercussions a disturbed parent was inflicting upon the school community, jeopardizing the school's survivability at its most vulnerable infancy. This parent was a non-Clifton-resident mother who had two children enrolled (both coming from Catholic schools) in the Classical Academy founding year. As early as the second month, while the school was still at the Greek Church, she accused one of our teachers of physically assaulting her 6th-grade son. Her daughter, a 7th-grader prone to frequent hysterical outbursts and panic attacks, accused other students of hating and mistreating her. My thorough investigations of the alleged "physical (kicking) attack" by the teacher and student bullying revealed that no such events occurred or were anywhere near the magnitude and frequency alleged. When I exonerated the teacher based on evidence and testimony of numerous witnesses, the parent and her two children turned their venom on me. The mother attempted to recruit other parents and students to support her claims and to admit falsely that the accused teacher had assaulted other students and that I ignored these serious allegations, thus abetting this teacher's assaultive behaviors.

Each day seemed to bring a new episode or event involving this mother and her two children that impacted the school and which required my repeated attentions. The aggregate of these malicious, irrationally motivated events and accusations could damage the fragile school, its reputation, and the ability to progress beyond its tender infancy. The parent complained bitterly both to the Clifton Public School District and the New Jersey Department of Education of "what terrible things were going on at the Classical Academy" and that the school's leadership was not doing its job at protecting students, punishing abusive teachers, or dealing with parent complaints.

She insisted to all who would listen that the Classical Academy was another "Columbine" school tragedy in the making. I received several concerned phone inquiries from the Office of Charter Schools seeking information about the reported incidents and my responsive actions to the parent's accusations. It was clear Trenton was concerned and monitoring the situation. If not controlled, the public-relations nightmare with possible headlines such as "Founder and Lead Person of Clifton's New Charter School Accused of Condoning Teacher Abuse and Ignoring Student Bullying" could well prove fatal to a school struggling for community acceptance and reputation.

This discordant tumult continued at the new Classical Academy building. To soothe the situation and allow parents to voice their concerns and opinions, we held several evening discussion sessions, inviting all parents. These meetings became acrimonious and heated. Parents understandably told this complaining and accusatory mother simply, "If you don't like the school, why don't you just take your children out?" Her reply was that she had a right to attend the school, that it was not her fault the school had hired some bad teachers, and that Mr. DeRosa is incapable or unwilling to solve the problems. At one such meeting, a student's father attended. He was a pastor and a counselor at the Passaic County Jail, and hoped to heal the acrimony by having everyone hold hands and sing some prayerful hymns.

The complaining parent never ceased to attempt to enlist the support of fellow parents and students, hoping to validate or create new stories of teacher misconduct and fabricated instances of my own malfeasance, continuing her groundless claims that the school allowed students to bully and harass her two children. On a school hike to Garret Mountain Reservation, for example, her son claimed to have "twisted" his ankle after having suffered an asthmatic attack. We transported him by car back to the school for rest and care (we always had a car not far from where our students were hiking in case of emergencies). That evening I received a threatening call from the boy's father. Based most likely on his son's lies about the incident, he accused me of negligence by allowing his son to be hurt and not doing anything to assist him. He said that if any further events of this sort happened, he would act, ominously stating: "Mr. DeRosa, you don't know who I am; I'm a 'made man' in my union." This, of course, is "Mafia talk," at which he thought I would be duly intimidated.

This mother's actions became more erratic and her accusations more bizarrely absurd, but they were also potentially dangerous. Frustrated in gaining allies to her cause, and stymied from convincing more parents of her malicious accusations, she began to act in harassing ways toward other parents and students. Several times, I witnessed her accelerating her car on the school driveway and coming close to striking pedestrians. On one occasion, she screamed at an African-American parent, "Watch out [N-word], or I'll hit you." She voiced, in the presence of others, similar racial vitriol against a black female student whom her daughter had accused of bullying. There was ample evidence that she was often inebriated or "out of sorts" when she picked up her children after school. At these after-school times, she would linger on school property with her own children and coax other students to enter her vehicle, all talking excitedly, as if sharing tales of what happened in school and what lies and accusations based on the day's events she could plausibly fabricate against teachers, other students, parents, and me.

It was obvious to us, after months of this sort of increasingly alarming behavior, that we had to act decisively. I filed several police reports with local authorities, who occasionally came after school to observe her behavior, but, being wise to their presence, she acted accordingly. For the sake of the school community, we hired an attorney, seeking to legally forbid her from school grounds and from any school event in which her children may be involved. Despite our near-exhausted funds, we believed, for the survival and general well-being of the school, such litigation must nevertheless be pursued.

Our court hearing was scheduled, and the attorney we hired was a welcome comfort to us. Her counseling and commitment to our success—not only in this matter but also for the school's future—was reassuring. Interestingly, this parent's attorney in this matter was a former Clifton School Board of Education attorney—no happenstance, because when the Clifton Board of Education got wind of this situation, it attempted to play a behind-the-scenes role in hurting the Classical Academy, perhaps even fostering its longed-craved for Classical Academy demise. I suspected, but never proved, that Clifton Public School District was paying her attorney's legal fees. Clifton school officials certainly believed that, if the Classical Academy's reputation became publicly tarnished so early in its existence, enrolling students (and thus possessing adequate school funding) would become even more difficult, and consequently the State Department of Education would terminate the school's charter for insolvency or not being financially or educationally viable.

At our first court session in seeking to bar this person from school grounds and events, the judge asked this parent in open court to rise and state her grievances and intentions. She said that she was here to sue the Commissioner of Education for $100 million. The Judge and all in the court were stunned, and it was then that I knew we would win our case, as she had demonstrated beyond all doubt that she was an unwell person whose veracity and emotional stability were dubious and untrustworthy. In the end, after sworn testimonies and a review of the incidents, evidence, and facts—which I scrupulously documented with eyewitness testimonies—the judge asserted that this was a serious matter of school safety and that this person had been proven to be a risk to the Classical Academy Charter School community. He even hinted at "restraining orders" and possible jail time. At this point, her husband and the former Clifton Board attorney negotiated a settlement with the judge and our attorney, to which we eagerly agreed: she was ordered never to come on school property or attend any school-sponsored function, day or evening, and have no contact with any school employee; violation would be a fine and possible jail time. Happily, in a few weeks, she voluntarily withdrew both her children from the Classical Academy. It was yet another favorable outcome to a difficult and threatening situation to the infant Classical Academy at its most fragile and vulnerable time.

Approaching Financial Collapse and Yet Another Miraculous Salvation

The other fact making the school's first-year survival doubtful, was, indeed, what the Clifton Board of Education had adduced as one of the reasons our charter application be rejected: the Classical Academy's budgetary income-expense figures for launching the school and to completing its first year successfully were inadequate and "speculative." Since New Jersey does not provide any funding for "start-up costs" or "seed money," nor could charter schools "float bonds" to raise money, the monetary resources, including facility renovative costs and all expenses for starting a charter school before student funding begins, must come from external sources.

Thus, before funding from Clifton School District (and other adjacent school districts from which we had enrolled students) for our enrolled students commenced in mid-September 1998, all Classical Academy start-up costs encompassing the 9-month period from charter approval (January 1998) to school opening in September of 1998, including legal fees to fight the litigations Clifton Board of Education initiated against the Classical Academy, were paid by me and my wife. In addition to the legal expenses, we paid for all other costs required by or incidental to the starting of the Classical Academy Charter School of Clifton, such as printing, advertising, renting venues for informational meetings, and a large portion of the building-renovation costs. Our apartment address and personal phone served as the Classical Academy's "developmental office" and contact information.

Added to what we actually paid, both from our own savings and in many lost-salary days devoted to the school's development, must also be calculated the income that we sacrificed in starting the school. Magda, my wife and school co-founder, quit, as previously stated, her full-time job in August, a month before our September 1998 school opening, and worked without pay the entire first year of the Classical Academy. For financial and health-insurance reasons, and all the uncertainty surrounding the school's first-year viability, I needed to keep my tenured teaching job at a school in Bergen County. However, in order to have time to devote to the school's founding year, my hours, by mutual agreement with my employer, were cut from full time to three-fifths. In all, we expended or otherwise contributed about $150,000 from our savings and lost income to start the Classical Academy Charter School of Clifton, not counting the fact that neither Magda nor I took a salary or any compensation whatsoever for working at the Classical Academy that entire first year of the school. Of course, Clifton, in its cost-estimate criticisms of our initial financial plan, could not have contemplated that there would be absolutely zero first-year "administration" costs (and comparatively little in subsequent years), and that its founders would be providing the majority of all funding for start-up expenses.

Despite our financial contributions in underwriting the launching of the Classical Academy, and notwithstanding the stringent frugality in our school expenditures, beginning in September 1998, the school's income revenue was becoming less than outgoing expenses. That we had less than half our anticipated first-year enrollment (and therefore less than half of expected funding) was a major factor for these revenue-shortfall and cash-flow problems, which were exacerbated by the loss of six students withdrawing in the first four months.

Our continually revised monthly internal budgets were further impacted by Clifton Public School District's refusal to provide charter-school funding for any Clifton-resident student attending a Catholic school who enrolled in the Classical Academy. We had 5 such students. Clifton's initial refusal was yet another way it could inflict damage on the Classical Academy. Eventually, through our persistent interactions with Clifton school bureaucracy on its charter-school-funding obligation, and with the state's clarification on this Catholic-school issue, the matter was resolved—but not before it added considerably to our first-year dwindling-cash-flow problems.

The $30,000 cost for facility renovations compared to other charter-school facility adaptations was relatively slight; our teacher salaries were considerably lower than the salaries of Clifton and area public-school teachers, but comparable to Catholic-school teacher compensation. Our monthly Greek Church rent and then the monthly lease cost (in which was included the property tax, as the school was not the owner of record) of $7,000 for the Classical Academy building were each rather steep for our meager incoming revenues. Teacher fringe benefits like health insurance, textbooks and learning resources, folding chairs and tables for student instruction, utility cost for the Classical Academy facility, legal fees, incidental start-up costs like a school office computer and accounting software, all comparatively minuscule for typical school expenditures of this sort, nevertheless added to our accumulating revenue deficit and constrained financial circumstances.

We had just celebrated our first "Spring Break" in mid-April 1999, when Magda and I, our prodigious self-sacrificing efforts and administrative frugality notwithstanding, after reviewing the school's most optimistic revenue projections, acknowledged we did not and would not have enough money to pay ongoing expenses and thus to complete the school year. If and when the Department of Education was informed of this financial failure, it would certainly mean that the Classical Academy's charter would be withdrawn for financial insolvency at the conclusion of our first year, June 1999.

The only possible salvation was to inform the teachers that we could not pay their salaries for May and June. We requested—indeed, *appealed* to them—that they continue working the last two months of their contracts without salary; we would, however, continue paying their health-insurance coverage. We provided each teacher with an addendum to their existing contracts stating that all "deferred" salary of May and June would be paid fully—assuming the school would continue into its second year—by September 30, 1999, even if the teacher did not continue as a Classical Academy employee next school year. All teachers but one agreed to this arrangement. Slightly rearranging the school-day schedule, I taught, in addition to my Latin classes, one class of the departing English teacher, and Magda, having a substitute's certification, was deployed to teach this teacher's other classes, the lessons for which I planned.

Even with these drastic fiscal measures, and even with my and Magda's already massive workload yet further increased, it was still uncertain if we could finish the year solvent and not be delinquent on outstanding bills and paying the monthly facility lease. Failure to pay bills and contractual obligations would mean insolvency and Classical Academy termination at the conclusion of the school's first year. Although we hoped the deferred teacher salaries would improve our money woes, we nevertheless braced for the Classical Academy's possible impending financial collapse. Contemplating with despair all possible sources of money, including our own remaining personal savings to avoid insolvency, we were visited by yet another miracle.

It was the conclusion of a lovely early-June school day of our first year, several months after we had successfully confronted the "plague of the disturbed parent" and had finally eliminated that fatal threat, but still fearing the school's probable and imminent financial insolvency. I was sitting in room #3, which had been the Dollymount nursing home's common room—remember the nursing-home ladies' crafts instruction room and the miracle of the "E" zoning designation? At the room's threshold, I noticed my wonderful, beautiful wife smiling with a joyful radiance which I had come to recognize as prelude to some welcome announcement. She retained that radiance all the while approaching me at the other end of the room, our eyes remaining fixed on each other's. Reaching me, she playfully thrust forward her hand and passed me a letter without saying a word. Paraphrasing the letter's contents: *"Congratulations. The Classical Academy Charter School of Clifton is hereby awarded an educational grant of $75,000 from the Walton Family Foundation."* I jumped up and embraced my beloved wife.

In December 1998, Magda, without my knowledge (sparing me false hope), had completed several grant applications; the one to the Walton Family Foundation was successful. The money resulting from Magda's initiative and her ever-uplifting *We'll find a way* attitude saved the school from dire financial straits and likely dissolution. We immediately paid the teachers for the weeks they had worked for deferred salary; we paid also the monthly lease payments for the summer months, and we had some money remaining to pay outstanding bills and purchase additional textbooks and necessary supplies for the new school year—a year the prospects for which just moments ago were bleak and uncertain, but now were excitedly anticipated with new challenges and successes, and, perhaps, with new miracles.

Such were the seemingly insurmountable obstacles and turbulent beginnings of an afflicted and beleaguered institution that, within 10 years, would become one of New Jersey's first charter schools to be nationally recognized with the "National Blue Ribbon School of Excellence Award" (2008), and a school consistently ranking in the top 5% of all New Jersey public schools in 8th-grade-student academic-learning outcomes. These noteworthy achievements were accomplished at a taxpayer cost of 50%-60% below neighboring school districts. How this near-unprecedented, remarkable New Jersey public-school educational feat was accomplished is described in the next several chapters.

Chapter V

THE CLASSICAL ACADEMY'S SYSTEMIC EDUCATION REFORMS LEADING TO HIGH ACADEMIC STUDENT LEARNING PROFICIENCIES 1997-2016

I here describe an actual New Jersey public middle school, grades 6-8. After this description, I ask the reader to speculate on how such a New Jersey school would be rated or ranked, and what would be this school's expected 8th-grade level of comparative student academic-learning outcomes, as measured by state-mandated tests.

The school, comprising grades 6, 7, and 8, is located in a northern New Jersey city (18 miles from New York City) that has both urban and suburban characteristics. The city has a Department of Education "district factor group" or "socio-economic" rating of "CD" ("J" being the most affluent and "A" the poorest urban areas). A "CD" district factor group rating can be described as "lower middle-class." The median household income in this city is slightly below the state's median household income. The school's 120 student population is 80%-90% children of immigrant families; a large percentage (about 75%) of its students are bi-lingual and speak or hear spoken a foreign language at home. Overwhelmingly, the parents of this school's students have only a high-school education or less (only about 10%-15% are college graduates). Ethnically, the school is predominantly "Hispanic" (60%-70%); the bulk of the remainder of the students are of Arabic, Asian, Turkish, Albanian, Bosnian, and Polish ancestries, whose parents immigrated to America. The school's "poverty rate" (percentage of students qualifying for "free or reduced school breakfasts and lunches") ranges annually between 25% and 40%. Its teachers are paid less than neighboring school district teachers. The school facility is a 100-year-old wood-frame structure, once the large home of a wealthy personage; it lacks many of the amenities and usual facilities of a typical public school. The school is documented to have among the lowest funding of any New Jersey public school; in some years, the state cited this school as having the lowest per-pupil cost of any public school in New Jersey. The school has relatively little technology.

I ask the reader again: With these school attributes and student-population profiles in mind, what would likely be such a school's ranking among all other New Jersey schools? And what would be the reader's conjecture regarding this school's 8th-grade student academic-achievement levels as measured on state-mandated tests?

The reader would understandably be incredulous when told that this school was ranked consistently in the *top 5% of all New Jersey public middle schools* and that its 8th-grade students' academic proficiencies, based on their state-mandated standardized tests scores, year after year *surpassed by huge margins the 8th-grade academic-learning proficiencies of their Clifton Public School peers.* Just as incredulous would one be to learn that this school's 8th-grade standardized-test scores show its students to be *comparable in academic-learning attainments to their much more advantaged counterparts in even the most affluent New Jersey schools and school districts;* and that its 8th-grade-student test outcomes yearly ranked the school *first or consistently among the top 10% of middle schools in all of Passaic County.* Furthermore, the school each year ranks scholastically in the *top 10% (occasionally number 1 or 2) of all New Jersey public charter schools in 8th-grade academic achievement.* The reader would undoubtedly react in disbelief to such absurd, preposterous claims so incongruous to known reality and public-education history.

However, what is here described and asserted are documented facts (see Appendix A); such a school does, or at least did, exist: The Classical Academy Charter School of Clifton (New Jersey), a public charter middle school (grades 6-8) whose unprecedented success offers a model of school reform and a cynosure to those desperately craving substantial changes in the way public education is done in this state. Simultaneously, The

Classical Academy Charter School of Clifton (New Jersey) during my school leadership was disdained by the established education interests, because the successes of this "Little School That Could" threaten their power, influence, and taxpayer-funded prosperity.

A Teacher-Founded and Teacher-Managed Public Charter School

Under my and my wife's leadership, and as the school's finances became stable and even, in time, robust, as Classical Academy students' scholastic-learning proficiencies burgeoned in excellence and consistency, and as the school's reputation grew, receiving two applications from Clifton residents for every vacant seat, the Clifton Public School District never again openly challenged or opposed the Classical Academy, or argued against its future charter renewals.

The Classical Academy Charter School of Clifton (New Jersey) became, as I had envisioned, the "proving ground" for implementing policies and practices which, based on my many years of close observation of and participation in the K-12 educational enterprise, both as a classroom teacher and principal, would achieve the overriding goal of increasing student academic-learning outcomes among middle-school children of mostly immigrant parents to unprecedented lofty levels. To this end, the school, by design and inception, is free of—as much as possible for a public school—the entrenched counterproductive student-learning practices which create and sustain the endemic "anti-academic school culture," which itself invariably produces the "high costs-low results" reality pervading public education. The school is, therefore, the consummation of my long-held ambition of creating an "academics-first" school as a laboratory and living demonstration of the merits and efficacies of my education-reform ideas.

Because of my reform ideas and the singular school policies and practices I implemented for bringing those ideas into reality from 1997 to 2016, the Classical Academy Charter School of Clifton (New Jersey), Passaic County's first public charter school, produced astounding learning-outcome results among a student population long associated with poor academic achievement. Amazingly, the Classical Academy accomplished this rare feat as one of New Jersey's lowest-funded public schools. How all this was accomplished will be explained in the next three chapters.

In this chapter, in addition to documenting my and my wife's school-managerial priorities and philosophy, I will delineate the Classical Academy's 13 unique—indeed, unprecedented—education-reform practices and policies. The education reforms that are described in this and the following chapters enabled the Classical Academy Charter School of Clifton (New Jersey) to create an "academics-first school culture," and thus to achieve consistently the remarkably high student academic-learning outcomes among students whose social-economic backgrounds and the schools they typically attend preclude scholastic excellence and suppress academic attainment.

1: Curriculum

The Latin word "curriculum" refers to a "racetrack or prescribed course" through which one must traverse to achieve a specified object or goal. In education, the curriculum, or *course of studies*, is, or at least *should be,* the heart of any school. What is studied? How often is it studied? What are the established marks of progress at agreed-upon intervals? What defines the achievement expectations at the end of the course? The answers to all these questions are crucial factors in the educative process.

The Latin components of the word *education* mean "the process of leading out of or out from." This "leading out of or out from" can be understood in two ways. First, as a *transformation out of adolescence and into adulthood*—a mere process of maturing, physically and emotionally. It is this definition of "education" that most schools, whether or not they acknowledge it, advocate and practice as their chief function and purpose. However, the other interpretation of *education* is the "leading out of or out from," as the *intellectual growth process leading from ignorance (darkness) to knowledge (light)*, or *from a condition of absence of knowledge and intellect to one of acquiring high knowledge and intellectual development.*

The Classical Academy is the rare public school that adheres to the latter definition of "education" and, thus, as an institutional imperative, replaces the typical "anti-academic school culture" with an "academics-first school culture." Academics-first schools are exemplars of the intellectual-growth definition of education for every one of its students (not only the most motivated, academically serious, or the most privileged), where the acquisition of academic knowledge compels intellectual development in every student, along with virtue and character, thereby defining their institutional purpose. The Classical Academy Charter School of Clifton exemplifies in its charter application and in its long practice under my guidance, of being a decidedly academics-first school with an intentionally constructed strong and manifest academics-first school culture.

A traditional "classical curriculum" is richly educative ("educative" in the sense of *leading out of the darkness of ignorance to the light of knowledge and understanding*). To quote from the Classical Academy's charter application of October 1997: "Centuries of scholastic history have demonstrated the worth and power of such a [classical] course of studies to educate, to inspire, to achieve. There is nothing experimental or speculative about the Classical Academy's curriculum; it is a well-traveled path toward solid learning and academic excellence. It is also a superb curriculum framework in which 1) to incorporate New Jersey's recently promulgated 'Core Curriculum Content and [Learning] Standards' and 2) to develop and sharpen the skills and proficiencies those content standards are intended to produce among all New Jersey youth."

The following subjects constitute the Classical Academy's prescribed 7-subject *mandatory* program of academic studies, or "curriculum" which *all* 6th- to 8th-grade students must traverse. Notice, in this curriculum, the absence of "elective" courses and non-academic subjects, which allows more school-day time for academic learning.

a) Latin

Again, quoting from the Classical Academy's charter application: "There is no finer pedagogical tool for a thorough understanding and acquisition of English grammar and English vocabulary than Latin. High in "transference" skills, Latin yields several important academic advantages: like mathematics, it creates a disposition for precision and teaches thinking skills; it is a marvelous foundation for study of modern languages, especially the Romance languages; it is the gateway language [and discipline] for understanding the ideals and principles of western culture; it assists in [English] reading and writing ability."

When teaching Latin, I myself utilized, and, pursuant to my directives to other Classical Academy Charter School teachers of Latin, an English-grammar book to be used in conjunction with the Latin-language textbooks. English grammar and the English language are deeply indebted to Latin; when learning Latin and Latin grammar, we are simultaneously learning English-grammar and English-language skills. Latin instruction should deliberately make the effort to transfer growing knowledge of Latin to the corresponding accumulation of English grammatical concepts, not only English vocabulary, of which approximately 70% is derived from Latin.

The belief that the ancient language of Latin has no use or place in today's curriculum—or that it serves no conceivable purpose or value for today's students—is absolute nonsense; it belies the indisputable fact that Latin is an unrivaled English-language learning tool. No one disputes the importance for all students to study and learn English well; it follows then, that, to deprive students of what arguably is the single most valuable tool for acquiring and reinforcing higher-proficiency English-language skills, is gross educational malpractice. Latin is also an outstanding vehicle for learning ancient Greek and Roman history and culture, and the immense contributions those societies have made both to modern Western and American cultures. It is also of incomparable value when, later or concurrently, one wishes to learn a modern Romance language, all of which are descendant tongues of Latin.

b) English Language Arts and Literacy

As an English teacher, I had found throughout the years that our students receive—to their detriment—very little instruction and experience in reading "non-fiction." Our students come to believe, after years of the typical middle- and high-school English courses, composed exclusively of fiction readings of short stories and novels, supplemented by occasional student "creative" writing assignments, that all writing and reading—indeed the entirety of the English language—is filled with "dialogue." In schools, the meager diet of "non-fiction" readings is invariably restricted to biographies. Using fictionalized characters and character development, with entertainingly imaginative plots of conflict, excitement, or mystery, fictional literature nurtures reading experiences that inculcate young minds toward a predisposition for "stories" or "fabulous" entertainments in adulthood. Nearly the entire consumption of what adolescents consume in TV, movies, and social media is fictionalized stories, often conveying the absurd and juvenile contortions of reality, thus inculcating the adolescent mind with incongruities of created, fictitious reality to appear normal and true.

On the other hand, non-fiction treatises, essays, descriptive narratives, expository writings, commentaries, and arguments offer invaluable instructional benefits and possess more lasting value in English-language instruction than the exclusive diet of imaginative fiction our students are forced to imbibe throughout their education. A truer, more-mature depiction of reality is expressed in non-fiction. Sentence structure, persuasive literary techniques, vocabulary usage, sharpening one's thoughts, and how to express those thoughts logically and convincingly are all critical dividends of well-selected non-fiction readings.

Non-fiction readings also strengthen rational-thinking skills; they exercise students' attentiveness to comprehend treatises, arguments, or narratives with logical order and supporting evidence, and they exercise reasoning ability. When non-fiction readings are related to other topics that students are studying in history, Latin, or science, for example, their knowledge of these subjects grows while their English-reading and expository (non-fiction) writing skills improve and expand. Non-fiction readings also better train students to discern "fact" from "opinion," to discriminate between weak and strong argumentation, and to produce the latter while recognizing the former. A wide variety of non-fiction readings broadens knowledge generally and more effectively teaches students to be better and more sophisticated readers and writers of English and, perhaps, in the end, better and smarter citizens.

During the school's initial years, I spent time in creating binders for each grade level of non-fiction readings. I selected readings, often relevant to students' grade-level topics being studied in Latin (ancient history), American history, science, and general-interest features. Using publications like *Reader's Digest*, *American History Magazine*, feature-length newspaper articles, editorials, and science journals, I reproduced for every student in each grade sufficient non-fiction readings to supplement and expand non-fiction readings appearing in their English- or language-arts textbooks. For many years, we also used newspapers, particularly extended news articles and editorials, and participated in the "NIE" (Newspapers in Education) programs to diversify our non-fiction reading sources and topics.

It is for these reasons—and to enable our students to experience the educative benefits of more "non-fiction" readings—that in the prescribed 7-subject curriculum I formulated, and as part of the Classical Academy Charter School of Clifton's mandatory English-language arts curricula, students must take 2 classes of English-language arts instruction each day. The class containing the "non-fiction" readings and writings I designated "English." The more traditional fiction readings of short stories and novels, as well as the ancient classical epics of Virgil, Homer, and classical mythology, are studied in the "Literature" classes.

This innovation addresses the absence or insufficiency of non-fiction readings in the typical public-school curricula. It also mandates the *doubling* of the amount of time during each school day Classical Academy students spend in English-language arts and literacy classes. This significant increase essentially means that, in 3 years of the Classical Academy Charter School of Clifton's academic middle-school program (grades 6-8), students will have undergone the equivalent in scope and application of *6 years* of instruction in English-language arts literacy compared with instructional programs typical in New Jersey middle schools! The same innovative doubling of instructional time, as the reader will learn, was done with mathematics instruction.

Some years later, while still the Classical Academy's principal and several years before retirement, I read recent studies on this very matter, expressing concern that American students simply do not receive sufficient instruction or classroom experience in non-fiction readings and writings. American students, the studies lamented, thereby remain woefully ignorant of models of logical argumentation, coherent and cogent expression, the role and different types of evidence, vocabulary usage, and sentence structure. These studies strongly admonished educators to quickly address this deficiency. It seems I and the Classical Academy were 20 years ahead in recognizing and rectifying this critical educational deficiency.

c) Mathematics: Pre-Algebra, Algebra I, and Middle School Mathematics

In the popular mind and modern world, mathematics has replaced Latin as the mark of an educated person; the more mathematics study one has pursued, the better educated one is believed to be. Mathematics is regarded as the language of science and technology; it is also the school subject many students find intimidating and fearfully challenging. But all students, through effective instruction and applied, mandated study, including regular class and mandatory tutorials, can overcome the difficulty of learning mathematics.

Most students who have achieved high math competencies, as did most Classical Academy graduates, upon middle-school (8th-grade) graduation are deemed qualified for high-school advanced mathematics courses and honors math classes. These same "math-competent" students, when entering college, will often pursue those "majors" which demand a superior mathematics knowledge, and, hence, are inclined to enter scientific and technological disciplines, which offer some of the greatest career and financial rewards. But because mathematics is such an accumulating discipline, where foundations for subsequent study must be firmly established before advancing successfully to higher levels, math instruction and competencies must begin in the earliest grades.

Students who have acquired a comparatively better-than-average level of mathematics knowledge through instruction have been imbued with the habits of mind for precision and abstraction, habits which mathematics so well teaches. All students will be well served by a serious, compulsory mathematics program of studies. It is vital, therefore, that a middle-school mathematics program, like that of the Classical Academy, lay a solid foundation for mathematics competence and assist all students toward the successful acquisition of mathematics knowledge and skills, whether mathematics is a key to their future pursuits and success or not.

A Second Math Class Each Day

After the first school year, it was clear that many of our newly admitted students, particularly in the 6th grade, were lacking the prerequisite mathematical knowledge to make acceptable progress in the 2-year (grades 6 and 7) "Pre-Algebra" sequence. I thus came to believe, based on student outcomes and teacher appraisals, that it would be highly beneficial to our students to incorporate a 3-year (grades 6-8) "Middle School Mathematics" program. This additional, mandatory 3-year mathematics course of studies would be taught parallel to and in conjunction with (not *in place of*) Classical Academy students' algebraic subjects.

By reducing each class and lunch period by about 5 minutes each, we were able to add a 7th required subject in 6th, 7th, and 8th grades—and to do so without extending the school day. This addition was a 3-year sequence called "Middle-School Mathematics." This new 3-year mathematics sequence was required of all students, and it was to be taken concurrently with the 3-year "Pre-Algebra/Algebra I" courses. By no means was it to be an "easier" alternative to or substitute for required instruction in algebraic mathematics. The 3-year "Middle School Mathematics" sequence provided a valuable vehicle for all students to acquire additional mathematics knowledge, and for many to bridge learning gaps in mathematical skills and concepts not learned in earlier grades. Not in any sense "remedial," it was intended generally to provide a stronger, broader, and more robust mathematics knowledge foundation; and it enabled the school to implement better both our "no-tracking policy" *and* our curricular mandate that *all* Classical Academy students take "Algebra I" in the 8th grade.

Interestingly, during Governor Christie's administration, it became a state-education objective to have every New Jersey student take "Algebra I" in or by the 8th grade. In this regard, I and the Classical Academy were yet again years ahead in already fully realizing this important educational goal. As expected, this state-education objective disintegrated soon after Governor Christie's term of office ended; little since has been said of reviving or implementing this worthy goal, a goal achieved and continued all during my Classical Academy leadership.

As in English-language arts literacy, the Classical Academy's academic mathematics program is mandatory and represents the *doubling*, each day, of the class time Classical Academy students spend in mathematics education. In addition to studying "Middle School Mathematics" in 6th, 7th, and 8th grades, our students take a two-year sequence of "Pre-Algebra" in the 6th and 7th grades, and *all* students—no exceptions based on grades or teacher recommendations—are required to study "Algebra I" in the 8th grade. Here again, by *doubling* the amount of time *each school day* our students study mathematics, our 3-year Classical Academy comprehensive, mandated study of mathematics is equivalent to *6 years* of mathematics study in any other typical New Jersey middle school.

d) Social Studies, American History

Occasionally, before starting the Classical Academy Charter School, I taught a 2-year middle-school "social studies" course. My primary student text contained 8 chapters, to which one marking period, more or less, was devoted to one chapter, for the entire 2-year or 8-marking-period sequence. Each chapter was devoted to one of the many subjects our schools have traditionally categorized as "social studies": economics, sociology, psychology, geography, government (civics), comparative cultures or religions, and a few others, but nowhere was history—or, *especially* American history—to be found.

Following my own predilections and well-founded reasons for the priority of subjects Classical Academy students should study, I determined that however worthy these traditional individual "social studies" topics may be, American history was paramount. This was particularly so in a school where 80%-90% of its students are children of immigrants or themselves born outside of America. America is their new country; as often is the case with immigrants, they don't know the history of one's new country or possess an emotional connection to it. Children of immigrant parents often feel a deep sense of "foreignness" or "alienation," particularly stinging when their own self-recriminations proclaim that they and their "people" have played no role in shaping their new country's culture or in contributing to its historic achievements.

Learning the matrix of circumstances and the flow of human events producing the rich fabric of American history, and the individuals and groups, prominent or obscure, who participate in that flow and fabric, makes that history relevant and meaningful, even to immigrant students. Knowledge of American history serves the vital function for immigrant children of making one's new country one's own. The importance of knowing the history of one's country, whether one is of "old-stock" lineage or recently arrived, cannot be underestimated in the process of Americanization and of national unity.

It used to be an important function of public education to facilitate the assimilation of foreign children or children born in America to immigrant parents. Public schools once facilitated the integration of new arrivals into American society and helped them and their children better acclimate themselves to American society and culture. We do not hear nowadays about this once-lauded duty of public education, but it still is, or should be, when done humanely and sensitively, an important public-education function achieved through the study of American history.

One dimension of American assimilation, and, indeed, helping the integrative process, apart from the common language of English, is a shared understanding and appreciation of American history. Eighty to ninety percent of Classical Academy students had been brought to America as children or infants, or were born in America to immigrant parents. I believed that Passaic County's first public charter school had an obligation to assist these new citizens in becoming Americans and engendering in them a feeling of common belonging. A knowledge and understanding of American history are effective for creating this common feeling of belonging, cemented with the bond of a shared history.

The establishing or imbuing of this "common American heritage" in children of immigrant parents is an important reason why the Classical Academy's "social studies" in the 6th and 7th grades is devoted solely to American history. The relevancy and nearness of American history is further demonstrated by a 2- to 3-week learning unit on "Local History," with classes and school trips devoted to the history of the city of Paterson, famous for immigration and industrialization, and to the rich history of our region during the U.S. American Revolution.

In the 8th grade, after achieving our expectations in the 6th and 7th grades of reaching the post-Civil War "Reconstruction Era" and progressing to America's industrial age of the late 19th to early 20th century, students then switch to a "World History and Culture" course during their 8th grade. During the last years as Classical Academy Lead Person, I, for several compelling and persuasive reasons, and considering also the greater value for our students of further study of American history, canceled this course and added a continuing 3rd year (8th grade) of American history, beginning with the Civil War, Reconstruction, and industrialization. Thus, Classical Academy students benefit from a full 3-year course in American history and cognate topics like civics.

e) Science

A 3-year coordinated program of science consisting of one year each of "Earth," "Astronomical," and "Biological" science comprised the essence of Classical Academy science instruction. This 3-year sequence of science subjects was supplemented by related non-fiction readings and science projects.

Summary of Classical Academy's 3-Year Middle School Curricula Mandatory for All Students

Adhering to the above curricula subjects, Classical Academy students undergo the same 3-year, 7-subject prescribed academic curricula or program of studies for all students:

1: "English" (non-fiction readings and writing), grades 6, 7, and 8

2: "Literature" (fiction readings and writing, including classical mythology and certain classical epics), grades 6, 7, and 8

3: "Pre-Algebra," grades 6 and 7

4: "Algebra I," grade 8 (required for all 8th-grade students)

5: "Middle School Mathematics," 3-year course, grades 6, 7, and 8

6: "Social Studies" (American History), grades 6, 7

("World History and Culture," grade 8, replaced by a 3rd year of American History [for some students, Supplemental English/Social Studies]

7: "Science," grades 6, 7, and 8

8: "Latin," (including classical epics, ancient Greek/Roman history and culture), grades 6, 7, and 8 [for some students, "Supplemental Pre-Algebra/Algebra I," instead of Latin]

(*NB*: The subject/courses "Supplemental English/Social Studies," and "Supplemental Pre-Algebra/Algebra I" will be explained below; see education reform #6).

2: Eliminating "Non-Academic Subjects," Thereby Increasing Dramatically School-Day Time Devoted to Scholastic Instruction and Academic Learning

Reflecting upon my New Jersey pre-Classical Academy public-school teaching experiences, from which, in large measure, emanate my critical analyses of our educational system described in previous chapters (and more fully in my companion narrative *"An Act of War Unresolved"*), it is not surprising that one finds in the Classical Academy's prescribed 7-academic-subject curricula certain unique elements, prominent among which are the absence of "non-academic" subjects or "co-curricular" elective classes.

Removing non-academic subjects and co-curricular classes from students' school schedules either as required courses *or* elective subjects allowed me to *double* the time, scope, and intensity every student must devote each day to serious learning, particularly in English-language arts and mathematics. That the same highly academic program of studies is prescribed for all students, with no mandated or elective non-academic subjects to seduce students away from academic learning, or compelling the egregious ill use of school-day time, is itself a major distinguishing feature of the Classical Academy, and one far different from all other New Jersey middle-school curricula.

The elimination of non-academic subjects from the Classical Academy's prescribed 7-academic-subject curriculum, and the resulting doubling of the time each day spent in English-language arts literacy and mathematics, is perhaps the single most important Classical Academy education reform. It accounts mightily for our students' astonishing academic achievements every year under my leadership. In eliminating non-academic subjects, and by finding creative ways to integrate state-mandated non-academic subjects into our high-powered academic program of studies without vitiating or weakening that program, the Classical Academy upheld the school's academics-first priorities for which it was granted a charter, and because of which it gained national recognition.

Some would hold that the Classical Academy boldly defied, indeed, violated the New Jersey Department of Education's non-academic "Core Curriculum Content or Learning Standards" represented in the board-mandated categories of "Visual and Performing Arts," "21st Century Careers and Life Education," "Physical and Health Education," and "Technology." The elevating of vacuous or less-critical non-academic subjects to the status of solid academic subjects and disciplines, and the learning time schools must devote to those non-academic subjects each day to be compliant with state curricular mandates—not to mention the degradation of the *meaning of education* in young minds—accounts for much of what is wrong in public education.

The state's requiring New Jersey schools to establish non-academic-subject classes, and thus to utilize so much of precious school-day time to comply with state non-academic-subject mandates, purportedly to educate the "whole child," contributes to New Jersey's chronically depressed student academic-learning outcomes, and accounts in no small way for the enduring education problem of "high costs, low results."

It must be affirmed that the Classical Academy's reduction or creative implementation of the state's "Core Curriculum Content and Learning Standards" for non-academic categories, conjoined with the Classical Academy's 3-year (grades 6, 7, and 8), 7-subject, richly academic middle-school program of prescribed studies for all students, is significantly responsible for the Classical Academy's consistently and remarkably high student academic achievement.

Furthermore, and of great import, the school's 7-academic-subject curricula mandatory for all students helped generate and sustain the Classical

Academy's "academics-first school culture," as it was impossible for students to misspend school-day time on non-academic pursuits or engage indiscriminately and excessively in school-sponsored opportunities for extra/co-curricular activities, particularly during the school day. The profusion of school-sponsored "fun" activities and non-academic classes present in most public schools not only does much to inculcate impressionable adolescents with a distorted—even *corrupt*—notion of what constitutes education, but also compels the pernicious misuse of precious school-day time. All this creates and reinforces a prevailing "anti-academic school culture" present in every public school.

Lastly, and most significant, by *doubling* class time each day in both mathematics and English-language arts literacy, every Classical Academy student received in *3 years*—and this cannot be emphasized enough—the scope of scholastic education and manifest learning benefits a typical student attending a Clifton, New Jersey, public middle school (or in any other New Jersey public middle school) would earn in *6 years*.

3: Selected and Preferred Learning Materials

In the early years of the school, I gave the responsibility of selecting the main textbooks to teachers, all of who were subject-matter specialists, with most having master's degrees in their teaching subject. Textbooks so selected were advanced and delivered a rigorous presentation of the subject, with many "learning extensions" within their lessons. Upon my review, I generally endorsed teachers' choices, acting in all instances as "district curriculum supervisor." I myself selected Latin and English-language arts literacy textbooks as well as an abundance of ancillary materials; I wrote also the curricula in these two subjects, which, for many years before the Classical Academy, I taught to middle- and high-school students.

In the first year of the Classical Academy, and while still employed part time at a Bergen County public school district, I received permission from the principal to take sets of disused books destined to be discarded for my charter-school students. These, like many textbooks and ancillary materials purchased throughout my leadership, I utilized at least one grade above their accustomed use—that is, books used in the 7th grade, I reserved for Classical Academy 6th-graders; 9th-grade English reading anthologies or other language-arts literacy materials, I employed for Classical Academy 8th-graders. This "at least one year ahead" use of learning materials was common for most Classical Academy subjects. It often was the case that newly graduated Classical Academy students would tell me: "Mr. DeRosa, we are using, in the 9th-grade English Honors class, the same English textbook(s) (or the same "Algebra" textbooks in 9th-grade Math Honors class) that we used in the Classical Academy 8th grade for all students."

Through the years, to meet modulating state-required academic-learning goals expressed, for example, in the "Core Curriculum Content and Learning Standards," other textbooks or readings would be added. When student learning materials of the kind we desired were not readily available, we amassed our own. This is particularly true of non-fiction supplemental readings and writing-task assignments, which became part of all "non-mathematics" subjects and classes.

During my long tenure as school leader (1997-2016), the school maintained an astonishingly consistent core of the same textbooks and supplemental learning materials for most subjects for many years. Why promiscuously change textbooks when our student academic goals were so magnificently being achieved as objectively evidenced by Classical Academy students' high performance on whatever state-mandated yearly assessments they took: "GEPA," "ASK," or "PARCC" assessments.

One school policy I established that illustrates the school's frugality and respect for taxpayers' money, as well as sensitiveness to client wishes— attributes for which the Classical Academy was almost as renowned as our students' high academic achievement—is our "textbook buy-back" program. Many parents complained that their children were carrying heavy bookbags. This, of course, was because of our nightly homework policy in every subject as well as the large number of academic subjects for which every Classical Academy student was responsible. Numerous parents asked the school for a set of textbooks to keep at home. Unless a doctor's note stated that the child's health required the child not to carry heavy burdens, the school could not comply, as it did not have nearly the surplus number of books to satisfy the many requests.

In response to this dilemma, I furnished to every parent at the beginning of each year a list of all our textbooks in each subject and grade. This information contained not only the specific ISBN numbers, publishers, and editions but also several online "used textbook" sellers. These books, used for only one or two years and in excellent condition, were priced at $1.00 to $5.00 each (often the shipping was more costly than the book). We recommended that parents buy as many books as they felt would alleviate the burden of heavy bookbags. At the end of the school year, the school would buy back the books at the parents' purchased price. This simple policy solved the problem of students struggling with heavy bookbags, while making sure also that students had books at home (the lack of homework completion could not always be easily justified with: "I forgot my book in school"). Equally important, the textbook buy-back policy was a cleverly effective way for the school to replenish its own stock of textbooks each year in a most inexpensive manner.

4: No-Tracking Policy

"Tracking" is the practice of placing students with poor academic records or school behavior into less-demanding, lower-expectation classes, and forbidding them from entering more-challenging, higher-level courses. "Tracking," which is tantamount to segregation determined by perceived—its proponents would say *proven*—academic ability, motivation, or conduct, often begins in the early grades and continues to most, if not all, of a student's public-school education.

"Tracking" is reserved for students who may not fall into a "learning handicap" classification and thus not eligible for "special education," but who, for whatever reasons, perform academically inferior, display little motivation, or exhibit non-conforming or disaffected behavior. For students so designated, "tracking," based on dubious grounds, remains a critical element in determining the quality of education while narrowing learning opportunities and expectations throughout one's middle- and high-school years. Such students often wade through their entire middle- and high-school years in the morass of anti-academic school culture and fun activities. When scholastically little is demanded or expected of them, little is given in return.

The Classical Academy rejected outright this abhorrent, segregationist practice, which so often permanently ruins the quality of a child's education and engenders that child's view of oneself as incapable or intellectually infirm. Contrary to other New Jersey public schools, the Classical Academy, by integrating all students in the same demanding classes, compelled high standards and rigorous academic expectations for all students.

The school's philosophy was based on the belief that higher-motivated and more-accomplished students would "pull up" the weaker or less-motivated students and classmates. This belief is further enhanced when education occurs in an "academics-first school culture," like that of the Classical Academy. One precept of teaching I invariably advocated among our faculty was to direct them to teach to the best cohort of students in each class, and compel the others to strive upward to meet, as best they could, the level of work and overall capabilities the best students in each class exhibited.

The Classical Academy's "no-tracking policy" understood that, even if the weaker students did not completely attain the superlative levels of achievement of their most motivated classmates, nevertheless, the elevated level of teaching, the demanding material, and the high expectations and requirements for *all* students would compellingly encourage the weaker students toward much higher scholastic progress and greater academic attainments than they would otherwise reach in schools where "tracking" was commonplace. Thus, Classical Academy students who, in other schools, were or would have been "tracked" into diminished expectations and less-challenging learning, and whose own expectations of themselves were correspondingly stunted, graduated our 8th grade with much higher skills, more knowledge, and greater confidence in their own abilities. (A glance at our 8th-grade standardized-test results detailed in Appendix A indubitably demonstrates the soundness of the Classical Academy's "no-tracking policy.")

5: "Mainstreaming" Classified Students

Closely related to "tracking" is so-called "special education." In New Jersey, students are routinely "classified" with some "handicap" or "disability." Justified by the *Americans with Disabilities Act of 1990* and its ensuing amendments, public schools exponentially inflate the number of students they interpret as "handicapped" or "disabled." Placed in "special-ed" classes, most students so designated seldom possess what the public associates with "handicapped": wheelchair-bound students, students with congenital cognitive impairment, or students suffering neurological disease.

Schools classify students as "handicapped" and eligible for "special education" services who merely perform poorly in school due to indolence, disinterest, an inadequate family emphasis on learning, or a lack of motivation impeding educational success. Students who behave disaffectedly from the norm, display undesirable attitudes toward schooling, exude a social awkwardness or difficulty integrating with their peers are all common reasons to diagnose students with "emotional disabilities" requiring "special education" classification and interventions.

In a stroke of marketing ingenuity, special-education students are given the definition "exceptional." Parents are enticed to allow their "exceptional" children to be classified, since, as they are told, their children would receive extra services, smaller classes, and an array of learning enhancements and advantages.

The number and vagueness of qualifying "classifications" or "handicaps" the New Jersey Department of Education permits under its own statutes, based on the federal "ADA" law, contributes to bloated numbers of "special education" students. In many New Jersey school districts, if one comes from a single-family home with low income, or simply exhibits a recalcitrant attitude, one is—by these metrics alone—deemed "disabled" or "handicapped," and thus eligible for "special education" classification. There are in New Jersey many urban and even suburban school districts which have 20% or more of their entire student body "classified" as "special education/handicapped" students. The state average percentage of "special education" students is nearly 17% (2020). If schools do not "classify" at least 5% to 10% of their student bodies as "handicapped," suspicions would arise that they were derelict in providing needed services to deserving students.

As with "tracking," teachers' unions cherish "special education." Statutorily, in New Jersey, "special-ed" classes can be no larger than 10 students (I often witnessed such classes with only 2 or 3 students). The total teaching load of a full-time special-education teacher is often as low as 15 to 30 students per day, while English or mathematics teachers regularly instruct 100 to 130 students. I have known numerous English and mathematics teachers who, frankly confessing their self-serving reasons, abandoned teaching academic subjects in favor of employment as a special-education teacher. The incentive to become certified as a "special education" teacher is irresistible. To any rational mind, gaining extraordinary reductions in workload and labor—with no diminishment of salary—has obvious attractions and is eminently justified.

For teachers' unions, smaller classes and the growth of "special education" means more teachers hired by school districts, hence, increased union dues and enhanced political power. Teachers' colleges and departments of education, illustrating the long-standing symbiotic relationship between themselves and teachers' unions, developed multiple programs to train and to certify "special-ed" teachers. Facilitating the growth of "special education," school districts receive additional state dollars for each special-education student it classifies.

When the Classical Academy received an application, usually for its 6th grade, from a student who was currently "classified," usually for an alleged emotional or learning disability, the parent agreed to "declassify" the student, as is the parents' right, and to "mainstream" the student in "regular" Classical Academy classes. These parents rightly believed, because of the Classical Academy's more disciplined environment, small school size, distinct academics-first school culture, and prescribed scholastic program of studies, that their student would be better served—emotionally and educationally—without a "special education" classification. In nearly 20 years of leading the Classical Academy, I can attest that "mainstreaming" of formerly "classified" students was a successful strategy for the school, students, and parents.

6: Supplemental Tutorial Classes in Mathematics and English Language Arts

The Classical Academy's "no-tracking" policy and its practice of "declassifying" or mainstreaming classified students posed some considerable challenges. How could those students who were poorly educated in their earlier grades because of special-education classification or because of "tracking," or the less-motivated students whose attainment of "grade-level" academic skills were lacking and less developed, participate successfully in the Classical Academy's 7-academic subject, no-tracking, rigorous, and demanding curricula?

How could such students better benefit from the school's distinct "academics-first" policies and culture? Would not such students be overwhelmed to the point of depression leading to self-harm, or driven to abysmally low self-esteem by a school and a curriculum of such unashamedly high caliber, one for which they are scholastically unprepared and emotionally unsuited? Would not weak students be destined to fail? Remember, by law, charter schools, as public schools, cannot select in any way their students. There can be no entrance requirements, academic or otherwise, for charter-school students; admission tests or evaluation of school records for admission purposes are strictly forbidden. Charter schools are public schools, and admission must be for all who seek it; if classroom space and school size are limited and cannot accommodate all who seek entrance, admission must be by blind lottery.

A number of Classical Academy students were entering the school with poorly developed scholastic skills and were simultaneously academically deficient, especially in mathematics and English (reading and writing). To such students, we would often issue a modified "classification" known as a "504." These students were allowed a mild reduction in homework, more time to take or retake tests, and other considerations to help them succeed in our single-track, high-demanding program of academic studies, all of which classes by most standards were advanced. Unused to disciplined study, never developing a propensity for scholastic pursuits, and never confronted with academic responsibility or school workload of any real kind, they consequently, even with an earnest attempt, struggled in the Classical Academy's demanding program of studies.

Early in the school's history, I realized this would be a continuing reality each year and that the measures implemented to this point were insufficient. A "no-tracking" school policy forbidding the placement of weakly motivated or poorly educated students in less-demanding classes with diminished expectations and the "mainstreaming" of formerly classified students in academically robust subjects required some programmatic changes—but changes that would not sacrifice or lower our academic rigor for every student, or adopt a student-segregation policy based on perceived capability or deficient scholastic knowledge and skills. I realized that a portion of Classical Academy entering students would always need additional learning reinforcements and interventions for both school and individual success.

Such programmatic changes would also make the teaching of classes with disparate student skills and knowledge less of a daunting pedagogical challenge—and my admonition to teachers to teach to the best students in each class less a difficult task or unreasonable expectation. I realized, too, that less-prepared students, unless some meaningful additional measure be introduced into our curricula, would not benefit as much as they could from the school's richly educative curricula.

To address these problems and answer these concerns, while not abandoning our "no-tracking" policy or promiscuously classifying students as "special education," I instituted our "Supplemental Pre-Algebra/Algebra I" tutorial classes and hired a "math supplemental teacher" (certified in mathematics, not special education). This I established as a regular, full-time position. To make room in our schedule and prescribed curricula for this necessary measure, struggling mathematics and "Algebra" students were removed from "Latin" and placed in a regularly scheduled, daily "Supplemental Math" class.

For the first several years and to my great pride, the Classical Academy was the only public middle school in New Jersey to require "Latin" of all its students beginning in the 6th grade, and continuing in 7th and 8th grades. I soon realized that our policies of "no-tracking" less-well-educated or -motivated students and the "mainstreaming" of classified students would force me to relinquish this proud distinction.

The purpose of this "Supplemental Math" class was not to conduct a separate, slower-paced class with less-demanding subject matter but, collaborating intimately with the regular mathematics and "Algebra" teachers, to offer school-mandated tutorial classes that were meaningful and effective in remediating each student's subject-specific learning needs, equipping them to better overcome their mathematics deficiencies and learning gaps, to better master the subject matter, and to succeed academically in the class by earning a passing or respectable class grade.

To reap the highest dividends from the tutorial or supplemental class, I required that the "mathematics supplemental teacher" meet every few days with the students' mathematics and "Pre-Algebra/Algebra I" teachers to know the students' homework assignments for each day, to know precisely the topics being studied, to know also the scope and pace of instruction, and to know what was being tested and when in-class tests were being administered. I required the mathematics and "Pre-Algebra/Algebra I" teachers to share their weekly "lesson plans" with the "Supplemental Math Teacher." The "Supplemental Math Teacher" would pinpoint one's instruction on the very matters being taught in the regular mathematics and "Algebra" classes and at the same time. The instruction would be delivered individually and in small-group settings of 5 to 7 students.

Our "math supplemental classes" fulfilled their function and purpose magnificently and permitted weaker mathematics students to better master subject matter, to confront successfully the demanding pace and material, to expand their level of mathematics skills and knowledge, and, lastly, to improve one's subject grade. We found, too, that our "Supplemental Mathematics/Pre-Algebra-Algebra I" classes were highly effective in enabling the weaker mathematics students to bridge their mathematics-knowledge gap and to keep up as much as possible with the best students in their classes. Finally, the precept of "teaching to the best students in the class" became a less-difficult task and not an unreasonable expectation. An objective measure of the success of our unique Supplemental Mathematics/Algebra courses, along with our "no-tracking" and "mainstreaming" policies, is amply evidenced in our outstanding 8th-grade mathematics and "Algebra I" yearly standardized-test outcomes (see Appendix A).

So remarkable was our success in attaining widespread mathematics proficiencies that, in a few years, we employed a similar supplemental/tutorial teacher for students showing English-literacy skills deficiencies in reading and writing. These students were taken from "social studies," a subject not tested on the state-mandated standardized tests. The "Supplemental English Language Arts/Social Studies" tutorial classes were conducted along the same lines as the "Supplemental Mathematics/Algebra I" tutorials. Non-fiction reading and writing materials often reflecting social studies topics were used in 6th, 7th, and 8th grades. It was not uncommon for the same student to be in both supplemental tutorial classes—mathematics *and* English-language literacy.

Students in these supplemental/tutorial classes therefore spent *3 class periods per day* in mathematics, and *3 class periods per day* in English-language arts. The supplemental tutorial classes essentially *tripled* the time each day weaker students spent in these two critical subjects. No other public-school curricula or program, in my experience, demanded such an academic requirement or such an application of school-day time for students characterized as underachievers.

Furthermore, students coming to the Classical Academy less-academically equipped and less-motivated, students who, under normal circumstances, would find the school's program of studies difficult and intimidating, could, by these mandatory supplemental tutorials in mathematics/"Pre-Algebra/Algebra I" and "English Language Arts Literacy," gain the knowledge, skills, and confidence to profit measurably by the Classical Academy's prescribed, rigorous curricula and academic-first policies and practices.

These supplemental/tutorial programs became a critical part of the school's learning culture. Students who, in other schools, were or would have been "tracked" in less-demanding subjects or "classified" as special education, were thus successfully challenged with higher learning expectations, made better able to benefit from the school's rigorous academic program, and find learning success therein. Such students often did not become "academic stars," but their knowledge, confidence, study habits, and scholastic skills were strongly improved and much better developed than they ever would have been if they had remained "tracked" or "classified" in a public school other than the Classical Academy.

7: *Mandatory Homework and Mid-Term/Final Exams*

Homework is a critical and vital vehicle for learning. It provides both practice and reinforcement for acquiring new skills and knowledge. Of course, assigning homework to students means more work for teachers, whether marking homework is done during the workday or at home. Dubious studies have been widely circulated claiming that homework does nothing to enhance learning and may be detrimental. Such studies are invariably sponsored or endorsed by teachers' unions, ever-dedicated to promote whatever can be done to lessen their members' work burdens. Even teachers who believe in the merits of homework have told me that they seldom, if ever, assign homework, because students simply refuse to comply and never do it.

Meaningful homework assignments (which, to students I referred to as one's "evening task") convey and inculcate crucial attributes for reinforcing and expanding learning. Homework also produces character building, as it teaches responsibility to students, setting priorities, fostering determination, discriminating between the momentary pleasurable and sacrificing that pleasure for a higher good. I therefore made it Classical Academy school-wide policy that every teacher must assign homework, usually nightly and on most weekends. To impress the importance of students doing homework and to provide an important incentive, the policy also stated that teachers must count homework completion as 20%-25% of a student's total marking-period grade in each subject for every 6th-, 7th-, and 8th-grader.

There are several ways to quantify homework over a span of time, such as a marking period. The way I and some of my Classical Academy colleagues accomplished this is by giving every homework assignment a numerical grade: "3," if the assignment was on time, complete, and done with good accuracy or quality; "2," if the assignment was done incompletely and/or a day late; "1," if the assignment was very poorly done or submitted more than two days late, and, finally, a "0," if the assignment was never submitted. In calculating a 10-week homework marking-period grade, the teacher adds up a student's homework grades for each assignment for that period. Let's say that a student earned a "110" for all assignments in that marking period and that there was a total of 40 assignments with a maximum total of 120 points (3 times 40, yielding a 100% score). That student's homework grade of "110" would be 92% (110 divided by 120 to get the percentage). The 92% would then be factored into the student's other grades on tests, quizzes, and other graded work the teacher assigned.

Teachers were also empowered to deny certain privileges to students who were too remiss in homework submissions. When we had regular "Friday Outdoor Activity Periods," for example, teachers could order students to remain indoors and under teacher supervision to complete missing assignments or to complete other unfinished scholastic obligations.

As with any beneficial practice, there are times when it can become controversial or even counterproductive if used without circumspection or inflexibly. Occasionally teachers would exceed good judgment and give long assignments, forgetting that students have homework in their other subjects for the same evening. Parent complaints were minor but regular: "Mr. DeRosa, my child begins her homework at 5:00 p.m. and does not stop until 11:00 p.m. or even midnight" or "Mr. DeRosa, my child wants to join a soccer club or take music lessons in the evening, and he cannot because of his fear that he will fail in school." My strong admonition to teachers, generally restated several times each school year, was that homework assignments should generally take no more than 20-30 minutes to complete for each subject. Classical Academy students should do, on average, no more than 2-3 hours of homework per night.

Similar to other Classical Academy innovations and reforms, our school-wide mandatory homework policy, whereby assigning homework and factoring homework completion into each student's grade in each subject, enabled our students to attain greater academic achievement. It also produced excellent results in learning outcomes and in sustaining an academics-first school culture, not to mention inculcating among students the notions and practice of obligation and responsibility.

To help teachers with the burden of mandatory homework and its assessment, we provided in our schedule two "free" or non-instructional periods per day for every teacher. Usually teachers have, by way of teachers-union approved collective-bargaining contracts, one "free" period per day, and one "duty" period. We dispensed with the latter. Sometimes, when forced to do so, we assigned one of the teacher's "free" periods to substitute for an absent teacher, for which we paid the substituting teacher a small stipend. This particularly occurred when Mrs. DeRosa could not, because of her urgent attention to one of her many other duties, provide teacher coverage, or on a day when we had more than one absent teacher. On such occasions, I often also substituted myself for a period or two of classes for an absent teacher. (During my last two years at the Classical Academy, I did hire several "on-call" substitute teachers).

Early in the school's history, my fellow teachers and I (I taught the two sections of 8th-grade Latin) discussed and decided upon the merits of administering teacher-made mid-term and final exams in each subject. We believed that these exams would serve several objectives and benefits. First, students would become accustomed to reviewing with some intensity and scope a larger body of learned subject knowledge comprising about a four-month period of instruction. Such reviews would better solidify learned knowledge and become part of each student's acquired scholastics skills.

Apart from the scholastic practice of reviewing or solidifying learned knowledge and skills, the mid-term and final exams required two to three class periods and were designed by teachers to mimic the sort of questions and activities our students would meet on standardized tests. As a sort of preview to the state standardized exams in science, English, and mathematics (or "Algebra I"), we restricted the mid-term and final exams to the 8th grade in each subject. Teachers provided students a syllabus of topics to be tested. The mid-term took place in early January (students had the opportunity to study for the mid-term during the December holiday vacation), and the mid-May final exam embraced subject material studied from the mid-term exam to May. The mid-term and final exams each represented 5% of a student's total subject grade; together, both exams totaled 10% of a student's subject grade. On average, both homework and the mid-term and final exams constituted 25%-30% of each 8th-grade student's final subject grade.

8: Teacher Financial Bonuses Based on Student Learning Outcomes Objectively Measured

Teachers' unions despise charter schools, but they loathe equally any sort of teacher-performance compensation or "merit pay," based on the learning outcomes their students (clients) demonstrate. A fundamental tenet of teacher unions, and for the well-being of union cohesion, is that every union member, whether teaching an academic or non-academic subject, or even providing a non-instructional student "support service," is equal to every other member; all are equally meritorious, all perform equally important functions, and all are paid accordingly.

By state statute, which was instigated by union political power, any person who works in a public school having "certification" in whatever field of specialty (and they are bountiful in number) and has "student contact," however cursory or irregular and in whatsoever manner or purpose, is a "teacher." All "teachers," whether they are academic-subject teachers or teachers of non-academic subjects, whether they have regular or irregular classroom instructional duties or no classroom functions, like nurses, counselors, librarians, and IT personnel, are all union and legally defined "teachers," and therefore must possess all the same union-sanctioned "teacher" protections and compensation features equally applied, per collective bargaining and negotiated contracts.

Accordingly, all teachers-union members must be compensated equally, and that compensation can be based only on "years of service" and "educational credits earned" post-hiring. Teacher unions vigorously enforce this belief and practice that all public-school unionized employees perform equally important work and deserve equal compensation, regardless of the catastrophic effects to motivation and morale on serious teachers of academic subjects. Performance, function, and compensation, so centrally linked in the true professions, is anathema to teachers' unions and thus absent from the work of teachers and their union-negotiated contracts.

In my estimation, so-called teacher "accountability" must and should be closely associated with teacher-merit or -performance pay, or, for that matter, with any proportion of teacher salary determined by student achievement. How can a fair and just salary bonus or performance pay be structured? Serious questions arise when salary bonus pay is linked to student standardized-test performance. If student success is measured solely or primarily on student outcomes on mandated standardized tests in mathematics, English-language arts, or science, how is eligibility for salary bonus or performance pay determined fairly and objectively for teachers of those tested subjects? What about the accountability or responsibility of the army of teachers and union members who do not teach standardized-tested subjects and therefore do not contribute directly to student performance on standardized tests? Are they to earn a salary bonus or performance pay? If so, on what grounds? Is it fair to mathematics, English, and science teachers that "teachers" of non-academic subjects and student service provider "teachers" who inhabit our public schools in great multitudes be eligible for salary bonuses or performance pay?

For teachers' union cohesion and solidarity, performance pay or salary bonuses based on student scholastic outcomes may well incite some union members to entertain divisive sentiments, perhaps even openly expressed, such as: "I am a superior teacher," or "I do more important work than you," or, most feared of all: "I am more skilled and talented, and I work harder than you and, thus, deserve greater salary based not on my years on the job, but on my skills, efforts, and work ethic evidenced in my students' academic-learning success, in which you, my dear non-academic-subject-teacher colleague, play no part."

Teachers' unions must dissuade and, indeed, *prevent* such divisive questions from being asked and such dissenting sentiments from being echoed. Unions and their local school-district associations must avoid any internal discord among members stemming from salary or performance-pay differential based on student learning outcomes. The best way to avoid discord surrounding any type of performance or merit pay is simply for the union to adamantly preclude it, never to be included or even contemplated in the collective-bargaining process.

It must also be acknowledged that teachers, even high-performing teachers of academic subjects who deserve greater compensation over one's non-academic-subject colleagues, do not yearn, judging from my personal experiences, for merit or performance pay. As academic teachers, they painfully realize that they have no control or responsibility over the many factors of their work that determine the extent and quality of their students' learning. They cannot make up the elements of the school day, or regulate how much time each day students squander on non-academic subjects or devote to extra-curricular activities during and after school hours. Often, they do not select the learning materials or develop the curricula. They have no role in determining and implementing broad policies and practices which de-emphasize academic learning over the prevailing emphasis on social and emotional development. Our unionized public-educational systems have emasculated serious, hard-working, high-performing academic-subject teachers from real influence, and stolen from them the power—which once they possessed at least to a modicum degree in the pre-teachers' union era—to govern and structure the educational system in which they work.

The Classical Academy Charter School was one of a very few, if not the only New Jersey public school, to make financial salary bonuses or performance pay based on student achievement a normal part of each teacher's contract. Being a newly created school and not unionized, the usual insurmountable obstacles to this commonplace professional type of compensation did not exist. I believe, also, in the strong motivating force, when properly correlated to desired outcomes, that additional salary in the form of performance pay or salary bonuses would play in achieving school goals and greater student learning outcomes. Teacher performance is especially critical in the free-market, non-monopolistic environment in which the Classical Academy and most charter schools operate, and is a crucial element for school success and, indeed, school survival.

It should be noted that, because of the Classical Academy's prescribed 7-academic-subject curricula for all students, and its "academics-first" credo, the school never hired, under my leadership, any non-academic teacher of a "non-academic" subject because, as I've emphasized often in these pages, our entire curricula *excluded* all non-academic subjects (how the Classical

Academy fulfilled state-mandated "physical education and health" and "visual and performing arts" will be discussed below). Without exception, all Classical Academy teachers were teachers of academic subjects and thereby contributed directly to student and school achievement as measured in state-mandated standardized tests; consequently, there was never an internecine dispute about bonus or performance-pay eligibility or merit.

One can with satisfaction imagine the depth of hostility and abhorrence with which the New Jersey Education Association (teachers' union) beheld the Classical Academy: here was an educational-choice public charter school, which in itself was enough to arouse its enmity, but a public school whose teachers were not only not-unionized, but boasted contractual teacher performance pay based on student learning outcomes, objectively measured. So much of what the teachers' union despises—and what it desperately strives to prevent—the Classical Academy showcased proudly, and to marvelous effect.

In my judgment, a teacher's performance pay or salary bonus should ideally comprise about 20%-25% of total compensation. During my long tenure as "Lead Person," teacher-performance compensation, or as I called it, "salary bonus," reached a maximum $6,000, about 15% of total compensation for most teachers. With each yearly teacher-employment contract, a "salary bonus-pay plan based on comparative student results" was attached, so every teacher knew well in advance the precise criteria for how the salary bonus, or part thereof, would be earned.

In all cases, the single objective measure upon which our "salary bonus" was based was comparative student test results: how Classical Academy students learning assessments compared with other relevant cohorts of students measured on annual state-mandated standardized assessments in English, mathematics (beginning in 2015, in "Algebra I"), and science. Only 8th-grade comparative student-outcome assessments in these subjects were employed, as the 8th grade, usually comprising 37-40 students, was the culmination of our richly educative 3-year middle-school curricula. 8th-grade assessments would, therefore, be the truest and fairest gauge of both our teachers' summative effectiveness and our students' achievement over time in the tested subjects. Except for our one 6th-grade generalist teacher, who taught several academic subjects to only 6th-grade students (who also was eligible for salary bonus based on 8th-grade test outcomes), all other Classical Academy teachers had 8th-grade students and teaching duties, and instructed the same students in the same subject for 2 or 3 years.

As the reader may be interested in the elements of an example "Salary Bonus Plan"—or performance (merit) pay based on student learning outcomes—one that is fashioned to motivate and reward deserving teachers, I here give a synopsis of the Classical Academy's salary-bonus or performance-pay plan as one of the school's many significant education reforms. It should be obvious that, to obviate dissension while projecting fairness, a salary-bonus or merit-pay plan must be organized around clearly objective, relevant, and quantifiable goals correlated to student learning outcomes.

Although minor, intermittent modifications were made during the years, the "Teacher Salary Bonus Plan based on 8th-Grade Comparative Student Results" most often contained the following 10 specific criteria; in the latest iterations of the salary-bonus plan, all teachers earned $600 for meeting each of the 10 criteria. Classical Academy teachers of English, literature, social studies, 6th-grade generalist, and supplemental English language arts teacher, based their bonus eligibility on student results on the 8th-grade "English Language Arts Literacy" state-mandated standardized assessment. Middle-school mathematics teachers, "Pre-Algebra" and "Algebra I" teachers, and the supplemental mathematics/Algebra teacher, based their salary bonus on the mathematics (beginning in 2015, on the PARCC "Algebra I") state assessment. Remember, consistent with the school's long practice of "no-tracking" and "mainstreaming" classified students—policies approved in its 1997 charter—all 8th-grade students were required to take the "Algebra I" course.

NB: In all instances of the following 10 comparative criteria, "Passing" is defined as the combined percentage of 8th-grade students earning either a "Proficiency" score or an "Advanced Proficiency" score.

NB: The state-mandated "Assessment of Skills and Knowledge" (ASK) was replaced in 2015 with the "PARCC" tests. The latter assessment used a numerical score of "1" through "5," with "passing" indicated by numerical scores of "4" ("met expectations," i.e., "proficient") and "5" ("exceeded expectations," i.e., "advanced proficiency"). "Passing" in PARCC subject assessments is the combined percentage of 8th-grade students earning either a "4 = Met Expectations," or a "5 = Exceeded Expectations."

Classical Academy's "Salary Bonus Plan" Based on Comparative Student Results

Measurement Category I: Comparing Classical Academy 8th-grader Student Outcomes with The Entire Clifton Public School District's 8th-grade "Passing" Percentage and Each of Clifton's Two Middle Schools

Criterion 1: The percentage of 8th-grade Classical Academy students *"Passing"* the Standardized Assessment by earning either a "proficiency" or "advanced proficiency" score will have exceeded the 8th-grade *"Passing"* rate percentage of Clifton's *Christopher Columbus Middle School* students in 8th-grade "mathematics" ("Algebra I" for PARCC tests beginning 2015) for mathematics and "Algebra I" teachers, and in English Language Arts Literacy for English and all other non-mathematics/non-"Algebra I" subject teachers.

Criterion 2: The *"Passing"* (proficiency and advanced proficiency) percentage of 8th-grade Classical Academy students will have surpassed or exceeded the 8th-grade "Passing" percentage of Clifton's *Woodrow Wilson Middle School* students in "mathematics"/"Algebra I," or in English Language Literacy.

Criterion 3: The *"Passing"* (proficiency and advanced proficiency) percentage of 8th-grade Classical Academy students will have surpassed or exceeded the 8th-grade "Passing" percentage of the entire Clifton School District (comprising its two middle schools) in "mathematics"/"Algebra I" (for teachers of these subjects), and in English Language Literacy for English teachers and all other teachers of non-mathematics subjects.

Measurement Category II: Comparing Classical Academy with Clifton Schools in 8th- grade "Advanced Proficiency" Percentage

Criteria 4, 5, and 6: Total percentage of 8th-graders earning "Advanced Proficiency" or "PARCC Level 5 Exceeding Expectations" for each Clifton middle school and for the entire Clifton Public School district. The same 3 comparative results as the above criteria 1, 2, and 3 are used for rewarding teachers, but here based on percentage of 8th-grade students earning the highest student level of standardized-test achievement: *"Advanced Proficiency"* or *"PARCC Level 5 (Exceeding Expectations)."*

Measurement Category III: Comparative New Jersey
Charter School Outcomes

Criterion 7: The combined percentage of Classical Academy 8th-graders achieving *"Passing"* (Proficiency or Advanced Proficiency) will be sufficiently high, in comparison with all other New Jersey public charter schools testing 8th-grade students, such that the Classical Academy, by virtue of its percentage of its 8th-grade students achieving "Passing," be ranked in the *top 20%* of all New Jersey charter schools in "mathematics"/"Algebra I" for teachers of these subjects, and English Language Literacy for all other subject teachers.

Criterion 8: The combined percentage of Classical Academy 8th-graders achieving *"Advanced Proficiency"* will be sufficiently high, in comparison with all other New Jersey public charter schools which test 8th-grade students, such that the Classical Academy be ranked in the *top 20%* of all New Jersey charter schools in "mathematics"/"Algebra I" (for teachers of these subjects), and English Language Literacy (for all other subject teachers).

Measurement Category IV: County-Wide Comparison: Passaic County

Criterion 9: The combined percentage of Classical Academy 8th-graders achieving *"Passing"* (Proficiency or Advanced Proficiency) is such that its students' standardized-test learning outcomes place the Classical Academy in the *top 5* of all 17 Passaic County middle/elementary schools or school districts testing 8th-graders in "mathematics"/"Algebra I" (for teachers of these subjects), and English Language Arts Literacy (for all other teachers).

<u>Measurement Category V:</u> State-Wide Comparison: New Jersey's "C/D" District Factor Group Schools

<u>Criterion 10:</u> The New Jersey Department of Education has designated the Classical Academy (and Clifton Public School District), based on "socio-economic" factors as average family income, levels of education, value of housing, rates of unemployment, and other factors, a "C/D" DFG (district factor group). A "C/D" district factor group illustrates attributes of an urban or low middle-class community. The combined percentage of Classical Academy 8th-graders achieving *"Passing"* (Proficiency or Advanced Proficiency) on state-mandated standardized-test learning outcomes will be such that its passing percentage will place the Classical Academy in the *top 20%* of all New Jersey schools possessing a "C/D" district factor group designation in "mathematics"/"Algebra I" achievement (for teachers of these subjects) and in English Language Literacy (for teachers of all other subjects). There are approximately 65 New Jersey schools or school districts with a "C/D" district factor group designation.

Summary, Classical Academy's "Salary Bonus Plan"

Except for one minor instance in the school's second year, and because of the remarkably high, consistent success of its 8th-grade students on state standardized tests in "mathematics"/"Algebra I" and English Language Arts Literacy, as well as 8th-grade science, every Classical Academy teacher for the 14-year period 2003 to 2016 met every criterion on the salary-bonus plan, and thus earned full salary bonus each year.

Overall, what is the purpose and value of teacher salary bonuses correlated to standardized assessment of student learning outcomes? First, it provides teacher motivation. It also affords tangible teacher recognition for a job well done. It also helps uphold an unambiguous academics-first school culture, a culture which needs to be sustained not only for adolescent students but also for teacher employees. The school's "Salary Bonus Plan," instead of causing dissension and disunity, ultimately enhances teacher collaboration and camaraderie for collectively striving for a common and important school objective of high academic student learning.

10: *"English Language Arts Literacy" Taught and Addressed in All Non-Mathematics (Non-Algebraic) Subjects*

In order for teachers of subjects not tested on state assessments, such as "social studies," to participate justifiably and fairly in the salary-bonus plan, they were required to contribute meaningfully to students' English language arts skills development. By contract and ongoing oversight, "social studies," "Latin," and "science" teachers, along with following the approved curricula objectives in their own subjects, incorporated regularly in their teaching lesson plans, student assignments and instructional materials intended to advance further English language literacy acquisition. Their lesson plans and student materials concentrated on non-fiction readings related to topics in their subjects which included enriched and expanded teacher-made reading-comprehension questions and writing tasks like those our students would encounter on state assessments.

"Social Studies" teachers, as well as teachers of "Latin" and "science," therefore participated fully in the school's salary-bonus scheme based on 8th-grade students' English language arts literacy achievement, even though their own subjects (except for "science") were not assessed on state standardized tests.

Selecting materials, developing lesson plans, and creating student learning activities, all toward promoting English language arts literacy while learning "Latin," "science," and "social studies," was an objective—indeed, a contractual teacher obligation—I carefully nurtured and oversaw. Not infrequently would I suggest and provide, occasionally even create myself, lesson plans and materials which would enhance English language arts literacy competencies and provide valuable standardized-test practice while concentrating on relevant subject matter and learning in the non-state-tested subjects. I frequently provided this service not only for teachers of subjects not tested on state assessments, but for English and literature teachers as well.

In this way, since "science" was state tested in the 8th grade, half of the "science" teacher's salary bonus was earned by students' achievement on the state "science" assessment, and half based on 8th-grade students' achievement on their English Language Literacy test. The same is true for "Latin" teachers, whose half salary bonus was based on pre-determined student results on the school-required 8th-grade standardized "Latin" and classical-mythology tests constructed and graded by the American Classical League, and half on 8th-grade state assessment in English Language Arts Literacy. "Social Studies" teachers have their entire bonus based on 8th-grade English language arts literacy. In all instances, the same 10 comparative objective criteria described above and constituting the school's salary-bonus plan was employed for determining the earned salary-bonus payments of all teachers.

The requirement that all non-mathematics teachers concern themselves with instructing, strengthening, and perfecting English language arts literacy was an innovation not only to justify meritorious eligibility for salary bonuses based on student achievement on state assessments, but also to make English language arts education and proficiency a systemic, school-wide instructional priority for all non-mathematics pedagogy during the entire 3-year middle-school program of studies.

With "science," "social studies," and "Latin" teachers' responsibility of addressing consistently English language arts literacy instruction primarily through non-fiction readings, and having students respond to teacher-made reading-comprehension questions of the type used in standardized tests, along with related writing assignments, the contributions of these teachers to students' growing proficiencies in English language literacy was meaningful and significant. These teachers' contributions to high English language literacy scores on standardized tests was obvious and their eligibility for salary bonuses undeniable.

11: Students Have the Same Teachers from Grade to Grade

Recent reports indicate the educative value of students having the same teacher for the same subject over consecutive years of schooling. Here, as in many of its policies and practices, the Classical Academy was a pioneering practitioner. All Classical Academy students had the same academic-subject teacher for at least 2 years in 7th and 8th grades, while half of all students had the same academic-subject teacher for all 3 middle-school years in 6th, 7th, and 8th grades. When students have the same teacher and teachers have the same students from year to year, each becomes much better acclimated to the other. For their part, students have greater experience with the teacher's instructional methods, expectations, requirements, personality, and disciplinary demands, while the teacher knows the strengths and weaknesses of every student and is well acquainted with each student's motivation, abilities, and degree of improvement attained as well as that which yet needs to be achieved.

12: Physical Education/Health; Visual and Performing Arts

In fashioning the Classical Academy charter school, I was resolute to exclude (or diminish as best I could) the anti-academic forces ubiquitous in public education, manifested most glaringly by the abbreviated time students spend each school day in academic learning. One way to address this systemic problem was to mandate for all students a rigorous academic curriculum devoid of non-academic course offerings ("home economics," "shop," "dance," "photography," and a raft of other such courses). In this way, most of the entire school day is employed in scholastic learning, not misused or misdirected for questionable, non-academic activities extraneous to intellectual growth and knowledge expansion, thus attaining the true meaning of "education": *"leading out of darkness and ignorance to light and understanding."*

Another way to apply more time to academic learning was to devise a different modality by which students could satisfy state requirements in "visual and performing arts," and "physical education and health," and do so with minimum interference and distraction from academic learning, or a weakening of our 7-academic-subject prescribed curriculum. In this way, too, the school would have no need to hire or spend its meager financial resources on art or physical-education teachers.

Instead of the usual separate courses or classes in "visual and performing arts," "art" would be integrated into academic courses; artistic or creative projects would become part of and relevant to the academic subject into which it was integrated. Not having separate, discrete classes in "art," but having it *integrated* into academic subjects was an innovation clearly annunciated in the Classical Academy's 1997 charter application and accorded state approval. And this "integrative approach" was how "art" instruction was delivered all during my Classical Academy leadership. In practice, "social studies" and "science" were the subjects most commonly enlisted for "art integration" projects, with occasional participation of English and Latin classes. Students would be assigned to produce projects with visual representations of the academic topics they were studying.

"Physical Education" and "Health" were also state curricular mandates. How the Classical Academy satisfied these instructional demands without significant impact on academic learning was achieved by resourceful and fortuitous means. By law, New Jersey K-8 students must spend about 200 minutes per week in some form of "physical education" and/or "health" instruction. No physical-education teacher is required (although most elementary and middle schools do have both gymnasia facilities and certified gym teachers).

Classical Academy "physical education" requirements were fulfilled by conducting, weather permitting, "Friday Field Days." By chance, a 20-minute walk from school was a Clifton municipal park, equipped with several baseball diamonds, open fields, and basketball and tennis courts. The school would receive a park permit for our use each fall and spring. I constructed during the morning of the event a "Field Day Schedule" showing which student groups would enjoy 2 activities, and which teachers, usually 2, would supervise each group. Activities included tennis, track and field events, soccer, kickball, dodgeball, volleyball, touch football (I usually supervised the 8th-grade boys in this event), among others.

On "Field Day Fridays," to minimize disruption to academic learning, all 7 academic classes were still held but reduced to 30 minutes each. Then there was a brief lunch period at noon, after which the entire school and all teachers sojourned to the park, enjoyed open-air activities, and walked back to school at about 3:00 p.m. In this way, we complied with the physical-education requirements all in one "end-of-the-week" fun event. I often reminded our students how fortunate they were to be outside on beautiful spring Friday afternoons, while their counterparts in Clifton schools were confined indoors (probably watching films). I also, jokingly, was wont to remind our teachers how lucky they were because they would not need to pay "spa" membership fees since they were getting their exercise at work—and being paid for it.

From about Thanksgiving to spring break in April, we discontinued the outdoor "Friday Field Days" and reverted to "health" instruction. Again, to minimize effects of non-academic distraction on academic-subject learning, I developed a weekly rotation of teachers and subjects which would comply with state-mandated "health" instruction. One half of the 50-minute class period was devoted to the teacher's academic subject and the remaining half to "health"-related topics. By this method, each teacher was responsible for health instruction once every 5-8 weeks; their academic subject and students' education therein was only minimally and briefly disrupted, and every student in every grade was provided "health" instruction as mandated. Health topics and materials were easy to find, and teachers worked among themselves to share ideas and resources.

As an alternative to the outdoor "Friday Field Days," the school made use of another nearby amenity, the Garret Mountain Reservation, a Passaic County 568-acre public-use "forever wild" property, which includes the famous Lambert Castle, built by a Paterson silk magnate. The reservation contains a pond, walking paths, deer, diverse wildlife, and lovely scenery. On an autumn afternoon, the school would take a two- to three-hour hike to and across Garret Mountain Reservation, where we delighted in the autumn leaves and the many deer and wild turkey that could be easily observed. We also took advantage of this nearby county-owned amenity for "nature hikes" in the spring, imbibing the glory of unfolding nature.

(My Latin students knew that our month of April owes its name to the Latin verb *aperire*, meaning "to open," as Nature begins to reveal her dormant majesty.)

During months when "Friday Field Days" were suspended because of weather, we instituted "Indoor/Outdoor Activity Periods." These activities were to reward students with deserved free time, while utilizing the school's pastoral setting of large open lawns under century-old walnut, mulberry, oak, and beech trees gracing both the rear and front of the building. With the majority of our students residing in the most urbanized sections of Clifton, the Classical Academy's bucolic setting provided a welcome environmental change.

Reducing slightly (about 5 minutes) each of the 7 academic periods and lunchtime, we accumulated a full period at the end of the day, usually Friday, to devote to these "Indoor/Outdoor Activity Periods." A student could decide whether to go outdoors on the school's pastoral grounds to engage in games (basketball, wall-ball, soccer, frisbee throwing, etc.) or in some convivial pastime with friends, or remain indoors to discharge scholastic responsibilities—perhaps to get a head start on the weekend's homework. Teachers had the right to usurp a student's use of the activity period and order a student to a classroom to make up homework, missed tests, or complete some other academic requirement for which the student was remiss.

"Indoor/Outdoor Activity Periods" were held on average 3 or 4 times per month, even in winter temperatures. Some teachers would monitor students outside to be sure behavior remained safe and merry, while others remained indoors, supervising students taking missed tests, doing homework voluntarily or ordered by a teacher, or for disciplinary reasons.

Lacking a cafeteria, students ate their lunches either provided by the school or brought from home. (For families who qualified, the school participated in the "Free or Reduced Lunch/Breakfast" program and purchased breakfast/lunches from a school food vendor, who delivered the food daily). Nearly every day, we permitted students, with several teachers monitoring, to take lunch period outdoors. A number of picnic tables were available for their comfort. This simple activity, much enjoyed by students, provided yet another way to ease the demands of our academic program, provide respite, and take advantage of our lovely, spacious grounds.

To continue our compliance with state mandates regarding "physical and health" education, at the beginning of May, we discontinued "health" instruction and resumed "physical education" in the form of outdoor "Friday Field Days."

By designing and employing these modalities, the Classical Academy fulfilled state-mandated non-academic requirements with the least amount of adverse impact on academic learning. Some believe that, because the Classical Academy facility lacked a gymnasium or sufficient building space for indoor physical-education classes, or surplus rooms for art classes, we reluctantly were compelled to satisfy state physical-education and arts requirements in the novel way we did. Frankly, this is completely erroneous. If our school building possessed all the gym facilities and additional rooms as a typical public school, I still would not have hired physical-education (or art) teachers. Discrete and separate classes in these non-academic subjects was not only contrary to our approved charter, but contrary to the school's long practice. Even if our building offered facilities to do so, I would have nevertheless devised similar unique ways that the non-academic state mandates would least affect students' use of school-day time for academics, and least detract from the school's strong academic emphasis and its academics-first culture.

13: School Calendar

During the school's first year, 1998-1999, the school day ended at 4:00 p.m. and had a 190 school-day year—10 days or two weeks longer than Clifton Public Schools and the state-required 180 school-day year. At the time of my writing the Classical Academy charter application, there was much "reform talk" of the purported benefits accruing from a longer school day and school year. Knowing full well that what truly matters is not how long the school day or school year is, but how much time students devote each day to serious academic learning within the traditional length of the school day and school year, I nonetheless specified an increased school-day and -year calendar, features more for enhancing the chances of charter approval than believing in the merits of these reforms.

Based on my wide public-school teaching experiences, I believe that, if a student misspends or misallocates a third or a half of a 7-hour school day in non-academic pursuits, as is the baneful reality of our public education, increasing the school day by one or more hours (or school year by more school days) will have no material benefit on student academic achievement, nor will this popular though specious education reform foster greater academic-learning outcomes. Additionally, and particularly for New Jersey residents, ineffective reforms such as increased school-day time or lengthening the school year will only cause the highest-in-the-nation's property taxes to increase even more intolerably and may well bankrupt the state—a steep cost for merely "keeping kids off the streets longer." The true and effective reform, which the Classical Academy Charter School so well demonstrated, is to reform *how* school-day time is used and *how* time is reallocated for increased student academic learning during traditional school hours.

After our first year, to the relief of all, we shortened the school day by one hour from 3:55 p.m. to the more-common 2:55 p.m. school-day ending time. However, we retained the two-week (10-instructional-day) longer school year not so much to extend academic learning, but to complete numerous "end-of-year tasks" and engage in student "fun" activities and school trips, which our students eagerly anticipated but which, at that late stage in the school year, would have no real adverse effect on academic-learning time.

Knowing also from long experience that "half days" are a bothersome disruption to academic learning, the number of "half days" in our school calendar were greatly reduced to about 7, much fewer than the 23-27 half days found in the typical school-year calendar. Most Classical Academy "half days" occurred in the last week of school, when their undesirable impact on learning would be very minimal.

Very occasionally, a "half day" was scheduled for teacher-informational sessions to instruct faculty on the implementation, security, and procedures for state-mandated standardized testing. Our two traditional half days before June were the last day of school before the Thanksgiving Day vacation and the last day before the December (End of Calendar Year) Holiday.

When we did have "half days" during the months before mid- to late June, they were scheduled so that students still attended all 7 academic subjects, albeit for 30 minutes each class, with elimination of lunch period and dismissal at 12:35 p.m. In this way, no serious abridgement to learning ensued from rare "half days," a statement which cannot be made by most New Jersey schools. (The only school days, full or half days, in which a Classical Academy student did not attend all 7 academic subjects was on "Delayed Opening" days due to snow or other weather-related events, or some other unusual circumstance.)

Further exemplifying our aversion to having a school calendar that militates against student progress and academic learning, the Classical Academy had fewer school holidays. Our students attended school during Columbus Day, the two-day teachers-union convention (vacation), Martin Luther King, Jr. Day, and had fewer "spring-vacation days." When questioned by students and parents, especially about being in school on Columbus or MLK day, I responded that I was certain both these great men would much prefer students honor them by being in school and having their knowledge expanded and their character improved, rather than sleeping till noon, watching TV, playing computer games, or engrossed in social-media activities.

The 13 radical and unprecedented education reforms described in this chapter collectively and in unison lead to and create not only greatly enhanced scholastic learning for every child, but also a school culture quite different from that found in most other New Jersey public middle and high schools. The function of the Classical Academy's "academics-first school culture" is so essential to the school's remarkable student learning outcomes, to the overall school camaraderie and school ethos, and, dare I say, to students' social-emotional development, that I devote the next chapter to its further elaboration.

Chapter VI

CLASSICAL ACADEMY'S DISTINCT, SCHOOL-WIDE "ACADEMICS-FIRST SCHOOL CULTURE" AND HOW IT WAS CREATED AND SUSTAINED (1997-2016)

When groups of people gather together in some organized endeavor, sharing a common purpose or objective through their interactions, we speak of that organization's "culture." Organizational culture arises haphazardly or with deliberate purpose. We identify, for instance, corporate culture, bureaucratic culture, military culture, or the particular culture of one's work environment. In most organizations, those responsible for its success are expected to create and to sustain a culture that strategically best promotes and achieves the goals for which the organization exists. It is no different in schools, and no less pregnant with consequences.

"Anti-Academic School Culture" and the Powers That Create and Sustain It

By deliberate intent, routine, or happenstance, every school has a culture. School organizations develop and perpetuate practices and policies which are intended to shape and to uphold the organization's goals and objectives. These goals and objectives may arise from administrative dictate, constituent wishes, or domineering external influences, or from all three. From these policies and practices, intended to achieve organizational goals and objectives, a school's culture emerges. The resulting interactions among school members as they perform their assigned work sustain that culture, thereby enabling the realization of the organization's goals and objectives.

A school culture tells adolescent students what adults believe is important in life and, thus, what they should believe important in their own lives. The most effective school cultures, even if one does not agree with their overriding goals and objectives, manifest and announce themselves in diverse ways to every student what are their preferred behaviors and actions, and what values the school culture prizes and what rewards are dispensed for conforming to that culture.

As public organizations, school cultures often mirror in their policies and practices the popular culture and public attitudes in which they exist. As such, American school cultures feature a plethora of non-academic diversions, extra/co-curricular activities, and interscholastic sports. These exist in our schools as edifying and wholesome preoccupations purported essential for adolescent social and emotional development, but the profusion of these non-academic learning diversions and the school culture they reflect and sustain overwhelm any pretext of serious academic learning. The saturation of non-academic diversions in our schools, to which I sometimes refer as "Club Med for Kids," necessarily relegates high academic and scholastic learning for most students to a decidedly secondary concern.

Our public schools and their school cultures create and envelop students in an irresistible propulsion away from academic learning to indulge themselves in school-sponsored, adult-endorsed, ubiquitous "fun" pursuits. These, of course, are fueled by popular expectations that demand our schools provide an infinity of non-academic but nonetheless, our culture asserts, valuable "learning opportunities." Since prevailing "anti-academic school cultures" reflect a popular culture that celebrates entertainments and honors those who give us the pleasure of spectacles, non-academic school diversions are often expressed by frequent musical concerts, theatrical productions, athletic competitions, and all manner of spectacles of stage and field. Popular culture is, thus, an active participant in establishing and perpetuating the "anti-academic school culture," and without its strong influence, teachers' unions and collegiate schools of education would have a much more difficult task in making academic learning a subordinate, ancillary function of public education, which is, even without the force of popular culture, an unavoidable consequence of their presence and influence in public education.

Education authorities and experts further support popular culture's non-academic demands with philosophies and theories of "well-rounded-ness," "proper balance," "comprehensive education," serving the needs of all students to better educate the "whole child," and "learning must be fun" educational theories, all of which have as their chief focus "social-emotional adolescent development." These educational philosophies have dominated and shaped public education and school operations since the first "Baby Boomers" entered school in the early 1950s, and when indiscriminately implemented, account for the saturation of non-academic priorities and preoccupations, creating an all-encompassing carnival-like school environment and school culture.

Can one think of a "movie" or "TV series" where education and adolescent students are the central setting and focus, but where academic learning or scholastic pursuits are not relegated to a non-entity, or even accorded a passing notice of importance in the plot, action, and behaviors of the actors? Is not the depiction of academic learning and its undertaking ignored completely, and even mocked and denigrated in popular entertainment in favor of song, dance, romance, and teenage angst as being the essence of American education?

What is seldom understood—or at least seldom admitted—is that, because our society demands that our schools offer and contain an endless array of extra/co-curricular activities and school sports, to which demands the widely accepted educational theories focusing on social-emotional development give intellectual justification, our schools exude a pronounced, deeply rooted "anti-academic school culture" as prevalent as it is destructive to serious academic learning—and one decidedly absent in Asian and European schools.

Adding to popular demands and their collaborating educational philosophies, the teachers' union and collegiate departments of education, for their mutual benefit and self-interest of training and advocating the hiring in schools of as many non-academic subject teachers and student-services school personnel as possible, uphold and protect the prevailing "anti-academic school culture."

The ultimate force sustaining and perpetuating the "anti-academic school culture" is, however, the New Jersey Department of Education, which, through the power of laws, rules, and regulations, entrenches the "anti-academic school culture" with its non-academic "content area" mandates.

These combined forces and influences generate the policies and practices that create and sustain the "anti-academic school culture" prevailing not only in New Jersey, but in American public education, while they insulate school culture from challenge, erosion, or even moderation, thereby setting in motion a never-ending cycle perpetuating the distorted enterprise hostile to academic learning we call the "educational process."

In most public-school "anti-academic school cultures," as I observed, confusing and contradictory messages co-exist at first for the new student, but soon that culture announces to all, plainly and clamorously, that academic learning is far from a priority objective. To adolescent students, each non-academic activity in the school environment yells: "Give me your time! Give me your interest!" It is the iconoclastic adolescent student, or the student with enlightened and determined parents, who, resisting both peer pressure and the adult-sponsored, enthralling force of the "anti-academic school culture," pursues instead, however unwittingly, the true meaning of education—*"leading out from ignorance and darkness to the light of knowledge, virtue, and truth."*

To the "anti-academic school culture" most adolescents, especially those whose parents lack insight or understanding, or heritages which prize above all academic learning, respond unhesitatingly and imbibe enthusiastically. But soon after attaining maturity, many will rue their enthusiastic indulgence and adult-sanctioned misuse of school time and attention, for fond memories of youthful frivolities cannot easily replace hard-won academic skills and knowledge proficiencies, or the enduring, life-enhancing dividends they confer.

Our typical and ubiquitous "anti-academic school cultures," especially in grades 6-12, are responsible for New Jersey's disappointing academic-learning outcomes, for impeding upward social and economic mobility, and for American students' poor academic standing in the world. If this is to ever change, American schools must defy, if not at minimum challenge and diminish the influences of those forces responsible for creating and sustaining our "anti-academic school cultures," namely, popular culture, teachers' unions, collegiate schools of education, social-emotional adolescent developmental priorities, and non-academic curricular content state mandates.

Classical Academy's "Academics-First School Culture"

I firmly attest that—from observation and experience—when placed in a school with a distinct "academics-first school culture," students from every socio-economic circumstance assimilate that culture and respond accordingly as that single-minded academics-first culture unswervingly propels them, however reluctantly or unwittingly, to develop their minds and character by prioritizing their time for and devoting their efforts to academic-learning success. In my view, it is the highest responsibility—a responsibility I executed to my fullest—of school authorities to resist the power of those forces suppressing high academic learning for every student, namely, the powers of popular culture, the prevailing social-emotional theories of child development, teacher-union demands, and, as much as possible, the New Jersey Department of Education's non-academic subject curricular mandates. In this way schools can adopt and implement, as did the Classical Academy, policies and practices which create and sustain a dominant "academics-first" school culture. In fact, schools with "academics-first" cultures are of especial necessity for students who are not blessed with enlightened parents, but such school cultures are woefully absent in those places that need them most.

Unabashedly and from its inception, the Classical Academy was an "academics first" educational institution as illustrated by the 13 unprecedented education reforms detailed in the previous chapter. The school abandoned almost the entirety of non-academic school activities that are commonplace features—if not the essence—of K-12 public-school education. It also subordinated the social-emotional priorities, the usual modalities and extensive practice of which militate against high academic-learning proficiencies, and it deemphasized those priorities for a school culture dedicated to advance academic learning for every student.

Non-academic subjects and pursuits, the abundance of "extra/co-curricular" activities, and school sports have little presence in the school

I founded. In this way, the Classical Academy's "academics-first school culture," supported by well-chosen policies and practices, would become a permeating, all-encompassing school ethos manifestly communicated to every student, teacher, and parent. Just as "anti-academic school cultures" drive students from serious scholastic learning, just so, a clear and distinct "academics-first school culture" propels students toward scholastic proficiency with the forceful message that academic learning is the unambiguous school priority to which all must give their devotion of time and effort.

Classical Academy objectives were clear from its beginning, enunciated in its state-approved charter-school application of 1997 and in all its policy pronouncements and implementations since that time under my leadership. With deliberate purpose and intention, the Classical Academy developed its school culture to sustain and to nourish both its academics-first principles and the attainment of its academic-educational objectives. Conversely, those principles and objectives manifested in the school's practices and policies coincide with and reinforce themselves in the school culture; each must enliven the other, continually and without ambiguity.

A school's culture, be it academic or anti-academic, is most effective when its policies and practices—and the culture they create—are calculated to achieve one prime objective rather than a multitude of confusing or contradictory purposes. School cultural power, for good or ill, influences student behavior, attitudes, beliefs, and actions, and it does so daily and powerfully.

By clear and quantifiable evidence, the Classical Academy's prime cultural objective was to demonstrate scholastic success by its students' devotion, or, better, their directed application to academic learning. This devotion and application are not contingent upon students' inborn or even cultivated love of learning, or their willing application of that devotion. For most adolescents, serious learning and the hard work to attain it is not natural or an innate propensity. "Academics-first school cultures" force all students, even the more reluctant or unwilling ones, toward working and attaining real academic-learning progress.

The Classical Academy's "academics-first school culture" and its effects are palpably reflected in its students academically outperforming by great margins their peers attending Clifton Public Schools, or, as referred by the state, its "resident district." In this regard, Classical Academy students, sharing the same socio-economic characteristics as Clifton Public School students, by the time of their 8th-grade graduation, attained demonstrably far-greater scholastic skills, higher proficiencies, and broader and deeper subject-matter knowledge than their Clifton counterparts (see Appendix A). Classical Academy students also demonstrated by the end of the 8th grade a well-developed habit of responsibility derived from meeting the demands and challenging standards of a highly academic curriculum supported by an "academics-first school culture."

As enumerated in the last chapter, the Classical Academy's 13 principal educational reforms in unison, each imparting force and effectiveness to the other, create and sustain the school's "academics-first school culture." The well-articulated Classical Academy "academics-first school culture" constitutes the learning environment which distinguishes the school I founded, and both cultivates and sustains the school's remarkable student scholastic achievements.

To summarize, an "academics-first school culture" focuses attention on academic learning and drives—indeed, *compels*—students of every motivational level and scholastic propensity (or lack therefor) toward higher learning achievement. It communicates to students unambiguously—without confusing messages—what the adults in their lives value and indeed what the school culture esteems; it delineates clearly for students the path to adult approbation and rewards, and even to peer acceptance. It also communicates to students what priorities their classmates pursue and upon which activities their fellow students focus their school time and application of effort. This school ethos or cultural force, generated and upheld by the school's policies and practices as reflected in the 13 education reforms described above, molded and sustained the "academics-first school culture." In large measure, that prevailing academic school culture enabled Classical Academy students to earn vastly superior scholastic outcomes than their peers for nearly two decades, but also was a force for engendering critical attributes of personal character.

In addition to the collective force the 13 prime school reforms discussed above had in creating the Classical Academy's "academics-first school culture," the school also fortified, sustained, and communicated its school culture in manifold other ways. Before discussing these additional school-culture reinforcing methods, it must be said that it is an easier challenge to establish an effective "academics-first school culture" in a small school. In fact, all essential elements of education are much better delivered in schools that have no more than 300 students. When student populations reach upwards of 300 (each Clifton middle school has more than 1,000 students), all aspects of educating youth become dauntingly problematic, and distinct, uniform school cultures fostering academic learning, presuming that is the goal of schools, are more difficult, though not impossible, to create or sustain. Interestingly, large public schools have no problem in perpetuating their dominant "anti-academic school cultures." In fact, the larger the school, the more pervasive and entrenched is its cultural hostility to serious academic study for every student, and to universal, school-wide high-level learning. However, the Classical Academy's small size of 120 middle-school students was conducive to the construction and cohesive promulgation of an effective school culture which fortified its "academics first" principles.

Re-Channeling Youthful Zest for Competition to Focus on Academics

Traditional school spirit, a kindred aspect of school culture, often emanates from non-academic competitions: interscholastic sports, marching-bands competitions, cheerleading contests, musical and dramatic presentations, and other non-academic team contests among vying schools. Channeling adolescent zest for competition from non-academics to serious school-wide academic learning was yet another way to establish and to sustain the Classical Academy's "academics-first school culture."

To excite students about the importance of the event, the Classical Academy re-channeled students' natural enthusiasm for competition from the sports field to the yearly state-mandated standardized student assessments. The "competitive contest" was between Classical Academy and the

2 Clifton middle schools; the "sport" was the state-mandated 8th-grade standardized assessments in mathematics (and later "Algebra I" in the PARCC tests), English language arts literacy, and science. In these state-mandated tests, our students, particularly 8th-graders, would be heroic participants and, when victorious, would bring rewards to themselves, happiness to their parents, honor to the school, and acclamation from all.

This rechanneling of competitive enthusiasm from non-academic endeavors to "taking the field for the big [academic] game" against rival Clifton schools (and rival charter schools), with the 8th-grade state-mandated assessments being the prime competitive contest itself, I made an integral and a conspicuous part of Classical Academy "academics-first school culture."

When adults in the school environment convincingly and unanimously convey to impressionable adolescent minds the clear priority of academics, students absorb that message and react positively. In addition to frequent exhortations for achievement, our "Wall of Honor," "Bestowing of the Cake," "Writing on School Walls," "Pep Rallies," "The Power of the Penguin," and "Advanced Proficiency Certificates" became school-wide celebratory traditions and examples of re-channeling youthful competitive inclinations to academics.

In a large exhibit prominently displayed on a central hallway wall, each August, I would affix the names and pictures of every Classical Academy student who had earned "Advanced Proficiency" (later, on PARCC tests, "Level 5"—"Exceeding Expectations") on state standardized tests taken the previous spring. The display was arranged according to student grade in school (6th, 7th, and 8th) and the tested subject(s) in which the student earned "Advanced Proficiency." Instead of a trophy case for athletic victories, the Classical Academy's proud display honoring and recognizing students for their academic successes—and the hard work that success required— would remain the entire school year. We designated it our "Wall of Honor."

Several weeks before starting the multi-day state-mandated testing, we would cover all the hallway walls with poster boards. I instructed students to write phrases exhorting Classical Academy victory or mocking rival schools, or to write encouraging statements to individual students. "Kick Ass on the ASK!"; "For Classical Academy students, success on the PARCC is a walk in the Park"; "Reach the top of the GEPA mountain"; "Briana, do your best"; "Abe, conquer the ASK"; "Humiliate Christopher Columbus!" and "Destroy Woodrow Wilson!" [names of both Clifton middle schools] were typical inscriptions. Students eagerly participated, as I reminded them that it is rare for a principal to allow—even to encourage—students to write on the walls, so use this unique opportunity freely and gratefully.

The "Bestowing of the Cake" was an event involving ice-cream cakes. Before the entire school, in an outdoor ceremony, several days before state testing began, each 7th-grade student would present a slice of ice-cream cake to an 8th-grader, while expressing sentiments of encouragement and best wishes for the 8th-grader's performance on state tests. This annual outdoor event also served as a "Pep Rally," encouraging students' best efforts for the state assessments.

During the second year of the school, at the end of one of my Latin classes, a student, while submitting his quiz, looked at me with some puzzlement and said, respectfully, "Mr. D, you have a shape like a penguin." The proverbial lightbulb flashed in my thoughts; from that point, we would be known as the "Classical Academy Penguins." The penguin would become the school mascot. As a quaint tradition, each year I placed a large, plush penguin in each standardized-testing room, and, before each day's test, I carried the mascot in the aisles and requested each student to pat the mascot for "good luck" and to invoke "penguin power" so they would perform their best on the test.

Certificates of "Advanced Proficiency" Achievement for students earning the highest category of standardized-test achievement in "mathematics" ("Algebra I"), "English language arts literacy," or "science," were given at the formal 8th-grade-graduation ceremony. Similar certificates were awarded to 6th- and 7th-graders at end-of-year outdoor ceremonies.

Existential Importance of Academics-First School Culture to the Classical Academy

Charter schools, in no small measure, rise or fall on how their students perform on state standardized exams. Repeated, abominably poor student standardized-test outcomes often led to charter termination or non-renewal, especially when wild spending or financial peculation accompanied low student performance. Classical Academy student performance on state subject-matter assessments was critical to its survival, particularly in so hostile an environment where powerful segments of Clifton's government, public-school officials, and community were rooting for Classical Academy's failure. The Classical Academy's educationally potent curricula and learning materials, our high academic standards and expectations, and all the educational reforms expressed in its policies and practices, assured, we firmly and accurately predicted, student academic-learning outcomes far superior to that of Clifton public schools and to most other charter schools. By establishing and maintaining those reforms, practices, and policies, a distinct and manifest "academics-first school culture" was created and became instrumental for school success *and*, indeed, survival. Traditional public schools never experience such existential pressures for achieving high school-wide student academic-learning results, and they never need to trouble themselves about it.

Debunking the "Anti-Academic School Culture's" Edifying Attributes

It is an accepted precept that "non-academic" subjects, school activities defined as "extra-" and "co-"curricular, and, most particularly, interscholastic sports, are most responsible for inculcating in the young person those virtues we prize in human beings: character, confidence, team building, fearlessly confronting challenges, striving toward a goal, creativity and imaginativeness, responsibility, honesty, respect, interpersonal skills, *ad infinitum*.

Athletic sports in schools was an honored feature of British private boarding schools, a tradition early American schools adopted. British school sports programs were aimed at developing strong bodies habituated to pain and discomfort ("caning" or beating students with a stick was also a feature of these British schools, and done so with parents' approbation, if not expectation). Graduates of these schools, all boys from aristocratic or titled British families, were destined to be officers in the British armed forces, especially the British navy. Their school training was intended to nurture the qualities of those destined to protect and expand the British Empire. Remember the often-quoted statement of Wellington, the British high commander who defeated Napoleon at Waterloo: "The Battle of Waterloo was won on the playing fields of Eton." Rugby, the forerunner of American football, was the primary sport most often played on those playing fields, and Eton is one of England's most historic and storied private boys boarding schools. The modern American purpose or justification for school sports is quite different from its British antecedents, is it not?

It amuses me, as it saddens, when those who justify, at the terrible expense of serious academic learning, the abundance of interscholastic sports programs in our schools by employing the bromide that "sports build character," endowing the sort of virtues and competitive spirit in its participants we desire to be inculcated in our children and fellow Americans. I am reminded that a school official once boasted to me that his average-size school district had no less than 54 organized team sports, presumably permitting so many of the school district's students to develop character and virtue. The academic learning student proficiencies of this school district's students were abysmal and well below the state average proficiencies levels, yet its school authorities bragged about providing extraordinary opportunities for supposed character development. Incidentally, if the benefits of competitive sports be so powerful in forming coveted personal traits, then the character and virtue of our professional athletes, those who have developed their athletic abilities to ultimate perfection, should be among our society's most admiral exemplars of high character. One only need look here to see that the lofty moral justifications for the saturation of interscholastic sports in our schools—and the putative power of sports to develop sterling personal character, respectable morality, and praiseworthy virtue—is as fictitious as it is fatuous.

In my long experiences as classroom teacher and school principal, as well as reflecting upon the developments of my own life, I believe that a rigorous academic education is much the superior way students develop true and permanent attributes of personal character and morality, the attributes people esteem as most commendable and praiseworthy, the very properties of character most responsible for successful, fulfilling lives, economically and personally.

Unless an adolescent is born into an erudite and scholarly family and guided by it, or is blessed with familial cultural imperatives prioritizing scholastic learning, most students do not come to academics naturally; it is not an innate propensity, like seeking and embracing "fun" activities. Serious academics is hard work. I always recoil from the foolish admonition we frequently hear that "learning must be fun." If there is no "fun" element to learning, as many educators and parents believe, their unhappy children will reject learning, and the acquisition of skills and knowledge is destined to be a failed, fruitless process, and social-emotional development stunted.

Schools, as is their common practice, apply sweet "honey" on the rim of the cup of learning to induce a child to ingest the bitter medicine of academic study—or what passes for academic learning in most schools. Yet, too often in our schools (and misinterpreting Lucretius's prescription who advised effecting a disagreeable but necessary act, like educating the young, with a tempting sweetener), our educational process and its typical school culture have, without restraint, applied copious amounts of "honey" which has slipped from the cup's rim into the cup itself, thereby diluting the medicine to the point where it no longer has therapeutic benefits. Indeed, in too many unfortunate cases, the young student has become giddy by many doses of the honey's natural sweetness and, over the course of many years in American schools, having now reached young adulthood, has developed tooth decay and other preventable disorders caused by professional malpractice of prioritizing the prevailing "anti-academic school culture" (the excessive honey) during one's adolescent education.

Educators who operate and influence our public schools (and responsible for putting too much honey on the rim of the cup of learning) believe rigorous academics is too stressful to be pursued assiduously. It is believed that our students require, in direct opposition to the philosophy and practice of Asian and European schools, frequent respites and pleasant diversions during the school day in order to be happy, and better to accept and assimilate the meager academic portion of their education. There is, of course, the hope and expectation that student immersion in extra-co/

curricular activities and sports, in addition to generating a "liking" for school, will also aid in reducing dropout rates and deterring adolescents from harmful indulgences like drugs, alcohol, and sexual proclivities. In many communities, the non-academic school diversions are intended to occupy students' time and interest as a prophylactic against juvenile criminal temptations and involvement.

Whatever the reasons for excessive non-academic preoccupations in our schools, one only need look at the international ranking of countries where, consistently, American students rank middling to low in academic proficiencies. One understandably also looks askance at the abundant importation into America of foreign engineers and scientists because American education does not educate sufficient numbers of its own citizens in these demanding academic subjects to maintain its technological and economic superiority. Such facts lead one to realize that the shockingly low assessment of American education and its dire consequences documented in the federal government's 1983 "A Nation at Risk" report, despite decades of education reform and massive funding, are still ominously accurate, and will always be accurate as long as the "anti-academic school culture" reigns supreme in American education.

It must be noted that, especially in New Jersey, where public education is a hyper-political and societal undertaking, the use of school-day time, allocation of resources, the extraordinary amount and diversity of "extra/co-curricular activities," and, indeed, the apotheosis of adolescent social-emotional education are matters in which political, ideological, societal, and financial self-interests coalesce in rare unanimity. Hardly anyone challenges the purported value of the non-academic over the academic, or the conspicuous subordination of academic learning to extolling the prevailing "wholesome fun" preoccupations of school. Few would confess that such a one-sided imbalance exists, or even that an "anti-academic culture" pervades and dominates schools. The woeful effects the prevailing "anti-academic school culture" inflicts on student academic-learning proficiencies, hindering the much-wider and deeper attainment of those proficiencies, are never acknowledged, except by those of us who witness the horrendous damage firsthand and close up.

The fatal consequences of the "anti-academic school culture" to young lives and to our society persist unabated and unquestioned, and that culture will forever inflict its pernicious power on academic learning while it dominates and pervades New Jersey public schools. No matter what educational reforms are undertaken, or how much taxpayer money is spent, as long as the "anti-academic school culture" is permitted to dominate education, those reforms and increased funding will be wholly ineffectual, if spreading and elevating student academic-learning proficiencies is their goal.

An "Academics-First School Culture" and Rigorous Academics Best Inculcates Strong Personal Character, Confidence, Self-Esteem, Responsibility, and Ambition

When school authorities foster above all else the pursuit of and devotion to serious academic learning and establish a palpable "academics-first school culture" supported by policies and practices, then every student will gain more lasting and more critical developmental benefits than gained by student immersion in non-academics, extra/co-curricular activities, and interscholastic sports, to which temptations students are daily exposed and unceasingly exhorted in our public schools.

In reality, student pursuit of school-mandated and enforced rigorous academic learning inculcates life-rewarding dividends more critical and enduring than those ephemeral memories of applause and momentary adulatory satisfactions gained from sports or the stage. Participation in a rigorous program of prescribed academic studies develops responsibility, self-reliance, and a habit of denial or postponement of immediate pleasure for a greater good. Serious academics nurtures enduringly the higher attributes of mind and spirit, and develops habits contributing to strong personal character which will forever better serve adolescent students in any future endeavor. Here, what is learned is secondary, but the personal attributes that are cultivated and required to attain that learning are what truly matter for strong adolescent character development.

Serious academic training produces what rational, thinking people extoll as paradigms of conduct and high emotional development. Many virtues and praiseworthy character traits are truly and permanently nurtured by the demanding *process* of serious academic learning—not solely by the attainment of knowledge itself. I sincerely believe that all adolescents, when challenged by some task that requires work, sacrifice, and dedication, and succeeds not only in its final attainment but by what they experience in the process of its acquisition, reap an indelible confidence in their abilities and an immense sense of accomplishment—and this is best and more lastingly rendered through serious academics, not by school sports or extra/co-curricular pursuits. This is not a fanciful theory but a fact of child development I witnessed unfailingly throughout my teaching career and during my Classical Academy leadership.

There is no better "confidence-building" tool than when a young person has benefited from a solidly academic education and becomes accustomed to strive for higher goals and invests in the conscious, ongoing effort to attain them. Habituating oneself to the practice of sacrificing immediate and transitory pleasures for a "higher good," even if at the time the adolescent may not recognize or appreciate that "higher good," is an edifying experience and a reliable source of "character building."

Academics breeds not only true character, but self-reliance, self-esteem, and ambition, too. It is my considered belief, in dealing with all manner of adolescents over many years, that serious academic study is the most potent element by far in the entire educative process; it cultivates genuinely strong character and imbues adolescents with those vigorous internal characteristics important for life success and personal happiness.

A strong, prescribed academic program of studies in an "academics-first school culture" accustoms one's embryonic character to curb natural inclinations to pursue fun; it teaches adolescents not to shun the hard work of rigorous scholastics in favor of cheerful, undemanding pastimes. If understanding of a "greater good" does not come from parents, our schools must provide it; if they do not, they are negligent, indeed, to my mind, *malfeasant* for not only not establishing "academics-first" emphasis as the school culture, but actually catering to the natural youthful inclination to avoid hard work of scholastics for headlong indulgence in school-sponsored "fun" and "frivolities." These unfortunate, assimilated adolescent attitudes, where the "fun" component must be present in all of one's endeavors, attitudes nurtured by and encouraged in our schools, are too frequently carried forward into young adulthood and which perforce enchain, perhaps forever, those who are incapable of breaking free from the distorted reality in which they were educated.

To succeed or merely meet basic requirements in serious academics, students must learn to use their time prudently, make decisions on how to deploy their efforts and, perhaps most of all, prioritize their responsibilities to meet the challenges serious academic learning requires. An "academics-first school culture" impresses unequivocally to young minds, without ambiguity or mixed messaging, that the purpose of their education and time in school is foremost that of academic learning and meeting the demands of their scholastic obligations. When this impression is firmly set in motion and practiced daily, so, too, is the *process* leading to the inculcation of personal character, confidence, ambition, self-esteem, and responsibility.

The pursuit of serious academics is, therefore, the truest, most potent method of building strong personal character traits and edifying habits in young people, the sort of inward and emotional strength that is lifelong and ever-present, not illusory, vacuous, or transitory. Rigorous academic learning nurtures and perfects more enduringly and valuably all the developmental attributes and esteemed personal character traits many foolishly and primarily ascribe as rewards of interscholastic sports and widespread student participation in "extra/co-curricular" school activities.

An "academics-first school culture" is especially needed when students do not come from households with parents having collegiate degrees and professional occupations, or are incapable of providing prudent or sagacious parental guidance. The more fortunate students, those with well-educated parents or born into cultures honoring academic learning, are often driven to academic achievements instilled in them by parents, ancestral culture, or familial imperatives. Schools, therefore, in less-affluent communities or communities having fewer parentally directed fortunate adolescents, are, therefore, more incumbent to develop and sustain an "academics-first school culture." Educational attainment remains a prime method for upward social and economic mobility for less-advantaged American youth, and much more reliably than fantasies of becoming a professional athlete or entertainer. Schools serving less-advantaged students which establish strong academics-first cultures and practices would truly be meaningful *in loco parentis* institutions, and provide lesser-advantaged students with similar guidance and parental direction for scholastic learning as students with cultural and familial impetuses which compel their offspring toward high academic achievement.

To summarize, for adolescents of all backgrounds, rigorous academics trains one to put forth the effort and the determination to meet successfully what may be construed as unpleasantly daunting, intimidating challenges. Rigorous academics inures the formative emotions to persevere when disappointments arise or motivation flags. It engenders an abiding confidence in oneself and in one's intellectual abilities, knowledge gained, and skills perfected, a confidence to strive for higher goals. It exercises the habit of personal responsibility, which is often the precursor to personal integrity. It teaches adolescents to forgo immediate satisfactions to labor for higher objectives, and develops the understanding and habit that procuring those higher objectives and greater goods may be a fun-less, arduous, and self-sacrificing endeavor. It promotes and sharpens the innate sense of drive to achieve whatever one's goals and objectives become in life. Rigorous academics enriches one's self-esteem and inculcates self-reliance. It incites lofty ambitions, as reflected in one of the Classical Academy mottos excerpted from the ancient Roman historian Livy, who wrote that the true purpose of education was: *"To be educated in those disciplines by which one's nature is aroused to the cultivation of a meaningful destiny."*

My close observations of the educational process as a teacher and school principal form my steadfast belief that all students and young people, even the more reluctant ones or those seemingly non-compliant or unsuited, when put in an "academics-first school culture," respond favorably and will benefit immensely from their experiences of a school-mandated pursuit of rigorous academics above all else.

Communicating "Academics-First School Culture" and Its Imperatives

Clear and frequent communication to both students and parents of what is expected of them, both scholastically and behaviorally, is paramount in sustaining an "academics-first school culture." I personally took the lead in these matters, but our teachers and parents contributed to my efforts. At the beginning of the school year, I always met both with students new to the school and with returning students. To them I delineated expectations: that study, doing their schoolwork, and striving for the best grades was their duty and obligation. All may not earn "A's" in all their subjects, but working hard for academic success and doing the best one can do were the behaviors we valued and what we rewarded. We also often communicated to parents that their children would be working harder in school than most had ever done previously, and parent support was essential in advocating and supporting their youthful labors in achieving scholastic progress and achievement.

Certainly, communications of the importance of academics and similar exhortations to students were not restricted to the start of school but continued regularly during the school year. They often took various forms and occurred in different situations. One method of conveying or reinforcing our "academics-first school culture" was to address periodically all 6th-graders at the beginning and throughout the school year. I asked students some strange questions: "Why would you want to come to a school where there is little else to do than to study and work hard on school subjects?" or, "Before coming to the Classical Academy, how much time did you spend doing homework?" or, "Did you know that, here, you must do 2-4 hours of homework nightly, and on weekends?" Students often responded that "I had to come here because my mother said I had to," or "Mr. DeRosa, do you recognize me? My brother graduated here last year, so my parents said I had to come." I would then make everyone feel easier and told the audience that success at the Classical Academy was within the power and abilities of every one of them, how fortunate they were to attend a school like the Classical Academy, and that I wish my mother had sent me to a school like this one. I then would detail what we expected of them, how they could succeed, why they should try hard in their studies, and that, when they are older, they will look back and say, "I am so glad that I attended the Classical Academy."

Another frequent "pep talk" method I was fond of employing was to enter a class (often with a day or two notice to the teacher) and address students. I would relate how important their work was to me, to their teachers, to their parents, and to their classmatesw—and how delighted we were to witness their efforts at studying and performing their schoolwork. I sometimes would note a particular student's grade on a test, or how well a student improved, and mention some names of students who had 100% homework submissions in a subject. If the teacher informed me that several students in class were flagging and not performing to teacher expectations, I took the opportunity to re-energize those students and reiterate the importance of their work, not to slack off, and how their determined labors will reward them now and in the future. It is a natural propensity that adolescents seek the praise and approval of adults, particularly adults whom they love, respect, or admire. The employment of adolescent desire for public approbation, peer recognition, and adult encouragement in order to sustain and reinforce an "academics-first school culture" is not only useful but necessary.

The Potency of Re-Directed "Peer Pressure"

Unremittingly communicating not merely verbally but by behaviors and interactions students daily witnessed in the school environment, and in which they themselves engaged, helped illustrate and indoctrinate students to our "academics-first school culture." Students' daily exposure to our school-wide academic priorities and expectations firmly established in each student's sensibilities our dominant "academics-first school culture." As students would remind me, "Mr. D, we have to study because there is nothing else here for us to do." Strictly speaking, this was not absolutely true, but it was generally a valid observation which always delighted me, for it proved that students were quite aware that they were in an "academics-first school culture."

Still, other methods were employed to reinforce our prevailing "academics-first culture." I encouraged teachers to provide diverse rewards as incitements for academic achievement or improvement, either individually or for the entire class. For example, when Jose or Abraham was chronically remiss in submitting homework, a teacher, often with my permission, might extend the proposition that if Jose and Abraham "do their homework" completely and on time for the next month, the entire class will have a "Pizza Friday." Another reward our teachers used regularly was that, if, on an upcoming test, every student in the class earned a 75% or above, or if no one failed the test, the entire class would earn two "free" nights without homework, or a free period outdoors.

Offers of similar group or individual rewards were integral to our program of studies as a method of enlisting "peer pressure" directed toward academics. "Peer-to-peer" tutoring or simply one student informally helping another for homework completion or studying for a test was encouraged and often rewarded.

Peer pressure is usually expressed exclusively within and about activities emanating from the anti-academic school culture's "Club Med for Kids" school environment, the reality of most public schools. But when peer pressure is redirected so students are incited (and excited) to encourage each other to focus on academic learning, and, indeed, cheering each other on, celebrating each other's academic victories, and assisting one another in matters scholastic, the "academics-first school culture" becomes a dynamic, visible phenomenon in fulfilling its organizational purpose. To the educator, this redirection of peer pressure toward academic learning is a most satisfying phenomenon, one that I witnessed all during my Classical Academy leadership, and one of my most gratifying experiences as an educator.

I can cite many other Classical Academy examples of academic-reward practices and of eliciting peer pressure for academic ends. The academic-encouragement methods initiated by teachers in individual classes or for particular students, or initiated by school leadership amongst the entire student body, are intended, along with adult exhortations and public rewards, to engage peer pressure toward academic achievement or improvement for their fellow students. The sum result of these practices was to communicate and to reinforce to every student, parent, and teacher, the Classical Academy's clear and unambiguous "academics-first school culture."

All during my long leadership, Classical Academy students never had any misconception or misunderstanding of why they were in school or what was expected of them, nor were they ever uncertain or confused—no mixed messages here—about what was valued and what engendered praise, earned rewards, and won admiration. This was the potent dividend of a distinct "academics-first school culture," the overall effectiveness of which was aided by a purposeful redirection of peer pressure from the trivial and frivolous to the essential and enduring.

To some, it may seem sadistic to put so much peer pressure on one or several particular students who were not upholding their scholastic responsibility to themselves and to their classmates. Nevertheless, it proved advantageous in motivating slacking students to achieve not just individual but "team" goals. How is this different than an athletic pep rally or the proposition that if the football team wins Saturday's big game, the school will have a Monday assembly (for which many will miss academic-subject classes), with the team members honored on stage? If exhortations and peer pressure are acceptable forms of encouragement for students in non-academic pursuits, why cannot similar methods be used for decidedly academic achievement and improvement—and not merely for a few students or for one class, but school-wide, as the Classical Academy amply demonstrated in its "academics-first school culture".

Student "Code of Conduct" Supporting "Academics-First School Culture"

I wrote and periodically revised a detailed "Student Code of Conduct" for Classical Academy students. It contained many commonplace statements of desired conduct, the treatment of fellow students, the "do's and don'ts" of school behavior. However, the most important, enduring admonition advancing the school's academics-first culture was simple and concise: "A student's classroom behavior must be such that it does not interfere with the teacher's ability to teach and other students' ability to learn." This foundational rule was as continually enunciated as it was steadfastly enforced. Whether a teacher or someone having experienced American education as a student, everyone can testify to the disastrous and fatal effects disruptive or disorderly classroom conduct has on academic instruction and learning. An academics-first school cannot realize its objectives, or produce the superior learning outcomes for which it was established, if classroom student conduct becomes contrary to its intent, and an erosive factor.

Enlisting Parents and Teachers: Pillars of School Culture

By its nature and intent, an "academics-first school culture" necessitates the willing involvement of all segments of the educative process. Teachers appreciative of a serious, orderly academic environment in which to practice their vocation, and parents who choose to have their children attend such a school, must uphold that culture by their committed and consensual participation in it.

Through written documents and verbal messages communicated to all parents and teachers, and through the well-distributed descriptions of our policies and practices, but most of all by actions and interactions of the school community, our "academics-first school culture" was well understood, and its daily, palpable presence was felt by all. Its positive consequences were visible in practice and manifested both in high student scholastic results and in maintaining a well-disciplined school environment conducive to those results.

Parents were essential to our school-of-choice institution. We regarded them our customers and clients, without whose satisfaction the school could not survive. As with all "educational choice" schools, the Classical Academy exists in a marketplace competing for customer-clients, so unlike the monopoly of traditional public schools, which, however chronic their egregious failings, are assured each year a client base, generous funding, and guaranteed existence.

Being by far the smallest New Jersey charter school, with only 120 students, and, for many years, the documented lowest-funded public school in the state, if the Classical Academy lost 20 or 30 dissatisfied students or parents during the year or not returning to the school the next year, serious financial distress would ensue. It was essential, therefore, that we provide to every parent and student the kind of high-quality academic education and learning environment we pledged, and, in turn, parents, by their educational choice understand and support our "academics-first" culture, and the policies and practices which sustained it.

In meeting with prospective parents and students, individually or in "Open House Informational Sessions," I would first recite in detail what the Classical Academy does *not* have and does *not* offer, and why. I described the curricula, homework requirements, scholastic expectations, the school's academics-first educational policies and practices, and the nature of our "academics-first school culture." No parent who chose to enroll a child ever did so without first possessing a full understanding of the Classical Academy and its educational aims and objectives.

Through the years, Classical Academy parents contributed to offering students extra-curricular activities which were not part of the mandated school program. Some years, a PTA was formed. Other years, parents unified more informally in arranging for events or organizing activities, but with measured congruence with the school's academics-first imperatives. It was, indeed, rare that I permitted a parent or teacher-initiated extra-curricular activity to be scheduled during the school day so not to interfere in academic instruction. At the Classical Academy, classroom instructional time was sacred and untouchable. Most parent-sponsored activities were either in the evening, on weekends, or after state-standardized testing concluded. Supporting and subscribing to our "academics-first school culture" was, apart from choosing to enroll their children, the single greatest contribution Classical Academy parents made to the school, and they did it for the sake of enhancing the prospects of their children's future.

Criticisms of an "Academics-First" School and Its Culture

Some critics of the Classical Academy's educational academics-first philosophy and school culture may proffer the assertion that our program neglects to provide growing adolescents the essential opportunities for social and emotional development. Furthermore, they may proclaim, my educational philosophy, of which I had the rare privilege of putting into actual practice, deprives children of valuable school-based experiences vital to their nurturing as human beings. An undiluted "academics-first school culture" may well serve a small group of motivated students with superlative academic learning and achievement, critics may pronounce, but it leaves the majority of diverse students without opportunity or encouragement to develop in ways more compatible with their natures and talents. An unmitigated "academics-first school culture" with a prescribed academic-centric program of rigorous studies for every student may well be tantamount to professional malfeasance and student deprivation. Growing children require more of a balance in education, this common view advocates, not an intense focus on academic learning to the harmful exclusion of other types of learning opportunities.

Learning comes from more than just books and academics, critics further declare. What I denounce as "anti-academic school culture" contains learning opportunities just as valid and valuable to the maturing adolescent as pure academics or unremitting study. Adolescents need experiences in dealing with other people to acquire socialization skills, and to discover and to understand themselves. Interacting with others in all manner of contexts provides lifelong skills that enhance adolescents' "emotional IQ." A rigorous, prescribed course of academic subjects to the exclusion of non-academic subjects and extra/co-curricular activities and school sports ignores the "whole child" and impedes emotional and social development.

A school that disregards common nurturing school experiences and puts too much emphasis on pure academic learning is a school that educates only half the child, leaving the other half to lie stunted and undeveloped, not to mention producing very unhappy children. Such a public-school program may well border on malpractice, if not actual child neglect.

To such critics, I respond that I am fully aware that life is more than academic learning. I always recommended to Classical Academy parents who felt that there were aspects of adolescent development they wished for their child but which were not available at the school, such as organized sports, theatrical productions, or dance or music lessons, that they explore such easily accessible opportunities outside the school. I never prohibited or discouraged students from participation in non-academic outside activities. The Clifton Recreation Department and Clifton's Boys and Girls Club sponsored a plethora of after-school activities, clubs, and sports programs, in which numerous Classical Academy students participated through the years.

We encouraged involvement of our Classical Academy students who found pleasure and satisfaction in participating in community-based programs for Clifton youth. But we always reminded both students and parents to be cautious that excessive participation or inordinate time devoted to outside school activities not interfere with Classical Academy students' paramount duty of application of time and effort to their academic studies. If a student's grades were declining because of the demands of outside activities, we quickly brought this to the attention of parents. In such cases, a resolution for more moderate participation was most often reached. Interestingly, when I first began to teach, and indeed when I was a high-school student many years ago, it was a common school policy that to participate in school sports or extracurricular activities, a student had to maintain a "C" academic average, otherwise, one was precluded. In New Jersey public schools, in my experience, few such academic requirements today exist or are enforced.

Incidentally, Classical Academy practices in this regard follow the European model. Students in Europe engage in sports, especially soccer teams; but the school does not sponsor interscholastic sports as an educational function of the school. Instead, students play on sport teams operated and organized by their communities or by other civic entities. Academic education or the school culture is, therefore, not corrupted or diminished by the preoccupation with interscholastic athletic competitions. Civic- and community-based cultural activities for students' involvement in music, art, and theater also abound in Europe, where schools are primarily for scholastic pursuits.

Ongoing healthy social and emotional development opportunities are, in my estimation, equally well provided, if not more so, by how children interact with each other in organized settings such as the school and class-room environment. Most Classical Academy students were together for three years in the same subjects and classes, and in the same scholastically demanding but mutually supportive, friendly environment. Most had the same teachers for the same subjects two or all three years of their Classical Academy education. All were immersed in the same "academics-first school culture," and nearly everyone responded to that culture positively.

Within our "academics-first school culture," there was a bonding amongst our students that was marvelous to behold and, to me, most personally gratifying. Students experienced nurturing associations, interacting with each other in matters typical of adolescents: music, rap stars, movies, electronic devices, but also much interacting about the homework, the upcoming test, teacher expectations, assisting one another with academic matters, the "academic star" informally but collaboratively tutoring the lesser achiever, much like team members assisting one another as they prepare collectively for the next game or upcoming school drama production. As a lifelong educator, it was wonderful to see students bonding within our "academics-first school culture" and responding to the "common mission" of academic learning that our school culture inculcated among all students. Of course, there was the occasional exception and disappointment, but these were minor and rare, as Classical Academy students routinely displayed responsible and amiable interpersonal relationships among classmates each day.

Strong friendships were formed in our "academics-first school culture," some, I understand, lasting to this day. I can recall on the last day of school each June, as Mrs. DeRosa and I waved to the buses departing our grounds, student tears were profuse. At first, I thought the students were weeping because they were leaving me, but, as I bade farewell to the buses filled with saddened and moist-eyed adolescents, an astute student standing nearby told me: "Mr. D, they are not crying for you, but because they won't see their friends until September." But more than a few graduating 8th-graders, I dare say, wept because they would not be returning to the school and its culture that had become their life and that they had learned to appreciate fondly. Our school environment proved that constructing valued personality traits, interpersonal skills, and emotional development can take root and grow magnificently in an "academics-first school culture" without a plethora of non-academic activities putatively thought to be the sole incubators of social and emotional adolescent development.

Readjusting the Balance in Education

The criticisms against the Classical Academy, its "academics-first culture," and its intense program of prescribed, 7-academic-subject curricula for every student, reflect Americans' erroneous belief that our students cannot endure, intellectually or emotionally, serious academic learning. Academic learning, as our public schools long have practiced, must be relieved from its tedium and stress with an intervening class or two of non-academic subjects or extracurricular activities. We have come to believe our students incapable of withstanding a rigorous educational program without suffering permanent psychic damage. Awkward social graces, emotional problems, low emotional IQ, isolation and loneliness, self-harm, drugs or alcohol, or merely a morose, gloomy outlook on life are all fearful consequences alleged when the school day and the educational environment are not liberally infused with a multiplicity of non-academic subjects, extracurricular pursuits and events.

The Classical Academy has proved false the near-universal belief that when the educational program lacks a plentitude of school-sponsored, extracurricular activities and opportunities intended to educate the "whole child," the most dreaded consequences will inevitably befall the deprived adolescent. During my 18-year leadership, the Classical Academy Charter School clearly put the lie to all these allegations and fearful assumptions, and showed that all students, including less-motivated, less-accomplished, and students born of immigrant parents benefit magnificently from a rigorous, prescribed academic-centric middle-school education in an academics-first school culture; and they are not emotionally injured or scared by an academics-first education.

I fully realize that children ages 11-14 years are not university graduate students, nor are they prodigies. They do require more for their emotional and social development than a constant, unremitting application of time and effort to academic learning. But it is a matter of *balance*. My overwhelming observation as a public-school teacher, of which I spoke in earlier chapters, was that, in our public schools, that balance has long been massively distorted to grossly favor the non-academic, the emotional, the social, the entertaining, the athletic, the myriad "fun" components of public education, to the point where all of these more frivolous preoccupations predominate education and have thus subverted any pretense of rigorous academic learning while perpetuating a school culture which denigrates serious scholastics.

The Classical Academy was founded in part to reassert the priority—to readjust the balance, if you will—of scholastics, and subordinate—not eliminate—the "fun" elements of adolescent education while catering less to the more ethereal aspects of child development. As the reader will see in the next chapter, the Classical Academy did provide students with pure "fun" diversions during the school year, many of which became school traditions, but we always did so in balanced moderation, never forgetting our primary purpose and objective of "academics first."

To see the effects of this re-balancing in practice, to witness how Classical Academy students acclimated themselves and responded so well to it and to our "academics-first school culture," was, indeed, one of the most gratifying feelings of vindication I experienced as an educator of adolescents and as a school founder.

From my own knowledge of our graduates as they grew to young adulthood, and based on our graduates' innumerable comments to me as they progressed in their lives, none of them ever suffered social or emotional maladjustment resulting from their Classical Academy Charter School attendance; nor did they feel deprived by the "academics-first school culture" in which they were immersed and by which they were shaped during their middle-school education. Indeed, nearly to the person, their matured reflections of their Classical Academy education can be condensed in this sentiment a Classical Academy graduate once expressed to me: "When I first came to the Classical Academy, I did not like it, but my attitude soon changed, and I found myself eager to come to school each day; now that I am older, I can say I'm so very glad [grateful and fortunate] that I attended the Classical Academy."

Chapter VII

PROGRESS, MILESTONE ACHIEVEMENTS, TRADITIONS, AND NOTEWORTHY EVENTS 1997-2016

In this chapter, I memorialize the Classical Academy's progress, traditions, milestone achievements, and noteworthy events under my leadership during the years 1997 to 2016. I record these achievements and events not in chronological order, since many of them are not discrete in time but mature or evolve over a period and, thus, better reveal a trend of development.

Mission

The comprehensive mission of the Classical Academy Charter School of Clifton (New Jersey) comprises the following objectives, to: provide a free educational choice to parents; create an "academics-first school and school culture"; demonstrate the worth and effectiveness of certain education reforms designed and implemented by the school's founder; produce 8th-grade student learning results superior to those of the resident public school district and which results place the Classical Academy in the top tier of New Jersey public charter schools. Further, from the school's 1997 charter: "The proposed Classical Academy Charter School's mission is to provide a public-school choice offering a "Humanities/Liberal Arts" orientation. To this end, the Classical Academy utilizes elements of the well-proven strength of a classical curriculum wherein, beginning in the 6th grade, Latin, readings in classical authors [in English translation, including classical mythology], and studies in the 'Great Books' [Homer, Virgil, and others] form the basis of a rigorous academic curriculum required for all students."

School Mottos

"To be educated in those studies by which one's nature is aroused to the cultivation of a meaningful destiny"
(Livy, Roman Historian)

"Nutriens Principes ad Saeclorum Posterum"
("Nurturing Leaders for the Next Generation")
(Vincent DeRosa, Classical Academy Founder)

Traditions and Extracurricular Events Enriching our Academics-First School Culture

Although deliberately excluding many of the extra/co-curricular activities found in public schools, nevertheless the Classical Academy's school year was punctuated with non-academic, "fun" events. The majority of these annual events became school traditions and were eagerly anticipated by our students, and most often scheduled well before or after state standardized testing.

One of our first school traditions began in June 1999. Nearing the end of our first year, having faced and succeeded in defeating so many potentially fatal situations, and having expended much energy in overcoming a multitude of challenges, we considered a suggestion from a parent that we celebrate not only the conclusion of the school's first tumultuous year of existence, but its very survival. She recommended a school trip to a "water park" to which she had once taken her family and knew that it was a popular destination for school outings. At first skeptical, believing the combination of "water and kids" a potential hazard to be avoided, I nonetheless agreed we all deserved a year-ending "fun" activity (as the reader will see, I am not opposed to a moderation of school "fun," properly spaced and judiciously selected). We made bus and park arrangements, and Magda and I purchased "barbecue" items comprising hamburgers and hotdogs. Several parents volunteered to help chaperone and cook the "barbecue."

Lake Tomahawk, in Sussex County, New Jersey, had a number of water slides, a swimming beach, outdoor grills, tables, a lovely setting, and plenty of lifeguards and park supervisors. The students had a wonderful time swimming and partaking of the long and varied slides into the lake. Given the large number of park supervisors and the volunteer parents, teachers could relax and enjoy themselves without the pressure or responsibility of monitoring students. This school trip proved to be a delightful way to end the year for both students and teachers, and it was well-chosen to become an end-of-school-year tradition.

Magda did not attend that first trip. Unhappy with their students' behavior at home and school, two parents forbade their students from attending the trip but refused to keep them home. Not to deny this deserved leisure outing to any of our teachers, Magda took it upon herself, as she and I often did to spare teachers from hardship or the specter of unfair treatment, to remain at school supervising these two students.

At times during that first Lake Tomahawk trip, I found myself alone, sitting at a park table among a grove of evergreen trees a bit distant from the main activities, hearing the faint background sounds of students excitedly enjoying themselves. There I contemplated the epic saga I and my wife had, for the last 17 months, gone through since that January 1998 phone call announcing our charter approval. I reflected on common thoughts which naturally intrude upon a person at the end of a tortuous but successful undertaking: *How did we do it? If we knew beforehand what we would endure and what efforts we would need to expend to be successful, would we have done it?* My simple, self-reflective response was perhaps trite but insightful nonetheless: "Grand dreams are not fulfilled without sacrifice, struggle, and effort, but a miracle or two doesn't hurt."

Our end-of-school-year trip to Lake Tomahawk became one of the Classical Academy's first traditions which we enjoyed for 18 years under my leadership. It was so popular and eagerly anticipated that, in subsequent years during my first-week-of-September meetings with new 6th-graders, at which time I would introduce them to the school and help acclimate them to their new surroundings and responsibilities, I would often be asked the question: "Mr. DeRosa, are we going to Lake Tomahawk this year?" They had learned about the June trip from neighbors or older siblings who had attended the school. My answer was always, "Yes, but only if you study hard, do your homework, and earn good grades!" Our Lake Tomahawk outing became an annual, much-beloved capstone of each school year as well as the longest Classical Academy tradition. (I sadly learned that this school tradition was replaced by other selected destinations soon after Magda and I retired).

School trips to other destinations became yearly Classical Academy traditions and, often, a reward for academic success. Annual school trips included the *"Faculty Scholar Trip to Six Flags Amusement Park"* for students recognized as *"Faculty Scholar,"* a distinction earned by having honor-roll grades for at least three of the four marking periods and the approving vote of three quarters of the faculty, as the award was in their name. "Faculty Scholar" Certificates would also be awarded to these deserving students at the conclusion of each school year. In addition, there was the *"Good Conduct"* trip or picnic for students whose grades were below Honor Roll qualification but whose school and classroom behavior was exemplary. The *"8th-Grade Trip"* to *"Dorney Park Amusement and Water Park* in Pennsylvania" for all graduating 8th-graders became another school tradition.

Additional school trips were taken to nearby Lambert Castle and to the Paterson Museum and Paterson Great Falls National Monument, as part of our unit on local history, which discussed the history of Paterson as one of America's first industrialized cities, the silk industry, and labor unrest for which Paterson is famous.

8th-Grade Graduation Ceremony and "Founder's Scholar Award"

The Classical Academy's first 8th-grade graduation was held in June 2000, with our first 14 graduates. It was held on the school's front lawn. Every June since then, we established another school tradition with our lavishly formal *8th-Grade Evening Graduation Ceremony*, held at an elegant catering facility. Here, our 8th-grade graduates, clad in blue caps and gowns, would enter, in slow procession, the splendid banquet hall to the "Pomp and Circumstance" tune, while their parents, relatives, and teachers brimmed with loving pride. Each teacher presented academic awards, not only for the best student in their subject, but for the most improved, most helpful, most trustworthy, most dependable, or other such awards the teacher thought fitting for academics or for character. Certificate awards were given also for students earning high or perfect scores on the National Latin and Classical Mythology tests.

As master-of-ceremonies of the 8th-Grade Graduation Ceremony, and as the Classical Academy's progenitor, I originated the *"Founder's Award."* Knowing well all students both as teacher and principal, I deliberated with myself to select the one 8th-grade student who, in my estimation, best encapsulated the traits of high grades, scholarly and intellectual propensities, commendable interpersonal aptitudes, and sterling personality enriched with high character. It was not an easy choice, as each year there were, at minimum, several meritorious students whose nomination would meet with universal approbation. Still, I was determined not to dilute my award with multiple recipients and select just one student. My "Founders Award" included a handsome wooden plaque suitably inscribed and a $300 check.

In those years when state-mandated tests results were provided to schools before school ended in June, school certificates for *"Advanced Proficiency"* in a tested subject were awarded at the 8th-grade graduation event (special certificates for "Perfect Score of 300," of which, through the years, we had more than a few, were also awarded to great applause). Each graduating 8th-grader was then awarded their "Classical Academy Charter School" graduation certificate, nicely encased in a blue folder. The formal evening ceremony having ended, the night was young while those assembled enjoyed the DJ, dancing, and dining till late in the evening. This deserving ceremonious tribute to our hard-working students invariably engendered a common reaction of attendees: it was, they affirmed, and in stark contrast to other 8th-grade graduation events where certificates were handed out in the gym, the nicest, most moving, and most elegant 8th-grade graduation they had ever experienced.

The 8th-grade graduating event was always a poignant ceremony for me and Mrs. DeRosa, made all the more so by the many comments of gratitude and indebtedness parents echoed at each graduation ceremony. Many parents wished to take pictures of me and my wife with them and their graduate. So many of the attendees thanked me "for my school," and expressed how happy they were that the Classical Academy was there for their children and that they had the opportunity to make so desirable an educational choice. Some even implored me to start a high school!

Halloween, Christmas, Easter Egg Hunt, Awards and Raffle, Charitable Activities

Still other "fun" or extracurricular activities interspersed during the school year included the annual *"Halloween or Fall Festival,"* in which students were encouraged to change into costumes at school, and everyone would partake of an outdoor festival that included games and costume-judging contests. This usually took place outside on a Friday afternoon in late October. Two months later, our in-school *Christmas festivities* took place, with snacks, a "Secret Santa" activity, and visits from Mr. and Mrs. Santa Claus. Students and their parents always displayed their generosity by presenting gifts of gratitude to me, Mrs. DeRosa, and teachers on this occasion.

Delighting students was our occasional *"Easter Egg Hunt"* on school grounds, with prizes such as a free homework pass, two points added to the next math test, and a $20 bill inside certain plastic eggs secreted on school grounds. During the last week of school, we held the annual *"6th- and 7th-Grade Awards Ceremony and Raffle."* On the front lawn, with parents attending, teachers distributed diverse academic awards and other meritorious recognitions to students. The school having purchased raffle prizes, like book bags, study lamps, lunch bags, and other school supplies, and, of course, coveted framed pictures of me in my traffic-warden garb, the raffle was held to the merriment of all. A highlight of the event was the presence of an ice-cream truck, where everyone was treated to an ice cream of their choice.

With some regularity, the school and students conducted a coat (winter clothing) collection or food drive for Eva's Kitchen, a well-known philanthropic organization assisting needy Paterson residents. The homeroom that collected the largest amount of donations was recognized with a pizza or "hoagie" party. Our annual *"St. Jude's Hospital Math-A-Thon"* was intended to improve students' math skills and homework completion, while the donated monetary proceeds from parents and friends benefited St. Jude's Hospital. Over the years, the small Classical Academy student body raised more than $15,000 for that worthy charity.

I cite these non-academic events and traditions to demonstrate that, with moderation and judgment, while interrupting as little as possible academic instruction, and to relieve academic intensity while giving our students "fun" things to anticipate, the Classical Academy always provided a judicious amount of extracurricular diversions and enrichment activities for our students' emotional and social health. All of these activities were compatible with our prevailing academics-first culture; they never took precedence over or interfered with the Classical Academy's priority of scholastic learning.

Total Enrollment from Clifton; Students from the Same Clifton Families

In the first years of the school, a number of our students were not Clifton residents, as much acrimony and distrust were sowed in the Clifton community against the school by our powerful enemies in the city. Charter-school law provided that, if a charter school had not filled all available seats from its resident school district, it could admit students from surrounding communities. Nearly half of our first-year enrollment of 48 students came from outside Clifton, primarily from Paterson and Passaic City.

As the school progressed, and as our reputation grew, within a few years the demand for admissions from Clifton residents grew. The school's greatest recruitment tool was the proverbial "word of mouth." Client satisfaction was so great throughout Clifton, to the chagrin of Clifton governmental and public-school officials, in a few years after its founding, all students were Clifton residents. For word had spread of the far-superior learning results

Classical Academy students demonstrated over Clifton Public Schools, and that the Classical Academy provided parents a documented-superior academic education in a small, orderly, well-disciplined, family-like school environment. By the mid-2000s, we were receiving, from Clifton residents, 2 applications for every available seat, especially for the 6th grade, the beginning middle-school grade. This resoundingly refuted Clifton Public School District's false assertions that the Classical Academy offered nothing new, was unwanted and unneeded in Clifton City, and, if the school started, it would soon fail to lack of enrollment and financial insolvency.

To acquiesce to parents' wishes, and to recognize them for their loyal support of the school (in the sea of hostility and opposition of potent community forces, growing parental support was one of our few weapons), I instituted our *"Alumni Admission Rule."* Simply stated, any student who currently had a sibling matriculating at the school, or whose sibling had graduated from the school (and was no longer in attendance), would circumvent the admission lottery and receive automatic enrollment. I knew this was bending (extending, if you please) the charter-school "sibling admission rule," but I recognized how vital it was to accede to the heartfelt pleadings of parents who, being so pleased with the educational experience of one child, desperately wanted those same educational experiences for their other children.

Nearly without exception, every parent who ever had one child attend and graduate the Classical Academy strongly desired to have their other children receive the benefits of a Classical Academy education. This was one of the most compelling testimonies to the qualities of the Classical Academy and to what it offered parents and students, namely, client satisfaction and high estimation. Most parents came to us because of recommendations from satisfied friends, neighbors, and relatives who had themselves experienced the Classical Academy. More than a few parents told me: "Mr. DeRosa, if my younger child cannot attend this school, as did my older child, then I will be forced to move out of Clifton." Such unremitting and profound demonstration of client satisfaction, in addition to Classical Academy students' remarkable standardized-test outcomes, was an indisputable vindication of my academics-first ideals, of the school policies and practices I implemented, of my philosophy of education, and of my and my wife's hard work and that of our teachers and staff.

When the state ordered in 2013 that I discontinue the "Alumni Admissions Rule" as being contrary to charter-school law, parents of Classical Academy graduates who did not have a student currently attending the school had to undergo the lottery admission process. On these occasions, some parents of Classical Academy alumni whose name/number was not chosen for admission by blind lottery actually wept, and their heart-wrenching disappointment had to be consoled.

Through the years, it was very common, especially due to the "Alumni Admissions Rule," that the Classical Academy provided middle-school education for multiple children from the same families, families for whom the Classical Academy was an educational choice, families who could have enrolled their children in the Clifton Public School system, but nevertheless without hesitation or reluctance, chose the Classical Academy. To have two or three children from the same family educated at the Classical Academy and graduate therefrom was very common. Indeed, we had some families who sent four or even five of their children to the Classical Academy; one family held the record with six Classical Academy graduates. Having children from the same family seek enrollment in the Classical Academy was supreme testimony of the school's merits, educational excellence, and astounding managerial success.

Each year, our *"Parent Satisfaction and Opinion Survey"* recorded 90%-100% overall parental satisfaction with one's Classical Academy education choice. The returned surveys were, as instructed, unsigned and contained questions such as: "Do you believe your child is receiving a superior education than if the child attended Clifton Public Schools?" "Would you recommend the Classical Academy to Clifton relatives, friends, or neighbors?" Responses were always in the 90%-100% range favorable to the Classical Academy.

9/11 (2001) Attack on World Trade Center

The searing impression on emotion and memory will forever be fresh for Americans who lived through this tragic episode in our country's life.

It was a beautiful early September day, and the Classical Academy, like other schools, was engrossed with the activities of launching a new school year. Mrs. DeRosa, who was in her basement office, first informed me of news reports that a plane had accidentally struck a large office complex in Manhattan. As events progressed, she soon told me in confidence that a second plane struck an adjacent building, and that these violent events, as news was now reporting, were deliberate.

From these morning events to the end of the school day, I was determined not to reveal to the student population the violent, unimaginable tragedy happening 18 miles away. I sent notes to all teachers not to reveal or discuss with students the Twin Towers destruction and the carnage and mayhem taking place in Manhattan. My actions were motivated by two salient considerations: First, I knew that a number of our students' parents worked in Manhattan. Informing the student body of horrendous violence happening there would immeasurably and unduly distress these students. It was my duty, as I conceived it, to protect students from agonizing thoughts of their parents' safety. Second, I believed that the best course was to continue calmly with normal instruction, lest an entire day of education be lost and students be unduly traumatized. I came to believe my decision all the more correct when I learned several days later that Clifton school leaders deemed it their obligation to inform their students of the events, even as the grim details of death and destruction unfolded during the day. One school principal took the censorious action by employing the school's public-address system to announce: "We are under attack." Students became understandably panic stricken, and all semblance of academic instruction was abandoned.

Soon after the second plane propelled itself into the other tower, a part-time teacher who was still at home called me to say she simply could not come to school, for she was too emotionally upset. During the day, parents called requesting to take their child out of school. Despite reassuring them that their children were safe, they insisted in coming to school to remove their children. Many expressed the desire that, as one parent poignantly pleaded, "Mr. DeRosa, I just want my child near me today." When students inquired why so many of their classmates were leaving school early, we used the excuse that they had a doctor's or dentist's appointment.

Being at the foot of Garret Mountain Reservation, the Classical Academy was on elevated terrain, and the prospect from the school to New York City was flat, without intervening obstacles. Going to the school's attic, I could see the plumes of dense smoke rising from the direction of Manhattan, 18 miles away.

It was not until the very end of that tragic day that Classical Academy students, through news reports being filtered to them (most students in those days did not have cell phones, and if they did, school policy prohibited their use in school), that the unbelievable events became generally known.

As we always have done on our trip home, Mrs. DeRosa and I took a road ascending to the top of Garret Mountain. The road was filled with parked vehicles; many spectators were out of their cars, transfixed on the destructive aftermath of this unprecedented attack on our homeland. Historical irony did not escape my thoughts as I recalled that, during the Revolutionary War, and using the same advantageous terrain features, colonial forces used the summit of Garret Mountain—a three-mile stretch extending from Paterson to Montclair, New Jersey, and which is part of the Watchung Mountain Range—as an outpost to monitor the movements of British military units as they sojourned out of New York City in pursuit of Washington's army, or to harass farmers and forage for foodstuffs. Now, the same advantageous location was being used 2½ centuries later to watch the smoky evidence of murderous violence of a more modern bloody conflict.

Purchasing the School Building and "Paying Off" Its Mortgage

The miraculous saga of how I obtained the former Dollymount Nursing facility by near-divine intervention to be the Classical Academy Charter School building was related in the foregoing. As with most charter schools, I leased the building from its owners. The four-year lease, 1998 to 2002, included the monthly lease payment plus property taxes (included in each monthly payment). Although a public school, we were not the owners of the property, therefore, despite the building being used by a tenant operating a "nonprofit" entity like a public charter school, Clifton legally charged the private owners of the building the assessed property tax, which they, in turn, passed on to the school. The monthly lease payment of $9,000 per month was a burdensome sum for a struggling enterprise responsible for all the other expenses of school operation. Having a very small student-body enrollment, ranging from 48 students the first year to its maximum of 120 students by the end of our fourth year, and, thus, correspondingly meager financial revenues compared with all other charter schools with larger school enrollments, husbanding of our resources by strict expenditure practices became a skill and managerial habit of which my wife, as school business administrator, and I became masters.

As the Classical Academy's four-year lease was near ending, and as the school was approaching its first charter-renewal application, I had ominous thoughts that the owners might decide not to renew the lease. We had genuine fears that lucrative offers from well-financed property developers to sell the property would entice the building owners. The property was slightly more than one acre on prime commercial real estate, two blocks from entrance and exit to Route 80, a major north Jersey artery. To property developers, it was an attractive parcel in size and location, possessing much profit potential. The dreadful mantra of those who opposed our establishment five years ago entered my consciousness with ever-terrifying reality: *"No building, no school."* The immense labor we devoted to the school during the first four years, and just now our successes were materializing with high demand for admission, high student test scores, the merits of my educational academics-first practices being proved and vindicated, all would be truncated if we now lost the school to property speculators.

I had the foresight to incorporate into our lease a provision that the Classical Academy, at the end of the four-year lease period, could exercise a priority option to purchase the building. Thankfully, the owners, after learning that our charter-renewal application was successful, were receptive to our possible purchase; if we could pay the assessed market price, they would not place the building on the open real-estate market.

Public-school buildings are owned by their municipal Boards of Education. Public schools do not pay rent or lease any of their facilities, which are paid for by the local property taxpayers or through municipal bonds. Capital or facility costs do not come out of public schools' operating budgets. For New Jersey public charter schools, however, facility costs are a major expenditure paid for by the same revenues it pays for teacher salaries and benefits, educational supplies, and all other everyday operational expenses.

Of the many advantages accruing to charter schools when its Board of Trustees owns the school building, the most important is security. Having a reliable "roof over one's head" is guaranteed when the school owns its facility and does not merely lease it. Charter-school facility ownership, although very rare among New Jersey charter schools, is among the most important considerations for responsible financial operations and for realizing a secure future. It is equivalent to the difference between renting one's home and owning it, with many of the same financial, emotional, and security advantages of the latter.

In 2002, the Classical Academy school building and property was assessed at $800,000. Desperate to exercise our purchase option before property developers swallowed up our beloved Classical Academy property and stand helpless at the school's demise, we sought a commercial mortgage. Bankers were impressed with our past financial management and in overcoming so many obstacles to make the school successful. Several of the more-understanding bankers, while deeming us a "good risk," nevertheless required that we put down at least 10% before they would grant a mortgage. One banker reduced it to 5%. But we simply did not have a surplus of $40,000 for a down payment, lest we jeopardize teachers' salaries and risk not having enough money for other essential expenditures for the new school year.

Working with several state organizations, such as the Department of Community Affairs and Department of Economic Development, a bank came forward willing to give us a 15-year $800,000 mortgage without requiring a down payment of any amount. We forthwith agreed to the terms and purchased the building.

The monthly mortgage payment, even with the interest, was somewhat less than our regular monthly lease payments, and as a public-school building owned by our Board of Trustees, we were exempt from property taxes. Most important, by purchasing the property, the Classical Academy was assured of a secure, ever-promising future.

With our accustomed strict control of spending, by performing ourselves many functions other schools delegate to hired personnel or pay vendors to perform, and by doubling the monthly mortgage-principal payments, Mrs. DeRosa and I were able to pay off the 15-year mortgage in just 7 years, less than half the mortgage length. In so doing, we saved for the school and the Clifton taxpayer 8 years worth of mortgage principal and interest, estimated to be $402,000. Thus, by 2009, The Classical Academy Charter School of Clifton's Board of Trustees owned *fully and mortgage-free* its own school building. I believe the Classical Academy is one of very few New Jersey charter schools to boast of the accomplishment of fully owning its own school facility free of mortgage and lease payments. Considering that the Classical Academy had the smallest revenues because of its small student size, and as the documented lowest-funded public school in New Jersey during this period, this accomplishment was all the more wondrous and praiseworthy.

Under Mrs. DeRosa's school business administrator's leadership, and practicing our usual frugality in spending, for the next 7 years and beyond, we continued to "bank" (i.e., to save) the monthly amount of money we would otherwise have allocated to mortgage payments and deposited these savings in our school bank account. In this way, we accumulated sufficient financial reserves to secure the school's financial future, to meet emergencies and unanticipated expenses, and to amass seed money for our planned grade and building expansion in future years.

Owning its own school facility is a rarity for New Jersey public charter schools. In a series of investigative reports (*The Record*, April 7, 2019) exposing the abuses of financing charter schools facilities and how some investors "cash in," making huge real-estate profits from taxpayer-funded charter-schools facilities, the Classical Academy is cited as one of only three New Jersey charter schools that owns its facility and is a charter school that "shows the way" for charter-school facility acquisition.

The Necessity for Frugality and Prudence in Spending

Husbanding our financial resources was paramount to Classical Academy success. Having the smallest student body of any New Jersey charter school at full development (120 students) and, thus, the lowest amount of yearly revenues, in addition to being in a low per-pupil funding public-school district, necessitated, if we were to be responsible school leaders, extreme frugality in spending. We were always vigilant against what we regarded as imprudent or unnecessary expenditures, and circumspect that our spending never exceeded our relatively meager incoming revenues.

We were keenly aware that a few New Jersey charter schools had succumbed to a deserved, ignominious fate by imprudent spending or flagrantly purchasing services and products based speculatively on "future student growth and revenues." These wayward charter schools were also guilty of prodigious, self-serving spending on capacious surroundings, and of vendor-provided or contracted school services to ease workload burdens on school administrators who selfishly enriched themselves with large "executive" salaries.

If a charter school became financially "stressed" or on the verge of bankruptcy, the state was adamant that it would not "bail out" ill-managed and overspending charter schools with state funds. Because of their profligacy, some charter schools ceased to operate. The Classical Academy was too precious to jeopardize financially, and having advanced this far in its development, I and Magda guarded against sharing an inglorious fate through fiscal irresponsibility. Foremost in our minds was the understanding that, if we became indebted or overspent, an eventuality easily foreseen in a school with a maximum of only 120 students, we could not rely on the state for financial assistance. These realities restrained our own spending habits and expenditure priorities, most visibly in Magda's and my work ethic whereby we both took it upon ourselves to perform very many tasks and duties for operating the school rather than hire additional personnel or pay for contracted or vendor services. This burden acceptance and multiple duties were a feature of our nearly two-decade Classical Academy leadership and was practiced even after the school became financially secure and had accrued a substantial financial surplus, particularly as these funds were intended for school expansion.

Graduates' Achievements: Honors, Advanced Placement, and Scholarships

Our reputation for being an academically focused school was built upon our 8th-grade graduates' comparative and documented greater-developed scholastic skills and deeper subject-matter knowledge, and their practiced habits of study. These attributes were demonstrated not only on standardized-test scores, but by our 8th-grade graduates' qualities of competence, motivation, and academic-subject proficiencies they brought to their high-school classrooms. Based on our students' high performance in high school, Classical Academy graduates acquired an outstanding reputation, which, in turn, reflected on the school.

To academic-subject teachers at Clifton High School and at area Catholic high schools, Classical Academy graduates were often described to me as: "really good kids," or "academically competent and advanced." Each year, 75%-80% of our 8th-grade graduates were placed in 9th-grade "Honors" or "Advanced Placement" in "English," "Algebra II," and science classes at Clifton High School. Even Classical Academy graduates with middling grades were esteemed by high-school officials to be educationally proficient or, in comparison to 8th-grade graduates from the two Clifton middle schools, "above average." It was a common sentiment often voiced to me by our returning graduates: "Mr. D, high school is much easier than the Classical Academy."

Each year, several Catholic high schools would visit the school to recruit students, discuss their programs, and outline financial-aid availability. Paramus Catholic and DePaul Catholic were frequent recruiters. Annually, a number of our graduates were offered scholarships to these schools amounting to one-quarter or one-half tuition; on a few occasions, a full-tuition scholarship, awarded to only two or three entering students each year, was offered to Classical Academy graduates. One all-girls high-school principal occasionally would call me, pleading: "Mr. DeRosa, send me more girls!" In all my years of leadership, no Classical Academy 8th-grade graduate was denied admission at a private or Catholic high school and, more often than not, with tuition-scholarship money.

During my long tenure, we had approximately 600 8th-grade graduates, from 2000 to 2016. In retrospect, I wished I had realized how important it would have been to conduct a more detailed, systematic, and ongoing study of all our graduates to better document the Classical Academy's inestimable value, witnessed in its graduates' triumphs and achievements as they progressed through high school and beyond. I know that such information would only reflect well on the school, its scholastic program of studies, and its academics-first culture and practices.

For knowledge of our graduates, I relied on students returning, which many often did, to school to visit with me and teachers, telling us of their school lives, accomplishments, and challenges. Often, in these occasions, they related information of other of their Classical Academy classmates. I and our teachers were always thrilled with a professional and personal feeling of achievement whenever we learned of our graduates' scholastic and non-scholastic successes. We were well pleased that our students profited by the rigors of a serious academic program of studies and the demanding pedagogy with which we challenged them. The requisite skills, confidence, and motivation to high achievement and future accomplishment were the inevitable rewards of their Classical Academy education. In this, we witnessed the fulfillment of our two school Latin mottos, as translated: "Nurturing Leaders for the Next Generation," and "To Be Educated in Those Disciplines by Which One's Nature Is Aroused to the Cultivation of a Meaningful Destiny." Of course, we felt regret when learning, however rarely, that a graduate's problems or weaknesses only worsened in a large, impersonal school environment.

Although their circle of friends expanded greatly upon graduation (Clifton High School is one of the largest in the state, with more than 4,000 students), many of our graduates remained friends with their fellow Classical Academy classmates in high school and beyond. I always smiled with sentimental satisfaction when I learned, as I often did, that many of our former students, who, upon entering the Classical Academy, were in the same 6th-grade "Pre-Algebra" class, and continued to advance together in the same mathematics classrooms during their three years at the Classical Academy. Remaining yet together in the same mathematics classes throughout Clifton High School, these same students found themselves classmates yet again in the same advanced "Calculus II," "Statistics," or "Geometry" Clifton High School honors classes in the 12th grade. I would remind our student visitors that such a marvelous, collaborative longevity of expanding mathematics knowledge all started in this room, in this building, seven years ago!

At our joyously elegant 8th-grade graduation ceremonies, which I mentioned earlier, we would often dedicate a table for invited Classical Academy alumni. At this table were seated Classical Academy graduates who graduated four years earlier and were now graduating high school. We invited some to speak about their accomplishments, their future studies or career goals, and what their Classical Academy experience meant to them, and in what ways it forged a foundation of confidence and inspiration for their prospective ambitions.

School Awards and Commendations: National, State, and Local Recognition

In October 2008, while teaching one of my two 8th-grade Latin classes, the school secretary came into the classroom notifying me that someone from the New Jersey Department of Education was on the phone, requesting my immediate attention. My first thought, as always when someone from the state education department called, was: "What's wrong now?" "What bureaucratic infraction did I commit?" "Of what innumerable state regulations did I now run afoul?" Answering the call with quavering trepidation evidently obvious to the person calling, she humorously said, "Don't worry, Mr. DeRosa, I have good news. I don't think you will regret this call." The New Jersey Department of Education, she announced, was nominating the Classical Academy Charter School of Clifton for the *"National Blue-Ribbon School of Excellence Award (2008).*

As with any school leader who received one of education's most coveted prizes, my elation was overwhelming. But this award had perhaps even more meaning for me than it might for other school leaders. The school being recognized nationally for its excellence in educating minority children of immigrant parents was my very own creation, my dream made manifest. The infinite labors I and my co-founder wife expended to overcome so much potent opposition, shepherding our small, ill-funded public charter school through so many daunting challenges to national prominence, was now indisputably acknowledged. Vindicated, too, was my educational philosophy. The "academics-first school culture" and the policies and practices I initiated to promulgate that culture; the educative power of the curricula and program of studies I designed; the ongoing, manifold decisions I implemented daily to maintain and enhance academic learning and institutional success—all were now accorded national recognition with this accolade.

My wife and I were invited to Washington, DC, for a three-day ceremony hosted by the Federal Department of Education and its "No Child Left Behind" division. Tours and dinners were planned for us and the other recipients. At one ceremony, we were given the "National Blue-Ribbon School of Excellence (2008)" plaque and certificates attesting to this national honor. Like conquering heroes, I and my wife brought these trophies of victory back to the school. We duly accorded recognition to our teachers and staff for their indispensable contributions to our mutual victory.

In previous years, some printed articles about the Classical Academy had referred to me as a *"passionate hero"* of charter schools and *"The Philosopher on the Hill"* (the school being on an elevated prominence). After receiving the national award, local newspapers featured the school in articles. Reporters visited the school to take photographs, interviewed teachers and students, and wrote front-page stories with headlines: *"National Honor for Academy,"* and *"Classical Method Rates Blue Ribbon."* This was, indeed, sweet vindication over all those who strove to prevent the school from being established; over all those doubters and maleficent skeptics who a decade earlier believed the Classical Academy would never open its doors or, if it did, would collapse in a year or two in utter failure.

Congratulating the Classical Academy for its "National Blue-Ribbon School of Excellence" award, *Public Commendations* and *Public Resolutions* were issued by the U.S. Senate, New Jersey General Assembly, the U.S. House of Representatives, and the Clifton Municipal City Council. This latter Public Resolution commending the Classical Academy for its achievements was of particular satisfaction to me, since it was signed by the Mayor and all city councilmen, a number of who were once adamant opponents of establishing Passaic County's first public charter school in Clifton, and who had advanced whatever obstacles they could devise to effectuate that opposition.

In 2008, charter schools had been in existence in New Jersey for 13 years. To that point, the Classical Academy had been just one of two other New Jersey charter schools to receive this national award. Princeton Charter School received the award the year before, and along with the Classical Academy, the Robert Treat Charter School of Newark, New Jersey, received the award the same year, 2008.

We certainly did not rest on these laurels; the strength of our academic program and high student-learning outcomes persisted year after year. In 2012, the New Jersey Department of Education designated the Classical Academy Charter School of Clifton a New Jersey *"REWARD SCHOOL."* This was the highest rating for a New Jersey public school; only about 40 schools or school districts among New Jersey's 500 schools were so designated. *"REWARD SCHOOLS"* were recognized for their success in achieving the kind of learning outcomes desired in all public schools. *"REWARD SCHOOLS"* were "doing things right," to which the New Jersey Department of Education pointed as models of public education. The designated rating was accompanied by a grant of $10,000. The next year, an independent evaluator of New Jersey public schools, the NJCAN, whose organizational aim is to improve public education in the state, particularly minority-student education, awarded the Classical Academy its *"TOP TEN SCHOOL"* award.

Hurricane Sandy: October 22, 2012; Saturday School

Complying with state orders, we closed the Classical Academy the day of and for two days after this disastrous weather event, one of the worst hurricanes ever to strike New Jersey. On the third day, my wife and I ventured out to see the degree of damage to the school. As we approached closer to the school, our fears of school damage grew as we witnessed surrounding destruction to structures and fallen trees. To our relief and amazement, our century-old building survived nature's onslaught with no damage, apart from a small piece of separated vinyl siding. A large tree on school property had fallen in a mass of tangled power lines across the front yard into and blocking the main thoroughfare. Upon entering the building, we discovered no appreciable interior damage, but all electrical utilities were out, as they were in most sections of Clifton, including the school's neighborhood. In speaking to utility crews cutting trees fallen onto roads and dealing with fallen power lines, they informed me that they could not predict when utilities would be working. I was given a phone number for inquiries regarding restoration progress.

Our personal situation was disruptive as well. Living in an "all-electric" home with well water, we lacked running water—the water pump operates electrically—no lights, and no heat, as the furnace and thermostats are electrically powered. For seven days, we lived in a part of our "sun room," using our wood-burning stove for heat and cooking, candles for illumination, a convertible couch for bed, and battery-operated radio for the latest hurricane-cleanup news.

We managed, by cell phone and other means, to notify the entire Classical Academy that the school would be closed until further notice. Electricity restoration in Clifton was conducted on a schedule which concentrated on those points of damage calculated to restoring utilities and power to as many residents as possible with each specific repair. Because the repairs needed to reestablish electrical service to the school would return service to only the Classical Academy building itself and a handful of adjacent residences, it was among the last scheduled repairs. Living in suburban Morris County, our home's electric service was restored in six days.

The Classical Academy utilities were not restored for a full two weeks, 10 school days, a much longer closing than the few days Clifton public schools endured. The Governor decided, possibly because most of New Jersey's electrical grid was restored in several days, that there would be no reduction to the 180 required school days. Our approved charter specified a 190-day instructional school year.

I pled with education officials and the Passaic County Office of Education, the latter no friend to charter schools, in light of the extreme "Act of God" circumstances no fault of our own, and because it took many days longer to restore power to the Classical Academy building than to Clifton public schools, to grant us a reduction in our 190-day charter requirement by several days—perhaps, on this one occasion, even to the state 180-day requirement. I argued that because of the two-week enforced school closure, it would be near impossible for the school to comply with its own 190-school day charter requirement. The Passaic County Office of Education denied my reasonable request, hoping perhaps I would defy the county school superintendent's order by unilaterally reducing our 190-day school year and become culpable of an infraction by our inability to solve our dilemma, ever eager was that office to find some violation it could lodge against the Classical Academy.

Once the Classical Academy resumed regular instruction in early November 2012, teachers and I worked on several schemes to fulfill our 190-instructional-day requirement. Our dilemma was apparent: If we used all four snow days and deducted most days from scheduled school vacations, we could, perhaps, meet our 190-day requirement. However, if we were forced to use any snow days for the approaching winter season, which was very likely, all remaining vacation days beginning January 2nd in our schedule would need to be canceled. This meant, even after returning from a reduced Christmas/New Year vacation, we would, in order to comply with the 190-instructional-day requirement, be in school for 6 months, from January 2 to June 26 continuously, without any vacation days intervening. This was a foreboding prospect to all concerned.

One way to prevent this real possibility was to schedule four "Saturday School Sessions." This unusual school-attendance scheme necessitated by urgency was agreed to by all concerned—teachers, students, and parents. Four Saturday half-day school sessions, from 8:00 a.m. to 12:30 p.m., which counted for a full day in school law, were scheduled for November and early December. Our regular school buses were contracted, though many parents transported their students to and from school on these days.

Teachers and I believed the best use of these Saturday half-day sessions was to concentrate on standardized-test prep in mathematics, English language arts, and science. For this instructional purpose, lesson plans were developed and materials prepared by teachers and myself to be used during the sessions. I developed a schedule in which not all teachers needed to be present on all four Saturdays, but which satisfied the instructional intentions and needs for all grades and students.

These four Saturday half-day sessions were attended, on average, by 92% of all students, almost equaling our normal daily attendance percentages. On the last scheduled Saturday half-day, to reward the positive attitude, classroom performance, and high attendance rates evinced by all, we delivered to the school for all students and teachers six, 6-foot-long Italian sub sandwiches, and one vegetarian sub, of which all partook heartily.

I informed state educational officials and the Passaic County Office of Education of our successful Saturday instructional sessions, our high rates of attendance, and a revised school schedule assuring that we would meet our 190-instructional day requirement, despite being closed by Hurricane Sandy for 10 school days. By ingenuity and determination, and with school-wide cooperation, we thus transformed a potentially hurtful consequence for the school of being held in violation of our 190-instructional-day mandate, into yet another unlikely victory.

Teachers and Board of Trustees Members

For all of the Classical Academy's history under my leadership, I strove to select academic teachers of quality whenever I could, teachers who displayed the potential to rise to the high demands of pedagogic excellence we demanded. Supporting the school's academics-first culture, policies, and practices, their instructional and workplace contributions to the school were critical for its successes.

The Classical Academy's serious academic ethos was appreciated by serious academic teachers. For most of the period from the school's founding to my retirement, I was not like all other public-school principals, secluded away in a commodious office, spewing directives and commands, but like my fellow pedagogues, I was a classroom teacher as well. I taught the two classes of 8th-grade Latin daily. There was never at the Classical Academy, until perhaps the last year of my tenure, an unbreachable demarcation between teachers and administrators. Seeing this, Classical Academy teachers understood that I was an active part of their own efforts in achieving common school goals, sharing their own instructional labors, experiencing the same classroom challenges, and helping effectuate agreed-upon notions of teaching excellence and school success.

As school principal, lead teacher, and school founder, it was my duty to realize our essential "academics-first school culture" and implement the policies and practices nurturing it, and to do all this collaboratively whenever possible. By word and deed, I strove to achieve student and school success, and realize our high institutional goals not by administrative dictate or directive, but by collective effort in a decidedly non-bureaucratic, collegial, collaborative, and amiable work environment. As leader, I endeavored to make all teachers feel valued as essential members of a successful team of educators.

On an emotional level, Classical Academy teachers felt pride in the school and in themselves. To be associated with a school of high recognition, and to be acknowledged as an important element for that recognition was a source of personal pride. Working in an orderly "academics-first" small-school environment, where even the principal was a fellow classroom teacher in a school nationally recognized for its excellence, provided our serious teachers workplace satisfaction and professional fulfillment.

Another reason for teacher satisfaction and low teacher turnover was the school leadership's strong maintenance of an orderly school environment and unquestioned support for teachers when dealing with unruly or disruptive classroom behavior. Indeed, one of the most distressing aspects of teaching—and one which incites many to seek different employment—is student misconduct and teachers' helplessness in dealing with it. In being interviewed for my first teaching job in an urban high school, the principal asked me: "Mr. DeRosa, what would you do if a student said to you: "F . . . k you, teacher, you M . . . F . . . er!" I callowly responded, "I would send him to you." The principal rolled his eyes, sighed, and turned his gaze away, clearly communicating to me that he did want me to send him my disciplinary problems.

Classical Academy teachers well knew that *their* classroom-misconduct problems were every bit *my* problems. Teachers welcomed my insistence that students' behavior bespeak an orderly classroom and expected my quick, supportive intervention if needed. Our golden rule of student classroom conduct was: "No student's behavior will become so unruly and disruptive that the teacher is unable to teach and other students unable to learn," and I enforced it compassionately but with persistence. Whenever a teacher notified me that a student was acting badly in class or defying teacher's authority, I took immediate action, by removing the malefactor, imposing penalties, and notifying parents of intolerable classroom conduct and of the immediate need for correction. Teachers and I routinely met after school with parents of students whose conduct needed correction or academic progress needed improvement. I empowered teachers with authority, barring school suspension, to impose any reasonable penalty for unruly student behavior in their classrooms.

Of course, for charter schools, especially a small, vulnerable charter school beset by powerful enemies eager to pounce upon every weakness, student classroom and school conduct have potentially real and adverse consequences. If students in a class are not learning because of a few unruly students, everyone's educational attainment may well be impeded, and their learning outcomes may thus be diminished, which eventually are likely to be reflected on lower standardized-test scores or student withdrawal. Inferior test scores, in turn, would jeopardize school standing and reputation, and provide school enemies with criticisms that may lead to charter non-renewal. Student withdrawal because of bullying or a disordered school environment would affect school finances. I had, therefore, strong reasons, apart from making classroom teaching a less stressful occupation, to maintain a well-ordered classroom learning environment.

This is the kind of positive pressure not known in monopoly public schools, and it is one reason why many public-school classrooms are often learning-free zones, marked by chaotic, dangerous, and simply uncontrollable behaviors. Situations like these continue because traditional public schools have no survival incentive, no compelling reasons to reduce or eradicate chronic misbehavior problems within their schools.

Being a Classical Academy teacher was generally regarded a satisfying position, in which serious teachers found gratification in their work. Little teacher turnover was a common feature of the school—in fact, there were consecutive years when we had zero teacher departures. When a teacher did not return to Classical Academy employment, it was due to unavoidable family circumstances or a spouse's job transfer. When a teacher left the school, regrets and sadness were often expressed. Indeed, one teacher left to return with her husband to India. Several years later, she and her family returned to the north Jersey region. The first school she sought teacher employment upon her return to America was at the Classical Academy. It so happened that a position was open, and she was rehired.

Rarely, but occasionally, a teacher reluctantly left the Classical Academy to seek a higher salary which, for sound financial reasons, we could not match. Our teacher salaries were below neighboring public-school districts, but generally on par with or slightly higher than area Catholic schools. From the beginning, the Classical Academy provided to its teachers the same or comparable fringe benefits common to all public-school teachers: excellent medical coverage, paid school-vacation days, paid sick days, paid professional-development days, one-half tuition reimbursement for employment-relevant graduate-school courses, state retirement contributions, tenure, and more.

Because of the yearly low rate of teacher departure, and being part of a collaborative effort producing a nationally and state acknowledged superior school, Classical Academy faculty bonded together in professional and even personal ways. Fraternizing outside of work took place regularly among segments of the faculty and staff.

Still, whenever disparate adults gather daily in a common enterprise, unwanted and troublesome human attributes may arise. Whatever the work, however satisfying the work environment, certain adults bring into the workplace their own unresolved frustrations, vindictive attitudes, and agitated emotions.

On one occasion, after receiving student reports of a first-year teacher putting hands on a child in an effort to discipline, and having substantiated those reports, I excluded that teacher from future classes that day. With continued investigations and numerous student firsthand accounts, which I fully documented, after interviewing the teacher, and discovering a pattern of physical interactions with students, I suspended and precluded the teacher on that very day from returning to school. I informed the person the due-process rights to which any teacher in a similar situation was entitled, and reported the matter to our Board of Trustees. I also notified the state, as required to do. The teacher did not pursue due-process legal action and did not return to the Classical Academy. For several weeks, until a replacement could be secured, I taught the dismissed teacher's classes, along with my own classes.

On another occasion, nearing the end of Christmas vacation, I received at home a call from a teacher telling me she was not returning to school. Her husband was starting a business, and it was vital, she informed me, that she assist him in this endeavor full-time. I responded I understood, and, as soon as we returned to school, I would seek an immediate replacement and abide by her 60-day contractual notification-of-termination period. She replied, "Mr. DeRosa, you don't understand—I am leaving immediately. I will not be returning to school at all after the Christmas vacation." Shocked at this, and reminding her of her contract obligation of a 60-day termination notice, she blithely said she did not care.

When school resumed, because of her sudden departure, I readjusted some schedules for teachers and classes, and, again, I taught, in addition to my classes, several of her classes by combining them into one large group of about 40 students. Although I had every right to report her to the Department of Education—not abiding by her 60-day termination notice is a serious violation of both contract and ethics—and request that her teaching license either be revoked or suspended, the usual penalty for this violation, I did not pursue that course, preferring to let matters rest. It took about a month to find a suitable replacement teacher; it was only then that I was relieved of the unimaginable burden of teaching so many classes while also managing the school.

In both these situations, and each day of the 18 years I was Classical Academy school leader, my devoted wife and co-founder was at my side, providing invaluable assistance in sharing and reducing my burdens of school management during both calm and troubled times.

In two instances, I denied a teacher contract for the following school year. Their demonstrated lack of overall performance, poor attitudes, and repeated defiance of complying with leadership's suggestions and even firm directives, convinced me that the person would not be a cooperative, contributing member of the faculty. For the good of school management and attaining both instructional and institutional objectives—critical concerns for a small charter school—there was no alternative but to dispense with their services and to do so before tenure was a concern.

Members of our Board of Trustees were, almost exclusively, parents of currently enrolled Classical Academy students. At first, we asked for volunteers, put their names on ballots, and had, as the state prescribed, only parents of enrolled Classical Academy students vote for Board candidates. In other years, I nominated select parents to be candidates to our Board of Trustees, and sent parents ballots to affirm or deny my selections. Parents always had a right to nominate another candidate, and parents were not required to sign returned ballots for validation, adhering to the accepted right of secrecy in voting.

During my years of school leadership, I received the confidence and trust of Board members. My courses of action, suggestions, decisions, policies, and practices were generally, and for the good of the school, Board-endorsed. I always justified and provided ample reasons to Board members why I made or would make any decision of consequence. In no small way, our Board of Trustees contributed to the success of the school by respecting my guidance and endorsing my seasoned authority and skill in managing the school. Supporting my vision of the school, and having confidence in my and Magda's managerial competencies, while respecting our determined efforts for school success, Board members provided sound governance and valuable advice in all matters, particularly in planning and holding school events, resolving problems, and suggesting actions to meet diverse challenges.

As parents of Classical Academy students, Board members felt both indebtedness and admiration to me and Magda for creating the school, educating children to high standards, overcoming challenges to school success, and for the effective policies and practices I implemented. Because of our vision and our work, their own children were benefited with a high-quality educational experience.

Regrettably, some Board members and teachers would harbor far-different and more-destructive intentions, exert divisive influences, and pursue antagonistic and vindictive policy decisions and actions during my last year at the helm of the Classical Academy, a story to be told next chapter.

Probation

After its initial four years of operations, a New Jersey Charter school must complete a "Charter Renewal Application" every five years. The Classical Academy had already successfully navigated two previous charter renewals when the school prepared for its third charter renewal for school years 2012-2017. The Charter Renewal Application must be completed and filed by September of the school's final year of last charter renewal. In September 2011, my charter-renewal application was duly submitted to the New Jersey Department of Education, Office of Charter Schools. As required, I submitted the document also to the County Office of Education and to the Superintendent of Clifton Public School District.

As part of the charter-renewal process, a team of education bureaucrats from the Office of Charter Schools visit the school to review documents, interview school leadership, teachers, Board members, students, and parents. Having been through the process successfully several times, reassured by the strength of my charter-renewal application, the extraordinary, consistently high achievement of our students on standardized tests and by all other metrics, our National Blue Ribbon status, the school's indisputable success financially and academically, I felt confident the charter renewal would be granted without hesitation and with universal commendation. So confident was I of charter renewal that I fully anticipated profuse laudatory remarks from these state education officials, remarks which I would glowingly quote in a newspaper article announcing our well-merited charter renewal.

The visit of the charter-renewal officials occurred in mid-November, 2011. As planned, they met with all representative segments of the Classical Academy community, as well as reviewed documents, textbooks, curricula, inspected the building and facilities, and whatever else they so desired, all of which consumed the entire school day. As the day ended, the visitors thanked me and Mrs. DeRosa for cheerfully enduring the disruption their presence had on the school and for the demands they made on our time and attention. Everyone seemed most cordial. Certain that all had gone well, we bade them a hearty farewell as they drove out from the school grounds waving and smiling. We awaited with happy anticipation the well-deserved awarding of our third charter renewal.

On the Friday evening the day following the charter renewal team's visit, I received at home a phone call from a news reporter from one of our larger north Jersey newspapers. I was always eager to speak with reporters, to whom I could recite the wondrous merits of the Classical Academy, and how and why its students achieved much superior academic-learning outcomes than Clifton schools, and even greater learning outcomes than most other charter schools, and how our little school who few thought would ever survive was performing educationally and financially so well. But he was not concerned about hearing any glowing, self-serving statements of that kind; instead, he was seeking my reaction to the state placing the Classical Academy on "probation."

The word "probation" reverberated in my mind, causing a mild trauma and massive disbelief. While I reeled in astonishment, struggling to keep my accelerating heartbeat at sub-cardiac-stroke levels, he continued mentioning some of the issues stated in a press release he had received from the Department of Education—a document I had not seen—which enumerated its reasons for probation. Too stunned to comprehend every detail in his monologue, what he recited seemed to indicate a number of "non-compliance" matters, certain reports not being submitted or submitted late, certain modalities of school operations deviating from prescribed practice, and other matters, none of which related to sound finances, prudent spending practices, and, above all, student learning proficiencies. Did such minor violations, I silently protested, justify *probation* for a school of such magnificent accomplishments?

From my knowledge of charter schools placed on probation or even those denied charter renewal, probation occurred when charter schools bankrupted themselves by profligate spending or school officials extracting school money to acquire personal enrichment. Most charter schools, however, earned probation for chronically and abysmally low student-learning outcomes, far inferior even to their resident district schools; in many cases probation was often a precursor to charter-school dissolution. But none of these failings could be charged against the Classical Academy. I could only wait until Monday, when I would gain a better understanding, if such were possible, about the state's reasons for its inconceivable action.

I slept little that weekend. My agonized thoughts were focused on what I would receive Monday by mail, fax, or email from our cordial Office of Charter Schools charter-renewal team (need I say "hit squad," which I increasingly regarded it). What horrendous findings did the education bureaucrats discover or interpret to inflict such a crippling injury to one of the state's highest-achieving charter schools, indeed one of the state's most successful public schools? Why could it not obtain its purpose without imposing the stigma of probation by simply declaring: "Vincent, the Classical Academy is admittedly a high-performing charter school, and we congratulate you for its success. However, according to certain education statutes and regulations, the school is in violation in specific areas of your school-management practices and compliance responsibilities. Please correct them and show us proof that you did so, otherwise, we will be forced to place the school on probation in several months"? Perhaps because this more-gentle but less-bureaucratic sledgehammer approach would not serve their true intention, which I came to believe was nothing less than to deliver a fatal blow to the school.

During those sleepless nights, I ruminated on these and two other reflections. First, I recalled the ominous utterance one of the Office of Charter Schools' employees made to me when he arrived to the school: "We read what you wrote about [education] bureaucrats." I found his comment odd, and no further elaboration by this official or me was exchanged on the statement. At that time, charter school renewal applications and the "annual reports" charter schools must produce invited Lead Person's views and opinions on the state's charter school program and on ways that program could be shaped to improve outcomes and operations, and about the school's educational philosophy and other "subjective" responses. Some of my commentary over several years in both reports on education-reform topics often contained uncomplimentary views and critical analyses of the role and function of non-teaching education bureaucrats whose authority dictated public education on all levels—in local public schools, in county offices of education, and state education departments. Were these persons insulted personally by my opinionated but honest remarks about bureaucrats? If so, were they willing, in retribution, to go so far as placing the school I had founded and operated on "probation"?

The other reflection concerned the presence with the charter-renewal evaluation team of an official of the Passaic County Office of Education. This office had been, from the school's beginning, hostile to the Classical Academy. For a number of years, the Classical Academy was the only charter school in the entire county. Unlike other county offices of education, such as Essex County, the Passaic County office never exercised its powers of office in any way to assist the Classical Academy, or any charter school attempting to begin in the county. Rather, it half-heartedly tolerated the Classical Academy and the charter-school movement, which it quietly opposed, reluctantly accepting this education-reform movement only because it was sanctioned, state-government education policy, and county education offices are branches of that government.

In recent years, there had been ongoing friction between me and the county office regarding the timely completion and, in its judgment, deficient content of certain reports, such as the annual "Teacher Professional Development Plan." The Classical Academy never was late or found wanting in its three most important state-required reports: the "Annual Report," "Charter Renewal Application," and its CAFRA (the yearly comprehensive audit and financial report) conducted by an outside, independent auditor. Although I spent much time on numerous other mandatory reports as well, the committee of unionized Passaic County teachers (Classical Academy teachers were not members of the teachers' union) reviewing my annual "Teacher Professional Development Plans," a document I often spent days in preparing, would often return it to me with "unacceptable" status ratings, together with an order to correct the report and resubmit, with which I routinely complied. But when my third revisions of each year's reports were returned as "unacceptable," I would ignore such unreasonable committee requests and its outrageous demands on my time.

After all, teacher professional development is intended to improve student instruction and learning, and if Classical Academy 8th-grade students are achieving among the highest proficiencies rates in all Passaic County schools, does this fact not indicate Classical Academy teachers are more than adequately professionally developed? Yet in all things public education, only "process" and "compliance" matter, not actual results, not to mention the antipathy unionized teachers harbored against a non-unionized public school.

I inferred that the county office complained to the Office of Charter Schools about what it viewed as my blatant, defiant recalcitrance and "non-compliance" regarding the submission of reports, and perhaps about other matters. The Classical Academy's upcoming charter renewal, I speculated, would be the ideal time the Passaic County Office of Education could best advance its complaints and covertly advocate, with the aid of the state Office of Charter Schools, its disdain for the school. The county knew that the Office of Charter Schools wielded the power to inflict harsh penalties upon the school the county office itself lacked. If the county education authority, with the collusion of the Office of Charter Schools, could hurt the Classical Academy in some way, perhaps even cause its demise, it would have achieved its tacit but desired purpose.

Returning to school on Monday, and receiving all the probationary documents from the New Jersey Department of Education's Office of Charter Schools, it was clear that the Classical Academy was facing yet another formidable battle for the school's survival. Probation documents cited 44 reasons wherein the school was in violation of statute or otherwise non-compliant with regulation and preferred practice, and therefore, in

its one-sided view, the Office of Charter Schools justifiably imposed probationary status upon the Classical Academy. Tellingly, not one of the 44
identified violations involved the two categories for which all other charter schools up to that point had led to probation or charter non-renewal:
financial irregularities or extortion of school funds, and persistently very
poor student-learning outcomes.

As asserted in the probation documents, the Office of Charter Schools
must verify that all 44 violations, non-compliance issues, and changed
governance or management practices must be resolved or well on their way
to satisfactory correction by June 2012, seven months from the probation
notice, or the school's charter renewal may well be denied. Some of these
"violations" could be quickly addressed; others would take significant time
and resources.

By the state's action, it became obvious to me that the new preferred type
of New Jersey charter school was that run by charter-school management
or "network" companies operating multiple charter schools. Such charter
schools were well represented in New Jersey. They were large schools with
500-3000 students, well-financed, housed in buildings offering ample
space and traditional school amenities. These schools possessed sufficient
personnel whose full-time jobs were to comply with timely submission of
innumerable reports and to fulfill and to process the mountains of education mandates and regulations. They, therefore, gratifyingly lessened the
monitoring and oversight workload burdens of state education bureaucrats.
Schools operated by charter-school network companies seemed to garner
the admiration and support of state education officials, who touted these
schools' abundant resources and lauded those who operated them as ideals of the charter-school concept while exhibiting high-level management
competencies. In their structure and operations, they closely resembled
traditional public schools. These were the type of charter schools New
Jersey education authorities increasingly prized and favored.

The Classical Academy, on the other hand, was a small, anachronistic
"Mom and Pop" charter school that, because of its remarkable success,
may well have brought upon itself the antagonism and opposition of
county and state education officials. To these evaluators, a school that

operates in an old, cramped, poorly equipped building where the chief school administrator has regularly assigned classroom-teaching duties, and his wife is the school's business administrator, and both function as day-time janitors, in-house substitute teachers, and traffic wardens, is a school deserving of termination. If regulatory reasons can be found to justify the elimination of such a disfavored kind of charter school as the Classical Academy, all the better. The fact that 8th-grade student academic-learning outcomes of this school placed it in the top 5% of all New Jersey middle schools (that is, showing superior student outcomes than 95% of all public middle schools) is completely irrelevant to these evaluators, to whom perceptions, process, and compliance is everything in education, not results, not student-learning outcomes.

The number and sort of probationary violations cited, and the heavy burden of complying with all of them would be so onerous, as these opponents to the Classical Academy likely intended, that I and the school's governing body may be tempted to take the easy way out and concede by voluntarily ending the school and surrendering its charter. But, as in starting the school, and knowing I again was on the right side of this struggle, I summoned all my energy, wits, and determination to fight these bureaucrats and emerge from this battle, as I did years before, vindicated and victorious.

One probation requirement was that the school must notify in writing the entire Classical Academy community of its probationary status, and prove to the Office of Charter Schools that this was done. Humiliating as it was, I was forthright in describing to the entire Classical Academy community our probationary status, what it entailed, and how we would respond. I assured all that we would succeed in overcoming this latest challenge, reassuring both worried parents that the school would continue to be here for their children and concerned teachers that I and Magda would spare no effort to save the school and their jobs.

From the beginning, I was confident the Classical Academy would emerge successfully from probationary status and receive its charter renewal, but that success would be contingent on my and my wife's unflagging efforts. The Office of Charter Schools found no financial fraud or financial malfeasance of any sort in the Classical Academy's fiscal history and practices.

The school's consistently high student-achievement levels had brought the school national and state awards and recognition. Again, not one of the 44 probation-cited violations or proscribed practices pertained to financial integrity or to student-learning outcomes. I conjectured that employees at the Office of Charter Schools, fearing repercussion and embarrassing news headlines as: *"State Denies Charter Renewal to Award-Winning Charter School,"* could not do otherwise but to grant our charter renewal, *unless* I gave them reasons for charter denial by my refusal or inaction to address fully all probationary "violations" and my failure to initiate the steps they cited for "corrective actions." I, therefore, committed myself wholly and earnestly to resolving all the issues the charter-renewal officials identified as reasons for probation, however petty and irrelevant to educational and school excellence were those "violations."

Embarrassing to members of the Office of Charter Schools, or perhaps not, several months after it placed the school on probation for certain violations and proscribed practices, its own New Jersey Department of Education accorded the Classical Academy its *"REWARD SCHOOL"* designation, attesting that the Classical Academy is a model school to which other New Jersey schools should aspire. A rational person must ask how could a deficient or ill-operated school assessed worthy of probation and possible non-renewal of charter be simultaneously judged by a branch of the same organization a model of achievement and effectiveness. A mere "bureaucratic mix-up," or does this gross inconsistency point to something more nefarious behind the suspiciously collusive intentions of certain county and Office of Charter School education officials?

With a few exceptions as illustrations, I shall not enumerate all 44 "violations." Suffice to say that, after devoting much of my time and effort to the crisis at hand, by September 1, 2012, 10 months after being placed on probation, I had executed the full and complete resolution of all 44 violations, recommendations, and deficient or proscribed practices, and demonstrated the school's full and complete compliance to the Office of Charter Schools. The school was, therefore, permitted to begin the 2012-2013 school year, but inexplicably did not receive formal notice of charter renewal until late spring of 2013, 16 months after being placed on probation.

Because of my work in assiduously addressing fully all probation items, the Office of Charter Schools had no choice but to grant, however belatedly, the Classical Academy its third charter renewal. The Office of Charter Schools perhaps did so with regret and a sense of "mission failure," perhaps also with apologies to the Passaic County Office of Education.

Before leaving this topic and by way of illustration, I want to mention a few of the issues the Office of Charter schools found so egregious. In this, the reader should gain some insight into the regulators' inflexible mindset; in my estimation, they willfully exceeded reasonable and fair determinations in order to find regulatory grounds to punish if not end the Classical Academy. In its action, the Office of Charter Schools, reflecting perhaps the sentiments of high-level education officials in government, revealed its disdain for a small charter school founded and operated by a teacher, not a charter-school network management company. Their inflexible attitude betrayed a belief that a charter school of only 120 students, whose chief administrator performs so many functions and duties without the assistance of numerous subordinate administrators and non-instructional personnel, as well as discharging regular classroom teaching duties, and whose wife serves as the school's business administrator, is simply not the preferred bureaucratic charter-school ideal and should not, therefore, be encouraged or permitted to continue functioning.

Violation: Out-of-Date Curriculum Guides: The Office of Charter Schools asserted our curriculum guides for all subjects were out-of-date. Curriculum guides are documents which more often than not remain on teachers' shelves and are of minimal use for actual instruction. I responded to the charter-renewal team that, given our students' extraordinary standardized-test results, *every* school should have the same sort of out-of-date curriculum guides as the Classical Academy. The evaluators were not amused or moved; we provided stipends to certain of our teachers to "re-write" or "update" our curriculum guides in all subjects. Even though the Classical Academy had no discrete physical-education classes and no physical-education teacher, nor did the school have specific classes in "Visual and Performing Arts," the Office of Charter Schools nevertheless demanded we produce "curricula guides" for these subjects which the school does not offer in its regular curricula, and pay outside consultants to produce them.

Violation: Full-Time Nurse and Use of Nurse's Room: According to the Office of Charter Schools, not having a full-time school nurse on the premises was a violation of state regulation. Since the Classical Academy began, it employed a part-time nurse several days a week. She performed all the state-required student-health mandates such as physical exams, record keeping, vaccination logs, height/weight measurements, eye exams, consultations with our contracted school doctor, and ongoing parent consultations for all of our 120 middle-school students. The school was always in full compliance with all student-health mandates and record keeping. The Office of Charter Schools nonetheless insisted that we have a full-time nurse and cited state regulations on which they based their order.

I retorted that first, our part-time nurse performed all state-required health checks and monitoring. Second, our parents who willingly send their children to the school know we do not have a full-time nurse, yet they have no fear that their child's health or safety while at the school is at risk. Thirdly, a number of our faculty, including Mrs. DeRosa, are trained in first aid and have certificates to prove that competence. Fourthly, one of north Jersey's largest hospitals and health centers is literally a two-minute drive down the road. Fifth, by school law, school nurses are not permitted medically to treat students; school nurses cannot even administer an over-the-counter aspirin to a child. Sixth, when a child is injured or becomes ill at school, we respond the same way as does any school with a full-time school nurse—we call the parent to bring medication or to remove the child from school. Seventh, I, Mrs. DeRosa, or a teacher, in response to more-critical student-health emergencies, do what all schools do, even those with full-time nurses, and call Clifton's Emergency Medical Team (EMT), who respond quickly and professionally to any summons from the school. Lastly, our one part-time nurse serves 120 students; yet, at Clifton middle schools, there is one full-time nurse for every 550 students. Thus, our nurse-to-student ratio is much superior to Clifton schools'.

These cogent reasons militating against hiring a full-time nurse (and the cost in salary and benefits our small school would incur) had no impact; a full-time nurse was the law, they adamantly asserted, which we callously ignore while jeopardizing our students' safety. Within a few months, we terminated the part-time school nurse and, in her place, hired a full-time person.

As if this were not enough, the Office of Charter Schools insisted that the bathroom in the nurse's room can no longer be used, as it had been for the last 13 years, exclusively for female teachers. The nurse's room, the team of evaluators proclaimed, was for sick children whose privacy would be infringed on if others entered the room (even though, for much of the time, there is no student convalescing in the nurse's room). Since that bathroom in the nurse's room was the only one in the building for teachers' use only, I had to tell our female teachers, to their shock and dismay, that they must henceforth, according to the decree from the Office of Charter Schools, use the school's three female-student bathrooms for their personal needs. (After our charter was renewed, I quietly informed female teachers that, in agreement with the new full-time nurse, teachers may begin to use the lavatory in the nurse's room once again, if there is no convalescing student therein.)

Violation: PARCC Tests and Building Inadequacies for Its Administration: The school lacked computers and internet connectivity for upcoming standardized assessments. The charter-renewal team urgently impressed upon me that the newly required PARCC tests to be implemented in less than two years would be taken by all students on computers. Our building must be wired for "WiFi" in every classroom and other rooms serving a school function, and we must add whatever other technical infrastructure-enhancements are needed for future standardized testing, for instruction, and for school management. (Perhaps members of the Office of Charter Schools did not know, as I did not until a year later, that a school could request to take the PARCC with pencil and paper.) I forthwith contracted with a firm to make our building "WiFi"- and PARCC-capable, and enlarge other technical capabilities for school-management purposes. We soon hired a part-time "IT" person to assist with PARCC preparations and school reports, and purchased 130 "Chromebook" laptops, enabling all students to take the PARCC on a computer. In the first year of the PARCC tests, 2015, the percentage of our 8th-graders achieving "Passing" was the highest of any Passaic County public school in both English Language Arts and "Algebra I."

Violation: Ending the Alumni Admission Rule: The "Alumni Admission Rule," of which I spoke earlier, was deemed contrary to charter-school admissions rule. Only siblings of *currently enrolled* students, not siblings of graduated students, can secure admissions outside the lottery mechanism. Whatever sound reasons I adduced for the purpose and worth of our Alumni Admission Rule, and its benefits to the school, all were summarily rejected. This admission rule, which served the school so well in building parental support and community-wide respect, was thus discontinued.

Concerns About My Teaching Duties and Nepotism: Although not listed or cited as "violations," it was made clear to me that a charter-school Lead Person is preferred not to have regular classroom-teaching duties. It was strongly intimated to me that my teaching two instructional classes daily may be interfering with the time I could devote to administering the school and accomplishing all management duties, in their evaluation, more competently, timely, and responsibly. Being the only New Jersey charter-school Lead Person to have regular teaching duties, and not wishing to provide any reason to regulatory bureaucrats of what they may construe my defiance or recalcitrance, at the beginning of the new school year, I reluctantly ceased teaching 8th-grade Latin, and hired another person to take on this Classical Academy duty that I had performed happily and well for 15 years.

Although we had taken every precaution and practiced complete transparency from even before the school was chartered and thereafter that my wife, as co-founder of the school and academically qualified to do so, would serve as the school's business administrator, it was nonetheless expressed verbally that having the two chief Classical Academy's administrators a married couple was suspicious, unprofessional, and unprecedented in a public school. This, in combination with Magda lately having difficulty in filing timely and accurately certain state financial reports—the state had changed significantly the content and methods for reporting and transmission, changes of which Magda was unaware, and the Passaic County Office of Education, instead of assisting us, likely bombarded the state with complaints—that another business administrator be hired part time with whom Magda could function collaboratively but in a secondary position. This "suggestion" was fulfilled beginning July 2013.

An Enviable Record of Distinction for Student Academic Achievement

Classical Academy Charter School of Clifton's record of student achievement, as recorded in objective, standardized testing of English language arts and mathematics, is well elaborated in Appendix A of this work, which I heartily invite the reader to peruse. By way of brief and illustrative evidence of the success of the Classical Academy 8th-grade students, the culminating grade of the school's middle-school program and, thus, the learning outcomes most indicative of programmatic strength and school performance, I note here the percentage of the Classical Academy's 8th-grade class earning a "passing" percentage each year during a 10-year period (2007-2016) on state-mandated standardized testing in English and mathematics (beginning in 2015 for the PARCC tests, "Algebra I").

State Mandated Standardized Assessment	Year	Percent of 8th Grade "Passing" English Language Arts	Percent of 8th Grade "Passing" "Mathematics"
GEPA	2007	91.2%	94.1%
ASK-8	2008	88.9%	85%
ASK-8	2009	100%	94%
ASK-8	2010	100%	100%
ASK-8	2011	100%	100%
ASK-8	2012	100%	100%
ASK-8	2013	100%	100%
ASK-8	2014	97.2%	94.5%
			"Algebra 1"
PARCC	2015	87%	94.7%
PARCC	2016	86.4%	89.1%

NB: "Passing" constitutes the combined percentage of 8th-grade students achieving either a "Proficient" or an "Advanced Proficiency" score. For PARCC tests, "passing" is the combined percentage of 8th-graders earning either a "Level 4-Meeting Expectations" or a "Level 5-Exceeding Expectations."

NB: The above data reflects the school's "no-tracking policy," which requires *every* 8th-grade student to take the Classical Academy's "Algebra I" course and, thus, the "Algebra I" PARCC test, not the less-demanding PARCC 8th-grade "mathematics" test.

The reader will note the string of successive years when *every* Classical Academy 8th-grade student "passed" English and mathematics; in those years when every student did not pass, our student 8th-grade passing rate was nevertheless in the high 80s to mid-90s percent, a passing percentage which most schools, traditional and charter, would greatly relish and regard a great accomplishment. The percentage of our 8th-graders achieving each year "Advanced Proficiency" is also quite impressive, and illustrated in Appendix A. The Classical Academy's 8th-grade class consistently numbered, beginning in 2002, between 36 and 40 students.

My Classical Academy Duties and Functions, and Those of Mrs. DeRosa

I would be remiss if this narrative memoir on the founding of the school and my 18-year Classical Academy leadership avoided mention of my diverse and many functions, as well as those of my wife and co-founder, Magda DeRosa. To biased traditionalists who despise and fear profound education reform, just two people shouldering the burden of performing so many diverse administrative and instructional responsibilities is not a feat to admire or elicit praise. Rather, to them it proves that the Classical Academy could not but be clumsily and poorly managed. New Jersey's massive corpus of public-school rules, statutes, and regulations, and the burden these and other school operations impose on just two people is reason enough for charter denial, reason enough to question its continued operations, despite its laudable fiscal strength and its remarkable student-learning outcomes.

To such critics, any small New Jersey charter school with a comparatively minuscule student enrollment because of building limitations, combined with all the state-imposed requirements for compliant school operations, would necessarily be encumbered with inadequate revenues, reduced resources, and insufficient personnel. Such a school is unlikely to be viable and, in fact, should not be viable. Charter schools of this type, their reasoning continues, cannot be otherwise than fraught with inherent, systemic managerial deficiencies caused by restricted revenues and insufficient non-teaching personnel, resulting in inadequate administrative infrastructure thereby inviting inevitable breaches in school law, in fulfilling regulatory mandates, and in reporting obligations.

In ascribing probationary status in 2012, it became apparent to me that the Office of Charter Schools was among those who believed the Classical Academy should never have been granted a charter in the first place. Critics affirm that, as a charter school administratively operated by a husband-and-wife team, the Classical Academy is decidedly not the preferred or desired sort of "professional" charter school deserving of state charter or charter renewal.

The management of a charter school, this view holds, should not depend so greatly on the monumental, manifold labors of just two people, however well-intentioned and willing they be. The demands for meeting the 2,000 pages of state education statutes, codes, regulations, and reporting obligations, from which charter schools are largely not exempt, are far beyond human capacity of any one or two people. Because of inevitable chronic compliance violations, deficient regulatory adherence, and a propensity to place actual results over mere process fulfillment, this type of school management will always find itself and the school in perpetual conflict with education authorities, and become an ongoing burdensome problem for bureaucratic monitoring and oversight.

My belief on this subject is, of course, quite different. As much as I was disgusted by the breadth and depth of the "anti-academic school culture" endemic in New Jersey public education, I was equally shocked by the bloated bureaucracy and abundant non-teaching personnel in every school and school district in which I was employed. Their positions and functions were always deemed essential to school management, to comply with state regulations, and to provide student "needs"; my own observations proved quite the contrary. Streamlining and reducing school bureaucracy and non-instructional functionaries was a Classical Academy objective not solely because of restricted funding, but because it would enhance academic instruction, uplift the status of academic-subject teachers, and provide better direct and immediate service for our client parents.

As I stated often, as a tenured and practicing classroom New Jersey teacher, I was given the very rare—if not unprecedented—opportunity of starting a public school, thereby fulfilling a long-held dream of actualizing my educational beliefs and philosophy in the everyday reality of a functioning school. New Jersey charter-school law gives little latitude for charter schools to become truly innovative and "laboratories of reform," demanding instead the same mandatory compliance with copious state education rules, regulations, and procedures as traditional public-school districts. In reality, New Jersey charter schools are forced into conformity with all other public schools, thereby castrating their potential for true innovation where actual student-learning results are the foremost goal.

I, therefore, realize more than anyone that compliance issues, innumerable reporting obligations, and school operational requirements make it most difficult for one person or two people to undertake the work of starting a charter school and, afterwards, to manage it successfully year after year. But if I and my wife did not struggle to overcome the challenges and hardships in starting a charter school, and if we did not enthusiastically undertake to perform every day of every year to the best of our abilities the infinite number of functions, duties, and tasks requisite for managerial success, there simply would not be, or ever could be, a Classical Academy Charter School of Clifton, New Jersey.

The best analogy, however it be ridiculed by New Jersey public education bureaucrats, is that of a couple possessing a dream to start a business, and, in so doing, the couple invests an unimaginable amount of time, energy, and often money to realize that dream. And when, against all odds, the dream materializes, they labor even harder not to let that dream perish. Such it was for me and my wife. I was motivated to accept the unprecedented opportunity and unique challenge of a New Jersey teacher starting and operating a New Jersey public school; my wife's motivation came from her love for me and wanting me to realize my dream.

A representative sampling of my primary duties, obligations, and functions as Classical Academy Chief School Administrator, Principal, and Lead Person/Teacher were:

Director of Curricula and Instruction; Teacher Performance Evaluator, including Production of Classroom Teacher Evaluations; Reviewer of Weekly Teacher Lesson Plans for All Subjects; Director of Personnel and Human

Resources; Officer in Charge of Hiring; Director of Public Relations; Grounds Custodian and On-Site Daytime Janitor; Director of Transportation; Events Planner and Coordinator for School Trips; Coordinator of all Extra/Co-Curricular Activities; Part-Time Teacher of Latin (1998-2013); Author of All Required School Reports (including Charter School Annual Reports and Charter Renewal Applications); Author of All School Policies and Practices; Compliance Officer; Director of Guidance and Student Counseling; Anti-Bullying Coordinator; Liaison with Clifton and County Police Departments; Communications Director; Director of Admissions and Admissions Lottery Supervisor; Special Education Supervisor; Director/Coordinator of all Standardized Testing; Supervisor of Student Preparations and Learning Materials for Standardized Tests; Board of Trustees Secretary Responsible for Writing and Dissemination of Board Minutes; Supervisor of Elections for Board of Trustees Members; Coordinator of Student and Teacher Scheduling; Director of School-Community Relations and Outreach; Web-Site Administrator; Information Technology Coordinator; Supervisor for Teacher Professional Development; Supervisor of Student Conduct and Code-of-Conduct Enforcement Officer; Guidance Director; Building Fabric, Maintenance, and Boiler Supervisor; Traffic Warden and Crossing Guard; Occasional Substitute Teacher; Evaluator for Dispensing Teacher Bonuses Based on Student Outcomes on Standardized Tests; Evaluator for Comparing and Ranking Yearly Student Standardized Tests Outcomes with all other New Jersey public and charter schools; Director of Food Services; Director of Physical Education and Health Instruction; Organizing and Scheduling of Teacher/Student Weekly Field Days in Fall and Spring; Director of Procurement of School Supplies and Equipment; Liaison with State Education and Local Officials on All Education Matters; Supervisor of Summer Preparations for the New School Year; Director for Resolution of Parent/Student Issues and Problems, and more.

Mrs. DeRosa, as school co-founder and the only other on-site school administrator, was the Classical Academy's School Business Administrator. As such, she was the chief person dealing with all aspects of the school's finances, a function for which she was duly state certified. At times, she had a part-time bookkeeper to assist in these duties. To reduce my administrative burdens, she regularly assisted me in many of my above-enumerated duties and functions. She was also the school's in-house substitute teacher to cover classes for absent teachers (she held county-issued substitute certification and is state certified to teach French). Mrs. DeRosa also supervised the school's food service. To obviate any charge of nepotism, we clearly stated in all founding documents and approved by state authorities that Mrs. DeRosa would be a Classical Academy paid employee as its founding "SBA." Mrs. DeRosa speaks both French and Arabic, the latter an asset to numerous Arabic-speaking immigrant families whose children attended the Classical Academy.

Even in the smallest New Jersey public schools, many of the above functions would be performed by a cadre of other employees. Still other functions and services would be provided by paid, school-contracted outside vendors.

Financial Practices and the Imperative for Spending Prudence

In addition to securing our initial goal of school survival and, subsequently, of sustaining its widely recognized success as one of the highest performing New Jersey public schools, we undertook so many functions and duties not only because the dearth of incoming revenues compelled us to do so, but to save enough money for emergencies and to achieve our goal of school expansion. Having the smallest enrollment of all New Jersey public schools, traditional and charter, and, hence, the fewest revenues by far with which to operate a public school, the Classical Academy from its beginning was beset by financial exigencies of school operations and, for the first 6 or 7 years of its life, by the ever-present specter of financial insolvency. That the Classical Academy was periodically the documented lowest-funded and lowest per-pupil cost public school in the state further constricted ample revenues.

Clifton Public School District, during my entire time at the Classical Academy, was among the lowest per-pupil cost districts in the state. Its school budgets were almost never passed by voters. As with all charter schools, we received from our resident school district for every Clifton student 90% of an already comparatively low per-pupil cost. When I started the school, we received about $6,500 for every student; by the time I retired, we received about $11,000 from Clifton per student. Because of this fact, and that we had only 120 students to generate revenues, our incoming revenues were scant compared with other charter schools. During the last few years of my leadership, our entire school budget revenues were approximately one million three-hundred thousand dollars ($1,300,000), likely the state's lowest school budget.

With such financial realities continually confronting us, and not to jeopardize financial soundness, the compulsion not to squander or to spend imprudently precious monetary resources on school personnel, functions, and services I and my wife could otherwise perform ourselves, became both a managerial imperative and our committed work ethic.

After some years, when school finances became stabilized and we even enjoyed small but accumulating revenue surpluses each year, especially after the facility mortgage was fully paid, I and Mrs. DeRosa continued to save school money each year by continuing to perform all the administrative and non-administrative tasks above enumerated. Our objective was to save enough money to realize our hopes of future building and grade expansion, and to meet any emergencies or necessary-but-unforeseen expenses.

For example, the unanticipated charter-probation episode of 2012 cost the school approximately $100,000 in immediate expenditures to resolve all 44 compliance violations and win our charter renewal; in the same year, the necessary refurbishing of the school building's deteriorating exterior with paint, carpentry, and vinyl siding cost another $70,000. These figures exclude the ongoing, increased state-mandated expenditures of a full-time nurse, part-time Latin teacher, part-time IT specialist, and part-time (off-site) school business administrator, all additional personnel probationary-status compelled or strongly advocated. These essential projects and additional mandated school personnel could not have been financed if we did not have sufficient money in the school's bank account, money which would not have been ready at hand if I and Mrs. DeRosa, during our long Classical Academy leadership, had spent school revenues imprudently on hiring additional personnel and contracting service vendors simply to reduce our own workload and make our professional lives less burdensome or onerous.

Under our school leadership, the Classical Academy held yet another distinction: it was ranked among the lowest New Jersey public schools for school administrative costs; the percentage of the Classical Academy's yearly school budget devoted to school-administration expenditures was likewise among the lowest, if not *the* lowest, in New Jersey.

Finally, in making financial decisions on school spending, we always respected and treated the taxpayers' money as if it were our own by practicing frugality and prudence in all school expenditures. We assiduously practiced the precept that, *"whenever a task or function could be performed in house, I, my wife, or together would undertake that task or function, rather than reflexively hire additional personnel or pay outside vendors to accomplish the work."*

My and Mrs. DeRosa's Monetary Compensation

Having founded the school with my ideas, money, and tireless efforts, by which the Classical Academy reached the pinnacle of institutional success, academic and financial, my highest yearly salary level, after 18 years at the school's helm, was earned during my last three years as Lead Person: $92,000 for my 12-month employment contract. For most years, my total salary was divided between 60% administration and 40% teaching. Interestingly, if I had never started the Classical Academy and had remained at my tenured teaching position with my affluent Bergen County school-district employer, I would be earning at time of retirement approximately $100,000 per year for a 10-month teaching contract (but I would never have enjoyed the priceless personal and professional satisfaction of operating "my own school" and seeing my educational philosophy and beliefs produce such remarkable success). The highest salary Mrs. DeRosa ever earned was $65,000 per 12-month contract, by far the lowest full-time school business administrator salary in New Jersey.

Chapter VIII

OUR LAST YEAR: VINDICTIVE TREACHERY VANQUISHES HOPES AND EXPECTATIONS

Retirement and School Expansion Plans

Emerging victorious from probationary status with charter renewal in hand after a yearlong arduous effort; after having arisen every workday morning for the past 17 years at 4:45 a.m., with seldom a day off from my labor of love; after overcoming steadfastly the many adverse forces and challenges to create a school of financial and educational success, and advancing past the age when most public-school personnel end their careers, my wife urged me, as she had done for the last several years, to consider retirement. Concurring now wholeheartedly with her wish, I announced to our Board of Trustees in January 2015, and soon thereafter to our faculty and staff, that both I and Mrs. DeRosa would retire in September 2016, about a year and a half after the announcement.

My and my wife's emotions swelled with anticipatory elation that our hopes and expectations, both personal and professional, for the next stage of our lives was about to begin. Personally, we would soon venture on two trips we had exhilaratingly contemplated for many years. First, I was eager to fulfill a promise I had made to her years ago about taking her to Rome, Italy, and to the Vatican. For one gloriously unforgettable summer, I had lived and studied in Rome. I often related to my wife the magic of the Eternal City and pledged to take her to all the ancient and romantic sites I came to know and love. After 10 days in Rome and the

Italian countryside, we would travel to Venice and board a Viking Cruise ship for a two-week Mediterranean Sea journey, visiting a number of ports around that fabled ocean. Our three-week Italian trip and cruise would take place in mid-August 2015.

As a retirement gift, my wife promised we would go to Quebec, Canada, for a three-week fly-fishing adventure in one of the largest private wildlife preserves in North America, filled with lakes, ponds, and rivers, and a place I had long yearned to visit. Here, one selects a most charming and idyllic cottage picturesquely situated on one of the many lakes or rivers in the preserve. With boat furnished, no other person is permitted on the body of water for fishing or recreation except the renter of the cottage associated with a particular body of water within the preserve. Luxurious accommodations, abounding natural beauty, and outstanding fishing for bass and trout are all unrivaled. We would embark on this nature and fishing adventure just two weeks after our scheduled retirement in September 2016.

By "professionally," I refer to the Classical Academy's future development—specifically, I intended to devote a large part of my final year to expanding both the school's building and adding grade levels. For its entire life, the Classical Academy had only the three traditional middle-school grades, 6, 7, and 8, the fewest grades of any New Jersey charter school. By adding grades 4 and 5, and thus be a school of grades 4-8, as are many New Jersey charter schools, we would not only have the benefit of more students and, thus, more revenues, but more importantly, students would enter our award-winning, scholastically rich program and "academics-first school culture" earlier, and matriculate longer.

In broaching this topic over the years, I pledged to Board members that if we added grades 4 and 5, the Classical Academy would, in my considered opinion, remain consistently in the top 5% of all middle schools in the entire state, regardless of socio-economic designations and notwithstanding our predominantly minority immigrant student body. After all, I reminded them, look at the high achievement our 8th-graders now demonstrate in just three years, or even two years for students entering the school in 7th grade. Our students would acquire and demonstrate exponentially greater learning and higher academic skills compared with their peers throughout the state, if they could benefit from a Classical Academy education beginning in the 4th grade and be educated in our excellent academic program for five years instead of just three or two years. In fact, I reasonably envisioned 80% of every 8th-grade class earning "advanced proficiency" ratings in every tested subject every year. Adding grades 4 and 5 would guarantee Classical Academy preeminence among all New Jersey public schools, charter and traditional, even consistently equaling or even surpassing Princeton Charter School, the state's perennially top charter school, for as long as the Classical Academy continues.

Outlining my projected course of action to initiate the beginning stages of Classical Academy expansion during my last year before retirement, I recommended to the Board that we hire someone by June 2015, to become my successor upon my retirement. I would train this person during the 2015-2016 school year to become knowledgeable about school operations and ready to assume my duties beginning September 2016. Just as important, the addition of a third trainee administrator would provide a small relief from my innumerable functions for me to undertake the initial, complex steps for school expansion.

Several New Non-Instructional Personnel Added to School

For the last several years, after having dispensed with the services of a part-time bookkeeper to assist Magda, and based on the strong suggestions of the Office of Charter Schools and the recommendation of our certified public accountant, whose firm performed the school's "Comprehensive Annual Report and Financial Audit," we hired a part-time business administrator to assume some of Magda DeRosa's School Business Administrator duties. This person came to school, often on weekends for only several hours per week, to work with financial documents Magda had prepared or otherwise supplied. Because of this person's full-time position at another charter school, presence at the Classical Academy even a few hours during the regular workday when Magda was present was impossible. We found this to be a poor arrangement for all concerned. After several years, we did not renew this person's contract but hired another part-time School Business Administrator whose contract clearly specified, and to which she agreed, to be in school during regular school hours at least 4 hours of her own choosing per week to collaborate directly with Magda, whose new job title was "Assistant SBA/Administrative Coordinator."

After several months, and contrary to her employment contract, our new part-time SBA insisted she work entirely off-site and discontinued coming to school, except intermittently to attend monthly evening Board of Trustees meetings. Refusing to appear in school even for those few hours during normal workdays as her contract demanded, she preferred to perform all her Classical Academy financial duties by computer and email. This mode of work was causing confusion, miscommunication, and severe ongoing problems needlessly impeding smooth fiscal operations, all of which nullified the very reason for which she was hired. I eventually discovered that she was the "full-time SBA" for two or three other charter schools, a workload which disinclined her from fulfilling her Classical Academy contract. I asked the Board to terminate her contract, if not immediately, then certainly by the time a new Lead Person commences duties, and hire a full-time, on-site school business administrator to replace Magda DeRosa and to assist the new Lead Person not only in financial matters but in administering the school generally.

To make the transition to a new Lead Person smoother, less abrupt, and more effective, we decided to hire my successor during my last year to serve a sort of apprenticeship. In this way, the person selected could better become acclimated to the school and its policies and practices, and be mentored by me and Magda before assuming full administrative capacity. Several applicants to be my successor were interviewed. Their resumes were loaded with "school administration" credits and experiences. I firmly felt that, as the Classical Academy is a teacher-centered, instructionally focused school, it should be led, as I led it, by a superior teacher, not by someone who had abandoned the classroom for the "executive educator's suite."

In the midst of our search, I recalled a person who taught English at the Classical Academy for one year, leaving to raise a family. She was a

Clifton resident, and she had visited the school a few times soon after she relinquished her teaching position to show us her new baby and give us some produce from her garden. In my estimation and memory, she was an excellent teacher, possessed a Master's Degree in English, harbored a winsome personality, and exuded level-headedness and responsibility in demeanor and attitude. When I contacted her about the possibility of becoming my successor, she was teaching at a nearby Catholic school. She expressed much interest in the position, and exhibited a willingness to acquire the understanding of the job and a confidence in her own abilities to become an effective Lead Person. She was willing to take the 4 graduate courses (for which the Classical Academy paid full tuition) leading to school "Supervisors Certificate," a basic state-required credential needed for charter-school leadership.

Despite her working one year as a teacher at the Classical Academy more than a decade ago, I noticed during our conversations that she knew very little about public education or about charter schools. She was herself educated in Catholic schools, worked in a Catholic school, and sent her own children to Catholic schools. The salient issues involving public education and the charter-school education-reform movement were largely foreign to her. Still, I thought this was a concerning but, on balance, minor drawback in her background. I strongly endorsed her candidacy to our Board of Trustees, who, in fact, hired her to begin July 1, 2015, to be my mentored assistant and the Classical Academy's new Lead Person beginning September 2016, contingent upon my and Magda's retirements.

It was now spring of 2015 and four months after our retirement announcement. My successor had been selected and would begin at the end of the school year, July 1, 2015. Our students had recently taken the newly required PARCC tests on Chromebook laptops, which we purchased for every student as a stipulation for charter renewal. A part time "IT" expert was hired about a year before the PARCC exams to assist in the technological complexities the administration of that exam required. Comforted by the confidence that our 8th-grade students' scores on the more difficult PARCC assessments would reflect our accustomed academic superiority to Clifton schools and, as usual, rank our student outcomes in the top

10% of all New Jersey charter schools, the end of the present school year was in sight, brimming with bright anticipation of future achievements and school expansion.

School Expansion Taking Shape

Mrs. DeRosa and I relished the prospect that our final year of Classical Academy leadership would soon be upon us. Amidst other tasks, my long-fomenting plan to expand the building capacity and add grades 4 and 5 was a vision beginning to take more definitive shape. That vision encompassed the development of a "Classical Academy campus" by expanding our existing building to accommodate additional students or, if that was not feasible, to construct a small classroom building on school property. The campus would house 200 students in grades 4 through 8, with 40 students in each grade level. When accomplished, this expansion of school building and student enrollment would not only ensure increased flow of revenues to pay for building construction, additional faculty, and increased teacher salaries, but would also solidify and perpetuate the Classical Academy's well-established standing as one of the highest academically performing public schools in New Jersey. By becoming a school encompassing grades 4-8, the Classical Academy's sterling reputation and high student academic performance would therefore continue and even grow well into the future, when I and my wife would no longer have formal or daily involvement in the school we founded and to which we had dedicated our lives.

I was cognizant that the entire expansion project must be done over two or three years in multiple, coordinated steps. With my mentored successor performing a portion of my administrative responsibilities along with my wife, and with me no longer teaching my two 8th-grade Latin classes, I would have at least a modicum of time during my last year, 2015-2016, to develop earnestly the initial stages of my school-expansion vision. I expected also that, after my retirement, the Board of Trustees would welcome my volunteer contributions in bringing this vital project to successful fruition. An organized "modus operandi" now formed in my mind to realize this vision, my final notable accomplishment as the Classical Academy founder and leader.

A rarity among New Jersey charter schools, our school building was a fully paid, mortgage-free facility, and now assessed with structure and property at about one million dollars. Our school's bank account, because of our habitual prudence in restraining expenditures, together with my wife and I performing so many school functions ourselves—thereby saving expenditures on additional personnel and service-provider vendors—contained one and a half million dollars ($1,500,000) in ready cash. These financial assets and collateral were more than adequate for making a substantial down payment on the expansion project's initial costs, while simultaneously operating the school in a sound fiscal manner. Our capital and liquid assets, along with proven reputation were also sufficient for securing bank financing for the remainder of the project's cost. Indeed, this long-desired school expansion was one reason we had accumulated a financial surplus over the years.

Once the project was completed, in two or three years, our greatly increased revenues would pay whatever bank loans were needed to finance the project. When all project costs were paid in about five years, a goodly percentage of our greatly increased yearly revenues would be saved or available for whatever reasonable expenses, such as significant increases in teacher salaries. I had always hoped to make Classical Academy teachers among the highest paid in the region; school expansion and greater revenues would realize that hope. Furthermore, the school's Board of Trustees and Clifton taxpayers would, upon the project's completion and outstanding expansion costs paid, themselves fully own the "Classical Academy campus," free from monthly mortgage expenses, repayment of bank-loan obligations, or from interminable and financially burdensome monthly lease payments to a private property owner.

According to my estimated time schedule of three years to complete school expansion, and after all expansion costs were fully paid, the Classical Academy would, in a few years, enjoy, as it had for years, the security and independence that attends full property ownership—again a rarity among New Jersey charter schools. The Classical Academy would, as I envisioned, assuredly become, in a relatively short period, one of the richest, most robustly financially endowed New Jersey charter schools, as well as sustaining its status as one of the state's highest academically performing public schools. Quite a happy prospect to contemplate for a school whose revenues in its first year were so depleted that it could not pay teacher salaries and its two co-founders functioning as teacher-administrators worked without compensation so that the school might survive its difficult birth year.

I arranged for an architect to assess my intentions. We spoke about how the building could be enlarged with "wings" and the comparative merits and cost differentials of constructing an additional, free-standing small classroom building, thus producing a two-building educational complex. Providentially, a property adjacent to the school had been recently placed on the "for sale" market. I spoke with the owner, informing him that the school was interested in the property. The increasing of school grounds after the home was demolished would give the school more expansion options in design and construction.

Of course, nothing could earnestly begin, no real progress made, no financial commitments transacted, without the New Jersey Department of Education first approving our grade-expansion plans. Our 1997 charter approval granted permission for grades 6-12, not 4-8, so a "charter amendment" would need to be filed and state approved. I often mentally conceived of a solid and rather convincing case to the New Jersey Department of Education why it should approve the Classical Academy's 80-student enrollment increase and adding 4th and 5th grades.

Knowing that Clifton would aggressively oppose any Classical Academy expansion, my advocacy, as I pondered it, would compellingly be based on these points: 1) the school's renowned program of studies for which it had earned national acclaim and state recognition for educational excellence; its consistent record of high student-learning outcomes as demonstrated on state assessments and by other quantifiable metrics of achievement; and by the wide margins Classical Academy students outperform their Clifton district peers in learning outcomes; 2) soundness of Classical Academy's finances and ability to pay for expansion project costs; 3) school expansion would be a demonstrative public good, as it expands educational choice and realizes large educational benefits to students, community, and to the

Classical Academy itself; 4) grade and school expansion would respond to high demand for Classical Academy attendance; 5) increasing opportunity for more Clifton youth to reap the acknowledged superior learning outcomes of a multi-award-winning, academics-first school; 6) expansion would have negligible adverse financial impact on Clifton schools; 7) expansion to be a school of grades 4-8, would allow the Classical Academy to join the great majority of New Jersey charter schools having this grade/school configuration. I would array other elements and points imparting still greater persuasion to my case such that if denial was the outcome, the reason(s) should be known and further adjudicated. Notably, even with this projected student expansion yielding a total 200 student body, the Classical Academy would still be one of the smallest New Jersey charter schools in one of the state's largest public-school districts.

Leaving the precise 4th and 5th grade curricula to others more versed in the education of this age group, I envisioned, and would insist, that 30%-40% of the school day be devoted to mathematics, 30%-40% to English language arts, and 20%-40% to enrichment studies and activities—art, physical education, geography, history, and other such disciplines, including suitable time for extracurricular pursuits during the day. With this rigorous two-year pre-middle-school education concentrating on mathematics and English literacy, Classical Academy students entering its 6th grade would be extraordinarily better prepared educationally than the typical student now entering 6th grade and would require less remediation. Upon completion, this grade-expansion project would guarantee that the Classical Academy continue to maintain far into the future its high student-learning proficiencies and even to augment them.

It was my intention during the summer (2015) to write, along with the required "Annual Report," a full charter-amendment application advancing the Classical Academy's case for increased enrollment by the addition of a 4th and a 5th grade. I anticipated the New Jersey Department of Education to take six to eight months on evaluating and rendering a verdict regarding my school- and grade-expansion application. If the state approved the addition of the 4th and 5th grades, financing and renovations on the building and grounds would begin during the summer of

2016, a few months before my and Mrs. DeRosa's scheduled retirement. After having thus made some early strides toward the school-expansion goal, I intended to join the Board of Trustees as a voting or non-voting member and work without compensation in retirement to spearhead, along with a few interested Board members, the project and see it through completion. For me and Magda, entering our last year at the school we had founded 17 years earlier, and foreseeing an even more glorious future for the Classical Academy, all things shone bright and expectant.

Treachery and the Enemy of Charter Schools Invade the Classical Academy

Alas, all this was not to be; my vision for the school's ultimate development of a Classical Academy campus enrolling 200 students in grades 4-8, and my final endeavor to perpetuate Classical Academy financial security and student-learning excellence was aborted in the harshest way conceivable. In mid-May, 2015, I received an email from the New Jersey Department of Education and the state Office of Ethics and Disputes, affirming that I was in violation of state law by not posting notices in various conspicuous areas of the school that the Classical Academy faculty, by vote of that faculty, was now a collective-bargaining unit of the New Jersey Education Association, the teachers' labor union.

Perplexed and bewildered, believing the message was mis-sent and meant for another school, I made several phone calls to state offices. From them I learned, to my horror and disgust, that Classical Academy teachers and staff had, by secret vote, welcomed into the midst of one of the most iconoclastic and highest-achieving charter schools, whose academics-first policies and practices were possible only because of teachers-union absence, the most vicious and vehement hater of charter schools, the NJEA (New Jersey Education Association, the state's largest teacher union).

Not only had Classical Academy teachers welcomed the detested enemy into the school, but they did so with the rankest conspiratorial secrecy. This "sworn secrecy" was demanded by the two teachers leading the conspiracy and, no doubt, by their union overlords. These teacher conspirators proclaimed forcefully to their colleagues that, if I knew about this effort at unionization and about the pending union vote, I would take opposing action or even retribution. Of course, I knew well that the laws of unionization are strict against any retaliation or hindrance of unionizing efforts, both for private and public employers and management. Never would I have acted in what would be unethical or criminal behavior leading to judicial consequences of one kind or another against me or the school.

Offering counterarguments against pending unionization is, however, well within the rights of management of any organization, rights which I was never afforded. In fact, unionization efforts without management knowing about them is rare and rather unprecedented. The true reason for absolute secrecy, maliciously concealed to their teacher colleagues, was the union leaders' fear that I would, before any union vote took place, offer, as was my acknowledged right, moving, persuasive reasons against the unionization of our teachers and staff. Secrecy denied me, as it was intended, any opportunity to convince teachers with passion and reason of the incompatibility of teacher unionization with successful Classical Academy policies and practices, while jeopardizing continued educational excellence. Unionization meant there would be innumerable, minute contract rules and stipulations, and a strict demarcation between teachers and administration, creating a work ethos quite different and anathema to the Classical Academy's informal, amiable, and collegial relations between management and teachers.

Without the perfidious tactic of secrecy, the union conspiracy leaders no doubt trembled at the prospect that I would underscore to teachers and staff that only a handful of the state's larger charter schools are teacher unionized, and that no outstanding charter school, no National Blue Ribbon School of Excellence, no highly successful New Jersey charter school is counted among them. I would highlight to Classical Academy teachers how the drastic step of teacher unionism militated against their best interests professionally and would degrade their collegial working environment. I would reveal why those few teachers most ardently advocating teacher unionism were not motivated by any true benefit to the school or to their colleagues' professional welfare, but rather animated by their vindictive animus directed against me, and against whom unionism is their weapon of attack. I would further argue that unionization may well weaken and damage the school and undermine the very attributes that made the Classical Academy unique by their own contributions of dedication and talent, an institution of distinct excellence and high standing. Such arguments might dissuade enough doubting employees from voting "Yes" on the proposed unionization vote, or possibly defect in large-enough numbers that a vote would not even occur. But I was never accorded the opportunity given to every organization whose workers were in the process of unionization, to counter fairly unionism or pending union vote with opposing arguments, facts, persuasion, and sentiments. The denial to me of such opportunity, indeed the contrived and deliberate silencing of my voice, was the true goal and purpose of enforced secrecy.

The prime conspirators for teacher unionism feared, too, that if I knew of their efforts, I would address any problems and alleged grievances, if any existed, to the satisfaction of teachers and staff who were only mildly inclined to follow the leading embittered agitators. But the conspiracy leaders' greatest fear was that I, with Board approval, in order to prevent the enemy of charter schools to have a presence in the Classical Academy, would re-open settled contracts and grant immediate higher-percentage salary increases to all employees, an action I would have certainly and instantly initiated, thus eliminating any and all possible monetary incentive to unionize, and, incidentally, save teachers from paying $1,000 in yearly union dues. In sum, if I had any opportunity of pleading my case against teacher unionism or satisfying whatever dissatisfaction teachers harbored, the conspiracy leaders feared their zeal to wreak vengeance upon me for their own personal gratification by unionizing Classical Academy teachers and staff would fail. So, keeping me and all others who might divulge their devilish machinations to me ignorant of their efforts was imperative to the success of their nefarious plot.

I soon learned that the unionization vote had taken place in April 2015. Owing to an error by the union, I received all the actual signed voter cards on which each teacher in favor of the union signed. Of the 12 eligible teachers and staff, 9 voted "Yes," and 3 voted "No." Included in the "Yes" vote was a teacher who was retiring in two months, and another whose non-tenured contract I did not renew for the next school year due to ongoing failures to follow instructional recommendations and a patently unenthusiastic attitude for the job. By law, however, these soon-to-be former employee votes for unionization were valid and had a legal say in entrenching the teacher union in the Classical Academy for perhaps years to come.

Most of the teachers at this time had been Classical Academy employees for five to ten years, and some longer than a decade. As mentioned earlier, we had relatively little teacher turnover, which in itself indicates a certain satisfaction with their employment. Mrs. DeRosa and I provided every amenity and workplace satisfaction to our employees as possible, even when it meant our own inconvenience or hardship. We treated employees respectfully and amiably; we were always receptive to their problems at work. Under our leadership, employees never hesitated to voice their concerns, suggestions, or proposed solutions, whether in after-school teacher meetings or privately. Teacher workplace issues, and even problems of a personal nature, we strove to address, if not satisfy whenever feasible.

One issue which teachers had understandably complained about in recent years was that, by state law, not school policy, teacher "bonuses" or "performance pay stipends" could not be counted as "salary" for retirement-pension contributions. To deal with this unfair state practice, I had devised an accounting scheme by which teacher bonuses based on student standardized-test performance, which was a Classical Academy-endorsed concept and long a Classical Academy practice for overall teacher compensation, could be included in teacher pension contributions. The school would include, as I intended, in teachers' regular pay, the anticipated maximum earned bonus amount of $6,000. For example, a teacher salary of $40,000 would be stated in the contract as $46,000. If, in the unlikely event a teacher did not earn the maximum bonus based on comparative student standardized-tests outcomes, that unearned portion of the total salary bonus would be subtracted from next year's salary-contract calculation. In this way, salary bonuses based on student standardized-test comparative performance would be counted for each teacher's yearly pension calculations. I was about to broach this plan to teachers just as I learned of their unionization. No longer believing the plan relevant to the circumstances, I never brought it before teachers for their opinion.

Still, given the way the school was operated in an amiable, open, and compassionate work environment, where free-exchange of opinions and problems was the appreciated rule, a system very much non-bureaucratic or hierarchical in structure, I was perplexed why the majority of teachers voted for unionization. If salary levels were a major source of dissatisfaction, I would, without hesitation, have increased salaries, even substantially, for the specter of unionization, had I been aware of its looming presence, would have spurred my eagerness to satisfy teachers fully in this regard. Ironically, as it relates to increasing teacher salaries because of the threat of unionism, the demanded secrecy of unionization efforts actually was counterproductive and worked to teachers' disadvantage.

But what workplace indignities or tyrannical victimization did our teachers believe they suffered or endured to justify the extreme measure of teacher unionism? Apart from the two spitefully motivated union agitators, I struggled to supply a reason, rational or irrational, for the inexplicable action of the majority of our teachers consenting to unionism, and even more, to do so in such an underhanded, concealed, and conspiratorially secret way.

A portion of our teachers socialized with each other outside of school. Among our employees, especially as many were long-serving teachers and staff, personal friendships formed over a number of years. This feeling of fraternity worked to the benefit of the two conspiratorial leaders. Even if the majority of teachers and staff may have been cool to the idea of unionization and not convinced of the value or benefit in it, the personal feeling of friendship and camaraderie among employees overrode hesitation, doubts, or disagreement. To some, fraternity and solidarity with friends and professional colleagues were more important than speculating about theoretical and possible deleterious consequences teacher unionization would inflict on school operations, on the school's worthwhile policies and practices, on workplace collegiality, and ultimately on student-learning outcomes. By cunning calculation and design, exploiting the strength of friendship and personal feelings, the secrecy demanded by the union conspiracy leaders and imposed on all employees before the unionization vote insured teachers would never hear anti-unionization arguments. Secrecy also precluded me from taking any mediation action, such as increasing salaries, which would dissuade teachers from voting for union membership and show them that unionization was not in their professional interests.

From the time when I became aware of the unionization vote, to my retirement 15 months later, I never assembled teachers to discuss their vote or to probe them on why they felt it necessary to proceed with this drastic course and to do so secretly. Nor did I ever question teachers singly about their motivation for voting to unionize or about what enhancements to their employment and work satisfactions which they did not already enjoy, they believed would now accrue to them by their action. I did not inquire into what festering, unresolved grievances, if any, they believed themselves to have endured and which, by not first affording me the opportunity to redress or solve, union membership would heal. At scheduled teachers' meetings, the unionization vote or the progress of collective bargaining negotiations was never a topic I broached or about which I sought more details—or even evinced an interest. What was done treacherously, conspiratorially, and furtively was final, and no amount of belated intervention or discussion could now, in my eyes, excuse or exonerate the faculty from such disloyalty, or dissolve or postpone the reality of Classical Academy teacher/staff NJEA unionization.

Understandably, I felt disdain for the two vindictive teachers who, nursing their own personal grievances against me, aggressively and malevolently advocated teacher unionization amongst their blind colleagues, but I lost respect and collegial affinity for all Classical Academy teachers, even the three who did not vote for union membership. By obeying the enforced secrecy demanded by the leading zealots, as they all compliantly did, all participated in the malicious conspiracy; all delivered the proverbial *"et tu, Brute?"* stab in the back, and all jeopardized the Classical Academy's future.

Some information about the agitation for teachers-union affiliation was provided to me, unsolicited. The two leading conspirators were long-time teacher employees in their 60s; one was an habitually embittered, disgruntled employee, and the other had become such more recently. In my experience in interacting with them both, each proved by their actions to possess ingrained vindictive natures, such that if they believed themselves wronged or treated unfairly, they would strike back in some maliciously deceitful, spiteful way. The one had a long employment history of poor judgment, intemperate actions, authority issues, and anger-management problems. Conflict with students, parents, and school management were common during her long Classical Academy employment, to whose infractions and censorious conduct I was compelled to respond with informal "advisories" and occasionally with formal administrative reprimands. Her enmity toward me grew more virulent with each reprimand or each administrative decision, however-much justified and well grounded, that displeased her.

The other conspiratorial leader felt aggrieved for certain decisions I made for the manifest good of the school, decisions touching her employment in ways she believed, incorrectly, to be attacks on her, but which I justified in writing with impartial, cogent points and sound pedagogic reasoning. One source of her grievance emanated from my cancelation of a traditional school trip which she led. Despite my expressed concerns for several years, she did not use the week or two of class time before the trip, as was customary, to establish with students the required pre-trip instructional foundation. It was not established because, as I protested for the last several years, the teacher chose to use the allotted one or two-week pre-trip classroom instruction in "local history" for other topics. Without the historic knowledge and preparatory information of the destination, the purpose of the trip would lose much of its intended instructional value.

She was aggrieved also because I felt it more important for our 8th-grade students, 80%-90% of who were children of immigrant parents, to learn more American history rather than the names of 15th-century Chinese Emperors or the attributes of Hindu deities. Equally important in my decision to replace a course this teacher taught with another more educationally relevant and profitable course, was that the unused textbooks and materials we had in storage for post-Civil War American history provided far better reading and writing PARCC-test English language-literacy preparation than the textbook materials used in the current 8th-grade course. My reasoning was amply justified when, one year after the third-year of 8th-grade American history was instituted, the percentage of our 8th-grade students earning English language-arts literacy "Level 5-Exceeding Expectations" (Advanced Proficiency) on the PARCC tests more than doubled, from 21% "Level-5" achievement on PARCC 2015, to 49% "Level 5-Exceeding Expectations" ("Advanced Proficiency") on PARCC 2016, thus proving the wisdom of my decision.

The natures of both these malcontented persons had quite similar and equally repugnant inclinations. Because of my actions and decisions, however appropriate and sound, involving them separately, I became to both a mutual and unsuspecting target against whom to satiate their own irrational grievances and to collaborate in spewing their venomous animosities.

I smiled when I recalled that, some years earlier, the one teacher of this pair complained to me privately that, since the other taught a subject not tested on the state standardized tests, that teacher should not be eligible for teacher-salary bonuses based on student-performance outcomes—that she was, therefore, getting "a free ride." This "free rider" person once came to me to complain that the other was severely berating and insulting another teacher in the teachers' room and to insist that yelling at a colleague is both unprofessional and illustrative of an anger-management syndrome. But now both were bound in common cause to inflict their combined vindictiveness upon me, and the best vehicle for their malignant, spiteful poison was, as they came to believe, teacher unionization. Both rabidly encouraged Classical Academy employees, blind to their true purpose, to become complicit in their malice by voting "Yes" on the union question and becoming members of the NJEA (New Jersey Education Association).

After learning of the dates of the unionization vote, I recalled that some weeks earlier, close to the time of the union vote, a young teacher new to the school became so distraught and upset before homeroom that she was unable to attend her first-period class. She remained in the nurse's room, being soothed and calmed by the nurse. At the end of the day, Mrs. DeRosa and I questioned her about the cause of her distress. She claimed that, while in the teachers' room before homeroom, a teacher (one of the union conspiracy leaders) was being "negative" about all things regarding the school, none with which this young teacher concurred. She recited the angry teacher's statements and allegations degrading both the school and its management, all pointing, according to this young victimized teacher, to a person deeply unhappy with one's circumstances. During this beratement, the young teacher finally became emotionally upset to the point of incapacity when the disgruntled teacher, as this teacher testified, referred to me and my wife as "crooks." Although the sensitive young teacher denied it, I believe this episode was pressure applied to overcome her reluctance to sign "Yes" on the union vote card, which she ultimately did.

All during my last year as Classical Academy Lead Person/Principal, simmering just below the surface was the disaffection and ill-feeling I felt for all teachers and staff, both for what they did but especially the maliciously deceptive way they did it. Since I worked both as school leader and fellow teacher with most of them for a number of years, I understandably felt betrayed. I confined this alienation and sense of undeserved betrayal within myself, and guarded against it surfacing or manifesting in any of my daily responsibilities and teacher interactions as Principal. I continued to operate the school and engage with teachers in the normal course of our mutual responsibilities; I even performed my teacher classroom evaluations. Nevertheless, the collegial, cordial, family-like work environment, long a Classical Academy feature, had dissipated into a cool, stiff institutional "matter-of-fact" atmosphere.

In late May 2015, I notified my recently hired successor that Classical Academy teachers had unionized, assuring her it was a situation about which I knew nothing when we were interviewing candidates for my position. She appeared quite unfazed by the news, leading me to surmise she knew little about teacher unions or their hatred for charter schools, or what troubling changes teacher unionism may inflict upon the school. I confessed to her that I was most uncertain what the future would bring to the school under these unforeseen and unprecedented circumstances. I mentioned to her that, because of such threats to the school, I may not retire and that the position for which she was hired may soon no longer exist, and her employment would be terminated according to contractual terms. However, waiting to see how matters would unfold, we deemed it best for the present to proceed with her initial contract amidst much uncertainty, and to do so as if teacher unionization had never happened.

The process of my successor's Classical Academy acclimation commenced on July 1, 2015, as planned. I began to mentor her by assigning my successor some administrative tasks which I or Mrs. DeRosa oversaw for a position which may not become permanent if I decided not to retire. In the latter eventuality, there would be few duties she could perform, certainly not enough to justify a full-time administrator's position and expenditure. If I rescinded my retirement intentions, I probably would recommend she not remain beyond this her initial year. The thought that my hired successor could replace Magda was never considered, since my wife would never consent to her own retirement while I remained at the Classical Academy—always having my welfare her major preoccupation, my wife would be adamant that I not work in an increasingly acrimonious workplace among employees who proved themselves untrustworthy without her able assistance and protection ready at hand when and if needed.

I had known of teacher unionization for less than two months when, toward the end of June 2015, we participated in our traditional end-of-year events: school outing and picnic to Lake Tomahawk, 8th-grade evening graduation ceremony, the 6th- and 7th-grade awards and raffle festivities. I did not feel the accustomed joy these events had always elicited, but I was determined that the troubling events at school would not affect my and my wife's long-planned three-week August trip to Rome, Italy, and our Mediterranean cruise. That summer (2015), before our trip, I executed my usual duties of completing the state-required charter-school "Annual Report," evaluating student test outcomes from the previous spring's state-mandated standardized assessments, and all other preparatory tasks for the new school year. While on our three-week Italian trip, I occasionally thought of the crisis at school but was largely able to bury the unpleasantness as I and my wife enjoyed immensely a vacation of a lifetime.

Since learning in mid-May 2015, that teachers had unionized, and the untoward consequences which would surely affect the direction of the school's future, I initiated nothing to realize my Classical Academy expansion vision. Adding grades 4 and 5, increasing total student enrollment to 200, expanding the building or constructing an additional small classroom building on school grounds, and transforming the school into the Classical Academy campus, was my grand hope and expectation as I began the concluding phase of Classical Academy leadership. However, by the beginning of the school year (2015-2016), in view of the upheaval and uncertainty teacher unionism presented, my vision of school expansion retreated from my immediate concerns.

As the 2015-2016 school year progressed and amidst the growing antagonistic uncertainties infecting the school, school expansion became an ever-diminishing goal for which I took no action to achieve. Indeed, grade and facility expansion became a suppressed ambition gradually losing all motivating force and prominence in my mind. Although blessed to have every one of my grandest dreams become reality, in this one ambition, deflated of drive and seized by a demoralizing morass, I was destined to be unfulfilled, obstructed by malicious vindictiveness in the guise of teacher unionism. Yet in wistful moments I could not but imagine that if my expansion plan, for which I had long prepared by accumulating sufficient finances and by earning superlative institutional reputation, were initiated and completed after several years, it would have been my final triumph as Classical Academy founder and long-time Lead Teacher/Principal. More important, the benefits to the school, students, teachers, and community would have been inestimable. But all came to naught. Evil forces vanquished this most glorious Classical Academy future.

Exclusion from Collective Bargaining Labor Negotiations

Responding to the more immediate traumatic events afflicting the school, I, with Board approval, selected, in the summer of 2015, an attorney experienced in public-sector union matters to assist the school with "negotiations" between the Board of Trustees and the "Classical Academy Education Association" (the school's newly minted teachers-union affiliate). As is common with traditional teacher labor negotiations, the school administration plays no visible role or part. However, following the precedent of Lead Persons of other unionized charter schools, I requested the school's governing body involve me in the recently commenced (late fall of 2015) labor negotiations in a non-voting advisory capacity. Surely, I would be an asset in these matters, for who knew more about the school than I, who could provide more valuable insights and advice in evaluating the union's many demands and their impact on school operations and outcomes than I, and who knew better the school's policies and practices than their very author.

Caring more about possible objections from teachers leading their side's negotiations, and complying with the school attorney's advice, the Board of Trustees chose to exclude me from taking any role in this new, threatening phase of Classical Academy history, or from contributing my views, insights, or suggestions in this critical matter of labor negotiations for the school I had founded, nurtured, and operated for nearly 18 years.

Amidst the destructive forces infecting the school and jeopardizing its future greatness, I dedicated myself instead of Classical Academy expansion to preserving as best I could the school's proven policies and practices, and the philosophy of education animating them. I feared that the demands of teacher unionism would chip away at the noble edifice of school effectiveness and excellence I had created, and render it all a mediocrity. I implored the Board of Trustees as it responded without my direct or welcome input to the recently transmitted "Classical Academy Education Association Collective Bargaining Proposals," and the school changes those proposals threatened, not to vitiate or weaken our long-existing policies and practices responsible for transforming the smallest and least-funded public school into one of New Jersey highest-performing schools.

There was, too, this unspoken but barely hidden Board of Trustees assumption that I was the cause for such apparent teacher dissatisfaction; that my leadership style and decisions had alienated teachers and caused workplace hostility. After all, why would teachers seek refuge and protection in unionism? What were the reasons for their actions and rebelliousness, were it not for my leadership arrogance and tyranny? This assumption was reinforced with comments and complaints to Board officials by those most responsible—and most vindictive—for inciting dissension and bringing teacher unionism to the school.

Still, one might well reason, if I were the cause of teacher woes, unhappiness, and dissatisfaction, why not simply endure the short time of my waning leadership and forestall or eliminate any thought of unionization? Unless, of course, the true reason was that those several teachers most seeking to injure me through teacher unionism and reputational degradation needed to do so before I retired, after which time it would be impossible for them to inflict the sort of malicious injury their vindictive anger craved (remember, the union vote occurred three months *after* I announced my retirement to the faculty).

Having returned in early September from our Italian sojourn, I was determined during my last year, 2015-2016, to fulfill all my duties and responsibilities as school leader, however downtrodden I might be. My task of preparing as best as possible our students for this year's standardized tests in the spring of 2016 was always a prime obligation. To initiate my vision of school expansion, however, was simply impossible in my forlorn and wounded state, feeling betrayed and victimized, such that I lost all motivation to effectuate this grand design. In this, at least, my foes—several embittered, vindictive teachers; NEJA (teacher union); potentially destructive, union-demanded changes in critical school policies and practices; unsupportive, belligerent Board members—won the day. Besides, Board members were completely disinterested in the project, salivating instead in increasing their governing power and in what changes they could bring to the school without my "interference." I feared most how the Board's dubious aspirations and its thoughtless willingness to accede to union demands would jeopardize the school's remarkable achievements.

Around the beginning of the calendar year (January, February 2016), teachers leading the union side were frustrated that collective-bargaining negotiations had not begun in earnest. Several members of the Board of Trustees organized as a "Board negotiations committee," which included the school attorney hired to deal with these negotiations, the Board president, and the part-time off-site school business administrator. The latter person, despite my recommendation that she be dismissed, if not as soon as possible, certainly by the time the new Lead Person replaces me, in recent months became a trusted ally of Board of Trustee leadership. In the fall of 2015 and early winter of 2016, several collective-bargaining meetings between teacher negotiators and the Board were held, but, in effect, no progress was advanced, and future negotiations were postponed indefinitely, for which teachers blamed the Classical Academy's Board of Trustees and, undoubtedly in their frustration, probably me, who had no involvement in the matter whatsoever.

Letters Reeking with False Accusations and Libelous Slander

About this time, two accusatory letters from two teachers were sent to the Board of Trustees President in December (2015) and January (2016), but this Board officer failed to notify me or supply me with copies until, with the permission of the Board attorney, late March 2016. One letter was anonymous (but it was easy to conclude who was the author), and the second letter was signed and, like the first letter, was from the other leader of the union conspiracy. Both letters contained maliciously gross, slanderous lies about me, my character, my leadership, and the integrity of some of my decisions. I refrain from according these foul slanders any semblance of truth by cataloging or providing here full details of their fraudulent, vitriolic nature.

However, by way of brief example, one typical lie accused me of changing a first-year teacher's contract willfully, and tyrannically making the employee ineligible for part of his teacher-salary bonus. His contract stipulated a half-salary bonus based on school-mandated standardized exams in his subject field, and half for the PARCC's 8th-grade English language arts literacy outcomes. As with all teachers of subjects not tested on state assessments, it was mandated by school policy and employee contract that he was to create ongoing special lessons related to his subject but emphasizing English language arts. By so doing he, like several other teachers of subjects not tested on state-mandated assessments, would be eligible for that portion of the salary bonus based on 8th-grade student English language arts-test outcomes. This was in keeping with our long practice of developing English-language skills in all non-mathematics subjects and in subjects not tested on the state-mandated tests.

In truth, this employee, new to teaching and all the challenges associated with the work, was, during his first year at the school, also preparing and sitting for his PhD-degree exams while simultaneously taking courses and satisfying requirements as a provisional teacher for the Alternate Route to Certification program. He was also struggling with classroom-control problems. When I realized this new employee was being confronted with such overwhelming challenges, I, with his understanding, removed the English language arts lesson-creation obligation as a dispensable burden so he could better concentrate on meeting his other, quite-challenging demands for his PhD-degree and teacher-certification requirements, and apply himself to improving classroom conduct. To be fair to other teachers, by removing the additional English language class-lesson preparation work the salary bonus required, he would be, as I informed him, ineligible for the English language arts portion of student-performance salary bonus. He thanked me for my concern and understanding, and appeared most relieved by my action. Far from mistreating an employee with indiscriminate, unilateral contract manipulation, as the slanderous letter asserted, I was demonstrating the actions of reasonable, compassionate, and judicious school leadership by responding empathetically to a teacher's conspicuous professional and personal difficulties.

Another blatant lie alleged that I had intimidated two recently hired teachers by suggesting to them that their new employment would not be pleasant or go well for them if they joined the union. The fact is that, after these two persons were hired in summer 2015, I informed them in a joint meeting prior to the start of the school year of the newly installed teachers union. Contrary to the lies in the letter, I clearly told both these new teachers that they could decide to join the union or not to join, and that whatever decision they make, I did not want to know. However, if either of them chose not to join, and if they were strongly pressured or intimidated during their employment because of their refusal, an action prohibited by law, then please apprise me of this improper conduct. After that brief meeting with them at the beginning of the school year (September 2015), I never spoke to either of them about the union or their membership, and it was never a topic or as much as a fleeting comment from me to either of them during the entire school year. Yet this innocent and appropriate several-minute interchange was intentionally distorted to be an example, as the letter's author asserted, of my persistent teacher intimidation, arrogance, and threatening anti-union behavior.

Still another egregious lie was that I continued to harass a teacher named in the anonymous letter—the name of this teacher I know to be herself the author of the letter. This allegation is as preposterous as it is ironically absurd. The so-called "harassment" was nothing other than my necessary, reasonable, and evidence-based responses to many of this teacher's ill-considered, anger-fueled, intemperate acts relating to student discipline and school policy. Despite granting her many work concessions because of her physical limitations and other personal considerations, her animosity against me also originated from my refusal for the good of the school and its operational effectiveness to consent to certain other of her numerous requests and demands over the course of her long employment. Doing my job competently and fairly in issuing recommendations, well-founded decisions, and deserved reprimands was twisted in this person's mind into "harassment," which was as paranoid as it was ridiculously false.

Adding to the ironic absurdity of these accusations of "harassment," both authors of these scurrilous letters, on not one but several occasions in the past, had publicly berated me, shouted angrily in my face, and loudly insulted me in front of fellow teachers and even in the presence of parents. Their unprofessional, humiliating actions against me were worthy of serious censor as blatant ethical breaches, even to the point of administrative suspension, if I had pursued their unethical conduct fully. Assuredly, if I had committed similar verbal assaults against either of these teacher employees, I would have faced Broad of Trustees reprimands, if not lawsuits for workplace bullying, or for abusing my authority by creating a "hostile workplace" intended to injure emotionally a subordinate employee. However, the extent of my reaction to their grossly unprofessional conduct was meekly to write a letter documenting the incidents to each of them on each occasion and placing the letters in their personnel files. I did not even bring these hostile, unprofessional episodes to the Board's attention or attempt to use my authority as Chief School Administrator to redress my victimization and impose sanctions on the guilty parties. Weighing these documented, public verbal assaults against me, and my inconsequential reactions to them, I ask, who was harassing whom?

All other slanderous lies in both letters were of the sort just described: despicable distortions and outright falsehoods, all calculated to besmirch my character, reputation, and leadership abilities. Not satisfied with ushering into the Classical Academy the fiercest enemy of charter schools, not satisfied by attacking me with the secret union vote, the two writers of these letters, their vindictiveness not yet satiated, fantasied that, if my legacy, both professional and personal, could be tainted and sullied before retirement, all the sweeter would be their vengeance-fueled victory. In their twisted minds, this was the primary purpose of their scurrilous letters. A subsidiary purpose was, perhaps, the hope that members of the Board of Trustees would invest some credence in their hateful lies against me, or perhaps, by their perverted logic, quicken the pace of negotiations for a union contract with employees, negotiations in which I had no role whatsoever.

Board of Trustees Disaffection and Belligerence

Still-greater worries arose from what I was experiencing at Board meetings: an adversarial relation between me and Board members was emerging. At several Board of Trustees meetings in spring 2016, I detected alarming indications that the Board was regarding my views and suggestions in responding to the school's situation and its future with little attention and credibility, often rejecting my views or suggested courses of action as unwise or counterproductive, or merely ignoring my advice contemptuously. It was clear to me that the Board, ignoring my suggestions and authority, preferred to take advice and make decisions regarding unionization and its impact on school management from the Board attorney. At one Board meeting, when I brought up the vitriolic letters against me, which all Board members had read, the school attorney, who was now attending Board meetings, actually interrogated me about each point in the "anonymous" letter, as if I needed to defend myself and prove each slanderous point untrue. Even the part-time, off-site school business administrator, who should have been terminated long ago, was taking an active part as a non-voting Board member in school leadership and operations, and influencing fellow Board members with recommendations contrary to my own opinions while denigrating my authority and strategy preferences.

When the Board of Trustees president publicly affirmed that teacher unionism "might be a good thing for the school," having prohibited me from any part in union negotiations, relegating my authority and advice below that of the attorney and off-site business administrator, and against the malicious letter-writing employees insulting my character with lies and vitriol took no action despite my pleas, together with my announced retirement, were events and developments which forced my conclusion that nothing less than a revolt, quite unprovoked on my part, was taking place, first among teachers and now the Board of Trustees.

Certain Board members saw the school's situation—and what they perceived as my weakened leadership position—as an opportunity to assume dominant control, assert its ill-directed authority, and run the school according to its own ill-advised preferences. Not a few charter schools have failed because their Boards, composed of people quite inexperienced in education or management, superseded or ignored their schools' Lead Person's authority, policies, and recommendations. Without me at the school's leadership helm, the Board could also, as I believed it intended, influence, if not dominate, my neophyte, non-tenured successor. It could then shape and change the school in ways and directions more favorably with its own poorly conceived objectives, uninformed notions, and questionable aspirations for the school's future direction, and to do so wielding its benighted authority.

The horrible truth now terrifying me was that people who knew little and cared even less about the Classical Academy's history, its trials and tribulations, its philosophy of education—people who may disagree with certain critical policies and practices, and people who were not seasoned educators or who understood little of the NJEA's vehement anti-charter-school sentiments—would now, without my involvement, be in complete control of the school I had built and loved. Those now leading the Board not only would likely negotiate ill-advised agreements and school policies with the despised enemy of all charter schools, but pursuing their own poorly considered decisions, desires, and dubious intentions would blindly steer the school into a troubled future. Without my presence or input, which they eagerly anticipated as much as they scorned and belittled my advice, there was no obstacle or damage limitation to their dismantlement of the foundation for educational excellence I had built. I understandably agonized that their actions and decisions would instigate a steady, inexorable decline in all things which made the Classical Academy exceptional.

Board of Trustees Corrupt Election:

As a desperate hope to limit the damage of unionism and questionable Board of Trustees motives and objectives injurious to the school's future, and to retain a voice in Classical Academy matters even in retirement, I decided to put myself on the ballot for Board membership in the upcoming June 2016 Board of Trustee elections. One Board member's term was expiring who chose not to seek reelection, and the Board decided to increase its number from 5 to 7 voting members. As in all past Board elections, I supervised the process, approached parents about their interest in being Board members, and constructed the election ballots and voting procedures. Although employees of a school cannot serve on its Board, I stated clearly on the election ballot under my name that, if elected, I would not become a Board member until I had retired three months hence, and, therefore, would legally be eligible as a non-employee to serve on the school's governing body.

Anticipating opposition or arguments against my Board membership upon retirement as being disallowed by state law, I sought confirmation from the New Jersey Department of Disputes and Ethics regarding the election of a former school employee seeking Board membership in a governmental entity (public school) in which one was formerly employed. A month before the June 2016 Board election, I presented at the Board meeting the department's written response affirming that no "conflict of interest or ethical breach" would be activated as long as the former

Board-employed person seeking Board election otherwise complied with the Board's bylaws for election eligibility. My Board membership would, thus, present no violation or ethical problem after retirement.

The June 2016, ballot contained 6 names, including my candidacy, for 3 vacant Board seats. The instructions on the ballot stated that a parent-voter should vote "Yes" or "No" for each of the 6 candidates listed. The three candidates with most "Yes" votes would be duly elected. As with all charter-school Board elections, only parents of enrolled students could vote.

Customary at the Classical Academy, Board of Trustees' election ballots were either mailed to parents, or students could obtain a ballot from the school office or homeroom teacher to bring home. For confidentiality in voting, parents were instructed not to sign ballots. All returned ballots were to be placed in envelopes with the word "Ballot" written on the envelope and collected by homeroom teachers, who would then deliver the ballots to the school office. For greater voter convenience, parents could also mail or personally hand in a ballot to the office or entrust their student to do so. There was an unsecured cardboard box in the office marked "Ballots," into which the office secretary, teachers, or myself would place and accumulate the ballots until ready to be opened and counted on the designated date.

The election period was about three weeks, during which time ballots were returned and placed in the unsecured "Ballot Box" in the school office. Toward the end of this Board-election period, several parents informed me that certain teachers, the same individuals who had agitated for teacher unionism, were intimidating students with threats like: "If you want to have a good school year next year, be sure to tell your parents not to vote for Mr. DeRosa," and similar threatening statements of this kind.

When the ballots were about to be opened and counted in public session at the June 2016 Board meeting, which teachers-union leaders attended, the Board president announced that my candidacy, according to the lawyer, was invalid, as I was still on the school's payroll, and any votes for me must be discounted. The lawyer interjected that any votes for Mr. DeRosa, whose candidacy is null and void, may nevertheless merely be calculated. So, even if I received the most "Yes" votes, the Board of Trustees was obviously unwilling to accept me on the Board, even after my retirement.

If this Board were composed of right-thinking adults free from petty motivations, it would have invited—if not *beseeched*—me to become a fellow Board member, appreciating my experiences, knowledge, and judgment in creating such an outstanding school. A responsible, enlightened, rancor-free Board of Trustees concerned for the continued excellence, stability, and good management of the school, would see me as an invaluable Board asset, rather than an impediment to their own ambitions and ill-conceived intentions. Still, they had no worries, for among the six Board candidates, several of who were entirely unknown to most parents and voters, I received by far the fewest "Yes" votes, only 6 or 7 out of about 70 returned voted ballots.

How could this be? I knew most of the parent voters, and their conversations, comments, and interactions with me bespoke of earned respect and high estimation. How could they vote for relatively unknown persons instead of the school founder and the only Classical Academy school leader for the entire life of the school? As many knew, I was presently on the Board as its non-voting Board secretary, responsible for the agenda and Board minutes, and had been for 18 years. I also was the person whom they incessantly thanked for the school and were so grateful that the school I founded and operated had been there for their child. I was the person parent voters called upon to resolve issues between teachers and students; I was the school official parent voters relied upon to intervene when their child was having problems, academic or personal; I was the person parents relied upon to maintain a safe, learning-conducive school environment; I was the person they saw as most responsible for their child's school success.

With these facts in mind, how could my Board candidacy be endorsed by so few parent voters? The answer is both simple and obvious: In addition to teachers' voter-intimidation tactics, the election process was corrupted: the ballot box was undoubtedly stuffed with false votes by false voters. It was so easy for anyone so inclined to obtain a blank ballot, copy it, fill the copies with marked "No" votes for Mr. DeRosa and "Yes" votes for other Board candidates, and place them in the unguarded ballot box. And just as simple was it to remove voted ballots with my name marked for voter approval from the office ballot box, to which everyone had easy access, and replace them with fraudulent ballots with a "No" vote for me, indicating disapproval. Remember, voters were always directed not to sign ballots, so brazen, malicious manipulation of this sort would be very easy to perpetrate and impossible to discover. It also bespeaks the same kind of unethical conduct consistent with the union conspiracy and slanderous letters.

The Reconsideration of My Retirement: Offers of Fame and Riches

I resolved not to bring my strong suspicions regarding Board-election corruption to any higher authority, or to pursue any investigative process. But at the end of this Board meeting, expressing my frustration after most attendees had departed, I announced to several Board members that, because of the increasingly alarming situation at the school and the despicable way I was being treated, I may not retire in September 2016. For the sake of the school, and until the upheaval now raging within it subsides with the aid of my voice, I may be compelled to remain in my long-tenured position indefinitely.

Soon after my pronouncement that I was reconsidering my and Mrs. DeRosa's September 2016 retirement, certain Board members in different settings, alarmed that I would cancel my scheduled retirement, offered me two grand enticements to keep my original retirement date, enticements which they likely regarded as irresistible. The one incentive was that, upon my retirement, the Board would change the name of the school to: "The Vincent DeRosa Charter School of Clifton." Initially I was impressed, indeed, honored that this Board member was moved by my long and distinguished service to the school that she felt it fitting it bear my name forevermore. But I quickly deduced, especially as it had been offered by a Board member who displayed open disdain for me, my opinions, and my situation, that it had nothing to do with honoring me or respect for my notable achievements as an educator and school founder. It was instead a crass, deceptive inducement to sway me from remaining at the Classical Academy beyond September 2016.

The other incentive not to rescind my approaching retirement was made by the Board president and the part-time, off-site school business administrator. These two public servants offered me and Mrs. DeRosa a combined "severance bonus" of $250,000. Though persons of lesser pride and dignity might regard such payment "due compensation" for "pain and suffering" ruthlessly inflicted upon us during our last year of employment, nevertheless, without a moment's delay or regret, I and Mrs. DeRosa scornfully rejected both offers.

I could only think how I and my wife strove for years, shouldering hardships and undertaking manifold work burdens, to save school money and practice circumspection and frugality in dispensing school funds, all to make the school financially stable and secure. That these two school functionaries were now willing to spend such a great sum in such an indiscriminate and foolhardy way only reinforced my notion of how greatly they desired my departure in order to have a free hand in managing school affairs themselves, while taking advantage of the willing compliance of an unexperienced, tentative, and malleable new Lead Person. It also reinforced my doubts of the Board's integrity and competence, and increased my trepidation about future profligate school-spending habits. Doubtful I was also that this governing Board and the new school leadership would pursue sound management and fiscal practices; nor was I hopeful that they would make, under the pressure of collective-bargaining demands, the kind of decisions and pursue actions which would sustain the school's distinctive policies and practices, while perpetuating its distinguished record of high student academic achievement.

My and my wife's 12-month employment contract always began July 1 of each year. To be consistent with our announced and still declared retirement date, we signed a three-month contract for July, August, and September, with our formal cessation of Classical Academy employment dated October 1, 2016. From that three-month contract, we could unilaterally withdraw, if we determined it necessary, and, as tenured employees, demand retention of our positions and sign a 12-month employment contract, should we rescind retirement intentions. As the Board agreed, we would work July and August, and take our paid three-week vacation not in

August as usual, but in September, directly after which our still-scheduled but increasingly doubtful retirement would commence.

Upon signing our three-month employment contract, the Board of Trustees attorney presented me and Mrs. DeRosa with an "End-of-Service or Severance Agreement." To "make things legal," this person suggested I have an attorney review it with me, at my cost, before we affixed our signatures. The document contained language and stipulations common to such agreements, and I saw nothing in them to which I or my wife objected. However, I wanted to specify clearly some aspects of any future role or privileges I may enjoy upon my pending retirement date and to which my status as school founder and long-serving Lead Person I believed entitled me.

After devoting nearly 20 years of my life to the Classical Academy, I had always expected that, upon my departure from the school, I would be passively involved in an "ex-officio," "emeritus," or, deservedly, an "esteemed adviser" capacity. I thus requested our attorney to affix these few innocuous, but to me and Mrs. DeRosa, meaningful stipulations as an addendum to the severance agreement. These stipulations included: 1) I could use and have access to school records and archives (nearly all of which were my own productions) for purposes of research and writing; 2) Mrs. DeRosa and I could attend school functions and events as we pleased, such as the 8th-grade graduation, the Lake Tomahawk Picnic, Awards Ceremony and Raffle; 3) that after my retirement, the Board of Trustees consider by majority vote my appointment to the Board as a voting or non-voting member, consistent with the Board's Bylaws.

I soon learned through our attorney that the Board of Trustees did not agree to include any of these inconsequential, minor privileges to the severance agreement. Although our attorney was befuddled as to the rejection of so innocuous but deserving stipulations, he did not know, as I certainly did, that the rejection was yet another blatant instance where this Board of Trustees, at least those most actively in control, adamantly intended to eliminate forever my post-retirement connection and my voice, however small it be, to the school I founded. Because the Board did not consent to these reasonable stipulations, neither I nor Magda signed the "severance agreement."

Considerations for Withdrawing Our Retirement

It was at this point, end of July 2016, that I concluded that, if I retired from the school as scheduled, I and my co-founder wife, who was instrumental to the school's success, would be forevermore excluded from any involvement in school affairs or even school events; never would we be afforded even a minor voice in the school we had created and guided to national and state distinction, except as ordinary public observers. On the other hand, by canceling my retirement and continuing to hold my Lead Person/Principal position, I could remain on the battlefield to combat all the destructive forces—teacher unionization, hostile, ill-motivated Board members, and several maliciously vindictive teachers—afflicting the school, and save it from what I believed to be its eventual decline caused by the weakening, if not abandonment, of those policies and practices that made the school a resounding success, academically and financially.

By not retiring and retaining my position of school leadership, I doubtless would hire an attorney to bring a private, financial-compensation litigation of libel against the two teachers who willfully injured me personally by conveying to our mutual employer, the Board of Trustees, malignant and defamatory lies and slanderous claims they knew to be false. As Chief School Administrator, I could not act in that capacity to address these slanders and libels, as I was myself the object of my accusers' viciousness and party to the matter. I speculated on suing the Board of Trustees as well, since, as my employer, it took no action against the vitriolic abuse of which I was victim but allowed, even *encouraged*, its continuance and thereby willingly fostered a hostile and persecutorial work environment in which I was victimized. Supporting my litigation against the two malicious teachers, abundant and incontrovertible evidence, proving my claims of deliberate slander and libelous accusations calculated to tarnish my reputation to the point of humiliation and dishonor, could easily be gathered through personal testimonies and documents, if I remained as Lead Person/Principal.

By rescinding my retirement, I could also demand a greater voice in collective-bargaining negotiations and, as far as my authority permitted, suggest modifications or counterproposals to the union's demands. A number of these demands, if fully granted, would inevitably weaken the school and bring about changes which could only lead to school detriment and decline, and recklessly complicate school operations. If I canceled my retirement, I could also be, or so I envisioned, an opposing or restraining presence to potentially injurious Board of Trustee decisions. I could be an influence in its deliberations in order to forestall or alter their actions which otherwise may prove detrimental to Classical Academy management and school performance generally.

During these days, I recollected that I had fought many "David and Goliath" battles to secure the Classical Academy against powerful foes who sought to injure it, hoping for its ultimate demise. In surmounting these battles, I and my wife succeeded in transforming the Classical Academy into one of the most outstanding public middle schools in New Jersey. Although the enemy in this struggle was within the school, not external foes, this would yet be another such battle, albeit I hoped my last, in which I would confidently and assuredly emerge victorious.

I foresaw that this struggle could take two or three years before prevailing, in which time the harmful aspects of teachers' collective-bargaining demands may be, with reason and compromise, somewhat blunted through the negotiations process and become assimilated into acceptable, unobtrusive school operations and accustomed practices. In that time period, any personal litigation against the two vindictive teachers for libel and defamation would be settled, almost certainly with an out-of-court financial settlement in my favor. Any litigation against the Board of Trustees for allowing workplace abuse and bullying to go unchecked, would likely also redound in my favor. In those two to three years, the composition of the Board of Trustees would be changed, welcoming less-disagreeable, more-reasonable parents as Board members, as we had in the past. After which time I, with the adverse consequences of teacher unionism mollified and least harmfully assimilated into school operations, could then retire, knowing the school was being well governed by retaining its traditional policies and practices, and that the school's recognized excellence would not be diminished, but sustained. I even toyed with the uplifting idea that I could, when the tumult had subsided, begin to undertake once again my dream of school expansion and creating a "Classical Academy Grades 4-8 Campus."

With some melancholy, I saw the painful irony that, in that very brief four-month period after announcing my retirement but before learning of the union conspiracy and vote, I was as exuberant with hope and expectation for my grand design and final triumph of creating a 200-student-body school, with grades 4-8 housed on a Classical Academy campus, as I was when, in January 1998, I had received notice that the state had approved the Classical Academy charter application. Now, as August 2016 approached, after more than a year of struggling against vindictive, malicious forces, being beaten down and hopes trodden upon, I needed to decide on my future course. I saw only two paths: stay and fight for what undoubtedly would be a full, victorious outcome, or quietly retreat from the field of battle, acknowledging defeat. In this, my wife was instrumental to my decision—my wife, without whom there would be no Classical Academy and whose constant support and loving counsel were in no small measure responsible for my strength and success.

Magda's Sage and Comforting Advice

Even prior to starting the Classical Academy, my wife, Magda, had been invariably at my side, giving support, encouragement, and wise counsel. She was with me every day for the last nearly 25 years, my constant, steadfast companion at work and at home. As I so often did with problems or decisions, or meditating what course of action I should pursue and why it was preferred, I turned to her to discuss the cancellation of our retirement, continuing to lead the school, and what I expected could be accomplished by so doing. I knew that if I did not retire, she, too, would certainly remain at the school, ever at my side; she would never consider for a moment that I engage in this struggle without her being with me at every step as both my counsel and my shield.

From our several, deeply personal discussions, I want to summarize to the reader in my own words what Magda's feelings and arguments were for keeping our retirement date, just two months hence. She impressed upon me that the malicious lies some vindictive, disgruntled teachers had proclaimed against me for their own wickedly spiteful purposes, were not truly believed by anyone. Through the years, the thousands of people—teachers, students, parents—who had come to know and respect me, would not and never would put any credence in the lies of these malicious slanderers. The phenomenal success, she reiterated, of the Classical Academy under my leadership; all the hard work I devoted to the school for nearly 20 years; the proven worth and fruitfulness of my ideas for education reform; my integrity, professionalism, and leadership abilities, are facts acknowledged by thousands over decades. There were so many grateful, admiring persons over many years who had witnessed and attested to my character, compassion, and competence, she said, qualities that no one, however malicious, can seriously impugn or refuse to admit without themselves being mocked as base liars.

She continued, saying that the solid educational foundation for academic success and personal advancement I had provided to nearly 600 Classical Academy graduates, most of whom were children of immigrant Americans, is a source of pride few can equal, and for which their families are eternally grateful, as so many have profusely expressed over the years.

We always realized, Magda reminded me, that, as a public institution, the Classical Academy is not our private business, despite investing the time, effort, ideas, and personal resources a dedicated private owner would devote to the success of one's enterprise. We always knew that whoever succeeded our leadership would not have the same emotional investment, not the same passionate commitment, not the same drive as we had as school founders. We endured the labor pains to bring forth the school, giving it birth and nourishing it during its troubled infancy. When attacked by hostile, ill-willed aggressors, we were the ones to protect it, and, when injured, struggle it back to health. For it we envisioned a brilliant future and worked diligently to have it reach its glorious destiny. Whoever follows us, Magda continued, would not have the same feelings, emotions, or motivations about the Classical Academy. In comparison to us, they would be mere employees, more interested in enhancing their own workplace amenities, reducing workload, and increasing compensation. New school leadership would not have the understanding or fortitude to withstand the worse impulses and poor decisions of a benighted Board of Trustees, nor the knowledge or motivation to advise the Board to adopt the wisest policies. We always knew this would be the case; now it was time to accept this reality. Of course, it is a shame we could not leave the school under more cordial, amiable, and hopeful circumstances, have our accomplishments celebrated openly and enthusiastically by the entire Classical Academy community, and enjoy a welcome involvement in future Classical Academy affairs, as we always had hoped and expected.

Magda asserted that I had accomplished so much, struggled successfully to attain my dream of running my own school, that I had a rare privilege very few teachers have ever possessed, and that no one can take from me the immeasurable satisfaction of seeing the undeniable worth of my sweeping education reforms yield equally astounding student-learning outcomes. Do you remember, Magda asked me, the desk plaque an 8th-grade student presented to you at our first 8th-grade graduation in June 2000, containing the well-known Caesarean quotation: *"Veni, vidi, vici"* ("I came, I saw, I conquered"). Well, that is exactly what you did! Let us now, after having achieved such remarkable accomplishments, begin the next phase of our lives, contented in the knowledge that we are blessed and will continue to be blessed with a life well spent.

She reminded me of her retirement gift to me, a glorious three-week fly-fishing adventure in Quebec, to one of North America's largest and most famous nature preserves, a trip for which I had long yearned and anticipated. Our September 2016 reservations for that trip would have to be canceled if I chose to rescind my retirement and remain Lead Person.

Pondering her words, and as I was beginning to be swayed by Magda's arguments, I thought also of her. That she was eagerly anticipating our mutual retirement was a sentiment she periodically over the last several years expressed to me, even before the tumult at the school had erupted. Of most concern, I was repulsed at the thought of her being in the midst of people who were hostile and creating an unfriendly, rancorous workplace atmosphere. Although our working life at the Classical Academy was replete with responsibilities and challenges demanding hard work, self-sacrifice, and dedication, it was also filled with jocularity, laughter, and fun which we shared and experienced each day together. I found it repugnant that if we remained, my wife and co-founder administrator would go to work every day in a contentious, acrimonious environment, among nasty people who disseminated vicious lies about me, and who conspired actively or passively by their silence to injure her husband and the school he loved, and by extension, injure her as well.

I thought, too, of our approaching charter renewal, to be granted in the spring of 2017 for the ensuing five years. Thankfully, the Office of Charter Schools no longer contained the same rule-bound, acerbic bureaucrats with whom I had contended, bent on punishing the Classical Academy, if not putting an end to it. Still, I could imagine the unfavorable impression conveyed to that office if, in the unsettled state of labor-contract negotiations of a newly teacher-unionized charter school, the Lead Person was suing for defamation and libel several teachers, and perhaps litigating against the Board of Trustees for not taking any action against his allegations of slander, workplace abuse, and wanton persecution. How would such bitter intramural school battles influence charter renewal, and how would ongoing litigation appear to bureaucrats who prize stability and predictability?

To charter-school renewal evaluators, such internal discord and internecine litigation would surely portray a school in utter tumult and disarray, and that the Classical Academy's governance was seriously, perhaps intractably disordered. I was concerned, too, about how the school's hard-won sterling reputation in the Clifton community would be tarnished if the school's upheavals and intramural antagonisms became widely known. I speculated also how the several disgruntled, vindictive employees would take advantage of the charter-renewal situation if I remained Lead Person/Principal: the fabricated complaints and lies sure to be transmitted to state officials by the same malicious malcontents infecting the school; lies against me, my integrity, and my school management (particularly in the heat of collective-bargaining negotiations), and groundless accusations against the school itself, could well further jeopardize the Classical Academy's charter-renewal prospects if I did not retire. However much personal satisfaction legal action against my persecutors would afford me, my foremost motivation behind all my actions and decisions was always the good of the school.

By the beginning of August 2016, weighing all factors in determining our preferred course of action, a course which was both the best decision for ourselves and for the school's charter-renewal prospects, and ranking the school's future higher than my own well-merited retribution, I, reluctantly, resolved to abide by our announced retirement date and thereby not to mount a further battle in this, my final Classical Academy struggle. Deferring to the persuasive arguments of my loving wife, wishing to protect the school's public image and high repute, and unwilling to jeopardize charter-renewal prospects, I decided to forgo legal action against my slanderers and those having Board of Trustees authority. Accepting the fact that my imminent retirement would eliminate my voice and involvement from future Classical Academy affairs, and would essentially foreclose litigation to redress my grievances, I chose nevertheless to ignore stoically the false, defamatory assaults on my character and reputation, and the contemptuous workplace treatment to which I had been subjected.

I took this withdrawal action, which my retirement as Lead Person would necessitate, despite having complete confidence that, if I remained to fight, I would prevail triumphant, with my slanderers duly cowed and rebuked with punishments richly deserved, and no longer a threat to me or to the school. I recognized, too, that, without my voice or involvement, my departure would allow injurious changes to the Classical Academy because of teachers-union demands, and because of shortsighted, incompetent governance decisions. But I also recognized that, for the sake of Magda and charter-school renewal, a life without the Classical Academy was our new reality. Nevertheless, even in quietly retreating from this final struggle, no one could, as Magda reminded me, dispute or falsify that in all things Classical Academy Charter School of Clifton, *"Veni, Vidi, Vici,"* and for my legacy and personal vindication, that was fulfillment aplenty, even if I did not leave the Classical Academy, as I was seductively invited, with a load of cash and the school bearing my name.

My Final Acts and Responsibilities

I asked the person who would be the Classical Academy's new Lead Person and who had been working at the school for a year, to undertake the charter-renewal application, due October 1, 2016. (The Classical Academy's charter renewal was successfully granted in 2017).

During my last two months, July and August 2016, as Classical Academy Lead Person, my labors were directed to accomplishing three projects. First, the state-required charter school "Annual Report" was due August 1, a document I had nearly completed by the time I resolved to retire. The second, to construct my annual detailed report on our "PARCC 2016 Standardized Test Comparative Student Outcomes," which were characteristically superlative (see Appendix A), and which was the last state-mandated student academic assessment taken under my leadership. My third project was a task I took upon myself for the good of the school, namely, to develop a "Labor/Collective Bargaining Negotiating Handbook" for all Board members.

I was duly alarmed at the many items included in the union's collective-bargaining proposal put forth to the Classical Academy's Board of Trustees. It was a document containing the union's extensive "wish list" demands, created not only by the school's union leaders and teachers, but by NJEA's officials, for it contained many of the same union-promulgated work rules and school policies found in most traditional public schools. It was patently obvious how potentially damaging many of these proposed demands would be for maintaining high student-learning outcomes, effective school operations, and financial soundness. Many of the union's collective-bargaining proposals, if adopted without modification, would dilute and emasculate the exceptionally remarkable Classical Academy education reform practices and policies to the same counter-productive operational features of every other unionized public school. The collective demands in their lengthy proposal for a desired labor agreement would strike at the heart of a number of programmatic and administrative innovations long an intrinsic part of the Classical Academy and because of which the Classical Academy became an astonishingly successful, highly meritorious public charter school.

I realized it would profit our own Board of Trustees to see, if they were so inclined, how the few other New Jersey charter schools that were unionized handled their unionization negotiations and collective-bargaining processes, and how they responded to many of the same issues that were part of the Classical Academy's union collective-bargaining demands. I developed a survey to be sent to all 11 or 12 charter schools (most of which were among the largest New Jersey charter schools) whose faculty and staff were members of the NJEA and who had, in the last several years, endured the labor-negotiation process. Five unionized charter schools returned to me the completed survey.

In the survey, I asked about certain topics appearing in Classical Academy teachers-union collective-bargaining proposal, and how these were resolved in their own charter-school contract negotiations. These topics included: longevity payments; teaching a 6th class; payment for unused or accumulated sick days; personal days; professional-development days and payments; tuition reimbursement for graduate courses; duty-free periods, teacher professional development, and other such topics. I then tabulated the survey results with Classical Academy teacher-union demands to what other charter schools agreed on the similar proposal issues or topics.

In the summarized survey results, which I furnished to all Board members, I went even further. I took it upon myself to comment on each and every demand in the Classical Academy teachers-union extensive collective-bargaining proposal, and whether, in my view, a demand could be granted, modified, or strongly opposed. I gave reasons for each and every one of my recommendations; if a proposed demand could be granted with modification, I specified my recommended modification as a counterproposal. I also identified particular union demands I believed should be rejected outright, and I stated why and how a particular demand would damage the school in its operations, student-learning outcomes, or in its finances. For such demands, I either recommended rejection or, when possible, adoption with significant modification.

This project was an extension of a previous document I had produced in March 2016, in response to the Classical Academy teachers-union collective-bargaining proposals, entitled: "The Classical Academy School Administration's Positions and Counterproposals to the Association

(Union's) Proposals." This document, now combined with the recent survey results and my additional commentary, was my last policy prescription I would ever write as Classical Academy Founder/Lead Person. I placed all 60 pages of my work in black one-inch binders, making enough copies for every Board of Trustee member, as well as the attorney. I mailed to all Board members and intended recipients this newly titled, updated Board resource: "Classical Academy Board Negotiators Collective Bargaining Handbook." It included my administration's positions and counterproposals on every teachers-union demand delineated in the union's bargaining proposals. I am sure, as a final rebuff, none of the Board members ever used my work for collective-bargaining purposes, and likely never opened their binder or read its contents. I knew this would be the case, but they could not deny me this final defensive effort to protect the institution I created and loved, and to which I had dedicated a good portion of my professional life.

At the time of my departure from the Classical Academy in September 2016, no settlement between teachers and the Board had been reached in negotiations, and the collective-bargaining process was ongoing.

Strikingly, the union's collective-bargaining contract proposal was silent on the fate of teacher monetary bonuses based on student standardized-test outcomes, a staple of Classical Academy teacher compensation for 15 years. Whether the union (or the majority of teachers) preferred the bonus payments continue under the same criteria, or that the current $6,000 maximum bonus payment be automatically added to each teacher's base salary annually without any required student-outcomes criteria, is unknown to me. Knowing how much the NJEA despises "teacher-performance compensation" of any sort, I was certain this would be a topic for later negotiations, but I was confident that any "performance pay" and the student-outcome criteria upon which the payments were based would likely be discontinued.

A Bountiful Bequeathal, Final Declaration of "No Confidence," and a New Life Begins

Lastly, I wish to proclaim as manifest testimony to my and my wife's indisputably remarkable success as charter-school founders and administrators, that no new school leadership or Board of Trustees ever assumed governance of a New Jersey charter school from its previous charter-school administration boasting a greater record of student academic accomplishment and greater financial bounty than that which I and Mrs. DeRosa bestowed upon our successors.

In 2016, the Classical Academy was ranked consistently in the top 5% academically of all New Jersey middle schools, and routinely in the top 10% of all New Jersey charter schools based on years of outstanding 8th-grade standardized-test outcomes. Each year, Classical Academy 8th-graders scholastically outperformed their Clifton Public School peers by huge margins (see Appendix A).

Financially, the Classical Academy's new leadership had inherited assets of two and a half million dollars ($2,500,000) and no outstanding debts or ongoing expenses it could not easily meet. This multi-million-dollar inheritance consisted of a fully paid, mortgage-free school facility fully owned by the school's Board of Trustees and assessed at about $1,000,000. I and my wife Magda also bestowed upon our successors approximately $1,500,000 in surplus funds residing in the school's bank account, a sizable amount, considering that our comparative minuscule funding through the years was generated on a very small school size of only 120 students. These surplus savings were the hard-earned proceeds accumulated under our long leadership by performing ourselves multiple school functions—thereby saving school costs on additional personnel and outside-vendor service providers—all while practicing prudential spending habits.

My final act was to write the Board of Trustees a valedictory letter, conceding that now it and the school's new administrative leadership had the responsibility to continue the school's outstanding attributes: high performance in student-learning outcomes; a distinct "academics-first school culture"; acknowledged financial integrity; and prudence in expenditures, all hallmarks of the Classical Academy Charter School of Clifton. Concluding in that letter, however, that I had little confidence in the aspirations, intentions, skills, motivations, judgment, competence, and dedication of those taking the mantle of Classical Academy leadership, nor much credibility or faith that they would perpetuate the remarkable attributes and profound accomplishments of the widely acclaimed educational institution affectionately referred to as "The Little School That Could."

In September 2016, with a thoroughly sublime contentment that ambitious dreams realized and hopes satiated beyond expectations impart to a purpose-driven life spent well, I and my wife merrily headed north to Quebec, where luxurious, bucolic surroundings and eager game fish awaited us as we commenced a new, rewarding phase of our lives.

Epilogue

Since my and my wife's retirement in September 2016, neither of us have had any interactions or contact with the school and its personnel. All our post-retirement information about the school which we founded and operated for 18 years (1997-2016) has been from a limited number of public sources, such as intermittent publication online of Classical Academy Board of Trustees Minutes, the yearly independent auditor's report (CAFR), newspaper accounts, the school's website, and state data. Admittedly my knowledge of school progress and changes is limited, but what little I have learned and corroborated is troubling. To my understanding, the Classical Academy has in the last six years adopted practices, executed decisions, and instituted changes the consequences of which have, without circumspect leadership, the propensity over time to erode the school's scholastic excellence and its financial security. Without the presence of my voice, it was such inadvisable developments and feared alterations in school policies and practices as I here describe that fed my dreadful foreboding when retiring from the school.

Move to a "Better" School Facility

About a year after our retirement, Classical Academy school leadership placed the school building on the For-Sale market. The school soon afterwards, a year before a sale transpired, moved its location to a defunct Clifton Catholic-school facility. The accommodations and amenities this new Classical Academy building offered and which the former building lacked are many and significant. The school now has a full cafeteria, a surplus of large classrooms, library, auditorium, gymnasium, traditional school lavatories, and commodious quarters for school leadership to perform its executive duties. For most people, this move was an obvious and indisputably superb choice for the entire Classical Academy community. However, this seemingly brilliant, widely applauded decision has come at real cost.

The fact that the Board of Trustees fully owned mortgage-free the original Classical Academy school building, and however much it lacked traditional school attributes, was a great asset only a very few New Jersey charter schools possess. It was in this same unlikely facility that the Classical Academy reached the apex of school excellence. To any charter school, full ownership of its own mortgage-paid facility is an immense advantage for both school security and low facility costs, and especially advantageous to the state's smallest and among the least funded-charter schools. The Classical Academy Board and school leadership were willing, without hesitation or deeper consideration, to sacrifice these important advantages.

For this greatly upgraded school facility, owned by the Paterson Diocese of the Catholic Church, the Classical Academy pays an annual lease of nearly three-hundred thousand dollars ($300,000). Since moving into its better-equipped facility in 2018, the school has paid to the Diocese of Paterson in the last four years more than a million dollars (a steep added expense when it formerly expended no facility costs, apart from basic upkeep and utilities for its original facility). The proceeds from the eventual sale of the original building amounted to about a million dollars, which has by now been totally consumed in lease payments for a facility the school does not own. Its facility-lease costs must now come from the per-pupil cost and basic operating funds, which, if expenditures are not prudently controlled, may present a financial problem in the years ahead.

The move from a fully owned school facility to one now owned by another entity, presents the problem of security. The facility owner, the Paterson Catholic Church Dioceses, may at any point after expiration of a 4- or 5-year lease contract, decide, for whatever financial or organizational purpose, not to renew the lease. The Classical Academy must then search for another facility, no easy task, and failing to secure another building may well lead to school discontinuation. Thus, this acclaimed "no-brainer" move into a much-enhanced, costly school facility does come at significant, ongoing risks and uncertainty, both to school security and to school finances.

Incidentally, Appendix B of this work contains an interesting historical sketch of the Classical Academy's former "Dollymount Mansion" school building (pictured on the cover of this book) and its original owner, William B. Gourley, one of the most illustrious individuals ever to have resided in Clifton, New Jersey.

Some Dubious Board of Trustees and School Leadership Actions

Soon after my retirement, certain Board of Trustees' actions came to my attention, actions which occurred in 2017 and 2018, and which further confirmed my low esteem for the Board's abilities and judgment (the leadership of this Board was yet unchanged from that with which I struggled my last year before retirement).

A teacher demanded that she was owed by the previous administration (that is I) $10,000 for some dubious matter or deprivation she incurred. I can unequivocally attest that there was no such payment or monies owed to this teacher, for whatever reason. The claimant happened to be a prime agitator for unionism and the suspected author of the scurrilous, anonymous letter against me. I was not contacted about the matter or about the validity of her claim, nor were, I believe, documents scrutinized. Seemingly without objection, and capitulating abjectly to her erroneous demand, the Board paid her the $10,000 she claimed was owed to her. When the independent auditor analyzed the payment, he concluded that this payment was without merit and that the Board is warned against paying employees without cause and beyond the specifications of employee contracts.

The same independent auditor conducting the 2018 and 2019 required yearly financial audits cited as "needing corrective action" the fact that the percentage of the school's "administrative costs" had exceeded the state-recommended percentage of school budget allocated for administrative functions, and had done so for several years. Imagine, under my Classical

Academy school leadership, our "administrative costs" relative to yearly school budget were cited as among the least in the state. Yet, within several years after my retirement, administrative costs had risen to beyond recommended state limits.

The part-time off-site School Business Administrator, whom I referenced earlier and who should have been forthrightly terminated, as I had repeatedly advised, for her blatant lack of compliance with critical contractual obligations, thereby causing financial-operational distress, was still employed, several years after my calls for her termination. In fact, her standing and influence had augmented as a close ally of the-then Board President. This person also owned a business services company. Well, would one be surprised that the Board authorized purchases for business services and products from her privately owned enterprise? Of course, it is common knowledge, except apparently to the Classical Academy Board and school leadership at that time, that a Board of Trustees is strictly prohibited from purchasing services or products from a person who is simultaneously their employee. It is universally known as "conflict of interest." When the state discovered this "conflict," the Board was reprimanded and compelled to attend School Board leadership training. After this episode, this person, who was so detrimental to the school, departed Classical Academy employment, whether voluntarily or not I do not know.

Increase in Students, but Not Grades

Requiring a hefty lease payment, and filling a school facility built for the accommodation of 300-400 students with only 120 students, necessitated an increase in Classical Academy enrollment. The additional revenues would be critical to manage its new substantial facility costs. Having failed in its first attempt (2018) to gain state approval to increase the number of Classical Academy students, the state came to the school's fiscal rescue in 2019-2020 and permitted an increase of 60 students, thereby adding to the school's revenues about $800,000 in annual funding. Without this life-saving, state-approved increase of students, the Classical Academy would have faced severe financial problems in a few years.

The addition of grades 4 and 5 and the huge benefits this change would afford to Classical Academy continued educational excellence and financial robustness, I described in the final chapter of my narrative. But school leadership sought merely to add students to its three existing grades, 6th, 7th, and 8th. The Classical Academy, for the last several years, has a maximum permitted school enrollment of 180 students, with 60 students in each middle-school grade. In total enrollment, the Classical Academy still remains one of, if not the smallest New Jersey charter schools, and regrettably, still the one with the fewest grade levels.

The Classical Academy's new facility would have provided nicely for the addition of grades 4 and 5, grades which would have proved extraordinarily valuable for sustaining and perpetuating Classical Academy's record of remarkable scholastic outcomes. But finding, perhaps, the addition of these grades too speculative in argument and onerous in preparation (needing to provide a curriculum, for example) for state approval, and choosing the easy way, the school administration elected merely to increase the number of students in existing grades. Again, like deciding to move from a fully owned to a leased facility, the decision not to focus school expansion on grades 4 and 5, and thereby assuring that Classical Academy 8th-grade students would achieve consistently superlative and unmatched academic excellence, was shortsighted and indicative of questionable school leadership. Financially, adding more students was a necessary action to increase revenues to handle heavy lease payments; educationally, however, by not adding students in newly-created 4th and 5th grades will, I fear, prove a most unwise decision in the years ahead.

Would it not have been far better, I muse, for new school leadership to attempt to realize my original intentions for adding the 4th and 5th grades and increase facility space by adding onto its fully owned school building or constructing a second, small school building on bucolic school property. After my contemplated project's completion in the school's original location, and in five or six years with all bank loans paid, the Classical Academy, as I envisioned, would have fully owned its own educational campus and would be generating large surplus revenues. In this way, its financial health with large reserves would be substantial, its student learning outcome proficiencies consistently extraordinary, and its building security absolute. All this is now lamentably lost forever.

Thus, whatever obstacles my plan for increased students and grade expansion in the school's fully-owned building would have entailed, and whatever work it would have required, this plan would have proved, in the final outcome, exceedingly worthwhile to pursue and to strive to overcome whatever difficulties it presented. Failing in this preferred direction of school development, only then would securing a larger building (preferably by purchase and not lease) be an alternate and justifiable course.

Violations of Charter and Long Practice

Hiring full-time teachers in art and physical education, as I understand is now the fact, and mandating in students' schedules and school-day time these subjects in discrete or dedicated classes, is contrary to long practice under my leadership, and contrary to the school's charter.

Tracking students in (8th-grade) mathematics is now also a common Classical Academy practice. This, too, is contrary to Classical Academy precedent and contrary to its "no-tracking" charter-approval provision. Instead of mandating all Classical Academy students take "Algebra I" in the 8th grade, as was the precedent and long-effective practice, now only the "better" mathematics students take an 8th-grade "Algebra I" course and standardized test, while the other 8th-grade students, deemed less math accomplished, take an "8th-grade Mathematics" course and the less-advanced 8th-grade non-Algebraic Mathematics standardized assessment.

Whether or not the school, before implementing these changes to its charter and long-standing practices, initiated formal charter amendments and sought state approval for the changes, I know not, but I think it unlikely.

Related to "tracking," the segregation or differentiation of students based on "ability" or "innate, distinguishable attributes," is further exacerbated by the school's newly-instituted "Talented and Gifted" program. Under my leadership, such a program would have been unthinkable and contrary to the fundamental philosophy underpinning a Classical Academy education. During my leadership, every one of our classes and academic subjects was sufficiently rigorous, accelerated, and demanding that even the most talented and gifted ("motivated") students were challenged. A "Talented and Gifted" program militates against the school-wide "academics-first school culture" embracing every student. It is also destructive to the school's long practice of teachers teaching to the best students (the so-called "talented and gifted") in the class, to which high levels of instruction and educational achievement all others must strive. A "Talented and Gifted" program appears to erode yet another basic anti-segregation Classical Academy school principle.

Increase of Half Days of School

Recalling the details of Classical Academy school calendars under my leadership, and how that calendar was constructed to maximize student instruction and learning, the number of half days and, thus, their corresponding harmful impact on student learning, numbered a mere 5 to 7 per year, and most half days were in late June so as not to adversely impact student instruction. More recent Classical Academy school calendars show an increase of 20-25 half days per year, averaging two per month, and thus exacerbating significantly their harmful effect on student learning. I presume this increase was a consequence of teachers-union collective bargaining and the union's demands for vacuous "teacher professional development" during normal working hours.

Standardized Assessment and Student Academic Outcomes

Perhaps most alarming is the decline in Classical Academy student-learning outcomes. Because of the Covid pandemic, standardized testing across the nation was suspended for two years, 2020 and 2021. New Jersey resumed standardized testing by administering the "New Jersey Student Learning Assessment" (NJSLA) in spring of 2022. The last pre-pandemic standardized testing of the NJSLA occurred in spring 2019. Let us compare

Classical Academy 8th-grade results of that 2019 test in "English language arts literacy," "Algebra I," and "8th-grade Mathematics" with the last standardized, more-challenging PARCC 2016 test taken during my final year of Classical Academy leadership.

PARCC 2016
8th Grade
Percent of 8th-grade class earning "Passing"
("Passing" is defined as the combined percentage of the 8th-grade class earning "Level 5" ["Exceeding Expectations"/ "Advanced Proficiency"] and "Level 4" ["Meeting Expectations"/"Proficiency"] in each tested subject).

PARCC 2016
8th-Grade Outcomes

Subject	Percent of 8th-grade Class "Passing"	Percent of 8th-grade class earning Level 5 ["Exceeding Expectations"] "Advanced Proficiency"
English Language Arts	86.4%	48.6%
"Algebra I"	89.1%	48.3%

NJSLA 2019
8th-Grade Outcomes

Subject	Percent of 8th-grade Class "Passing"	Percent of 8th-grade class earning "Advanced Proficiency"
English Language Arts	85%	40%
"Algebra I"	88.9%	18.5%
8th-grade Mathematics	53.8%	0%

It appears from the above comparative data that, although slightly lower than PARCC 2016 8th-grade test results, the NJSLA 2019 English language arts scores, both in "passing" and "advanced proficiency" percentages have been upheld, somewhat. I anticipate that future Classical Academy 8th-grade standardized assessment English scores will decline. However, this chart shows a distinct decrease in "Algebra I" and "8th-grade Mathematics" student outcomes.

Remember, as of 2019, "mathematics tracking" had only recently begun as a Classical Academy policy, and yet we see its quick, deplorable results. When reviewing the PARCC 2016 scores, remember also that every 8th-grade student was mandated to take the "Algebra I" course and, hence, the "Algebra I" standardized test. "Tracking"—the exclusion of less-capable students from taking more-demanding subjects—was a specifically prohibited Classical Academy practice. In the NJSLA 2019 Classical Academy "Algebra I" test outcomes, a test taken by the school's better mathematics students because of the Classical Academy's newly-instituted mathematics "Tracking," we observe a clear declined from the PARC 2016 in the percentage of 8th-graders earning "Advanced Proficiency,"—only 18.5% (an unprecedented low "Algebra I" 8th-grade "Advanced Proficiency" rate)—whereas, in PARCC 2016, nearly half the 8th-grade class (48.3%) earned "Advanced Proficiency" scores.

More alarming is the performance of the 13 8th-grade "Mathematics-tracked" students excluded from taking "Algebra I," with barely half (53.8%) of them passing the 8th-grade Mathematics test, and not one student (0%) earning "Advanced Proficiency." These percentages are the embarrassingly deficient 8th-grade mathematics attainment scores typically earned by Clifton District Public middle-school students, and *never* by Classical Academy 8th-graders, until now.

If we consider the total mathematics performance of Classical Academy 8th-graders on the NJSLA 2019, we see that 71.3% of all 8th-graders "passed" and that 18.5% achieved "Advanced Proficiency." These numbers for total Classical Academy 8th-grade mathematics learning performance represent the *lowest* mathematics achievement the school *ever* recorded on state-mandated assessments.

In 2019, the destructive deviations from fundamental Classical Academy practices and policies had recently commenced, and their full erosive impact, indeed, assault on the Classical Academy's long-documented academic excellence and on its academics-first school culture has yet to be fully seen. I, therefore, anticipate witnessing even clearer and widespread evidence of Classical Academy academic deterioration in the next several years as demonstrated on state-mandated test assessments. Upon retirement, it is what I feared most, and, regrettably, I tremble that it is now inevitably coming to pass.

If declines in the long record of Classical Academy superlative student-learning academic outcomes become manifest in future state-mandated assessments, these cannot and should not be attributed to Covid or remote learning. Future Classical Academy standardized-test outcomes should be compared not only with past outcomes attained during my leadership (see Appendix A) but also, beginning with the 2022 NJSLA testing, with other 8th-grade learning outcomes of charter schools and Clifton Public School District's standardized 8th-grade test results, all of which endured the same Covid-induced learning interruptions as the Classical Academy.

In fact, on that NJSLA 2022 state assessment, a disappointing 67.7% of Classical Academy 8th-graders "Passed" English Language Arts Literacy, while 20.6% achieved "Advanced Proficiency." These unprecedented low Classical Academy 8th-grade "Passing" and "Advanced Proficiency" percentages rank its 8th-grade students 25% and 27% respectively among all New Jersey charter-school 8th-graders. However respectable these charter-school comparative rankings may be, they are still quite a worrisome decline from past comparative charter-school performance levels which consistently ranked Classical Academy 8th-graders in the "Top 1%-10%" of all New Jersey charter schools in English Language Arts Literacy standardized assessment outcomes during my school leadership.

If, on future state-mandated assessments, beginning with the NJSLA 2022, Classical Academy 8th-grade test outcomes in English language arts, mathematics, "Algebra I," and even in science, do not place the school in the top 10% of all New Jersey charter schools, and if those same results do not surpass Clifton Public School 8th-graders by the Classical Academy's accustomed large margins, then those leading the Classical Academy must act to regain the school's high academic learning excellence and superiority, and before learning declines become habitual and irretrievably depressed.

Final Thoughts and Recommendations

One wonders whether the above-cited adulterations of and departures from proven Classical Academy policies and practices were adopted primarily because the new facility made them possible. If so, are we to conclude that occupying a commodious, well-endowed school facility prompts or excuses Classical Academy student-learning decline? Is paying $300,000 a year of school and taxpayer money for a well-equipped, spacious facility not owned by the school's Board of Trustees, and the willful abandonment of proven school practices and policies, defensible reasons to cause potentially an inexorable descent to mediocre levels of student-learning proficiencies?

Of course, no institution remains exactly the same over time or when other school leaders with their own ideas and professional convictions assume control. Institutional stagnation and refusal to change or to satisfy client preferences can lead to diminished success and unwanted outcomes. But former and current Classical Academy leadership, projecting a fundamentally different Classical Academy operating emphasis and educational philosophy upon which the school was founded and managed for nearly 20 years, and because of which the Classical Academy rose to the apex of student-learning performance, are nonetheless responsible for whatever undesirable consequences departures from proven school policies, practices, and programs have produced or may produce. For such departures or programmatic changes may well result in lower 8th-grade learning outcomes, as we are beginning to witness, and may precipitate an overall decline in the school-wide academic excellence for which the Classical Academy was once renowned. School decline happens rapidly; rebuilding or reasserting school-wide academic excellence is a much slower, arduous process. The Classical Academy must therefore guard against transforming itself from a high-performing high-academic outcome school, into a competent but very ordinary and unremarkable public school.

However much I may disagree with certain rather fundamental changes adopted and implemented in the school over the last six years, I commend the Classical Academy's new leadership, Lead Person, and current Board of Trustees, for their honorable efforts and dedication to students and to the school I founded and long directed.

If I were to address the current Board of Trustees and the school's new leadership, I would wholeheartedly offer these three recommendations:

1: Make every attempt to purchase the building. Offer above (even far above) assessed value to entice the Paterson Diocese to sell its school building to the Classical Academy. In the long term, such purchase will save money, contribute to solid future school finances, and provide near-absolute school facility security.

2: To maintain an academics-first school culture and to perpetuate the Classical Academy's accustomed high student academic outcomes for every student, adhere as much as possible to each of the 13 reforms and practices delineated in Chapter V of this narrative.

3: Construct and file as soon as possible a charter amendment seeking state permission to add grades 4 and 5 to the Classical Academy program of studies, preferably 60 students in 4th grade and 60 students in 5th grade; and employ the persuasive reasons (before those reasons lose their validity) stated in this narrative (Chapter VIII) to help secure State Department of Education approval. A maximum size of 320 students in a grades 4-8 school, although a bit larger than ideal, is still conducive to sustain an "academics-first school culture" (including the school policies and practices that uphold that culture) and for attaining high levels of scholastic outcomes and academic excellence.

If these three recommendations are followed, the excellence in high student academic achievement, the maintenance of sound finances, and school facility security, all of which we abundantly bestowed to our successors upon my and Mrs. DeRosa's retirement from Classical Academy leadership six years ago, will not further deteriorate but be recaptured and sustained far into the future as the Classical Academy begins in 2023 its second quarter-century of high academic excellence in education.

THE CLASSICAL ACADEMY CHARTER SCHOOL OF CLIFTON'S SUPERIOR 5-YEAR RECORD OF COMPARATIVE 8TH-GRADE STUDENT ACADEMIC-LEARNING OUTCOMES ON STATE-MANDATED STANDARDIZED TESTS OF ENGLISH LANGUAGE ARTS AND MATHEMATICS (2012-2016)

Introduction

Classical Academy students undertook state-mandated standardized testing from the school's beginning in 1998. The following data represent the last 5 years of test results during my leadership tenure. Because the information in this Appendix A is excerpted or duplicated from my "Comparative Student Outcome Reports" produced annually over 15 years, the data cited, though uniform in their employment and import, are varied in their presentation and format. This variation in format in no way detracts from the understanding or interpretation of Classical Academy comparative student standardized-tests results relative to their meaningful student-peer outcomes.

2014 was the last year of the state-mandated "Assessment of Skills and Knowledge," acronymically known as the "ASK," a test which had supplanted in 2008 the "GEPA" or "Grade Eight Proficiency Assessment." As the "Core Curriculum Content Standards" was becoming a national movement, the "ASK" was replaced in 2015 by the "PARCC" assessments ("Partnership for the Assessment of Readiness for College and Careers"). The PARCC was intended to better advance and reflect the Core Curriculum. In the last several years, as the opposition and near abandonment of the Core

Curriculum became widespread, and complaints that the PARCC was too time consuming and too difficult, New Jersey replaced it in 2018, two years after my retirement, with its "New Jersey Student Learning Assessments (NJSLA)," by all estimates, a test not only requiring less school time, but one that is a less academically challenging assessment as well.

All state-mandated standardized-test comparative outcomes in this Appendix A feature only Classical Academy 8th-graders as they compare to their 8th-grade peers in other schools. The 8th grade is the most meaningful segment to measure, as it is the middle-school culmination of the accumulated effectiveness, or ineffectiveness, of a middle-school's policies and practices, and to which 8th-graders bear best testimony. Classical Academy 8th-grade enrollment numbered 37-40 students each year.

Classical Academy Charter School student-outcome comparison reports have always been comprehensive, encompassing a number of comparative benchmarks by which to measure our students' learning results with meaningful cohorts or relevant peer groups. However, the most imperative of these, as with any charter school, is how a charter school's student outcomes measure against its resident, or home public-school, district. I have long declared that if a charter school's students are not minimally demonstrating equal, preferably superior, learning outcomes to their peers in the home public school district, then the continuance of such an ill-performing charter school must be questioned and, lacking improvement over a reasonable period of time, its charter should be in jeopardy.

With this declaration in mind, and ever since the Classical Academy was established in 1998, and for every year under my leadership ending in September 2016, its 8th-grade students, as the reader will see, outperformed their Clifton Public School 8th-grade peers not barely or slightly, but by immense margins. Such that, when it was time for charter renewals every 5 years, Clifton school officials, although they had the right to oppose the Classical Academy's continuance, never proffered any arguments against the school's charter being renewed. This was a decision not out of any affection for the Classical Academy, but out of reticence of opposing a school whose students not only perform academically so magnificently, but also from the ensuing embarrassment surely to accrue to Clifton school officials if they advocated charter non-renewal for a school whose student academic performance is so much superior to the schools they themselves manage.

Above all, at least for those who believe academic learning is the primary purpose and goal of public school K-12 education, the data provided in this Appendix A prove the cumulative value and effectiveness of the Classical Academy Charter School of Clifton's policies and practices, and reveal statistically and objectively the overwhelming worth of its "academics-first school culture" those practices and policies created and sustained.

Although "science" is a tested subject on the GEPA and ASK, it is not generally included or cited in commentaries on school performance, as it is a subject not tested yearly, but only in the 4th, 8th, and 11th grades. It is for that reason that I here omit "science" outcomes in these charts and data. Suffice to say that Classical Academy student "Passing" outcomes on standardized 8th-grade science tests ranged from 85% to 100% consistently, with 50%-75% of 8th-graders routinely earning an "Advanced Proficiency" science score.

In most of the 5-year "Comparative Student Learning Outcome Data" here presented, there are charts comparing Classical Academy student outcomes with those students and communities having much higher socio-economic advantages than Classical Academy students. These are presented to show how exceedingly well the Classical Academy has succeeded in closing the "learning gap" between the most-advantaged and much-less-advantaged students.

The comparative test data also include data showing that Classical Academy students persistently outperformed 90% of all New Jersey charter schools in 8th-grade learning proficiencies. Classical Academy 8th-graders, as the following data shows, also significantly outperform statewide students having the same "C/D" District Factor Group designations, that is, with their peers statewide having the same socio-economic characteristics. Classical Academy 8th graders also surpass every year the state's "passing" and "advanced proficiency" averages. Comparative 8th-grade standardized-test outcomes data also show how well (often in top or second place) Classical Academy students perform among all Passaic County public schools.

All data and statistics for Appendix A are based on "Total Students Tested" and sourced from New Jersey Department of Education publicly available websites. State-mandated assessment results and data are available at websites accessed under general category: *"New Jersey Department of Education Assessment Results."*

For those who believe academic-learning outcomes is the paramount objective of public education, and to further substantiate, as well as to document, the Classical Academy's long record of high student academic-learning outcomes, even a quick perusal of the following comparative statistical evidence will demonstrate to what profound and enduring degree Classical Academy Charter School of Clifton 8th-grade students achieved academic excellence during my long tenure (1997-2016) of Lead Teacher/Principal.

ASK-8, 2012

"Assessment of Skills and Knowledge"
Standardized Test Student Outcomes Comparison Between Classical Academy Charter School of Clifton and Clifton Public Schools

"PASSING"

Percent of 8th graders "Passing" English Language Arts and Mathematics. "Passing" is defined as the combined percentage of a school's 8th-grade students earning either a "Proficient" score or an "Advanced Proficiency" score on each tested subject.

School	Percent of 8th-grade Students "Passing" English Language Arts	Percent of 8th-grade Students "Passing" Mathematics
Classical Academy Charter School of Clifton	100%	100%
Woodrow Wilson Middle School of Clifton	78.2%	58.6%
C. Columbus Middle School of Clifton	66.6%	47.4%
Clifton Public School District 8th Grade Passing Average	72.4%	53%

"ADVANCED PROFICIENCY"

Percent of 8th-graders earning the highest ASK-8 Outcome of "Advanced Proficiency" in each tested subject.

School	Percent of 8th-grade Students "Advanced Proficiency" English Language Arts	Percent of 8th-grade Students "Advanced Proficiency" Mathematics
Classical Academy Charter School of Clifton	27%	70.3%
W. Wilson Middle School of Clifton	11.1%	14.9%
C. Columbus Middle School of Clifton	1.5%	6.9%
Clifton School District's 8th grade	6.1%	10.9%

Total Mean Scale Score Comparisons between Clifton School District's 8th-grade students and Classical Academy 8th-grade students in English Language Arts and Mathematics:

School	English Language Arts	Mathematics
Classical Academy Charter School of Clifton	234.8	260.5
W. Wilson Middle School of Clifton	217.7	205.3
C. Columbus Middle School of Clifton	206.5	195.9

Observations: In the above data charts, we see Classical Academy 8th-graders outperform their Clifton Public School District 8th-grade peers by large margins in "passing" and in achieving "advanced proficiency" in both English language arts and mathematics. Notice especially the hugely superior Classical Academy student margins in achieving "advance proficiency" in English and mathematics, with the latter being *7 times greater* than the Clifton Public School District 8th-grade mathematics "advanced proficiency" achievement.

Statewide ASK-8 2012 Outcomes

"PASSING"

("Passing" is the combined percentage of 8th-graders earning either a "Proficient" score or an "Advanced Proficiency" score in the tested subject).

	English Language Arts	Mathematics
Classical Academy Charter School of Clifton	100%	100%
Statewide "Passing" Percent for all 8th-Grade Students	67.7%	41.5%

"ADVANCED PROFICIENCY"

	English Language Arts	Mathematics
Classical Academy Charter School of Clifton	27%	70.3%
Statewide Percent for all 8th-Grade Students Achieving "Advanced Proficiency"	14.5%	30.1%

ASK-8 2012
"C/D" District Factor Group 8th-grade Statewide Student Socio-Economic Peer Comparisons

"PASSING"

	English Language Arts	Mathematics
"C/D" Classical Academy Charter School of Clifton	100%	100%
Passing Percentage Average for All New Jersey's 128 "C/D" DFG Schools Educating 9,816 8th-Grade Students	78.8%	65.4%

"ADVANCED PROFICIENCY"

	English Language Arts	Mathematics
"C/D" Classical Academy Charter School of Clifton	27%	70.3%
"Advanced Proficiency" Percent for All New Jersey's 128 "C/D" DFG Schools Educating 9,816 8th-Grade Students	8.2%	21.2%

ASK-8, 2012
"J" Schools
8th-Grade "J" School Student ASK-8 2012 Test Outcomes Compared with "C/D" Classical Academy Outcomes

"J" schools are designated as New Jersey's most affluent communities, having the most advantaged socio-economic characteristics: highest household incomes, most expensive real estate, highest levels of parent education, etc. "J" schools' educational student outcomes are always among the highest in the state. As a "C/D" socio-economic (lower middle-class) designated school, and having a socio-economic (District Factor Group) designation 5 steps below the wealthiest "J" schools, the Classical Academy Charter School of Clifton student body is largely children of immigrant parents. Students from a school having this student profile and an average 30% "free/reduced" school lunch student eligibility, invariably perform academically much lower on standardized-test outcomes than their much wealthier and privileged "J" school students.

"Closing the Learning Gap" is a Classical Academy Charter School of Clifton mission and a natural outgrowth of its "Academics-First" school culture. Its array and collective force of policies and practices (described in previous chapters) both create and sustain that culture of high academic student-learning outcomes well beyond what their demographic (socio-economic) characteristics would predict, or what, in fact, are the typical learning outcomes of students in all other New Jersey "C/D" schools.

In the following two "J" school data charts, the ten "J" schools listed and included were selected completely at random from state data.

"PASSING"

("Passing" is defined as the combined percentage of a school's 8th-grade class earning either a "Proficient" score or an "Advanced Proficiency" score on each tested subject). (*NB*: The following 10 "J" schools were selected from ASK-8 2012 state data completely at random.)

DFG	School	Percent of 8th-grade Students "Passing" English Language Arts	Percent of 8th-grade Students "Passing" Mathematics
"C/D"	Classical Academy C.S. of Clifton	100%	100%
"J"	Mendham Twp. M.S., Mendham Twp.	100%	97.2%
"J"	Black River M.S., Chester Twp.	96.6%	90.2%
"J"	Haddonfield M.S., Haddonfield	94.1%	89.2%
"J"	Markham Place Sch., Little Silver	97.6%	96.3%
"J"	Milburn M.S., Milburn Twp.	96.2%	91.8%
"J"	Montgomery M.S., Montgomery Twp.	95.6%	92.8%
"J"	G. Washington M.S., Ridgewood Village	95%	91.7%
"J"	Old Turnpike School, Tewksbury Twp.	96%	95.9%
"J"	Thomas R. Grover M.S., West-Windsor Pl.	94.1%	89.6%
"J"	Woodcliff M.S., Woodcliff Lake Boro	96.9%	91.6%

"J" Schools Comparisons with Classical Academy ASK-8 2012 Outcomes in "Advanced Proficiency"

DFG	School	Percent of 8th-grade Students "Advanced Proficiency" English Language Arts	Percent of 8th-grade Students "Advanced Proficiency" Mathematics
"C/D"	Classical Academy C.S. of Clifton	27%	70.3%
"J"	Black River M.S., Chester Twp.	37.6%	53.6%
"J"	Haddonfield M.S., Haddonfield Boro	29.9%	53%
"J"	Markham Place School, Little Silver Boro	41%	61.4%
"J"	Milburn M.S., Milburn Twp.	39.9%	59.9%
"J"	Montgomery M.S., Montgomery Twp.	38.5%	68.1%
"J"	G. Washington M.S., Ridgewood Village	25.8%	60%
"J"	Old Turnpike School, Tewksbury Twp.	41.9%	68.9%
"J"	Thomas R. Grover M.S., West Windsor-Pl.	37.9%	69%
"J"	Woodcliff M.S., Woodcliff Lake Boro	25.3%	63.2%
"J"	Mendham Twp. M.S., Mendham Twp.	49.5%	70%

Observations: In the above two charts, we see that Classical Academy students, mostly children of immigrant parents with socio-economic factors far below those of New Jersey's most-advantaged families and children, compare very favorably. In Mathematics "Passing" and "Advanced Proficiency," Classical Academy 8th-graders surpassed the 10 "J" schools listed. Quite an achievement in which the "Learning Gap" between highly advantaged students and decidedly less-advantaged students has been eliminated!

ASK-8 2012
Charter School Comparisons
Charter School Rankings (in descending order) Based on Each School's 8th-Grade Student "Passing" Percentages and Each School's "Advanced Proficiency" Student Achievement in Tested Subjects of English Language Arts and Mathematics

"PASSING"
"Passing" is defined as the combined percentage of a school's 8th-grade class earning either a "Proficient" score or an "Advanced Proficiency" score on the tested subject.

Charter School	Percent of 8th-grade Students "Passing" English Language Arts	Charter School	Percent of 8th-grade Students "Passing" Mathematics
Classical Academy C.S. of Clifton	100%	Classical Academy C.S. of Clifton	100%
Discovery C.S.	100%	Princeton C.S.	100%
Princeton C.S.	100%	North Star Acad. C.S. of Newark	96.8%
Robert Treat Academy C.S.	100%	Elysian C.S. of Hoboken	90.3%
North Star Acad. C.S. of Newark	97.6%	Robert Treat Academy C.S.	87.5%
Elysian C.S. of Hoboken	96.8%	Greater Brunswick C.S.	85%
Learning Community C.S.	94.6%	Unity C.S.	84.6%
Gray C.S.	93.8%	Foundation Academy C.S.	83.7%
Bergen Arts and Sciences C.S.	91.7%	Gray C.S.	81.3%
Renaissance Reg. Leadership C.S.	91.6%	Red Bank C.S.	81.3%
Teaneck Community C.S.	91.2%	Learning Community C.S.	78.4%
Soaring Heights C.S.	90%	Greater Newark C.S.	77.1%
Queen City Academy C.S.	88.6%	Bergen Arts & Sciences C.S.	76.7%
Red Bank C.S.	87.6%	Teaneck Community C.S.	76.5%
Unity C.S.	84.6%	Maria L. Varisco-Rogers C.S.	74.2%
Foundation Academy C.S.	83.7%	Discovery C.S.	72.8%
Union County Teams C.S.	81.5%	Marion P. Thomas C.S.	72.5%
Greater Brunswick C.S.	80%	Camden's Promise C.S.	71%
Marion P. Thomas C.S.	80%	Renaissance Reg. Leadership C.S.	66.7%
Sussex County C.S. for Tech.	77.3%	Soaring Heights C.S.	65%
Pride Academy C.S.	76.7%	Paterson C.S. for Sci. & Tech.	63%
Team Academy C.S.	76.6%	Team Academy C.S.	61.1%
Camden's Promise C.S.	74.7%	Pride Academy C.S.	59.4%
Maria L. Varisco-Rogers C.S.	74.2%	Central Jersey College Prep. C.S.	55.8%
Greater Newark C.S.	71.5%	Jersey City Golden Door C.S.	54.6%
Hoboken C.S.	70.6%	Union County Teams C.S.	52.6%
Jersey City Golden Door C.S.	70.5%	Village C.S.	52.5%
Dr. Leana Edwards C.S.	69.5%	Ridge and Valley C.S.	50%
Paterson C.S. for Sci. and Tech.	69.1%	Sussex County C.S. for Tech.	49.4%
Village C.S.	67.5%	Lady Liberty Academy C.S.	49.2%
Central Jersey College Prep. C.S.	66.6%	Oceanside C.S.	48.1%

Charter School	Percent of 8th-grade Students "Passing" English Language Arts	Charter School	Percent of 8th-grade Students "Passing" Mathematics
LEAP Academy University C.S.	66.1%	Hope Academy C.S.	47.1%
Lady Liberty Academy C.S.	62.7%	Hoboken C.S.	47%
Galloway Community C.S.	60.9%	Paul Robeson C.S. for Humanities	46.5%
Oceanside C.S.	59.3%	LEAP Academy University C.S.	45.8%
Hope Academy C.S.	58.8%	Jersey City Community C.S.	45%
Paul Robeson C.S. for Humanities	58.6%	Galloway Community C.S.	39.1%
Jersey City Community C.S.	58.3%	METS. C.S.	38%
Ridge and Valley C.S.	57.1%	Emily Fisher C.S. for Adv. Studies	32.7%
Emily Fisher C.S. for Adv. Studies	56.6%	Queen City Academy C.S.	31.4%
PleasanTech Academy C.S.	54.5%	Liberty Academy C.S.	31.3%
METS C.S.	53.2%	DUE Seasons C.S.	26.4%
Central Jersey Arts C.S.	51.4%	Central Jersey Arts C.S.	25.8%
DUE Seasons C.S.	50%	Freedom Academy C.S.	17.9%
Freedom Academy C.S.	44.8%	PleasanTech Academy C.S.	17.9%
Liberty Academy C.S.	43.7%	Dr. Leana Edwards C.S.	(no scores recorded)

Observations: The above charter-school 8th-grade outcome rankings of 46 charter schools place the Classical Academy 8th graders in **Top 1%** (tied with 3 other charter schools) in achieving "Passing" English Language Arts Literacy, and in the **Top 1%** (tied with Princeton Charter School) with "Passing" Mathematics.

ASK-8 2012
Charter Schools
Percent of 8th-Grade Class Achieving "Advanced Proficiency" Scores in English Language Arts and Mathematics

NB: Since more than half of the 46 charter schools administering this exam to their 8th-graders recorded less than 20% earning "Advance Proficiency" in both English Language Arts and Mathematics, with many producing single-digit or zero percentages for "Advanced Proficiency" in both subjects, I here list only the top 10 "Advanced Proficiency"-producing charter schools in each subject and where within that top-10 list the Classical Academy Charter School ranks or places.

Charter School	Percent of 8th-grade Students "Advanced Proficiency" English Language Arts	Charter School	Percent of 8th-grade Students "Advanced Proficiency" Mathematics
Princeton C.S.	45.5%	Princeton C.S.	79.5%
Discovery C.S.	36.4%	**Classical Academy C.S. of Clifton**	70.3%
Classical Academy C.S. of Clifton	27%	North Star Acad. C.S of Newark	56.8%
Robert Treat Academy C.S.	25%	Elysian C.S. of Hoboken	54.8%
Bergen Arts and Sciences C.S.	21.7%	Robert Treat Academy C.S.	47.9%
Learning Community C.S.	21.6%	Teaneck Community C.S.	41.2%
Teaneck Community C.S.	20.6%	Discovery C.S.	36.4%
North Star Acad. C.S. of Newark	19.2%	Foundation Academy C.S.	34.9%
Soaring Heights C.S.	15%	Bergen Arts and Sciences C.S.	26.7%
Elysian C.S. of Hoboken	12.9%	Greater Newark C.S.	25.7%

Observations: From the above ASK-8 2012 Charter School "Advanced Proficiency" outcome chart, the Classical Academy, among all 46 charter schools, has the **third-highest** percentage of its students earning "Advanced Proficiency" in English Language Arts, and the **second-highest** for students attaining Mathematics "Advanced Proficiency." That places the Classical Academy in the **top 6%** of all New Jersey charter schools in producing "Advanced Proficiency" students in English Language Arts, and in the **top 4%** for producing "Advanced Proficiency" students in Mathematics! Interestingly, when the Classical Academy Charter School of Clifton produced these superlative academic results, it was in its 6th month of "Probation."

ASK-8 2013

The Classical Academy Charter School of Clifton, Inc.

A Comparison Ranking of 8th-Grade Student Outcomes on the 2013
"Assessment of Skills and Knowledge" (ASK-8) State-Required Tests

Comparing the Classical Academy's 8th-Grade Student Outcomes
in English Language Arts and Mathematics with

1: Clifton Public Schools
2: All New Jersey Charter Schools
3: All Passaic County Public Schools

CLASSICAL ACADEMY CHARTER SCHOOL OF CLIFTON
VS.
CLIFTON DISTRICT SCHOOLS

"PASSING"
Percent of school's 8th-Grade class "Passing" each of the tested subjects of
English Language Arts and Mathematics
Along with "Statewide" 8th-Grade Student "Passing" Percentages

"Passing" is defined as the combined percentage of a school's 8th-graders
achieving either a "Proficient" score or an "Advanced Proficiency" score
in the tested subject.

8TH-GRADE "PASSING" PERCENTAGES

	English Language Arts	Mathematics
Classical Academy Charter School of Clifton	100%	100%
Clifton: W. Wilson M.S.	78.6%	52.1%
Clifton: C. Columbus M.S.	71.0%	45.6%
Clifton District Passing Average	74.8%	48.9%
State Passing Average	70.5%	38.0%

ASK-8, 2013 "ADVANCED PROFICIENCY" IN
ENGLISH LANGUAGE ARTS AND MATHEMATICS

ASK-8 2013 School	Advanced Proficiency: English Language Arts	Advanced Proficiency: Mathematics
Classical Academy Charter School of Clifton	12.8%	84.6%
Clifton: W. Wilson M.S.	4.3%	14.4%
Clifton: C. Columbus M.S.	1.7%	11.1%
Clifton District "Advanced Proficiency" Average	3.0%	12.8%
State Advanced Proficiency Average	11.4%	31.3%

Observations: In ASK-8 2013, Classical Academy students surpassed their Clifton Public School peers by wide margins in every category. The "Advanced Proficiency" superior margin in Mathematics over Clifton Public School students is truly "eye popping," as its 8th-grade students exceeded Clifton's 8th-graders by *7 times greater,* and surpassed the statewide 8th-grade "Advanced Proficiency" attainment by nearly *3 times*!

Charter Schools

Ranking in descending order of New Jersey Charter Schools based on each school's percentage of its 8th-grade class achieving a "passing score" on the ASK-8 2013 exam-English Language Arts. "Passing" is defined as the combined percentage of a school's 8th-grade class achieving either a "Proficient" score or an "Advanced Proficiency" score in the tested subject.

"PASSING"

ASK-8 2013, ENGLISH LANGUAGE ARTS

School	Percent of 8th grade "Passing" English Language Arts
Classical Academy Charter School of Clifton	100%
Discovery Charter	100%
Princeton Charter	100%
Red Bank Charter	100%
Robert Treat Academy Charter	97.9%
North Star Academy Charter	91.7%
Gray Charter	90.0%
Queen City Academy Charter	88.6%
Elysian Charter	87.5%
Jersey City Golden Door Charter	86.3%
Maria L. Varisco-Rogers Charter	86.1%
Learning Community Charter	85.3%
Teaneck Community Charter	85.3%
Sussex County Charter	85.3%
Marion P. Thomas Charter	85.0%
Soaring Heights Charter	80%
Union County Teams Charter	80%
Galloway Community Charter	78.9%
Pride Academy Charter	78.8%
Hoboken Charter	77.3%
Greater Newark Charter	75.0%
Team Academy Charter	74.4%
Foundation Academy Charter	70.0%
Freedom Academy Charter	68.1%

Camden's Promise Charter	67.3%
Lady Liberty Academy Charter	66.1%
Hope Academy Charter	65.2%
Oceanside Charter	64.9%
Jersey City Community Charter	64.8%
Village Charter	64.1%
Paterson Charter of Science and Technology	63.1%
Central Jersey Charter	60.5%
Central Jersey Arts Charter	60.5%
Leap Academy Charter	59.7%
Liberty Academy Charter	53.3%
DUE Season Charter	40.9%
Greater Brunswick Charter	36.8%
PleasanTech Academy Charter	Scores not recorded
Trenton Community Charter	Scores not reported
CREATE Charter School	Scores not recorded
Emily Fisher Charter	Scores not recorded

Charter Schools

Ranking in descending order of New Jersey Charter Schools based on each school's percentage of its 8th-grade class achieving a "passing score" on the ASK-8 2013 assessment in Mathematics.

"PASSING"

ASK-8 2013, MATHEMATICS

School	Percent of 8th grade "Passing" Mathematics
Classical Academy Charter School of Clifton	100%
Robert Treat Academy Charter	100%
Princeton Charter	100%
Discovery Charter	100%
North Star Academy Charter	89.5%
Red Bank Charter	89.5%
Central Jersey College Prep Charter	85.4%
Maria L. Varisco-Rogers Charter	80.6%
Teaneck Community Charter	79.4%
Hoboken Charter School	72.7%
Elysian Charter of Hoboken	71.9%
Camden's Promise Charter	70.1%
Jersey City Golden Door Charter	68.2%
Foundation Academy Charter	66%
Learning Community Charter	64.7%
Soaring Heights Charter	60%
Pride Academy	63.7%
Galloway Community Charter	57.9%
Team Academy Charter	57.3%
Queen City Academy Charter	57.2%
Gray Charter	55%
Sussex County Charter for Tech	54.7%
Village Charter	53.9%
Oceanside Charter	51.3%
Jersey City Community Charter	50%
Leap Academy Charter	46%
Union County Teams Charter	45%

Paterson Charter for Sci and Tech	42.9%
Lady Liberty Academy Charter	42.4%
Marion P. Thomas Charter	40%
Freedom Academy Charter	36.2%
DUE Season Charter	34%
Central Jersey Arts Charter	31.6%
Hope Academy Charter	30.4%
Greater Newark Academy Charter	27.3%
Greater Brunswick Charter	23.7%
Liberty Academy Charter	20%
PleasanTech Academy Charter	Scores not reported
Trenton Community Charter	Scores not reported
CREATE Charter School	Scores not reported
Emily Fisher Charter	Scores not reported

Charter Schools

Ranking in descending order of New Jersey Charter Schools based on each school's percentage of its 8th-graders achieving an "**Advanced Proficiency**" score on the ASK-8 2013 exam-English Language Arts

"ADVANCED PROFICIENCY"

ASK-8 2013-ENGLISH LANGUAGE ARTS

School	Percent of 8th-Graders Earning "Advanced Proficiency"
Princeton Charter	40.9%
Robert Treat Academy Charter	30.6%
Discovery Charter	18.8%
Red Bank Charter	15.8%
Classical Academy Charter School of Clifton	**12.8%**
Teaneck Community Charter	11.8%
Learning Community Charter	11.8%
Soaring Heights Charter	10%
Hoboken Charter	9.1%
North Star Academy	9%
Freedom Academy Charter	5.8%
Jersey City Golden Door Charter	4.5%
Foundation Academy Charter	4%
Queen City Academy Charter	2.9%
TEAM Academy Charter	2.5%
Paterson Charter of Sci & Tech	2.4%
Lady Liberty Academy Charter	1.7%
Pride Academy Charter	1.5%
Sussex County Charter	1.3%
Camden's Promise Charter	.9%
Elysian Charter	0%
Central Jersey Charter	0%
Greater Newark Charter	0%
Union County Teams Charter	0%
Greater Brunswick Charter	0%
Maria L Varisco-Rogers Charter	0%

Marion P. Thomas Charter	0%
Village Charter	0%
DUE Season Charter	0%
Jersey City Community Charter	0%
Central Jersey Arts Charter	0%
Galloway Community Charter	0%
Gray Charter	0%
Hope Academy Charter	0%
Leap Academy Charter	0%
Liberty Academy Charter	0%
Oceanside Charter	0%
PleasanTech Academy Charter	Scores not recorded
Trenton Community Charter	Scores not recorded
CREATE Charter School	Scores not recorded
Emily Fisher Charter	Scores not recorded

Charter Schools

Ranking in descending order of New Jersey Charter Schools based on each school's percentage of its 8th-graders achieving an "**Advanced Proficiency**" score on the ASK-8 2013 assessment in Mathematics

"ADVANCED PROFICIENCY"

ASK-8 2013-MATHEMATICS

School	Percent of 8th-Graders Earning "Advanced Proficiency"
Princeton Charter	90.9%
Classical Academy Charter School of Clifton	84.6%
Discovery Charter	68.8%
Robert Treat Academy Charter	67.3%
Red Bank Charter	47.4%
North Star Academy Charter	43.6%
Teaneck Community Charter	41.2%
Central Jersey College Prep Charter	39.6%
Learning Community Charter	35.3%
Elysian Charter of Hoboken	34.4%
Hoboken Charter	31.8%
Maria L. Varisco-Rogers Charter	27.8%
Pride Academy Charter	27.3%
Camden's Promise Charter	27.1%
Foundation Academy Charter	26%
Soaring Heights Charter	25%
Queen City Academy Charter	22.9%
Galloway Community Charter	21.1%
Jersey City Golden Door	18.2%
Gray Charter	15%
Team Charter Academy	14.5%
Oceanside Charter	13.5%
Sussex County Charter for Tech	12%
Jersey City Community Charter	11.1%
Greater Newark Academy Charter	9.1%
Hope Academy Charter	8.7%

Union County TEAMS Charter	7.5%
Freedom Academy Charter	7.2%
Leap Academy Charter	6.3%
Paterson Charter for Sci & Tech	6%
Central Jersey Arts Center	5.3%
Lady Liberty Academy Charter	5.1%
Marion P. Thomas Charter	5%
DUE Season Community Charter	4.5%
Greater Brunswick Charter	2.6%
Village Charter	2.6%
Liberty Academy Charter	0%
PleasanTech Academy Charter	Scores not recorded
Trenton Community Charter	Scores not recorded
CREATE Charter School	Scores not recorded
Emily Fisher Charter	Scores not recorded

Observations: The above four charter school comparison charts for the ASK-8, 2013, show that Classical Academy 8th-graders ranked: 1) **Top 1%** (tied with 2 other charter schools) in "Passing" English Language Arts; 2) **Top 1%** (tied with 3 other charter schools) in "Passing" Mathematics; 3) **Top 12%** (5th place out of 41 charter schools) in achieving "Advanced Proficiency" in English Language Arts; 4) **Top 5%** (2nd place out of 41 charter schools) in achieving "Advanced Proficiency" in Mathematics.

ASK-8, 2013

Passaic County Public Schools

Percent of Each School's 8th-Grade Class "Passing" Tested Subject

Charter School	Percent of 8th-grade Students "Passing" English Language Arts	Charter School	Percent of 8th-grade Students "Passing" Mathematics
Classical Academy C.S. of Clifton	100%	Classical Academy C.S. of Clifton	100%
Wayne-Schuyler Colfax M.S.	95.3%	North Haledon Boro	88.8%
Wayne-Anthony Wayne M.S.	93.2%	Wayne-Schuyler Colfax M.S.	88.5%
Wayne-Geo. Washington M.S.	92.8%	Wayne-Anthony Wayne M.S.	86.6%
Totowa Boro	92.5%	Wayne-Geo. Washington M.S.	81.2%
Pompton Lakes Boro	91.3%	Ringwood Boro	79.5%
Ringwood Boro	90.7%	Totowa Boro	76.6%
North Haledon Boro	90.1%	Little Falls Boro	75.9%
Wanaque Boro	87.9%	Wanaque (Haskell)	75.5%
Hawthorne Boro	87.9%	Bloomingdale Boro	74.4%
Bloomingdale Boro	87.2%	Wanaque Boro	74.2%
West Milford Boro	86.5%	Pompton Lakes Boro	71.7%
Little Falls Boro	83.5%	Woodland Park Boro	69.2%
Clifton-Woodrow Wilson M.S.	78.6%	West Milford Boro	69.1%
Woodland Park Boro	78.2%	Haledon Boro	68.5%
Wanaque (Haskell)	73.4%	Hawthorn Boro	63.3%
Haledon Boro	72.9%	Clifton-Woodrow Wilson M.S.	52.1%
Prospect Boro	72.9%	Prospect Park Boro	51.6%
Clifton-C. Columbus M.S.	71%	Paterson City-District Average	45.7%
Paterson City-District Average	61.6%	Clifton-C. Columbus M.S.	45.6%
Passaic City	58.5%	Passaic City	44.6%

Passaic County Public School Rankings
Based on Percentage of Each School's 8th-Grade Class Earning
"Advanced Proficiency" in English Language Arts and Mathematics

ASK-8 2013
Passaic County Schools
8th-Grade English Language Arts, "Advanced Proficiency" Attainment

School and Municipality	Percent of 8th-Grade Students Achieving English Language Arts "Advanced Proficiency"
G. Washington M.S., Wayne	19%
Anthony Wayne M.S., Wayne	17.8%
Classical Academy Charter School of Clifton	**12.8%**
Macopin M.S., West Milford Twp.	11.4%
High Mountain M.S., North Haledon	11.3%
Martin J. Ryerson School, Ringwood	10.6%
Wanaque School, Wanaque Boro	10.4%
Lakeside School, Pompton Lakes	10.1%
Washington Park School, Totowa Boro	8.6%
Walter T. Bergen M.S., Bloomingdale	7.7%
Memorial School, Woodlawn Park	7.5%
Haskell Elementary School, Wanaque Boro	6.1%
W. Wilson M.S., Clifton	4.3%
Prospect Park School #1, Prospect Park	3.3%
Lincoln M.S., Hawthorne	2.6%
Haledon Public School, Haledon	1.8%
Lincoln M.S. #4, Passaic City	1.8%
C. Columbus M.S., Clifton	1.7%
Paterson School District (Advanced Proficiency Total for District)	1.3%

ASK-8 2013

Passaic County Schools

Rankings Based on Percentage of Each School's 8th-Graders Achieving
"Advanced Proficiency" Score in Mathematics

School and Municipality	Percent of 8th-Grade Students Achieving Mathematics "Advanced Proficiency"
Classical Academy Charter School of Clifton	84.6%
High Mountain School, North Haledon	57.5%
Schuyler-Colfax M.S., Wayne	46.2%
Anthony Wayne M.S., Wayne	45.8%
Martin J. Ryerson School, Ringwood	40.4%
G. Washington M.S., Wayne	38.3%
Wanaque School, Wanaque Boro	34.5%
Walter T. Bergen School, Bloomingdale	32.1%
Memorial School, Woodlawn Park	31.6%
Washington Park School, Totowa Boro	29.8%
Haskell School, Wanaque Boro	28.6%
Little Falls School #1, Little Falls Boro	26.4%
Haledon Public School, Haledon	24.6%
Lakeside School, Pompton Lakes	20.3%
Macopin School, West Milford Twp.	17.1%
Lincoln M.S., Hawthorne	15.7%
W. Wilson M.S., Clifton	14.4%
Prospect Park School #1, Prospect Park	12.9%
Lincoln School #4, Passaic City	12.3%
Paterson District (Total "Advanced Proficiency" for Entire District)	11.8%
C. Columbus M.S., Clifton	11.1%

Observations: In the above Passaic County public school comparison charts, Classical Academy Charter School 8th-graders outperformed *every* Passaic County public school in its percentage of 8th-graders "Passing" English language arts *and* Mathematics—**tops in the county!** *Classical Academy produced the highest percentage of 8th-graders achieving "Advanced Proficiency" scores than any other Passaic County school by far in the ASK-8 2013 Mathematics Test,* and placed 3rd highest out of all 19 Passaic County schools (top 15%) in English language arts "Advanced Proficiency." Notice also how extraordinarily higher its 8th-grade "Advanced Proficiency" percentage is compared with the two Clifton Middle Schools (W. Wilson and C. Columbus).

ASK-8 2014
CLASSICAL ACADEMY STUDENT OUTCOMES
A Broad Comparative Analysis and Rankings of Classical Academy 8th-Grade Student "Passing" Percentage and "Advanced Proficiency" Outcomes in Tested Subjects of English Language Arts and Mathematics on the ASK-8 2014 Classical Academy Student State-Mandated Standardized Assessment

Outcome Comparisons with:
1: Clifton District and Clifton District Middle Schools
2: All New Jersey Charter Schools Administering
the ASK-8 2014 assessment
3: All New Jersey "C/D" District Factor Schools
4: All Passaic County Public Schools
5: Statewide Passing and Advanced Proficiency Outcomes

1: Classical Academy Charter School of Clifton
vs.
Clifton Public Schools (and Statewide Comparisons):
Student Assessment Outcomes in the ASK-8 2014 test of
English Language Arts and Mathematics

"Passing" constitutes the combined percent of a school's 8th-grade class achieving in each tested subject either a "Proficient" score or an "Advanced Proficiency" outcome.

ASK-8 2014
"PASSING" PERCENTAGES

School	Percent of 8th-Grade Students "Passing" English Language Arts	Percent of 8th-Grade Students "Passing" Mathematics
Classical Academy C.S. of Clifton	97.2%	94.5%
Clifton's W. Wilson Middle School	72%	54.6%
Clifton's C. Columbus Middle School	62.5%	51.7%
Clifton School District Average Passing %	67.2%	53.1%
New Jersey Statewide Passing Average	67.2%	35.9%

ASK-8 2014
"ADVANCED PROFICIENCY" PERCENTAGES

School	Percent of 8th-Grade Students "Advanced Proficiency" English Language Arts	Percent of 8th-Grade Students "Advanced Proficiency" Mathematics
Classical Academy C.S of Clifton	25%	66.7%
Clifton's W. Wilson Middle School	6.2%	20.%
Clifton's C. Columbus Middle School	1.6%	16.2%
Clifton School District Average "Advanced Proficiency" %	3.9%	18.1%
NJ Statewide "Advanced Proficiency" %	12.6%	35.6%

<u>Observations:</u> In all categories, as the above 2 charts document, Classical Academy students massively outperform academically their Clifton peers, with a "passing" rate nearly 30 percentage points greater in English Language Arts and near doubling the "passing" rate in Mathematics. In "Advanced Proficiency," the margins are even greater, with Classical Academy students scoring near *4 times* Clifton district's levels in both English Language Arts and Mathematics. In statewide outcomes, the percentage of 8th-grade Classical Academy students achieving "Passing" and "Advance Proficiency" was significantly greater than the percentage of the state's 8th-graders in every category on state-mandated assessments.

2: Charter-School Student Outcome Comparisons and Rankings

Percentage of 8th-Grade Class Achieving a "Passing" Score in ASK-8 2014 Tested Subjects of English Language Arts and Mathematics

N.B. "Passing" percentage is the combined percentage of 8th-grade students in each listed charter school scoring either a "Proficient" or "Advanced Proficiency" outcome. All charter percentages are cited in descending order—from highest "Passing" rate to lowest.

ENGLISH LANGUAGE ARTS		MATHEMATICS	
School	Percent Passing	School	Percent Passing
Discovery Carter School	100%	Robert Treat Academy	95.6%
Gray Charter School	100%	**Classical Academy Charter**	**94.5%**
Red Bank Charter School	100%	Princeton Charter School	93.3%
Unity Charter School	100%	Discovery Charter School	93.3%
Classical Academy Charter	**97.2%**	Bergen Arts and Science Center	93.2%
Princeton Charter School	95.5%	North Star Academy Charter	93.1%
Bergen Arts & Sciences	94.9%	Unity Charter School	90.9%
Queen City Charter School	94.4%	Red Bank Charter School	90.0%
Robert Treat Academy Charter	93.5%	Central Jersey College Prep	89.9%
Soaring Heights Charter	92.7%	Hoboken Charter School	86.4%
Hoboken Charter School	90.9%	Gray Charter School	85.7%
Leap Academy Univ. Charter	87.9%	Maria L. Varisco-Rogers Charter	83.4%
Phillips Academy Charter	87.5%	Foundation Academy Charter	83.3%
Maria L. Varisco-Rogers Charter	87.1%	Phillips Academy Charter	77.5%
Ridge & Valley Charter School	85.7%	Great Oaks Charter	77.3%
Central Jersey College Prep	84.8%	Camden's Promise Charter	75.8%
Jersey City Golden Door	83.8%	Soaring Heights Charter	75.6%
Learning Community Charter	82.7%	Jersey City Golden Door	75.0%
Foundation Academy Charter	81.5%	Teaneck Community Charter	70.6%
Renaissance Regional Charter	81.3%	Renaissance Regional Charter	68.8%
Lady Liberty Academy Charter	80.9%	Queen City Charter School	66.7%
Teaneck Community Charter	79.4%	Elysian Charter School Hoboken	65.6%
Greater Newark Charter	77.5%	Ridge & Valley Charter	64.3%
Camden's Promise Charter	74.7%	Leap Academy Univ. Charter	62.1%
Sussex Cty Charter for Tech	73.3%	Pride Academy Charter	59.1%

Marion P. Thomas Charter	72.1%	TEAM Academy Charter	59.1%
TEAM Academy Charter School	72.1%	Learning Community Charter	58.6%
Great Oaks Charter School	69.7%	Central Jersey Arts	57.9%
Pride Academy Charter School	68.2%	Lady Liberty Academy Charter	53.2%
Union County Teams Charter	67.6%	Paterson Charter for Sci & Tech	52.6%
Dr. Lena Edwards Academic	66.7%	Jersey City Community Charter	51.8%
Benjamin Banneker Prep	66. 6%	Benjamin Banneker Prep	51.7%
Elysian Charter School	65.6%	Marion P. Thomas Charter	51.2%
Galloway Community Charter	64.2%	METS Charter School	48.3%
Greater Brunswick Charter	62.2%	Dr. Lena Edwards Academy	46.6%
Hope Academy Charter	60.8%	Galloway Community Charter	46.4%
METS Charter School	60.7%	DUE Season Charter	43.6%
Village Charter School	59.0 %	Sussex County Charter for Tech	43.1%
Jersey City Community Charter	58.6%	Union County Teams Charter	38.3%
Central Jersey Arts Charter	57.9%	John P. Holland Charter	36.9%
Paterson Charter for Sci & Tech	56.6%	Paul Robeson Charter School	34.7%
John P. Holland Charter	52.6%	Village Charter School	33.3%
DUE Season Charter School	50.9%	Greater Brunswick Charter	32.4%
Freedom Academy Charter	48.1%	Hope Charter School	30.4%
Paul Robeson Charter	46.4%	Freedom Academy Charter	29.5%

Observations: Of the 46 New Jersey charter schools in the above chart, Classical Academy Charter School placed *fifth-highest* (**top 10%**) in its English Language Arts "passing" percentage, and *second highest* (**top 4%**) in Mathematics "passing" percentage.

NEW JERSEY CHARTER SCHOOL RANKINGS
"ADVANCED PROFICIENCY"

Percentage of 8th-Grade Class Achieving an "Advanced Proficiency" Score in Ask-8 2014

Tested Subjects of English Language Arts and Mathematics

ENGLISH LANGUAGE ARTS		MATHEMATICS	
School	Adv. Prof. %	School	Adv. Prof. %
Classical Academy Charter	25.0%	Unity Charter School	81.8%
Princeton Charter School	24.4%	Red Bank Charter School	75.0%
North Star Academy Charter	20.9%	Princeton Charter School	73.3%
Discovery Charter School	20.0%	Classical Academy Charter	66.7%
Soaring Heights Charter School	19.5%	Central Jersey College Prep	63.0%
Unity Charter School	18.2%	North Star Academy	55.1%
Bergen Arts & Sciences Charter	16.9%	Bergen Arts & Sciences Charter	52.5%
Robert Treat Academy Charter	15.2%	Maria L. Varisco-Rogers Charter	51.9%
Gray Charter School	14.3%	Robert Treat Academy Charter	47.8%
Ridge & Valley Charter School	14.3%	Foundation Academy Charter	46.3%
Hoboken Charter School	13.6%	Hoboken Charter School	45.5%
Red Bank Charter School	10.0%	Discovery Charter School	40.0%
Teaneck Community Charter	8.8%	Great Oaks Charter School	39.4%
Queen City Charter School	8.3%	Elysian Charter School	37.5%
Galloway Community Charter	7.1%	Soaring Heights Charter	31.7%
Central Jersey College Prep Charter	6.5%	Camden's Promise Charter	31.6%
Foundation Academy Charter	5.6%	Teaneck Community Charter	29.4%
Maria L. Varisco-Rogers Charter	5.6%	Gray Charter School	28.6%
Hope Academy Charter School	4.3%	Jersey City Golden Door Charter	27.9%
Lady Liberty Academy Charter	4.3%	Queen City Charter School	27.8%
METS Charter School	3.4%	Phillips Academy Charter	22.5%
Benjamin Banneker Prep Charter	3.3%	Ridge & Valley Charter School	21.4%
Elysian Charter School of Hoboken	3.1%	Pride Academy Charter	21.2%
Great Oaks Charter School	3.0%	Learning Community Charter Sch.	17.2%
Pride Academy Charter School	3.0%	Paterson Charter for Sci & Tech	16.7%
Paul Robeson Charter School	2.9%	Marion P. Thomas Charter	16.3%
Jersey City Golden Door Charter	2.9%	Galloway Community Charter	14.3%
Team Academy Charter School	2.9%	Leap Academy Univ. Charter Sch.	13.8%

Greater Brunswick Charter School	2.7%	METS Charter School	13.5%
Phillips Academy Charter School	2.5%	Central Jersey Arts Charter	13.2%
Marion P. Thomas Charter School	2.3%	Renaissance Regional Charter	12.5%
Camden's Promise Charter School	2.1%	Jersey City Community Charter	12.1%
Greater Newark Charter School	2.0%	Team Academy Charter School	11.1%
Learning Community Charter School	1.7%	DUE Season Charter	10.9%
Paterson Charter for Sci & Tech	1.3%	Lady Liberty Academy Charter	10.6%
Sussex County Charter for Tech	1.3%	Greater Newark Charter	10.2%
Central Jersey Arts Charter	0%	Greater Brunswick Charter	8.1%
Dr. Lena Edwards Academic Charter	0%	Village Charter School	7.7%
DUE Season Charter	0%	Paul Robeson Charter School	7.2%
Freedom Academy Charter	0%	Freedom Academy Charter	6.4%
Jersey City Community Charter	0%	Union County Teams Charter	5.9%
John Holland Charter School	0%	John Holland Charter School	5.3%
Leap Academy Univ. Charter	0%	Sussex County Charter for Tech	5.3%
Renaissance Regional Charter	0%	Benjamin Banneker Prep Charter	5.0%
Union County Teams	0%	Hope Charter School	4.3%
Village Charter School	0%	Dr. Lena Edwards Academic C.S.	3.3%

<u>Observations:</u> As the above chart illustrates, Classical Academy Charter School of Clifton's 8th-graders placed *first* (*top 1%*) of all 46 New Jersey charter schools in the percentage of its 8th-graders earning English Language Arts "Advanced Proficiency" scores on the ASK-8 2014, and placed *fourth* (*top 8%*) of all 46 charter schools in earning "Advanced Proficiency" scores in 8th-grade Mathematics.

4: ASK-8 2014 Outcome Comparison of
"CD" District Factor Group Schools and School Districts

Explanation: The New Jersey Department of Education has long grouped New Jersey schools and school districts by their "socio-economic" characteristics and similarities of population or shared demographic attributes. These "factors" are generally seen to compare more fairly educational outcomes, as they better account for differences in advantages and disadvantages, and therefore educational achievement (and potential) of adolescents. These "factors" include such measurements as household income, price of real estate, the average educational attainment of a community, percentage of minorities and immigrants in a community, and other similar demographic and economic information. The state relies heavily, though not exclusively, for their statewide *District Factor Group (DFG)* analysis and groupings on national census data complied every 10 years. For example, when the Classical Academy Charter School of Clifton began in 1998, Clifton was a "D/E" District Factor Group school. A year after the 2000 census, Clifton was "downgraded" to a "C/D" District Factor Group school district, as it had and was experiencing demographic changes justifying a lower group rating.

The state uses letter markings to distinguish the various groups, from "A" to "J," with "A" being communities of the lowest socio-economic measurements and "J" the state's most affluent communities. For example, Paterson, New Jersey (Passaic County), Public School District is designated an "A" DFG, but Glen Rock, New Jersey (Bergen County), only a few miles distant, is a "J" DFG school district.

If a community and its school district contain enough "factors" where specific socio-economic factors don't dominate or permeate a community exclusively, and sufficient "shared" attributes prevail, the state often designates a community or school district with a divided District Factor Group rating, as Clifton's "C/D" DFG. Since the Classical Academy Charter School of Clifton enrolls only Clifton resident students, it, too, is a "C/D" public charter school, and, therefore, standardized-test academic outcome comparisons with all other 131 New Jersey public "C/D" schools are fair and eminently justifiable.

ASK-8 2014

Classical Academy and Statewide Peer-to-Peer Comparison

C/D District Factor Group (DFG) Student Achievement: Comparing Classical Academy, a "C/D" School, with the Statewide "C/D" Student "Passing" Achievement on Tested Subjects

C/D DFG Schools	Percent of 8th-Grade Students "Passing" English Language Arts	Percent of 8th-Grade Students "Passing" Mathematics
Classical Academy Charter School of Clifton (C/D)	97.2%	94.5%
Statewide Average Percentage of C/D (DFG) 8th-graders achieving "Passing"	75.8%	65%

ASK-8 2014

C/D District Factor Group (DFG) Student Achievement: Comparing Classical Academy, a C/D School, with the Statewide "C/D" Student "Advanced Proficiency" Achievement. "Advanced Proficiency" C/D (DFG) score statewide represents 131 C/D schools and school districts educating 9,880 students.

C/D DFG Schools	Percent of 8th-Grade Students "Advanced Proficiency" English Language Arts	Percent of 8th-Grade Students "Advanced Proficiency" Mathematics
Classical Academy Charter School of Clifton (C/D)	25%	66.7%
Statewide Percent of C/D 8th-Graders Achieving "Advanced Proficiency" score statewide represents 131 C/D schools and school districts educating 9,880 students.	6.6%	26.2%

ASK-8 2014

C/D School and School Districts: Average Total Mean Scale Score: C/D DFG Schools English Language Arts Mathematics

C/D DFG Schools	English Language Arts	Mathematics
Classical Academy Charter School of Clifton (C/D)	234.5	260.5
Average Total Mean Scale Score for All 131 New Jersey C/D Schools and School Districts.	215	215.6

<u>Observations:</u> As the above charts show, the Classical Academy Charter School's 8th-grade students are about *25 to 30 percentage points higher* in their passing

percentage average than their 9,880 New Jersey 8th-grade peers enrolled in all New Jersey's 131 C/D schools and school districts.

Classical Academy 8th-grade students also earn an "Advanced Proficiency" achievement rate *4 times higher* in English Language Arts, and an "Advanced Proficiency" percentage nearly *3 times higher* in Mathematics than their C/D 8th-grade peers statewide.

Furthermore, a close examination of the state's ASK-8 2014 data reveals that, of the 131 C/D District Factor Group schools and school districts educating 9,880 students, the Classical Academy Charter School of Clifton places or ranks *number 1 in all test percentage outcomes for both English Language Arts and Mathematics*. The Classical Academy Charter School of Clifton, by virtue of its 8th graders' performance on state-mandated academic assessment, is the **top performing C/D school in the state, and its 8th-graders prove themselves to be the highest academically achieving C/D District Factor Group school in New Jersey based on ASK-8 2014 student outcomes.**

5: Passaic County Public Schools
Rankings Based on 8th-Grade English Language Arts
tested in the ASK-8 2014
8th-Grade English Language Arts "Passing" Percentage Outcomes

(*N.B.* "Passing" is calculated by the combined percentage of students earning either a "Proficient" score or an "Advanced Proficiency" score)

District Factor Group	Name of School and School District	8th-Grade Passing Percent
ENGLISH LANGUAGE ARTS		
C/D	Classical Academy Charter School of Clifton	97.2%
F/G	High Mountain Middle School (No. Haledon)	92.1%
F/G	Lakeside Middle School (Pompton Lakes)	91.5%
G/H	Martin J. Ryerson Middle School (Ringwood)	91.0%
G/H	George Washington Middle School (Wayne)	91.0%
G/H	Anthony Wayne Middle School (Wayne)	90.7%
G/H	Schuyler Colfax Middle School (Wayne)	90.7%
C/D	Washington Park Middle School (Totowa Boro)	88.0%
D/E	Lincoln Middle School (Hawthorne)	84.6%
F/G	Walter Bergen Middle School (Bloomingdale)	84.2%
F/G	Macopin Middle School (West Milford)	83.2%
D/E	Haskell Middle School (Wanaque Boro)	82.9%
F/G	School # 1 (Little Falls)	81.7%
B	School # 1 (Prospect Park)	72.1%
C/D	Woodrow Wilson Middle School (Clifton)	72.0%
B	Haledon Public Schools (Haledon)	71.6%
D/E	Memorial School (Woodland Park)	68.1%
C/D	Christopher Columbus Middle School (Clifton)	62.5%
A	Paterson Charter School for Science & Technology (Paterson)	56.6%
A	Paterson (District-Wide 8th-Grade Passing %)	54.4%
A	Lincoln Middle School (Passaic City)	52.6%
A	John P. Holland Charter School (Paterson)	52.6%
A	Dr. Frank Napier Jr. School (Paterson)	39.7%

Observation: Classical Academy Charter School of Clifton earned the **highest** *(top 1%)* "8th-Grade Percentage Passing Rate" in English Language Arts of all Passaic County public and charter schools administering the 8th-grade ASK-8 2014 standardized test.

ASK-8 2014
Passaic County Public Schools
Rankings Based on ASK-8 2014 8th-Grade Mathematics
"Passing" Percentage Outcomes

N.B. "Passing" is calculated by the combined percentage of 8th-grade students earning either a "Proficient" score or an "Advanced Proficiency" score).

MATHEMATICS		
District Factor Group	Name of School and School District	8th-Grade Passing Percent
C/D	Classical Academy Charter School of Clifton	94.5%
F/G	High Mountain School (North Haledon)	89.9%
G/H	Anthony Wayne Middle School (Wayne)	87.2%
G/H	Schuyler-Colfax Middle School (Wayne)	85.1%
G/H	George Washington Middle School (Wayne)	84.7%
F/G	School Number 1 (Little Falls)	83.7%
G/H	Martin J. Ryerson School (Ringwood)	78.4%
D/E	Haskell School (Wanaque Boro)	77.1%
C/D	Washington Park School (Totowa Boro)	77.1%
D/E	Lincoln Middle School (Hawthorne)	75.0 %
F/G	Lakeside School (Pompton Lakes)	74.6%
D/E	Wanaque School (Wanaque)	72.2%
F/G	Walter Bergen Middle School (Bloomingdale)	72.0%
F/G	Macopin School (West Milford)	71.1%
B	Haledon Public Schools (Haledon)	68.4%
C/D	Woodrow Wilson Middle School (Clifton)	54.6%
D/E	Memorial School (Woodland Park)	53.3%
A	Paterson Charter School for Science and Technology (Paterson)	52.6%
C/D	Christopher Columbus Middle School (Clifton)	51.7%
A	Lincoln Middle School (Passaic City)	48.1%
A	Paterson (District-Wide 8th-grade passing percentage	45.9%
B	School Number 1 (Prospect Park)	42.9%
A	John P. Holland Charter School (Paterson)	36.9%
A	Dr. Frank Napier Jr. School (Paterson)	28.2%

<u>Observations:</u> 1) The above chart shows that Classical Academy Charter School of Clifton earned the **highest (top 1%)** 8th-grade Mathematics "passing" percentage of all Passaic County schools administering the 8th-grade ASK-8 2014 test. 2) The above chart also shows that the Classical Academy's 8th-grade Mathematics "Passing" percentage is nearly *twice* that of either of the two Clifton middle schools.

ASK-8 2014
Passaic County Public Schools "Advanced Proficiency"
Each Passaic County Public School's Percent of 8th-Grade Class
Earning "Advanced Proficiency" on ASK-8 2014 for
English Language Arts and Mathematics

	ENGLISH LANGUAGE ARTS	
District Factor Group	Name of School and School District	8th-Grade "Advanced Proficiency" Percentage
C/D	Classical Academy Charter School of Clifton (Clifton)	25.0%
G/H	Anthony Wayne Middle School (Wayne)	22.2%
G/H	Schuyler-Colfax Middle School (Wayne)	19.4%
G/H	George Washington Middle School (Wayne)	15.9%
F/G	High Mountain School (North Haledon)	15.7%
G/H	Martin J. Ryerson School (Ringwood)	13.9%
F/G	Macopin School (West Milford)	10.8%
F/G	Lakeside School (Pompton Lakes)	10.1%
F/G	Walter Bergen School (Bloomingdale)	9.2%
D/E	Wanaque School (Wanaque Boro)	6.6%
C/D	Woodrow Wilson Middle School (Clifton)	6.2%
D/E	Haledon Public School (Haledon)	5.8%
F/G	School Number 1 (Little Falls)	5.4%
D/E	Memorial School (Woodland Park)	4.4%
C/D	Washington Park School (Totowa)	2.9%
D/E	Haskell School (Wanaque Boro)	2.9%
A	Paterson (District-Wide 8th-Grade Average)	2.1%
C/D	Christopher Columbus Middle School (Clifton)	1.6%
A	Lincoln Middle School (Passaic City)	1.5%
A	Paterson Charter School for Science and Technology (Paterson)	1.3%
B	School Number 1 (Prospect Park)	1.0%
A	John P. Holland Charter School (Paterson)	0%
A	Dr. Frank J. Napier Jr. School (Paterson)	0%

PASSAIC COUNTY SCHOOLS: ADVANCED PROFICIENCY RANKINGS IN MATHEMATICS

Passaic County Public Schools Rankings Based on Percent of 8th-Grade Class
Earning Advanced Proficiency Scores in Mathematics on the ASK-8 2014

MATHEMATICS		
District Factor Group	Name of School and School District	8th-Grade "Advanced Proficiency" Percentage
C/D	Classical Academy Charter School of Clifton	66.7%
G/H	George Washington Middle School (Wayne)	50.8%
F/G	High Mountain School (North Haledon)	50.6%
G/H	Anthony Wayne Middle School (Wayne)	49.4%
G/H	Schuyler–Colfax Middle School (Wayne)	47.0%
G/H	Martin J. Ryerson School (Ringwood)	45.8%
F/G	School Number 1 (Little Falls)	43.5%
C/D	Washington Park School (Totowa Boro)	38.0%
D/E	Haskell School (Wanaque Boro)	37.1%
D/E	Wanaque School (Wanaque Boro)	36.1%
F/G	Walter Bergen School (Bloomingdale)	29.3%
B	Haledon Public School (Haledon)	29.2%
D/E	Memorial School (Woodland Park)	25.9%
F/G	Macopin School (West Milford)	25.1%
C/D	Woodrow Wilson Middle School (Clifton)	20.0%
F/G	Lakeside School (Pompton Lakes)	17.7%
A	Paterson Charter School for Science and Technology (Paterson)	16.7%
C/D	Christopher Columbus Middle School (Clifton)	16.2%
D/E	Lincoln Middle School (Hawthorne)	16.0 %
B	School Number 1 (Prospect Park)	15.3%
A	Paterson (District-Wide 8th-Grade Average)	14.1%
A	Lincoln Middle School (Passaic City)	12.6%
A	Dr. Frank J. Napier Jr. School (Paterson)	6.4%
A	John P. Holland Charter School (Paterson)	5.3%

<u>Observation:</u> *Tops in Passaic County, Again!* By their "Passing" and "Advanced Proficiency" rates, as the above charts show, a higher percentage of Classical Academy 8th-graders demonstrated greater learning in English Language Arts and Mathematics on ASK-8, 2014, than 8th-grade students *in any other Passaic County public school!*

ASK-8 2014
New Jersey's "J" Schools

I have often asserted that Classical Academy Charter School of Clifton 8th-grade students, largely children of immigrant parents, who hear spoken, or speak themselves at home a language other than English, and whose parents' educational levels, for the most part, do not extend beyond high school, and whose household incomes are below or barely meet the state average household income, nevertheless produce standardized-test outcomes and high academic-learning results comparable to those of New Jersey's most affluent school districts and wealthiest communities. These schools and communities possessing the highest wealth and greatest assets are state-designated as "J" schools; they are home to the state's most advantaged adolescents. The following chart, comparing Classical Academy ASK-8 2014 student outcomes to 10 New Jersey "J" schools selected randomly, will support my assertion.

ASK-8 2014

"PASSING"

Percent of a school's 8th-grade class "Passing" each tested subject. "Passing" is defined as the combined percent of a school's 8th-grade class earning either a "Proficient" score or an "Advanced Proficiency" outcome.

DFG	School/Community	Percent of "Passing" English Language Arts	Percent of "Passing" Mathematics
"C/D"	Classical Academy C.S. of Clifton	97.2%	94.5%
"J"	William Annin M.S., Bernards Twp.	97.1%	95.3%
"J"	Glen Rock M.S., Glen Rock	98.1%	92.3%
"J"	Briarcliff School, Mountain Lakes	98.9%	93.3%
"J"	Mendham Twp. M.S., Mendham Twp.	99.1%	97.2%
"J"	Ho-Ho-Kus School, Ho-Ho-Kus Boro	98.8%	82.5%
"J"	Old Turnpike School, Tewksbury Twp.	96.4%	97.6%
"J"	Community M.S., West Windsor-Plainsboro	95.5%	90.9%
"J"	G. Washington M.S., Ridgewood Village	92.1%	92.8%
"J"	Milburn M.S., Milburn Twp.	97.1%	92.8%
"J"	Forestdale School, Rumson Boro	95.8%	85.5%
"J"	Statewide 8th-Grade Passing Percent for 4,381 "J" School Students	96%	92.1%

ASK-8 2014
New Jersey's "J" Schools
"Advanced Proficiency"

Percent of each "J" District Factor Group school's 8th-grade class achieving an "Advanced Proficiency" (the highest-level outcome) score on each tested subject.

DFG	School/Community	Percent of "Advanced Proficiency" English Language Arts	Percent of "Advanced Proficiency" Mathematics
"C/D"	Classical Academy Charter Sch. of Clifton	25%	66.7%
"J"	William Annin M.S. Bernards Twp.	33.1%	69%
"J"	Glen Rock M.S., Glen Rock	30%	63.5%
"J"	Briarcliff School, Mountain Lakes	30%	64.4%
"J"	Mendham Twp. M.S., Mendham Twp.	39.6%	83.6%
"J"	Ho-Ho-Kus School, Ho-Ho-Kus Boro.	17.5%	45%
"J"	Old Turnpike School, Tewksbury Twp.	25%	63.1%
"J"	Community M.S., West Windsor-Plainsboro	49.9%	77.7%
"J"	G. Washington M.S., Ridgewood Village	28.8%	56.8%
"J"	Milburn M.S., Milburn Twp.	36.2%	62.5%
"J"	Forrestdale School, Rumson Boro.	26.3%	48.7%
"J"	Schools Statewide Average Percent of 4,381 8th-Grade Students Achieving an "Advanced Proficiency"	33.2%	65.5%

Observations: "Learning Gap" much narrowed if not eliminated: The above "J" school student-performance chart comparisons for 8th-grade "Passing" and "Advanced Proficiency" attainment in English and mathematics, substantiate my assertion that Classical Academy students' attainment equals that of New Jersey's most affluent and most advantaged 8th-graders. Here, yet again, it proves that the Classical Academy Charter School of Clifton, whose students' parents are decidedly characterized as lower middle-class in income and educational levels, and a school whose students are 75%-80% children of immigrant parents, *has closed, indisputably and magnificently, the "learning gap" between advantaged and less-advantaged students in learning achievement.*

PARCC 2015
The Classical Academy Charter School of Clifton (Est. 1998)
National Blue-Ribbon School of Excellence (2008)
New Jersey "REWARDS" School (NJDOE, 2012)
A "Top Ten New Jersey School" (NJCAN, 2013)
New Jersey "Title I Exemplary Rewards School" (NJDOE, 2016)

CLASSICAL ACADEMY PARCC 2015 RESULTS
AND
COMPREHENSIVE COMPARATIVE STUDENT OUTCOMES
Comparisons Based on the Percentage of a School
or School District's 8th Grade Students Attaining
Level 4 ("Meeting Expectations") and
Level 5 ("Exceeding Expectations")
Vincent De Rosa, Founder, Lead Person/Principal
Magda De Rosa, Co-Founder, Administrative Assistant

Introduction

The Classical Academy Charter School of Clifton (New Jersey) is a middle school comprising grades 6, 7, and 8. Its 118 students for the 2014-2015 school year are all residents of Clifton, New Jersey. It operates on funding levels approximately 50%-60% below the per-pupil costs prevailing among neighboring public-school districts. Typically, 80% to 90% of its students are immigrants or children of immigrant parents, with the great majority (70% on average) being "bilingual" and speaking or hearing spoken a foreign language at home. The percentage of the school's student body qualifying for "Free/Reduced Federal School Food Program" is normally 25% to 40%.

The New Jersey Department of Education has designated Clifton, New Jersey, based on "socio-economic census and other data," a "C/D" District Factor Group ("DFG") school district and community. C/D District Factor Group schools are communities like Clifton, New Jersey, which can best be described as lower middle-class, with household incomes below or minimally meeting the state average.

This PARCC 2015 student-performance data represents a rather complete and accurate compendium of comparisons showing how the Classical Academy Charter School of Clifton 8th-graders performed on the state-mandated PARCC 2015 assessment, the first year this assessment was used in New Jersey. Classical Academy student academic performance is compared in the following data to student outcomes of pertinent student counterparts and relevant peer institutions. Specifically, this report compares Classical Academy PARCC 2015 student results in English Language Arts (8th grade), and "Algebra I" (8th grade), with the following 6 relevant and indicative categories:

1: Clifton Public Schools and School District

2: All New Jersey Charter Schools

3: Passaic County Public schools (traditional and charter)

4: New Jersey "C/D" District Factor Group Schools and School Districts

5: Statewide PARCC 2015 Results

6: "J" Schools Comparison

Contextual Background

The New Jersey Department of Education's Office of Charter Schools questionably imposed "Probation" on the Classical Academy, thus withholding its charter renewal in 2012. The Probation period lasted nearly two years, and the school's renewal charter was finally granted in spring of 2014. One of its "complaints" was that the Classical Academy, housed in an antiquated 115-year-old wood-frame structure, and having very little in the way of technology infrastructure, would never meet the technological demands and infrastructure requirements of modern education, and could never satisfy the digital and electronic requirements needed for the upcoming state-mandated student PARCC assessments, an entirely "online" computer-based test. Complying with that office's demands, the school installed the mandated technology infrastructure.

The student-learning outcomes in this (PARCC 2015) report should forever bury the Office of Charter Schools' dire predictions and show how wrong was its shallowly critical, disdainful, and prejudicial assessment of the Classical Academy's long-demonstrated capabilities. The contents of this PARCC 2015 report must also put to shame the Office of Charter Schools' derisive characterization that the Classical Academy is a mere "small Mom-and-Pop School," incongruous with the state's preferred and admired type of charter school: charter schools founded and operated by "network" companies. This report displaying the Classical Academy's high student PARCC results also belies the Office of Charter Schools' low assessment of the Classical Academy's educational effectiveness and value to students and community. Lastly, Office of Charter Schools underestimated the fierce determination of the school's leadership to meet successfully, if the Classical Academy was to continue as a charter school, the 44 "corrective action" mandates—none of which related to educational results or student-learning outcomes, or financial irregularities, but only to "procedures," or what it assessed as operational weaknesses which the Office of Charter Schools challenged the Classical Academy to rectify, if it wanted to continue as a charter school.

After a long, arduous struggle, the Classical Academy met all those demands to, what appeared to us, the reluctant satisfaction and grudging concession of its Office of Charter School critics. Having no other choice because of our successful efforts and determination, state bureaucrats finally and formally ratified the Classical Academy's continuance to educate its students to the very high levels this report documents. In the year prior to the PARCC's first administration, the Office of Charter Schools granted the school its third charter renewal in Spring of 2014, thus permitting "The Little School That Could" to continue its position as one of New Jersey's top-ranked public schools.

PARCC Measurement of Student Outcomes

In expressing standardized-test outcomes, PARCC discarded the term "Proficient" and replaced it with "Expectations." It also replaced the long-used three standardized-test outcomes of "Partial Proficiency," "Proficient," and "Advanced Proficiency" with 5 levels of "Expectations": Level 1 = Not Yet Meeting Expectations; Level 2 = Partially Meeting Expectations; Level 3 = Approaching Expectations; Level 4 = Meeting Expectations; Level 5 = Exceeding Expectations. A school's "Passing Percentage" is the combined percentage of students earning either a "Level 4" (Meeting Expectations) or "Level 5" (Exceeding Expectations) outcome.

Executive Summary and Synopsis

Based on the percentage of 8th-grade students achieving a PARCC 2015 Level 4 ("Meeting Expectations") and Level 5 ("Exceeding Expectations")— the two highest levels of PARCC outcomes—Classical Academy 8th-grade students outperformed its resident Clifton District Schools 8th-graders *"Passing Percentage"* by more than *4 times* (94.7% to 21.1%) in "Algebra I." Comparing "Algebra I" results among New Jersey charter schools, Classical Academy students scored 34 percentage points higher than the average percentage of students earning levels 4 and 5 among all New Jersey charter schools: 94.7% to 60.6%. Compared to all New Jersey charter schools in its "Algebra I" Level 4 and Level 5 outcomes, the Classical Academy ranks in *2nd place* (**Top 6%**) among the 30 charter schools administering the "Algebra I" PARCC 2015 test. Furthermore, the Classical Academy's "Algebra I" outcomes are the *highest* among *all public schools in Passaic County.*

In 8th-grade English Language Arts, highly commendable and superior Classical Academy PARCC 2015 outcomes are as prevalent as they are striking. The combined percentage of its 8th-graders scoring either a Level 4 ("Meeting Expectations") or a Level 5 ("Exceeding Expectations") in English Language Arts, that is, "Passing," is *nearly two and a half times greater than that of the Clifton Public School District: 87% to 36.5%.* Classical Academy PARCC 2015 8th-grade Level 4 and Level 5 English Language Arts "Passing" outcomes surpass statewide outcomes, 87% to 51.6%, and are *4 times the statewide percentage of 8th-graders scoring at the highest Level 5 (Exceeding Expectations): 21.1% to 5.3%.* Of the 45 New Jersey charter schools administering the English Language Arts PARCC 2015 to 8th-graders, the Classical Academy ranks in ***third place (top 6%),*** that is, it has the third-highest "Passing" percentage of all 8th-grade New Jersey charter-school students earning PARCC 2015 Levels 4 and 5 combined, and it placed in ***5th place (or top 11%)*** out of all 45 charter schools in its Level 5 "Exceeding Expectations" English Language Arts achievement.

Purpose of Report

This report intends not only to document the learning outcomes of Classical Academy students on the newly inaugurated PARCC 2015 assessment, an assessment believed to be considerably more challenging than its ASK predecessor, and, as all standardized assessments, a vital "performance measure" for charter schools, but also to detail the comparative criteria upon which is based and validated Classical Academy teachers' pre-established salary-bonus payments.

Authorship

The school's Founder and long-time Lead Person, Vincent DeRosa, with help from the school's co-founder and administrative assistant, Magda DeRosa, is responsible for this report and its accuracy. All the PARCC 2015 data, which were collated, extracted, and calculated forming the comparisons, figures (percentages), and statements constituting this report, were based on schools' "total students" tested and sourced from the publicly accessible New Jersey Department of Education assessment websites: www.nj.gov/education/schools/achievement/15, and www.nj.gov/njded/schools/achievement. State-mandated assessment results and data are available at websites accessed under general category: "New Jersey Department of Education Assessment Results."

PARCC 2015
Algebra I
Algebra I: 8th-Grade Student Results

Problem with Comparing Classical Academy "Algebra I"
Student Results with Other Schools'

Consistent with Classical Academy policy and "no-tracking practice," all 8th-grade Classical Academy students have long taken simultaneously both "Algebra I" and "8th-grade Middle-School Mathematics" courses (see Chapter V). PARCC testing rules require that any student who is enrolled in an "Algebra I" course must take the "Algebra I" PARCC test, even if they are simultaneously taking another mathematics course. Since PARCC considers "Algebra I" the higher-level mathematics subject, its rules require that all Classical Academy 8th-graders must, therefore, take the more-rigorous "Algebra I" PARCC test, not the less-demanding 8th-Grade Mathematics test. Months before students were to take the actual PARCC 2015 test, I beseeched state testing officials to permit Classical Academy students to take both exams, "Algebra I" and "8th-Grade Mathematics," since all our students take both courses in the 8th grade. They denied our request and restated their rule that any 8th-grade student taking "Algebra I" in the 8th grade must take only one exam, and that one exam must be the PARCC "Algebra I."

Unlike many public schools, including charter schools which employ "tracking" and segregate students based on achievement or motivational level into different or lower mathematics courses, the Classical Academy has always mandated that all 8th-grade students take "Algebra I," even the weakest 8th-grade mathematics students. Again, less-accomplished or -skilled mathematics students in most New Jersey public schools are forbidden to enroll in an "Algebra I" course in the 8th grade. In these schools, because of restricting only their best 8th-grade mathematics students to take "Algebra I" and, hence, the PARCC-8, 2015 "Algebra I" test, their school's success on 8th-grade "Algebra I" assessment outcomes are thus artificially, though deliberately, inflated.

For example, in the two Clifton middle schools, tracking is intense. The distorted effects of test outcomes by restricting "Algebra I" 8th-grade enrollment to only the most mathematically accomplished students can tellingly be depicted in the following chart:

The Reality and Consequences of Mathematics "Tracking" on PARCC 2015 "Algebra I" Student Outcomes
and
Comparing Those Outcomes with Classical Academy Charter School of Clifton Student Outcomes:

School	Number of 8th-Grade Students Enrolled in 8th Grade	Number of 8th-Grade Students Taking PARCC Algebra I Test	Percent of 8th-Grade Taking PARCC Algebra I Test	Percent Passing	Percent Level 5
W. Wilson	371	55	15%	98.2%	12.7%
C. Columbus	332	52	16%	73.3%	6.7%
Clifton District's	703	107	15.2%	85.7%	9.7%
Classical Academy Charter School of Clifton, all 8th-grade students	38	38	100%	94.7%	18.4%

Observations: We see in the above chart the highly commendable Clifton public school student outcomes in PARCC 2015 "Algebra I" tests, but only 15% of the district's 8th-grade students, the most outstanding mathematics students in each school, took the test, while 85% of its students took the less-demanding PARCC 8th-grade Mathematics test, the student results of which were very much not commendable. In stark contradiction to Clifton Public Schools' rampantly restrictive or "tracking" policy, 100% of all Classical Academy 8th-graders were required to take the test! Furthermore, and redounding to the Classical Academy's educational effectiveness and academics-first policies, it should be observed in the above chart that, even with severe "tracking" by which only the top Clifton school district's 8th-grade mathematics students were permitted to sit for the PARCC 2015 "Algebra I" test, the Classical Academy Charter School of Clifton *still surpassed* the Clifton School District's "Algebra I" passing percentage and exceeded its Level 5-"Exceeding Expectations" performance!

In the chart below, let us compare Classical Academy PARCC 2015 "Algebra I" results with the Clifton Public Schools *overall* PARCC 2015 8th-grade Mathematics outcomes to see the true quality of 8th-grade Clifton students' Mathematics learning outcomes.

PARCC 2015

Classical Academy "Algebra I" outcomes compared with Clifton's 8th-grade Mathematics results:

"Passing" percentage is defined as the combined percentage of 8th-graders attaining either a Level 4 ("Meeting Expectations") score or a Level 5 ("Exceeding Expectations")

School	Percent of 8th-graders Passing	Percent of 8th-graders Exceeding Expectations (Level 5)
Classical Academy	94.7%	18.4%
Woodrow Wilson M.S.	23.4%	0%
C. Columbus M.S.	11.3%	0%
Clifton School District 8th-Graders	18.8%	0%

Of the approximately 700 Clifton 8th-graders taking the test, a dismal 81.3% of all Clifton 8th-graders did *not* achieve a Passing score on the PARCC 2015 8th-Grade Mathematics, and not one Clifton School District 8th-grade student (0%) achieved a Level 5 ("Exceeding Expectations" or "Advanced Proficiency"), while only 5% of Classical Students failed to Pass the harder PARCC "Algebra I" test! And this is the school district, along with its allies in the community and in municipal government, which proclaimed loudly that "there was no need in Clifton for a charter school," and that the Classical Academy's "program of studies is not only incompatible with the Clifton community, but also non-compliant with New Jersey Department of Education standards," and, finally, "will be incapable of providing for the needs of all its students."

Limiting 8th-grade "Algebra I" subject enrollment and making only a very small minority of the best 8th-grade students eligible to take the PARCC "Algebra I" test is a widespread occurrence, especially in middle schools' 8th grade. This practice and reality should be remembered when evaluating Classical Academy's PARCC 2015 high "Algebra I" student outcomes, particularly with K-8 schools, traditional or charter.

If all middle schools were required to enroll all their students in "Algebra I," as did the Classical Academy under my leadership, then comparing their outcomes with those of Classical Academy students would be fair and meaningful. In the absence of that circumstance, and to better balance the unfairness to non-tracking schools like the Classical Academy when comparing "Algebra I" outcomes, I elect here to measure Classical Academy Charter School's 8th-grade PARCC 2015 "Algebra I" student outcomes with the "Algebra I" entire school-district outcomes, when a school or school district has grades beyond that of the 8th grade in which high-school students take the PARCC "Algebra I" test.

However, in comparing the Classical Academy Charter School "Algebra I" outcomes with other charter schools, if a charter school has grades beyond the 8th grade and administered the PARCC 2015 "Algebra I" test to students in those upper grades, we compared only the achievement demonstrated in their 8th grade, notwithstanding the likely presence of the practice of 8th-grade "tracking."

"Algebra I" PARCC 2015
Comparisons with Clifton Public School District-Wide "Algebra I" Outcomes

I: Outcome Criterion: "Passing": Defined as combined percentage of students taking the "Algebra I" tests who achieved either a Level 4 ("Meeting Expectations") or Level 5 ("Exceeding Expectations")—the two highest achievement levels on PARCC assessment tests.

	Passing: Combined Percentage of "Algebra I" Students Achieving Level 4 or Level 5
Classical Academy Charter School of Clifton	94.7%
Clifton Public School District (All "Algebra I" Test Takers, grades 8-12)	21.1%

PARCC 2015
"Algebra I"
Classical Academy C.S. vs. Clifton Public School District:
Level 5 ("Exceeding Expectations") Achievement

II: Outcome Criterion: Percentage of Students Taking the "Algebra I" Test
Who Achieved a Level 5 ("Exceeding Expectations") Outcome:

	"Exceeding Expectations" Percentage of 8th-Grade Students Achieving Level 5 (Exceeding Expectations)
Classical Academy Charter School of Clifton	18.4%
Clifton Public School District (All "Algebra I" Test Takers, grades 8-12)	1.2%

Algebra I
Statewide Comparison
Classical Academy Student Outcome Comparison with Statewide
Passing Percent: Combined Percent of Students Statewide Earning
a Level 4 ("Meeting Expectations") or a Level 5 ("Exceeding
Expectations") "Algebra I" Score

PARCC-2015

	"Passing": Combined Percentage of Students Achieving Level 4 ("Meeting Expectations") or Level 5 ("Exceeding Expectations")
Classical Academy C. S. of Clifton's "Algebra I" 8th-Grade Passing Percent	94.7%
New Jersey Statewide "Algebra I" Student Passing Percent	36%

PARCC 2015
"Algebra I"

	"Exceeding Expectations": Percent of Students Statewide Achieving Level 5 ("Exceeding Expectations") <u>on "Algebra I" (PARCC 2015)</u>
Classical Academy C.S. of Clifton's "Algebra I" 8th-Grade Level 5 ("Exceeding Expectations")	18.4%
New Jersey Statewide "Algebra I" Level 5 ("Exceeding Expectations")	3.1%

Algebra I
PARCC 2015
8th-Grade Test Takers
"C/D" District Factor Group ('DFG') Comparison

The Classical Academy Charter School of Clifton is designated, as is the Clifton Public School District, a "C/D" District Factor Group (DFG) school. The following figures are useful to see how the Classical Academy 8th-graders compare in their "Algebra I" results to all of New Jersey's 8th-graders attending "C/D" DFG schools, of which there are approximately 140 in the state. Keep in mind when evaluating the below data that most, if not all, public "C/D" DFG schools permitted only their best mathematics students to take a class designated "Algebra I" in the 8th grade, and only these exceptional mathematics students took the PARCC 2015 "Algebra I" test.

	Passing: "Algebra I" Combined Percentage of Students Achieving Level 4 ("Meeting Expectations") <u>or Level 5 ("Exceeding Expectations")</u>
Classical Academy Charter School of Clifton C/D	94.7%
All New Jersey Public Schools Designated as "C/D" District Factor Group Schools Average Passing Percent	66.7%

	Level 5: "Exceeding Expectations" Percent of "Algebra I" Test Takers <u>Achieving Level 5 ("Exceeding Expectations")</u>
Classical Academy Charter School of Clifton C/D	18.4%
All New Jersey Public Schools Designated as "C/D" District Factor Group, Level 5 Average	1.3%

Algebra I
PARCC 2015
Charter Schools

"Passing" Percentage: Defined as a school's combined percentage of
students earning either Level 4 ("Meeting Expectations")
or Level 5 ("Exceeding Expectations")

Comparing Classical Academy 8th-Grade "Algebra I" Outcomes with
the Combined Percentage of Students Earning Level 4 or Level 5 for all
New Jersey Charter Schools Administering the PARCC 2015 Algebra I
Test to Their 8th-Graders.

	"Passing": "Algebra I" Combined Percentage of Students Achieving Level 4 ("Meeting Expectations") or Level 5 ("Exceeding Expectations")
Classical Academy Charter School of Clifton	94.7%
Combined Aggregate Percentage of all New Jersey Charter School 8th-Graders Achieving Level 4 or Level 5	60.6%

Algebra I
PARCC 2015
Charter Schools: Level 5 ("Exceeding Expectations")

Comparing Percentage of Classical Academy 8th-Graders Achieving
Level 5 ("Exceeding Expectations") on the PARCC 2015 "Algebra I"
Test with New Jersey Charter Schools' Aggregate Percentage of Students
Earning Level 5 ("Exceeding Expectations")

	"Exceeding Expectations": "Algebra I" Percentage of 8th-Grade Students Achieving Level 5 ("Exceeding Expectations")
Classical Academy Charter School of Clifton (8th-Grade Class)	18.4%
Percentage of All New Jersey Charter Schools' 8th-Grade Students Earning Level 5 ("Exceeding Expectations")	4.5%

Observations: In the above comparisons of "C/D" DFG schools and "Charter
Schools 8th-Graders," we see Classical Academy 8th-graders in these comparisons

surpassing the combined Level 4 and Level 5 percentages by large margins. However, these large margins would be even significantly greater if "tracking," which the Classical Academy does not practice but which is widespread in nearly every New Jersey middle school, including a number of charter schools, was not a reality of New Jersey educational systems. We estimate that, for most, if not all, New Jersey middle schools, including charter schools, only the top 15%-30% of 8th-grade mathematics students are permitted to take an "Algebra I" course in the 8th grade, and thus be compelled to take the PARCC "Algebra I" test, while the great majority of 8th-graders in these schools take the PARCC middle-school 8th-grade Mathematics test, a less-demanding assessment.

Contrary to the prevailing "tracking" mentality and reality, for many years, and as stated often in this narrative, the Classical Academy has required all students, from the most competent to those who struggle with mathematics, or who have come to the Classical Academy with poor foundational skills in mathematics, to take the school's "Algebra I" course in the 8th grade. As described above, by state directive, any student enrolled in a class called "Algebra I" must take the PARCC 2015 "Algebra I" assessment test. So when comparisons are made with all other 8th-graders in New Jersey public schools, including most charter schools having the 8th grade, we should never forget that 100% of Classical Academy students—typically a third to half of who would, in other middle schools, not be allowed to take or be placed in an 8th-grade Algebra I" class—are competing with the 15%-30% mathematically elite of a school's 8th-grade class.

"Algebra I"
PARCC 2015
New Jersey Charter School "Passing" Rankings

Based on a School's "Passing" Percentage, Where "Passing" Is Defined as the Total Combined Percentage of a Charter School's "Algebra I" Test Takers Who Achieved Either a Level 4 ("Meeting Expectations") or Level 5 ("Exceeding Expectations")

The following chart includes every New Jersey charter school administering the PARCC 2015

School	"Algebra I" PASSING Percentage: Combined Percentage of 8th-Grade Students Achieving Either a Level 4 or Level 5
*Robert Treat Charter School	100%
Classical Academy Charter School of Clifton	**97.4%**
Princeton Charter School	92.7%
Elysian Charter School (Hoboken)	82.4%
Central Jersey College Prep. Charter School	73.5%
North Star Academy Charter School (Newark)	65.2%
Foundation Charter School	52.6%
Great Oaks Charter School	36.5%
Camden's Promise Charter School	34.1%
Bergen Arts and Sciences Charter School	26.7%
Benjamin Banneker Prep. Charter School	26.3%
Hoboken Charter School	25.7%
Freedom Prep. Charter School	24.7%
METS Charter School	23. %
Greater Brunswick Charter School	21.4%
University Academy Charter School High School	20.5%
Lap Academy University Charter School	17.5%
Great Futures Charter School	16.5%
Trenton STEM-to-Civics Charter School	14.3%
Marion P. Thomas Charter School	13.7%
Academy for Urban Leadership Charter School	11.8%
Team Academy Charter School	11.3%
Camden Academy Charter School	8.3%
Paulo Freire Charter School	5.1%
Peoples Preparatory Charter School	4.8%
Charter Tech High School for the Performing Arts	2.7%
Paterson Charter School for Science and Tech.	1.2%
Barack Obama Green Charter School	0%
Newark Prep. Charter School	0%
Union County Teams Charter School	0%

*From state data, it appears only the top 12 math students, or 24% of its 8th-grade class, were enrolled in Robert Treat Charter School's 8th-grade "Algebra I" class out of a total 8th-grade enrollment of 49 students. Only these 12 elite or "tracked" students took the PARCC 2015 "Algebra I" test. The remaining 37 Robert Treat Charter School 8th-graders were enrolled in an "8th-grade Math" class and thus took the PARCC 2015 8th-Grade Math Test (presumably a less-demanding test).

There is nothing sinister in this; in fact, "tracking" is to most educators a quite acceptable practice and common in every public New Jersey school, but anathema to Classical Academy philosophy and its own practices since its founding in 1998 and all during my leadership. However, in school-outcome comparisons such as here delineated, "tracking" unfairly disadvantages schools like the Classical Academy, which does not "track" students into less-demanding or advanced subjects. We note, yet again, that every year, every Classical Academy 8th-grader, from the weakest math students to the most competent ones, were, during my 18-year Classical Academy leadership, required to take the "Algebra I" class, and all these students— that is, the entirety (100%) of the Classical Academy's 8th-grade class—underwent the more difficult PARCC 2015 "Algebra I" test. If the Classical Academy "tracked" students and only its best mathematics students were permitted to take the "Algebra I" course and, thus, required to sit for the state-mandated PARCC 2015 "Algebra I" test, it, too, would easily have a "100% Passing Percentage," and I speculate an 80% Level 5 ("Exceeding Expectations") student performance! Incidentally, of those 37 Robert Treat Charter School 8th-grade students, only 54.1% achieved Level 4 or Level 5 (that is, "passed") the PARCC 2015 8th-Grade Mathematics Test.

"Alegbra I"
PARCC 2015
Passaic County Public Schools

Classical Academy Charter School of Clifton

vs.

Passaic County Public Schools and School Districts

PASSING PERCENTAGE

"Passing" is defined as the combined percentage of a Passaic County School or School District's students earning either a Level 4 ("Meeting Expectations") or a Level 5 ("Exceeding Expectations") on the PARCC 2015 "Algebra I" Test Assessment. The following schools or school districts are listed from highest passing percentage to lowest passing percentage.

Passaic County School or School District	Passing: "Algebra I" Combined Percentage of Students Earning a Level 4 ("Meeting Expectations") or Level 5 ("Exceeding Expectations")
Classical Academy Charter School of Clifton	94.7%
Pompton Lakes Boro Public Schools	49.7%
Wayne Township District Schools	45.5%
Passaic County Technical Institute	39.7%
West Milford District Schools	25.1%
Hawthorne Boro Public School District	23.6%
Clifton Public School District	21.1%
Passaic City Public Schools	18.4%
Paterson City Public Schools	16.6%
Lakeland Regional High School District	10.2%
Passaic Valley Regional High School District	7%
Manchester Regional High School District	1.8%
Paterson Charter School for Science and Technology	1.2%

As described above, when a municipality, such as the City of Clifton or the Township of Wayne, has a district-operated high school, the "total district students" category of PARCC 2015 "Algebra I" data is utilized to calculate and to compare figures. The "total district students" category represents all the students in that same city or town who took the "Algebra I" exam, regardless of their grade level in school. A number of municipalities in Passaic County do not have a high school but send their students to a "Regional High School," which, by agreement, serves students from several towns. In order to capture a true picture of the PARCC "Algebra I" test results for towns not having their own high school, the PARCC's "Algebra I" "total students" category was also used—but for the Regional High School. This method compensates for the unfair and inaccurate PARCC 2015 "Algebra I" assessment outcomes inherent when comparing the entire (100%) Classical Academy 8th-grade class, each member of which must take the "Algebra I" course, with all other middle schools in which only the top 10%-30% of their 8th-graders take an "Algebra I" course, and thus sat for the PARCC 2015 "Algebra I" test.

PARCC 2015
8th-GRADE
ENGLISH LANGUAGE ARTS ("ELA")
Classical Academy Charter School of Clifton's Comparative Student 8th-Grade Outcomes for English Language Arts

I: Resident (Clifton) District: Comparing Classical Academy Charter School of Clifton's 8th-grade English Language Arts outcomes on the PARCC-8 ELA state-mandated assessment with those same outcomes for Clifton Public Middle Schools and the Clifton Public School District.

"Passing" is defined as the combined percentage of a school's 8th-grade students earning a Level 4 ("Meeting Expectations") or a Level 5 ("Exceeding Expectations") PARCC 2015 outcome. Achievement Levels 4 and 5 of the 5 levels for possible PARCC student outcomes are popularly, and not without reason, considered "passing."

N.B. Because "tracking" has no impact on the kind or level of PARCC test taken, it is not an issue in comparing Classical Academy 8th-grade English Language Arts student outcomes with outcomes of all other relevant cohort or peer schools.

School	Passing: English Language Arts Combined Percentage of 8th-Grade Students Earning Level 4 ("Meeting Expectations") or Level 5 ("Exceeding Expectations")
Classical Academy Charter School of Clifton	87%
Clifton's Christopher Columbus M.S.	19.5%
Clifton's Woodrow Wilson M.S.	47%
Clifton Public School District Total 8th Grade PARCC ELA Level 4 and Level 5 Combined Average	36.5%

II: Resident (Clifton) District Level 5 ("Exceeding Expectations"):
The percentage of 8th-grade students earning the highest PARCC English
Language Arts assessment outcome: Level 5 ("Exceeding Expectations");
PARCC Level 5 is equated with "Advanced Proficiency" achievement of
previous state-mandated standardized subject tests.

School	"Exceeding Expectations" Percent of 8th-Grade Students Earning the Highest PARCC Outcome Level 5 ("Exceeding Expectations")
Classical Academy Charter School of Clifton	21.1%
Clifton's Christopher Columbus M.S.	1.6%
Clifton's Woodrow Wilson M.S.	7.5%
Clifton Public School District Percent of Students Attaining PARCC Level 5 ("Exceeding Expectations")	5.3%

Observations: In the above two "resident district" charts, we see that Classical
Academy Charter School of Clifton's 8th-grade English Language Arts "Passing"
percentage is more than *twice* that of Clifton school district; the Classical
Academy's percent of its 8th-graders achieving the highest PARCC Level 5
outcome ("Exceeding Expectations") is *4 times* that of Clifton school district's
8th-graders.

PARCC 2015: 8th Grade: English Language Arts
"C/D" DISTRICT FACTOR GROUP (DFG) STATEWIDE "PASSING" COMPARISONS

III: District Factor Group ("DFG") of "C/D": Comparing the "Passing" percent average (see "passing" definition, above) of all New Jersey public schools having a "C/D" District Factor Group state designation with that of the Classical Academy Charter School of Clifton. Such comparison may be described as a relevant, meaningful "statewide peer-to-peer" comparison, as all of the Classical Academy's students are Clifton residents and share the same socio-economic characteristics as students in Clifton Public School District, a state-designated "C/D" District Factor Group school district.

	"Passing Percent": 8th Grade PARCC 2015 English Language Arts Statewide Percentage of 8th-Graders in "C/D" District Factor Group (DFG) Schools and School Districts Achieving Either a Level 4 ("Meeting Expectations") or a Level 5 ("Exceeding Expectations")
C/D: Classical Academy Charter School of Clifton	87%
Statewide Average 8th-Grade "Passing" Percent for all "C/D" Schools and School Districts total of 9,537 students	44.4%

	"Level 5" (Exceeding Expectations) C/D DFG 8th-Graders, Statewide, English Language Arts
C/D: Classical Academy Charter School of Clifton	21.1%
Statewide C/D "Level 5" (Exceeding Expectations); Percentage for all "C/D' Schools and School Districts; Total of 9,537 8th-grade students	7.6%

Observations: The above "C/D" DFG comparison displays the statistical fact that the Classical Academy's PARCC 2015 English Language Arts 8th-grade student "Passing Percentage" outcome is *twice* that of its statewide student peers sharing the same socio-economic characteristics. (The state identified and designated 131 public schools and school districts having a "C/D" DFG with a total of 9,537 students at the time of PARCC 2015). Another distinction, the percentage of Classical Academy 8th-graders earning a PARCC 2015 Level 5 of 21.2%, is the *highest English Language Arts Level 5 attainment of any other New Jersey "C/D" District Factor Group school.*

"J" School Comparison with Classical Academy

An "Academics-First School" Can Level the Playing Field and Close the Learning Gap Between the Less- and Greater-Advantaged Students

I have often, in my long tenure as Classical Academy Principal/Lead Teacher, asserted, based on Classical Academy consistently high student outcomes on state tests—the "GEPA," the "ASK-8," and now the PARCC, in 2015—that Classical Academy students in their educational outcomes mirror the academic attainment of children of affluent, well-educated, often professional parents who live in New Jersey's most lavishly expensive communities. We all know the adamant, well-documented, invariable correlation between wealth and school achievement: the richest achieve the highest academically, and the poorest achieve the least.

Classical Academy students are most often children of immigrant parents who do not have college educations, who often speak a language other than English at home, who, on average, earn lower middle-class incomes, and reside in apartments or own very modest homes in neighborhoods where lawns and trees are rare but cement and asphalt ubiquitous. If the unbreakable connection between wealth and academic achievement were inevitable and beyond human intervention, then Classical Academy students would show, at best, a very mediocre level of educational achievement, typically displayed in most C/D school districts, and producing test results always inferior to their more-prosperous fellow students in affluent "J" schools. But Classical Academy students never showed, while I was their school leader, "mediocre" education achievement or low standardized-test scores, but instead broke free from the chains of low socio-economic scholastic determinants.

In writing this narrative, I thought it illuminating to compare Classical Academy PARCC 2015 8th-grade English Language Arts outcomes with those of our state's richest communities, which educate our most-advantaged adolescents, the enviable "J" schools.

Public schools and school districts in the wealthiest New Jersey communities, with household incomes in the several hundred thousands, if not much more, and entry-level homes starting at a million dollars or more, are some of the socio-economic factors qualifying for a state-designated "J" school district, the most-affluent and highest District Factor Group school or community rating.

Selecting very randomly, and to validate my assertion, I present this list of 14 public "J" schools existing in several counties along with our modest Classical Academy lower middle-class C/D District Factor Group status. The following chart cites 14 randomly selected "J" schools' PARCC 2015 8th-Grade English Language Arts "Passing" and "Level 5 Attainment" outcomes, along with those of the Classical Academy. Of most significance, this chart shows how marvelously well the Classical Academy has closed the "learning gap" or "achievement gap" between majority-advantaged students and far-less advantaged minority children of mostly immigrant parents.

PARCC 2015
"J" Schools
vs.
Classical Academy Charter School of Clifton ("C/D") Comparisons
"J" (DFG) School Comparison with Classical Academy Charter School of Clifton "C/D" (DFG)

8th-Grade English Language Arts Attainment: PARCC 2015

ENGLISH LANGUAGE ARTS

DFG "C/D"	County	School or Community	Percent of 8th Grade Passing	Percent of 8th Grade Achieving Level 5
"C/D"	Passaic	Classical Academy C. S. of Clifton	87%	21.1%
"J"	Bergen	Glen Rock M.S.	84.6%	37.8%
"J"	Bergen	Ho-Ho-Kus	79.2%	39.6%
"J"	Bergen	Ridgewood Village Ben. Franklin M.S.	80.9%	30.6%
"J"	Bergen	Upper Saddle River Emil Cavallini M.S.	78.1%	28.6%
"J"	Camden	Haddonfield Boro	79.5%	25.3%
"J"	Essex	Milburn Middle School	69.2%	23.9%
"J"	Hunterdon	Tewksbury Twp.	74%	35.6%
"J"	Mercer	West Windsor-Plainsboro Community M.S.	83%	37.6%
"J"	Monmouth	Little Silver Boro	88.4%	37.2%
"J"	Monmouth	Rumson Boro	89.3%	28.6%
"J"	Morris	School District of the Chathams	72%	18.6%
"J"	Morris	Harding Twp. School	83.3%	33.3%
"J"	Morris	Mendham Boro Mountain View School	84.5%	45.1%
"J"	Somerset	Bernardsville; W. Annin M.S.	72.7%	31.5%
New Jersey Statewide "J" School District "Passing" and Level 5 ("Exceeding Expectations") Average 8th-Grade Percentages			80.4%	33.5%

Observations: Notice in the above chart, where schools are listed in no order of performance, how favorably less-advantaged Classical Academy students compare in their academic achievements with 8th-grade students in the most affluent communities and most advantaged households in New Jersey. For most Classical Academy students of immigrant parents, English is not their native language, and many speak or hear spoken a foreign language at home regularly. Yet the Classical Academy, its program, practices, policies, and "Academics-First Culture" has enabled its minority and less-advantaged students to compete scholastically with New Jersey's best and most privileged youth.

PARCC 2015
8th-GRADE ENGLISH LANGUAGE ARTS

Comparing Classical Academy Outcomes to New Jersey Statewide
Student Outcomes in 8th-Grade "English Language Arts"

CLASSICAL ACADEMY VS. STATEWIDE
PASSING PERCENTAGES

"Passing" is defined as the combined percentage of students earning either a
Level 4 ("Meeting Expectations") or Level 5 ("Exceeding Expectations")

Classical Academy vs. Statewide Outcomes	English Language Arts PARCC 2015, 8th-Grade English Language Arts Passing Percentage
Classical Academy Charter School of Clifton 8th-Grade English Language Arts Outcomes	87.0%
New Jersey Statewide Average "Passing" Percentage for 8th-Grade English Language Arts	51.6%

Statewide Comparison

Percent of 8th-Grade Students Earning Level 5
("Exceeding Expectations" [Performance Equivalent to Advanced
Proficiency]) on PARCC 2015 English Language Arts

CLASSICAL ACADEMY VS. STATEWIDE PARCC LEVEL 5
"EXCEEDING EXPECTATIONS"

Classical Academy vs. Statewide	8th-Grade English Language Arts: Percent of 8th-Graders Achieving Level 5 (Exceeding Expectations)
Classical Academy Charter School of Clifton 8th Grade English Language Arts Level 5 Outcome:	21.1%
New Jersey Statewide Average of Students Achieving a Level 5 ("Exceeding Expectations") PARCC 2015 8th-Grade English Language Arts Outcome:	12.5%

PARCC 2015
8th-Grade ENGLISH LANGUAGE ARTS
CHARTER SCHOOL RANKINGS

The following Charter School rankings are arranged from the highest to lowest "Passing" outcomes among New Jersey charter schools administering the PARCC 2015 to 8th-graders. The rankings are based on each charter school's combined percentage of 8th-grade students earning either a Level 4 ("Meeting Expectations") or a Level 5 ("Exceeding Expectations") on PARCC 2015 8th-Grade English Language Arts. This "Combined Percentage" is defined as "Passing."

New Jersey Charter School	English Language Arts "Passing" Percent: Combined Percentage of Each School's 8th-Graders Achieving Level 4 ("Meeting Expectations") or Level 5 ("Exceeding Expectations")
1: Princeton Charter School	91.7%
2: Central Jersey College Prep. C.S.	89.8%
3: Classical Academy Charter School of Clifton	**87%**
4: Queen City Academy Charter School	77.2%
5: Passaic Arts and Sciences Charter School	76.8%
6: Gray Charter School	76.4%
7: North Star Academy C.S. of Newark	74.6%
8: Discovery Charter School	73.7%
9: Bergen Arts and Sciences Charter School	71.3%
10: Hoboken Charter School	70%
11: Elysian Charter School of Hoboken	68.8%
12: Robert Treat Charter School (Newark)	67.3%
13: Learning Community Charter School	65.3%
14: Foundation Academy Charter School	63.4%
15: Dr. Lena Edwards Charter School	61.3%
16: Maria L. Varisco-Rogers Charter School	59%
17: Great Oaks Charter School	57.1%
18: Soaring Heights Charter School	52.1%
19: Red Bank Charter School	50%
20: Jersey City Golden Door Charter School	52.1%
21: Leap Academy University Charter School	50%
22: John P. Holland Charter School (Paterson)	45%
23: Jersey City Charter School	44.1%
24: Camden's Promise Charter School	42.1%
25: Pride Charter School	40.9%
26: Paterson Charter School of Science & Tech.	40.5%
27: Teaneck Community Charter School	40%
28: Lady Liberty Academy Charter School	38.6%
29: METS Charter School	37%

30: Union County Teams Charter School	34.4%
31: Link Community Charter School	33.3%
32: Marion P. Thomas Charter School	33.3%
33: Freedom Academy Charter School	31.6%
34: Phillips Academy Charter School	30.8%
35: Greater Brunswick Charter School	28.6%
36: Hope Academy Charter School	27.8%
37: Team Academy Charter School	27.5%
38: Village Charter School	27 %
39: Sussex County Charter School of Technology	25.4%
40: Benjamin Banneker Prep. Charter School	22.8%
41: Galloway Community Charter School	22.6%
42: Paul Robeson Charter School	15.5%
43: Central Jersey Arts Charter School	15.4%
44: Merit Prep. Charter School (Newark)	8.3%

Observation: The Classical Academy placed *third (top 6%)* among 44 charter schools in percent of 8th-grade class earning a "Passing" score on PARCC 2015 English Language Arts—that is, it *outperformed 94% of all other New Jersey charter schools in this comparison.*

PARCC 2015
8th-Grade English Language Arts
Level 5 ("Exceeding Expectations")
Charter School Rankings

The chart below ranks New Jersey Charter Schools from highest to lowest based on the percent of each school's 8th-grade class earning Level 5 ("Exceeding Expectations") on English Language Arts PARCC 2015 assessment. Level 5 ("Exceeding Expectations") is equivalent to "Advanced Proficiency" of previous state-mandated assessments.

	PARCC 2015 Percent of 8th-Grade Class Achieving English Language Arts Level 5
New Jersey Charter School	**("Exceeding Expectations")**
1: Princeton C.S.	43.8%
2: Central Jersey College Prep. C.S.	26.5%
3: Bergen Arts and Sciences C.S.	23.8%
4: Gray C.S.	23.5%
5: Classical Academy Charter School of Clifton	**21.1%**
6: Elysian Charter School of Hoboken	18.8%
7: Learning Community C.S.	16.3%
8: Foundation Academy C.S.	15.6%

9: Queen City Academy C.S.   14.3%
10: Passaic Arts and Sciences C.S.   14.3%
11: North Star Academy C.S. of Newark   14.2%
12: Dr. Lena Edwards Academic C.S.   12.9%
13: Robert Treat Academy C.S.   12.2%
14: Discovery Charter School   10.5%
15: Great Oaks Charter School   9.5%
16: Paterson CS for Science and Technology   7.2%
17: Lady Liberty Academy C.S.   6.8%
18: Maria L. Varisco-Rogers C.S.   5.4%
19: Camden's Promise C.S.   5.3%
20: Freedom Academy C. S.   5.1%
21: John P. Holland C.S.   5%
22: Soaring Heights C.S.   4.3%
23: University Heights C.S.   4.3%
24: Jersey City Golden Door C.S.   3.6%
25: Jersey City Community C.S.   3.4%
26: LEAP Academy University C.S.   3.2%
27: Union County Teams C.S.   3.1%
28: Pride Academy C.S.   3%
29: TEAMS Academy C.S.   2.9%
30: Greater Brunswick C.S.   2.9%
31: Link Community C.S.   2.9%
32: METS C.S.   2.2%
33: Sussex County C.S. for Technology   1.5%
34: Teaneck Community C.S.   0%
35: Red Bank C.S.   0%
36: Village C.S.   0%
37: Marion P. Thomas C.S.   0%
38: Hope Academy C.S.   0%
39: Galloway Community C.S.   0%
40: Central Jersey Arts C.S.   0%
41: Phillips Academy C.S.   0%
42: Merit Prep. C.S. of Newark   0%
43: Benjamin Banneker Prep. C.S.   0%
44: Paul Robeson Humanities C.S.   0%
(No scores were reported for Unity C.S. and Ridge and Valley C.S.)

Observation: The Classical Academy Charter School of Clifton ranks in *fifth (5th)* *place* or the *top 11%* of all 44 charter schools in the percentage of its 8th-graders achieving Level 5 ("Exceeding Expectations" ["Advanced Proficiency"]) on the PARCC 2015 8th-grade English Language Arts assessment.

Passaic County Schools
PARCC 2015
8th Grade ENGLISH LANGUAGE ARTS

"PASSING"

Comparative Rankings of Passaic County Public Schools
and School Districts

The following ranking of Passaic County public schools and school districts is based on each school or school district's 8th-grade English language arts PARCC 2015 attainment, specifically on the percentage of each 8th-grade class earning a "Passing" score, where "Passing" is defined as the combined percentage of 8th-grade students achieving a Level 4 ("Meeting Expectations") or Level 5 ("Exceeding Expectations"). Schools listed in descending order based on the percentage of each school's 8th-graders who "Passed" the PARCC 2015 English Language Arts

DFG	Passaic County School	"Passing": English Language Arts Combined Percentage of 8th-Graders Achieving Level 4 ("Meeting Expectations") and Level 5 ("Exceeding Expectations")
1: C/D	Classical Academy Charter School of Clifton	87%
2: F/G	Lakeside School (Pompton Lakes)	79.4%
3: D/E	Wanaque Elementary School (Wanaque)	75%
4: G/H	George Washington Middle School (Wayne)	71%
5: D/E	Haskell Elementary School (Wanaque Boro)	68.3%
6: F/G	Walter T. Bergen Middle School (Bloomingdale)	66.7%
7: F/G	Little Falls Public School #1 (Little Falls)	66.7%
8: G/H	Anthony Wayne Middle School (Wayne)	66.3%
9: G/H	Martin J. Ryerson School (Ringwood)	64.5%
10: F/G	High Mountain Middle School (North Haledon)	64%
11: G/H	Schuyler-Colfax Middle School (Wayne)	56.4%
12: B	Haledon Public School (Haledon Boro)	49.6%
13: F/G	Macopin Middle School (West Milford)	49.5%
14: D/E	Lincoln Middle School (Hawthorne)	47%
15: C/D	W. Wilson Middle School, Clifton	47%
16: A	John P. Holland Charter School (Paterson)	45%
17: C/D	Washington Park School (Totowa Boro)	44.8%
18: B	Prospect Park School #1 (Prospect Park)	42.2%
19: A	Paterson Charter School for Sci & Tech (Paterson)	40.5%
20: D/E	Memorial Middle School (Woodlawn Park)	34.2%
21: A	Philips Academy Charter School (Paterson)	30.8%

22: A	Paterson Public School District (all 8th-graders)	30%
23: C/D	C. Columbus Middle School, Clifton	19.5%
23: A	Lincoln Middle School #1 (Passaic City)	19.2%

Passaic County Schools
PARRC 2015
English Language Arts 8th Grade

LEVEL 5-"EXCEEDING EXPECTATIONS"

DFG	School	"Exceeding Expectations" Percent of Each School or School District's 8th-Grade Students Achieving a Level 5 Score ("Exceeding Expectations")
D/E	Wanaque Elementary School, Wanaque	26.8%
G/H	Anthony Wayne Middle School, Wayne	24.6%
F/G	High Mountain Middle School, North Haledon	22.7%
C/D	**Classical Academy Charter School of Clifton**	21.1%
G/H	Schuyler-Colfax Middle School, Wayne	20.7%
G/H	G. Washington Middle School, Wayne	19.5%
F/G	Lakeside School, Pompton Lakes	19.4%
D/E	Haskell Elementary School, Wanaque Boro	14.6%
F/G	Little Falls Twp. Public School #1, Little Falls	12.5%
G/H	Martin J. Ryerson School, Ringwood	10.5%
F/G	Macopin Middle School, West Milford	9.4%
C/D	Washington Park School, Totowa Boro	8.6%
C/D	W. Wilson Middle School, Clifton	7.5%
F/G	Walter T. Bergen Middle School, Bloomingdale	7.4%
A	Paterson Charter School of Sci. and Tech., Paterson	7.2%
B	Haledon Public School, Haledon Boro	6.1%
A	John Holland Charter School (Paterson)	5%
D/E	Lincoln Middle School, Hawthorne	4.9%
D/E	Memorial Middle School, Woodland Park	4.6%
A	Paterson City (total for district)	3.7%
C/D	C. Columbus Middle School, Clifton	1.6%
A	Lincoln Middle School #1, Passaic City	1.2%
B	Prospect Park School #1, Prospect Park	1.1%
A	Philips Academy Charter School (Paterson)	0%

Observations: The above two charts show the Classical Academy Charter School of Clifton possessed the *highest* (*top 1%*) 8th-grade English Language Arts "passing" percentage rate than any other Passaic County school, traditional or charter; and placed *fourth* (*top 17%*) out of 23 Passaic County public schools in educating its students to achieve the highest PARCC outcome of Level 5 ("Exceeding Expectations") in English Language Arts.

It must also be noted that the majority of Classical Academy Charter School of Clifton students would be attending, because of their residency locations in Clifton, Clifton's Christopher Columbus Middle School, if not enrolling in the Classical Academy. When comparing the standardized-test outcomes between Classical Academy and Clifton's C. Columbus Middle School, or of Passaic County schools generally, this fact should be noted, especially as one sees the vast difference in student academic attainment between the Classical Academy and Clifton's C. Columbus Middle School.

PARCC 2016
("Partnership for the Assessment of Readiness for College and Careers")

"PASSING" ENGLISH LANGUAGE ARTS
Comparing: 1) "Passing" percentages for Clifton Public Middle Schools and Clifton School District, New Jersey, 8th-grade students; 2) "C/D" (DFG) schools' statewide 8th-grade "passing" average percentage; 3) New Jersey statewide 8th-grade "passing" percentage; and 4) New Jersey charter schools' "percent of 8th-grade class" achieving a "passing" performance on English Language Arts.

"Passing" is defined as the combined percentage of each school's 8th-grade students earning either a Level 4 ("Meeting Expectations") or a Level 5 ("Exceeding Expectations") in the tested subject.

DFG	School	Percent of 8th-Grade Students "Passing" English Language Arts
"C/D"	Classical Academy Charter School of Clifton	86.4%
"C/D"	Woodrow Wilson M.S., Clifton	42.7%
"C/D"	Christopher Columbus M.S., Clifton	42%
"C/D"	Clifton Public School District's 8th-graders	42.1%
"C/D"	Average 8th-grade Passing Percentage for	
	All students statewide attending "C/D" District Factor Group' schools (128 "C/D" schools educating 10,000 students)	47.6%
	Statewide 8th-grade "passing" percentage	55.2%
	New Jersey Charter Schools' 8th-grade average "passing" percentage	53.8%

Level 5 ("Exceeding Expectations") Attainment:
PARCC 2016 English Language Arts

Level 5 ("Exceeding Expectations") is the highest student outcome on the PARCC tests and is, in that regard, comparable to the ASK test's "Advanced Proficiency" outcome.

DFG	School	Percent of 8th-Grade Students Achieving Level 5 ("Exceeding Expectations") in English Language Arts
"C/D"	Classical Academy Charter School of Clifton	48.6%
"C/D"	Woodrow Wilson M.S., Clifton	9.7%
"C/D"	Christopher Columbus M.S., Clifton	5.4%
"C/D"	Clifton Public School District's 8th-graders	7.4%
Statewide Percentage of 8th grade students attending C/D District Factor Group schools and achieving ("Exceeding Expectations") [there are 128 "C/D" schools educating 10,000 students)		8.9%
Statewide 8th-Grade Level 5 ("Exceeding Expectations") percentage		14.5%
New Jersey 8th-grade Charter Schools' Average Percentage of Level 5 ("Exceeding Expectations") Attainment		12.7%

Observations: In the above two charts, we show that Classical Academy 8th-graders surpassed by very significant margins all meaningful student-outcome comparisons both for "passing" and Level 5 ("Exceeding Expectations/Advanced Proficiency") attainment on the PARCC 2016 English Language Arts.

New Jersey Charter School Comparisons: PARCC 2016

In the following two charts, I list only the top-10 New Jersey Charter Schools (out of the 47 charter schools administering the PARCC 2016 to 8th-graders) having the highest percentage of their 8th-grade class "Passing" English Language Arts, and where, in that top-10 ranking, the Classical Academy Charter School of Clifton places. "Passing" is defined as the combined percent of 8th-grade students earning either a Level 4 ("Meeting Expectations") or a Level 5 ("Exceeding Expectations") outcome score in the tested subject, English Language Arts.

Charter School	Percent of 8th-Grade Students "Passing" English Language Arts
Central Jersey College Prep. C. S.	97.9%
Princeton C.S.	97.8%
Soaring Heights C.S.	91.3%
Gray C.S.	88.3%
Classical Academy Charter School of Clifton	**86.4%**
North Star Academy Charter School of Newark	86.2%
Queen City Academy C.S.	85.7%
Hoboken C.S.	81.8%
Elysian C.S. of Hoboken	77.4%
Vineland Public Charter School	75.7%

New Jersey Charter Schools
PARCC 2016

LEVEL 5 ("EXCEEDING EXPECTATIONS") ACHIEVEMENT

In the chart below I list only the top-10 New Jersey Charter Schools (out of the 47 charter schools administering the PARCC 2016 assessment to 8th-graders) having the highest percentages of their school's 8th-graders who achieved Level 5 ("Exceeding Expectations") outcomes in English Language Arts.

Charter School	Percent of 8th-Grade Students Achieving Level 5 ("Exceeding Expectations") in English Language Arts
Princeton C.S.	69.9%
Soaring Heights C.S.	52.2%
Classical Academy Charter School of Clifton	**48.6%**
Central Jersey College Prep. C.S.	45.8%
Elysian C.S. of Hoboken	35.5%
North Star Academy Charter School of Newark	31.8%
Ridge and Valley C.S.	23.1%
Maria L. Varisco-Rogers C.S.	21.8%
Foundation Academy C.S.	21.5%
Vineland Public Charter School	21.2%

Observations: There were 47 New Jersey charter schools administering the PARCC 2016 to 8th-graders. The Classical Academy Charter School of Clifton placed in the top *10% (5th place out of 47 charter schools)* of all charter schools having the highest percentage of its 8th-grade students "Pass" English Language Arts, and in the *top 6% (3rd place out of 47 charter schools)* for the highest percent of Level 5 ("Exceeding Expectations") in English Language Arts student achievement.

PARCC 2016
Passaic County Public Schools Comparisons
English Language Arts

The following chart shows, in descending order, Classical Academy ranking among all Passaic County public schools (including Charter Schools) based on the "Passing" percent of each school's 8th-grade students in English Language Arts. "Passing" is defined as the combined percentage of each school's 8th-grade students earning either a Level 4 ("Meeting Expectations") or Level 5 ("Exceeding Expectations") score on PARCC 2016 English Language Arts.

DFG	School and Municipality	Percent of 8th-Grade Students Earning a "Passing" Score on PARCC 2016 English Language Arts
D/E	Wanaque Elementary School, Wanaque Boro	89.4%
C/D	**Classical Academy Charter School of Clifton**	86.4%
A	Passaic Gifted and Talented Academy School #20, Passaic City	77.2%
F/G	High Mountain M.S., North Haledon	75.5%
G/H	Anthony Wayne M.S., Wayne	74.5%
G/H	G. Washington M.S., Wayne	74.1%
F/G	Walter T. Bergen M.S., Bloomingdale	72.2%
F/G	Lakeside School, Pompton Lakes	71.9%
G/H	Schuyler-Colfax M.S., Wayne	70.9%
F/G	Little Falls Public School #1, Little Falls	70%
D/E	Haskell Elementary School, Wanaque Boro	69.3%
G/H	Martin J. Ryerson School, Ringwood	60.5%
B	Prospect Park School #1, Prospect Park	58.8%
A	John P. Holland Charter School, Paterson	57.1%
C/D	Washington Park School, Totowa Boro	56.7%
D/E	Memorial M.S., Woodlawn Park	54.4%
A	Community Charter School of Paterson, Paterson	54.2%
D/E	Macopin M.S., West Milford	53.3%
D/E	Lincoln M.S., Hawthorne Boro	53%
B	Haledon Public School, Haledon Boro	53%
A	Paterson Charter School for Science and Tech, Paterson	51.3%
C/D	Woodrow Wilson M.S., Clifton	42.7%
C/D	Christopher Columbus M.S., Clifton	42%
A	Paterson Public School District-Wide Passing Percent	36.6%
A	Phillips Academy Charter School of Paterson	35.3%
A	Lincoln Middle School #4, Passaic City	26.7%

Passaic County Public Schools
PARCC 2016
Level 5 ("Exceeding Expectations")

The chart below records all Passaic County Public Schools, including charter schools, in descending order based on the percentage of each school's 8th-grade student achievement of Level 5 ("Exceeding Expectations") outcomes on PARCC 2016 English Language Arts.

DFG	School and Municipality	Percent of 8th-Grade Students Earning Level 5 ("Exceeding Expectations") on PARCC 2016 English Language Arts
D/E	Wanaque Elementary School, Wanaque Boro	51.1%
C/D	**Classical Academy Charter School of Clifton**	**48.6%**
G/H	Anthony Wayne M.S., Wayne	31.1%
G/H	Schuyler-Colfax M.S., Wayne	25.7%
G/H	George Washington M.S., Wayne	24.9%
F/G	Lakeside School, Pompton Lakes	23.1%
G/H	High Mountain M.S., North Haledon	22%
A	Passaic Gifted and Talented Academy School #2, Passaic City	21.9%
F/G	Walter T. Bergen M.S., Bloomingdale	19%
C/D	Washington Park School, Totowa Boro	15.3%
D/E	Haskell Elementary School, Wanaque Boro	12.2%
A	Learning Community Charter School, Paterson	12.1%
D/E	Memorial Middle School, Woodlawn Park Boro	10.7%
C/D	Woodrow Wilson Middle School, Clifton City	9.7%
A	John P. Holland Charter School, Paterson	9.5%
B	Haledon Public School, Haledon Boro	9.4%
B	Prospect Park School #1, Prospect Park Boro	9.4%
F/G	Macopin Middle School, West Milford Twp.	8.2%
F/G	Public School #1, Little Falls Twp.	8%
G/H	Martin J. Ryerson School, Ringwood Boro	7.6%
D/E	Lincoln Middle School, Hawthorne Boro	7%
A	Community Charter School of Paterson	6%
C/D	Christopher Columbus Middle School, Clifton	5.4%
A	Paterson Charter School for Sci./Tech.	5.1%
A	Paterson Public School District's Percentage of 8th Graders Earning Level 5 ("Exceeding Expectations")	4.7%
A	Lincoln Middle School #4, Passaic City	3.5%
A	Phillips Academy Charter School, Paterson	0%

Observations: The above two charts show that, out of 27 Passaic County public schools (traditional and charter), the Classical Academy Charter School of Clifton placed *second (2nd)* or *top 7%* in Passaic County in having the greatest percentage of its students *both* "Passing" and achieving Level 5 ("Exceeding Expectations") on PARCC 2016 in English Language Arts. Its 8th-graders outperformed (often by very large margins) 93% of all Passaic County public schools.

"J" District Factor Group Schools
The Classical Academy Charter School of Clifton
(a "C/D" District Factor Group School)

Comparison with the state's "J" District Factor Group schools.

Based on a number of socio-economic factors, the New Jersey Department of Education has long designated every public school and school district in the state with a letter indicating relative wealth and student socio-economic advantages. These District Factor Group (DFG) designations are: "J," "I," "G/H," "F/G," "D/E," "C/D," "B" and "A," with "A" schools in communities of the greatest levels of poverty, lowest household incomes, and other disadvantageous socio-economic factors. "J" schools, on the other hand, are New Jersey schools with the highest level of wealth and prosperity. "J" school communities contain the state's highest household incomes, most expensive homes, greatest levels of parent education, and a host of other socio-economic factors reflecting enviable affluence, factors which also provide children in these communities the privileges and material advantages their fellow students in less-wealthy communities do not possess.

The correlation between family wealth and educational achievement has long been a fact of American life and New Jersey public education; the higher the wealth, the greater the academic achievement. This unwavering correlation between wealth and academic achievement can be seen in the chart below, depicting each New Jersey's DFG's 8th-grade statewide "Passing" and Level 5 ("Exceeding Expectations") success in English Language Arts on the PARCC 2016. As we proceed from the top ("J") to the bottom ("A") socio-economic group, there is a palpable decline in student academic achievement at each step downward.

DFG Designation	Average 8th-Grade "Passing" Percentage in English Language Arts	Average 8th-Grade Level 5 ("Exceeding Expectations") Percentage in English Language Arts
"J"	82.7%	35.5%
"I"	72%	24.1%
"G/H"	65.4%	21.1%
"F/G"	58.9%	14%
"D/E"	49.9%	11.1%
"C/D"	47.6%	8.9%
"B"	42.8%	6.4%
"A"	35.4%	5.2%

As seen above, the lowest four DFG schools (from "D/E" to "A") do not succeed in educating to acceptable levels half their students, and the percentage of their students earning Level 5 ("Exceeding Expectations") on the PARCC 2016 is minuscule compared to the number of students in these schools. One could examine state educational-assessment data results since state-mandated standardized tests began many years ago, and one would find very similarly striking correlations between wealth and student academic achievement as that demonstrated in PARCC 2016 English Language Arts.

What does this steadfast relationship between wealth and student-learning outcomes say about public-education systems? About schools' inability to meet the challenge of educating to modestly acceptable standards the children of parents of modest or less means? What do these "etched-in-stone numbers" say about how schools are structured and operated? About the state spending massively as it fecklessly attempts to improve academic-learning outcomes in the lowest-performing schools and school districts? About the educational bureaucratic priority on compliance and process rather than outcomes and results? About the ills of school monopolies? About the lack of "educational choice"? About the "anti-academic school culture" dominating and prevailing in all our schools?

We often hear of the goal of "closing the achievement or learning gap." Charter schools are among those institutions for which this school mission is an everyday challenge. The most successful of New Jersey charter schools—and there are a number of them in urban or lower middle-class communities—have succeeded in this seemingly impossible task. The Classical Academy Charter School is one such charter school that has, year in and year out, succeeded remarkably in closing that intractable student achievement or learning gap between more-advantaged students and their less-advantaged peers. As a school whose student body is largely that of children of immigrant parents of very modest incomes and lower educational levels (on average, 25%-40% of Classical Academy students qualify for "Free/Reduced Breakfast and Lunch" programs), Classical Academy student-learning outcomes have been extolled, justifiably, as remarkable and exceedingly impressive. By its "C/D" District Factor Group rating, it would be expected barely to educate successfully only half, if not less than half, of its largely immigrant or minority student body to achieve even a low-passing-rate score in English and mathematics, and if it reached that 50% student-body "passing" percentage rate, it would be deemed a most successful school.

Let us see, therefore, where Classical Academy students, the majority of whom speak or hear a foreign language spoken at home, and many who are themselves bi-lingual, be their familial language Spanish, Arabic, Croatian, or some other ancestral language, rank with the enviable "J" school students in PARCC 2016 English Language Arts.

"J" Schools vs. Classical Academy:

"PASSING"

The following 15 "J" schools' and their performance data were selected completely at random from state-assessment results detailing 8th-grade PARCC 2016 English Language Arts. "Passing" is defined as percent of 8th-grade class earning either a Level 4 ("Meeting Expectations") or a Level 5 ("Exceeding Expectations") on PARCC 2016 English Language Arts. The following schools are listed in their descending order of "passing percentage" and "Level 5 percentage."

DFG	School and Municipality	Percent of 8th-Grade "Passing" English Language Arts
"J"	Cranbury School, Cranbury Twp.	94%
"J"	Woodcliff M.S., Woodcliff Lake Boro	91.3%
"J"	Briarcliff M.S., Mountain Lakes Boro	90.8%
"J"	Emil J. Cavallini M.S., Upper Saddle River	88.3%
"C/D"	**Classical Academy Charter School of Clifton**	**86.4%**
"J"	Chatham M.S., School District of the Chathams	84.2%
"J"	George Washington M.S., Ridgewood Village	85.3%
"J"	Millburn M.S., Millburn Twp.	82.7%
"J"	Glen Rock M.S., Glen Rock	82.6%
"J"	William Annin M.S., Bernards Twp.	82.4%
"J"	Haddonfield M.S., Haddonfield	82%
"J"	Mountainview School, Mendham Boro	76.5%
"J"	Black River M.S., Chester Twp.	76%
"J"	Montgomery Upper M.S., Montgomery Twp.	74.8%
"J"	Old Turnpike School, Tewksbury Twp.	74.1%
"J"	Harding Township M.S., Harding Twp.	72%

"J" Schools vs. Classical Academy
PARCC 2016, English Language Arts:
Level 5 ("Exceeding Expectations")

Percent of each school's 8th-graders earning a Level 5 ("Exceeding Expectations"): (The same 15 "J" schools cited in the chart above are listed below in descending order, by each school's 8th-grade Level 5 ("Exceeding Expectations") achievement.

DFG	School and Municipality	Percent of 8th-Grade Achieving Level 5 ("Exceeding Expectations") in English Language Arts
"J"	Briarcliff M.S., Mountain Lakes	57.1%
"J'	Woodcliff M.S., Woodcliff Lake	52.2%
"C/D"	**Classical Academy Charter School of Clifton**	**48.6%**
"J"	Cranbury School, Cranbury Twp.	48.5%
"J"	Emil J. Cavallini M.S., Upper Saddle River	44.5%
"J"	Glen Rock M.S., Glen Rock	38.3%
"J"	Millburn M.S., Millburn Twp.	35.7%
"J"	George Washington M.S., Ridgewood Village	29.5%
"J"	Mountainview School, Mendham Boro	29.4%
"J"	Old Turnpike School, Tewksbury Twp.	28.6%
"J"	Black River M.S., Chester Twp.	27.9%
"J"	William Annin M.S., Bernards Twp.	27.9%
"J"	Chatham M.S., School District of the Chathams	27.3%
"J"	Haddonfield M.S., Haddonfield	25.6%
"J"	Harding Township M.S., Harding Twp.	22.2%

Student "Mean Scale Score"
PARCC 2016, English Language Arts

"C/D"	Classical Academy Charter School of Clifton	790
"J"	State Average "J" Schools' "Mean Scale Score"	779

Observations: Digesting the information in the above three charts, I trust the reviewer will agree that the Classical Academy Charter School of Clifton has performed magnificently in "closing the achievement or learning gap," and has provided immigrant children and those from very modest backgrounds the robust and honed academic skills and knowledge to pursue, as their desires and ambitions dictate, a little piece of the American dream, and to seek, on equal academic grounds with their more-advantaged contemporaries, a productive, satisfying future.

PARCC 2016
"Algebra I"

The problem with comparing Classical Academy Charter School of Clifton "Algebra I" student outcomes with those of most other public schools on PARCC tests was discussed when detailing PARCC 2015 "Algebra I" outcomes in this Appendix A (see PARCC 2015 "Algebra I"). To briefly reiterate, the prevailing practice of "tracking" allows schools to inflate artificially their PARCC standardized-test "Algebra I" outcomes and renders Classical Academy "Algebra I" student-outcome comparisons unfairly distorted.

"Tracking" is the practice whereby, based on grades and test results, only the better or best mathematics students take "Algebra I" in the 8th grade, while the majority of poor to mediocre students take "8th-Grade Mathematics." "Tracking" occurs in other academic subjects as well, notably English and science, but unlike "Algebra I," "tracked" students must still take the same English Language Arts PARCC test.

Consistent with its 1997 charter and long practice, as described in the foregoing chapters, the Classical Academy, under my school leadership, never practiced "Tracking." During its three-year prescribed middle-school program of studies, all students take the same demanding academic courses, and all undergo the same high standards and expectations each course entails. So, too, all Classical Academy students, from the mathematically accomplished to the least-performing mathematics student, take the same high-level, demanding mathematics courses, including "Algebra I" in the 8th grade.

PARCC rules specify that any student in the 8th grade taking an "Algebra I" course must, therefore, take the PARCC "Algebra I" test, a test more difficult than its "8th Grade Mathematics" assessment. "Tracking," therefore, precludes weaker mathematics students from taking "Algebra I" in the 8th grade, which is reserved for only the school's most-elite and highest-performing mathematics students. Consequently, "tracking" funnels the majority (like Clifton Public Schools, where only 15% of the district's 8th-graders take "Algebra I") of a school's students into non-Algebraic 8th-grade mathematics courses. The Classical Academy is a unique non-"tracking" school which mandates that every one of its 8th-graders take the "Algebra I" course.

When comparing, therefore, non-tracking Classical Academy results in "Algebra I," the innate unfairness lies in comparing Classical Academy's 100% of 8th-graders taking "Algebra I" PARCC tests, with a small percentage of the best mathematics students in rival schools, even in charter schools.

The following chart on PARCC 2016 "Algebra I" school outcomes between the Classical Academy and Clifton Public Schools conspicuously shows the deceptiveness in student-learning outcomes "tracking" permits schools to practice (note in the following chart the small percentage of each Clifton's school's 8th-grade class taking the "Algebra I" PARCC assessment).

School	Percent of 8th-Graders "Passing"	Percent of 8th-Graders Earning Level 5 ("Exceeding Expectations")
W. Wilson Middle School (Only 18% of total 8th-grade class took the "Algebra I" test)	96.5%	15.8%
C. Columbus Middle School (Only 13% of total 8th-grade class took the "Algebra I" test)	91.3%	2.2%
Clifton Public School District's 8th-graders (Only 15% of the entire district's 8th-graders took the "Algebra I" test)	94.2%	9.7%
Classical Academy Charter School of Clifton (100% of 8th-graders took the "Algebra I" test)	89.1%	48.3%

Observations: Despite "tracking" and the disadvantage in outcome comparison it presents to non-tracking schools like the Classical Academy, notice, even with having only their best 15% of mathematics students take the "Algebra I" test, how much greater the Classical Academy performed over Clifton's public schools in educating nearly *half* of all its 8th-graders to attain the highest PARCC level of achievement, Level 5 ("Exceeding Expectations"). Even with employing a severe eligibility "tracking" program for students to take the "Algebra I" test, Clifton public schools could still not even come close to achieving Classical Academy levels of Level 5 ("Exceeding Expectations") achievement!

To reduce the artificial achievement inflation "tracking" creates regarding the "Algebra I" comparisons results with a non-tracking school and to rectify the false picture "tracking" paints of a school's recorded mathematics performance, I compare Classical Academy's PARCC 2016 "Algebra I" student outcomes with the "Algebra I" student outcomes of the entire Clifton Public School District. Students take the "Algebra I" course and the PARCC test in grades anywhere from 8th to 12th. It is, thus, meaningful to compare the quality of "Algebra I" instruction and outcomes for the entire Clifton Public School District with the Classical Academy's 8th-graders. This better reflects comparative outcomes and represents a truer "index" of overall student "Algebra I" instruction and attainment.

PARCC 2016
"Algebra I"
Comparing District-Wide Clifton School District's "Algebra I" Outcomes with Classical Academy 8th-Graders "Passing" and Level 5 ("Exceeding Expectations")

School	Percent of 8th-Graders "Passing"	Percent of 8th-Graders Earning Level 5 ("Exceeding Expectations")
Classical Academy Charter School of Clifton	89.1%	48.3

	Percent of Students in Entire Clifton School District "Passing" "Algebra I"	Percent of Students in Entire Clifton School District Earning a Level 5 ("Exceeding Expectations")
Clifton Public School District's "Algebra I" Achievement (Grades 8-12)	26.1%	1.3%

Observation: The chart above better captures the true comparative educational quality between Classical Academy 8th-graders and that of Clifton Public School District's "Algebra I" PARCC 2016 student attainment, or should I say, non-attainment!

"Tracking" is similar to playing a baseball game where one side fields only its best 9 players for the entire game, while its competitor, because of its own lofty principles and unique understanding of the game, allows all 30 members of its team, some of whom may limp, use crutches, or have severe vision impairment, play portions of the game. How would one assess the score of the game? Would one say the "game" or competition was fair?

Unfortunately, "tracking" also occurs in many charter schools. The list below represents the "Top Ten" performing New Jersey Charter Schools in the PARCC 2016 "Algebra I" assessment.

If only a portion of a charter school's 8th-graders took the PARCC "8th-Grade Mathematics" test, then "tracking" occurred in that school. From state data, one may calculate the relative percentages of each school's student body who took PARCC 2016 "Algebra I" or the "8th-Grade PARCC Mathematics" test.

The Top Ten Performing Charter Schools on the PARCC 2016 "Algebra I"

Charter School	Percent of 8th-Graders Passing "Algebra I"
1: Foundation Academy C.S. (Tracking: Only 39% of its 8th-grade students took "Algebra I" test)	100%
2: Princeton C.S. (No Tracking: 100% of its 8th-grade students took "Algebra I" test)	95.3%
3: Bergen Arts and Sciences C.S. (Tracking: Only 26% of its 8th-grade students took "Algebra I" test)	95%
4: Classical Academy Charter School of Clifton (No Tracking: 100% of its 8th-grade students took "Algebra I" test)	**89.1%**
5: Elysian Charter School of Hoboken (Tracking: Only 42% of its 8th-grade students took "Algebra I" test	88.9%
6: North Star Academy Charter School of Newark (No Tracking: 100% of its 8th-grade students took "Algebra I" test)	76.6%
7: Team Academy Charter School (Tracking: Only 39% of its 8th-grade students took "Algebra I" test)	64.1%
8: Red Bank Charter School (Tracking: Only 50% of its 8th-grade students took "Algebra I" test	63.6%
9: Benjamin Banneker Preparatory Charter School (Tracking: Only 30% of its 8th-grade students took "Algebra I" test)	62.5%
10: Central Jersey College Prep. Charter School (No Tracking: 100% of its 8th-grade students took "Algebra I" test)	62.1%

Observations: Of the top ten charter schools which earned the highest percentage of their 8th-grade class "Pass" "Algebra I" on the PARCC 2016, only four did not "track" students and required their entire 8th-grade class to take the PARCC 2016 "Algebra I" test. The Classical Academy is among those four.

PARCC 2016 "Algebra I"
Level 5 ("Exceeding Expectations")

Whether charter schools "tracked" students or not, no charter school, except the Classical Academy and Princeton, broke into double-digits in the percentage of their 8th-grade students achieving Level 5 ("Exceeding Expectations"), except one "tracking" charter school with 27.3% of its 8th-grade students earning Level 5.

The two highest-performing PARCC 2016 "Algebra I" Level 5 ("Exceeding Expectations") charter schools were the Classical Academy Charter and Princeton Charter schools.

School	Percent of 8th-Graders Earning Level 5 "Exceeding Expectations"
The Classical Academy Charter School of Clifton	48.3%
The Princeton Charter School	39.5%

Observations: On the PARCC 2016, the last standardized test Classical Academy students took under my school leadership, **Classical Academy earned the highest 8th-grade class percentage achieving "Algebra I" Level 5 ("Exceeding Expectations") of all New Jersey Charter School 8th-grade students!** The top two charter schools with the highest percentage of 8th-graders earning "Algebra I" Level 5 ("Exceeding Expectations"), the Classical Academy and the Princeton Charter School are both "non-tracking" schools, requiring 100% of their 8th-grade students to take the "Algebra I" PARCC test. Both schools greatly surpassed in Level 5 ("Exceeding Expectations") attainment all other charter schools, most of which allowed only their best mathematics students to take the "Algebra I" test!

Concluding My "Little School That Could" Narrative Memoir with a Final "Gloat"

All during my Classical Academy 18-year leadership, our 8th-grade standardized-test scores in English and Mathematics ("Algebra I" for the PARCC tests) were very often second or third, behind top-ranked Princeton Charter School—and occasionally *tied* with Princeton Charter School, rightly esteemed as one of the best charter schools in the nation. It is, therefore, rather satisfying to record that, *on PARCC 2016 "Algebra I" results, a greater percentage of Classical Academy 8th-graders earned "Algebra I" Level 5 ("Exceeding Expectations") outcomes than did Princeton Charter School.* This comparative result and high student-learning outcome surpassing New Jersey's top charter school are especially and personally gratifying because PARCC 2016 was the last standardized test our students undertook during my long, 18-year career as Classical Academy Founder and Lead Teacher/Principal. Pardon my gloating.

APPENDIX B

WILLIAM B. GOURLEY (1857–1935)
AN EMINENT AND WIDELY ADMIRED MAN, HIS BELOVED
DOLLYMOUNT ESTATE, AND A ROMANTIC LEGEND

The Man

For nearly 20 years of my professional and personal life in operating Passaic County's first public charter school, I spent every day in that pursuit in a building which for more than a century was known as the "Dollymount" mansion. I heard rumors and intriguing stories about William B. Gourley, the squire and original owner of "Dollymount," all of which seemed to connect me with him. This, not only because I spent so much of my professional life "in his home" (indeed, teaching 8th-grade Latin in the converted classroom which reportedly was his bedroom), but because of the reputed nature of the man himself: a lover of books; a scholar of the classics and ancient Greek and Roman literature; a man of culture; a man of sterling character, deep humanity, and high ideals, but also a man of action and considerable influence in politics, government, commerce, law, and community affairs.

The life of Mr. William B. Gourley (also known as Dr. Gourley by virtue of an honorific "Doctor of Laws" degree bestowed upon him in 1915 by Seton Hall College because of his noteworthy accomplishments in law and government, and for supporting religious causes) spanned that period in history from when the principal mode of transportation was horse and carriage, to when travel by automobile became commonplace;

the same time span in which Paterson, New Jersey, the city in which he most exercised his aspirations and talents, was well along its development into an industrial city of national significance.

Apart from the momentous external changes his long life witnessed, and through his own determined efforts and boundless energies, he built for himself a truly magnificent life of personal accomplishment and reputation which would be remarkable for any era. In addition to his professional and personal success, he gave of himself unwaveringly to worthy causes not only by mere financial contribution, but more admirably by his own attention, devotion, and personal involvement, and actively engaged in activities which enriched the lives of those in his community, and for the betterment of mankind.

From the brief life sketches in Mr. Auger's 1917 "Passaic County New Jersey Biographies"[of notable individuals] we read that Dr. Gourley's

> ... natural ability soon gave him rank among the best [lawyers] in Passaic County, and today there are no lawyers in New Jersey who are above him in ability and accomplishment. In 1885, he was elected to the [state] Assembly on the Democratic ticket. That same year he was appointed Prosecutor [for Paterson and Passaic County] by Governor Leon Abbett and was in office two terms. He has always maintained his leadership in the Democratic Party and today no one is oftener called in as counsel when anything is contemplated which requires the direction of a skilled man. His [law] practice is very large and is constantly growing. Few lawyers in the state have a larger one. His home ['Dollymount'] under the shadow of Garret Mountain is a beauty spot, and it is there that his friends love to visit him since they find him at his best. As a brilliant scholar, he is much sought for addresses which are always filled with scintillating wit and profound knowledge. His work will live long after him, for men like he leave their impression upon the communities in which they spend their lives.

His was the classic "rags to riches" American story. Born in Gilford, County Down, Ireland, in 1857, William B. Gourley immigrated to Paterson, New Jersey, at the age of 11 with his parents. He soon thereafter sought employment as a "bobbin boy" in the textile and silk mills for which that city had garnered international acclaim. At that early age he fell in love with books, taking advantage of several Paterson bookstores that offered at a very small cost a lending service. He would walk to nearby Garret Mountain and there look for one of the many spots of solitude for reading, and tranquility for dreaming. That love of books would grow and last a lifetime; he was said to be "a bibliophile of nation-wide fame" and of possessing one of the best privately owned libraries in America. Indeed, William B. Gourley possessed great pride in his collection of books, many of which were rare first editions which he amassed during his annual trips to European capitals. His favorites were the Irish and Scottish poets, especially Robert Burns, and the Latin and Greek classics. One gets the feeling that he built his fine Dollymount mansion, once described in a news article as "his literary treasure house on the slopes of Garret Mountain," primarily to house his beloved books and library in an elegant ambience befitting their noble character.

After acquiring a "common school" education both here and later in a return trip to Ireland, a formal education generally comparable, at least in years in school but not necessarily in diminished quality of a high-school education today, young William B. Gourley determined to become a lawyer, an ambition he early conceived as best fitting his intellect and aspirations, both of which his voracious reading progressively and keenly sharpened. As was common in his era, entrance to the legal profession entailed "reading the law" with a practicing lawyer for three to five years. Upon successful completion of this apprentice or mentoring preparation, not unlike a young lawyer's "clerkship" today, and after the requisite knowledge and skills were acquired to the satisfaction of the mentoring practitioner, the hopeful attorney stood to pass the state bar exam. Having been mentored by two notable Paterson attorneys, and having advanced successfully through this process, William B. Gourley became a licensed attorney in 1880, aged 23.

William B. Gourley spent his long 55-year legal, political, and governmental career primarily in Paterson, New Jersey, the same city which benefited from his dedicated civic and community involvement, but also as a highly respected resident of nearby Clifton, New Jersey. He was a founding organizer in the formation of the Passaic County Bar Association in 1889. Strengthening and representing the Democratic party in Passaic County, and occupying state elective office while undertaking leading roles in party functions—he was the state chairman of the Democratic committee for some years—were yet further professional life accomplishments. He administered justice and upheld safety for residents as his responsibilities as Passaic County Prosecutor for a decade. He organized the "Gourley Guards," a popular social and political club dedicated to supporting Democratic candidates for elective office, advancing Democratic Party ideals, and hosting social gatherings and festivities, often at the Paterson Great Falls. His private law practice flourished as his reputation quickly grew for integrity, intellect, and professional excellence. He was a corporation attorney for the Public Service Utility Corporation and Lackawanna Railroad, and was a member of the Board of Directors for several Paterson banks. All during the 1920s he served as Clifton's city attorney and was instrumental for achieving its municipal independence and incorporation as a city in 1917.

Combining such legal and commercial interests with cultural and intel-lectual pursuits was an especial gift of Dr. Gourley. He was a noted orator and lecturer, giving frequent "talks" and addresses to audiences on current events or the lives and writings of great authors. His erudite lectures on whatever topic were often given at fraternal and cultural organizations, and always incited rave reviews with his ability to enthrall and educate an audience. No one, judging from the newspaper reports at the time, ever left a "Dr. Gourley talk" disappointed or feeling that they in some way were not improved.

He devoted himself as well to religious causes and Roman Catholic charities and institutions, for Dr. Gourley was a devote practitioner and staunch supporter of that faith. He was a close friend of Bishop McNulty, the famed leader of Paterson's St. John's Cathedral Church, which, in the the decades following the Civil War, was built to serve the spiritual and social needs of the many Irish Catholic residents and other immigrants of Paterson and beyond. He was involved in the early establishing of St. Joseph's Hospital, today one of New Jersey's largest medical complexes, when it had only 10 beds for the sick. He advanced the interests of St. Anthony's Guild, a Catholic charitable organization whose mission was to help the needy and provide humanitarian betterment to Paterson's and the area's growing Catholic community. He helped start and long supported the "Friendly Sons of St. Patrick," and was selected to deliver a moving oration at the unveiling and dedication ceremonies for Gaetano Federici's "Boy at the Dublin Spring" statue in the Little Dublin section of Paterson in 1931. He unabashedly loved his ancestral homeland, his Irish heritage, and his Roman Catholic faith.

In 1930, to celebrate his distinguished 50-year career as a lawyer and civic and political leader, he, at the age of 73, was feted with a splendid testimonial dinner in the grand ballroom of the Alexander Hamilton Hotel in Paterson. To this event many of Paterson's and New Jersey's leaders of the Bar, industry, and government eagerly attended to pay tribute to this most excellent of men. One of the testimonial's speakers referred to Dr. Gourley as the universally recognized "Dean of the Passaic County Bar" and "an upright man in his public and private life, possessed of qualities such as make leaders of the Bar, a foremost citizen of a community, a leader of men and so inspiration to the young and an example of proper ambitions carried to a proper conclusion." The day after this event there appeared in *The Paterson Morning Call* newspaper (May 26, 1930), the following article titled "A Deserved Tribute":

> Fifty years in the harness as one of the leading members of the bar in the state, and still going strong. That is the record of Dr. William B. Gourley whose golden anniversary in the legal profession was celebrated with a testimonial dinner given the veteran barrister on Saturday night by leading members of his profession from this city and surrounding communities. The various speakers at the dinner dwelt on the ability of the honored guest in his chosen profession, on his splendid record not only as a lawyer but as a citizen; on his studiousness which has made him one of the most cultured men of the community and the state; on the fact

that he stood before the bar of the state and the nation as an example of what a member of his profession should be, a man without a blemish on his record after half a century of work in a profession which offered temptations which all too many found unable to resist. The tribute was one of which Dr. Gourley may well be proud and happy, but at the same time, it is one of which Paterson, also, may be proud in that it was offered to one of its leading citizens, and that it was deserved. Dr. Gourley's beginnings were humble. He was not a rich man's son whose way to a profession was made easy by a college education. He earned his living by the sweat of his brow in manual labor while through hours of study while others rested, he gained his knowledge of the law that eventually brought him admission to the Bar. Paterson is as proud of Dr. Gourley as a citizen, as one the members of his own profession are as of the fact that he is one of its finest exponents.

Five years after this tribute event, Dr. Gourley, in the summer of 1935, a month after allowing use of his palatial Dollymount estate as he so often did to the annual St. Agnes Altar Society's garden card party to raise funds for Catholic causes, an event to which 1,000 attended, embarked on one his many annual trips by ocean liner to Europe. The purpose of these trips, which he undertook regularly for the last forty years, was often to visit the places and homes of his favorite authors, to purchase books and other articles such as paintings and sculptures to adorn his beloved Dollymount home, and to educate himself in different cultures, national histories, and governmental systems. On this trip, which would be his last European excursion, he took ill while in London. The doctor at the Savoy Hotel, where he was residing, recommended that Dr. Gourley return home for rest and recuperation, which he did, boarding the *Normandie* ocean liner to New York. For the final time he made his way back to his beloved Dollymount, in which he lived continuously for 45 years. There he succumbed to his illness several months later at the age of 79 on October 19, 1935, amidst the beautiful and serene surroundings of his cherished estate, which reflected so much upon the man himself and his life's interests.

His passing was front-page news throughout the state. The headline of *The Paterson Morning Call* of October 21, 1935, simply read: "*Dr. William B. Gourley is Dead!*" It went on to say that his death was: " . . . a great shock to his friends here and in all parts of the state, for no lawyer in New Jersey was better known and more respected than Dr. William B. Gourley, statesman, lawyer, poet and lecturer, a man for whom there was always universal acclaim and whose opinion both in politics and law was looked upon as ever conclusive."

Perhaps one of the best descriptions of Dr. Gourley's life and the high esteem in which all others regarded him is reflected in his obituary appearing in *The Paterson Evening News* (October 21, 1935):

> His life's story was one which was filled with inspiration for those who battle against great odds and achieve outstanding success. There was every reason in the world why Dr. Gourley should not have been able to succeed. His boyhood was spent in poverty, but despite innumerable apparently insurmountable difficulties, he molded his success out of trying obstacles and disadvantages, surmounting them all by indomitable will power and the desire to do [i.e. to achieve]. . . . No man in the city's [Paterson] history was ever more deserving of the honors and encomiums . . . Success never spoiled his simplicity of heart nor warped his congenial and lovely soul. His mind was rapier like in its keenness and perception and he ranked high among New Jersey's best educated and best-read men. His library was the pride of his heart and his collection of rare volumes at Dollymount ranks with America's best. He was a natural leader and in the legal profession was recognized as among the country's most brilliant attorneys. Grief there will be at his passing but grief assuaged by beautiful memories of his exemplary and fine life.

His funeral was an affair of great sadness as outpourings of grief and encomiums of praise filled his Dollymount home in which his body reposed in a casket adorned with flowers, and to which mourners flocked to express sorrow and admiration. Those who paid homage to him as he lay in his casket in the library of his beloved Dollymount composed a long list of prominent figures in New Jersey: eminent attorneys, former state governors, serving elected officials, industrial leaders, city mayors, high Catholic church dignitaries, including the President of Seton Hall College. At his passing, Rutgers Alumni Club of Passaic County, and Democratic political societies issued public Resolutions attesting to the high qualities of the deceased scholar and public servant (Dr. Gourley served for many years on the Board of Trustees of Rutgers University).

As reported in *The Paterson Evening News* (October 21, 1935): "... government officials, neighbors and friends of long standing, wept unashamed and unrestrainedly [as] the body of Dr. William B. Gourley, dean of the Passaic County bar and a leading figure in state affairs for many years, was carried through his beloved library in beautiful Dollymount, his Clifton estate, on the way to his last resting place."

As his funeral cortege, escorted by police cars from Clifton and Paterson, departed Dollymount and proceeded to St. John's Cathedral Church, flags were lowered to half-staff, and spectators lined the short route to the church as men respectfully tipped their hats for the "Sage of Dollymount" while bells solemnly told that they and the world had lost a man of the highest qualities. The church was full with mourners as several thousand remained outside during the High Requiem Mass, at the conclusion of which Dr. Gourley's remains were interred in Holy Sepulcher Cemetery in Totowa, New Jersey.

His Beloved "Dollymount"

In addition to his cherished library, William B. Gourley's most treasured possession was his beloved home, "Dollymount." That it was on a sloping prominence of Garret Mountain was no happenstance, for from his boyhood these hundreds of acres of unspoiled nature comprising this mountainous area (originally named Weasel Mountain by the earliest Dutch settlers) helped form his character, and induced a love for the poetic serenity they afforded, and which were, with his books, an incubator to his dreams and ambitions. In fact, years later, Dr. Gourley was foremost in advocating that Garret Mountain become a public amenity for all to enjoy. We read in *The Paterson Morning Call* of July 3, 1929, that the principal dignitary at the July Fourth Ceremonies designating Garret Mountain Reservation the first county park in a system of planned Passaic County public parks was:

> Dr. William B. Gourley, noted orator, whose beautiful home, Dollymount, adjoins the Reservation on the south slope of the mountain, will be the [principal] speaker. . . Living in the shadow of the mountain, Dr. Gourley has roamed about the tract for many years enjoying its rough natural beauty and probably knows its every contour better than any other person.

The earliest reference in newspaper accounts to his living at Dollymount was 1902, in which was noted that "Lawyer William B. Gourley is recuperating from an illness at his Dollymount home." Here the name "Dollymount" first appears in conjunction with his affirmed residence in it. But an even earlier 1892 newspaper notice humorously states: "Prosecutor William B. Gourley is as brown as a berry from working on his farm on the Notch [Road]. What vacation the prosecutor takes he spends around his beautiful grounds." Those beautiful grounds indisputably are the Dollymount estate upon which its original owner, prosecutor William B. Gourley, resided, and which was on "Notch Road." The name "Notch Road" was changed to "Valley Road" in Clifton circa 1917. The original name signifies that the "Notch Road" led from the then-border of south Paterson to the "Great Notch" or natural opening in the Watchung Mountain Range (of which Garret Mountain is a part) between Paterson and present-day Montclair. The Notch Road traversed Clifton, as does Valley Road today, to the point where Route 46 now passes through the "Great Notch."

The evidence supports the conclusion that circa 1890, when he was about 33 years of age and serving as Passaic County Prosecutor, and as his private law practice was growing as was his prosperity, William B. Gourley purchased 12 acres of woodlands on the downward slope of Garret Mountain on the Notch Road (then in Paterson). It is probable that he purchased the land from silk industrialist Catholina Lambert, creator and owner of "Lambert's Castle," who at that time owned much acreage in that vicinity and to whose own estate the Dollymount property would be adjacent.

In 1917, when Clifton was incorporated as a municipality replacing its former governmental association with Aquackanonk Township (a political and legal process in which William B. Gourley was significantly involved), and due to a slight change in boundary between Paterson and Clifton, William B. Gourley's home and property would thereafter be in Clifton, and, as said above, the name of the road upon which his Dollymount home faced was renamed "Valley Road."

In his obituary in *The Paterson Morning Call* of October 21, 1935, the writer reported that: "Mr. Gourley loved the country and that is the reason he built the cozy home at the edge of Garret Mountain on the Valley Road, which is one of the beauty spots of Passaic County. To get away from the noise and din of a busy city, his haven of rest a short distance from the center of the town [Paterson] was one of the delights of the hard-working lawyer."

The features of his Dollymount estate became over time more elaborate and impressively grand such that no one could except at its earliest beginnings describe it as a "farm." The imposing main house with its bold front Greek columns supporting a pediment and expansive portico, redolent of classical architecture, certainly was due to Dr. Gourley's wishes that his home bespeak the grandeur of the classical age, of which he was a lover. (The picture of the Dollymount mansion is on the front cover of this book, and from 1998 to 2018 the home to the Classical Academy Charter School of Clifton, Passaic County's first public charter school; the picture was taken in 2013).

Unlike many wealthy individuals of our age, who see their grand homes as sources of profit or envy, and flit from one abode to another, possessing no emotional investment in the property save to wallow briefly in its ostentatious luxury, Dr. Gourley's Dollymount was an inseparable part of his very being, a lifelong encapsulation of and testimony to the fine qualities of the man himself, of his love of beauty, nature, and tranquil surroundings. A year after Dr. Gourley's passing, a friend from his youth wrote in *The Paterson Morning Call* (May 4, 1936) that "his Dollymount will ever be a monument to his taste."

Assessments of Dr. Gourley's Dollymount estate are unanimous in their descriptions as it being "a beauty spot," as one of the "showcases of Passaic County," and "one of the most beautiful plots of ground in northern New Jersey." We know that upon those 12 acres during Dr. Gourley's 45-year habitation would be erected not only the elegant main residence, but also a gatekeeper's cottage (where the person or family employed by Dr. Gourley in assisting him in the property's upkeep and development would reside), a carriage house with living quarters above, a summer house, a teahouse, and a barn. Formal gardens, colorful flowers and bushes, grape arbors, and selected shade trees, some of which are now well over a century in age and constitute some of the oldest living trees in Clifton, adorned the property. Around the summer house there were Italian marble busts of Plato, Demosthenes, and Socrates as well as stone benches throughout the property upon which to relax after strolling its paradise-like grounds so pleasing to the eye as they were edifying to the soul. There was too an orchard of 110 trees bearing fruits of different sorts, and a small herd of 6 Guernsey cows, the milk of which Dr. Gourley donated to nearby hospitals.

The interior of the home was just as elegant as the grounds: walls covered with ornate brocades and gold-leaf embellishments, chestnut and oak wood moldings and paneling throughout the home, large oak sliding doors, interior columns, elegant furnishings, marble and mosaic-tiled fireplaces with striking mantles, many large, expertly-crafted stained-glass windows producing an interior light of wondrous effect, and, of course, his large, richly-appointed library which occupied nearly one-half of the home's first floor. Oriental rugs, antique sculptures, and noteworthy paintings, many of which Dr. Gourley acquired on his annual European trips, also decorated the main residence.

William B. Gourley never married and never produced children. He had two sisters, Katherine Gourley, herself never wed and lived with her younger brother, William B. Gourley, at Dollymount, predeceasing him by many years. Another sister did marry a Mr. Boyle and had three children, William Boyle, Harry Boyle, and a daughter, Mary Clare. These two nephews and one niece were the principal "residuary legatees" of Dr. Gourley's estate, each having an equal share. According to his will, he left generous bequeathals to religious institutions like St. Joseph Hospital, St. Agnes Church, and St. Anthony's Guild in Paterson, but also to relatives and several churches for repair, improvement, and adornment in his ancestral county in Ireland. He also bequeathed a respectable sum to each of his four employees at Dollymount: a secretary, gardener and grounds-keeper, housekeeper, and chauffeur.

Five months after his death, his estate executors held a two-day auction at the Dollymount to sell objects from his home. Oriental rugs, china, oil paintings, furnishings, objects of art, silverware and table settings, many of which were purchased in Europe, represented the bulk of his domestic possessions which his discerning taste had accumulated over the years. Dr. Gourley's famed library, however, was not included for auction or sale. In fact several years before his death, he expressed in a letter to Paterson officials that he would like to donate his library to some institution in Paterson, but insisted that the books be kept together in one place and not be sold collectively or individually, or made available for lending, as many were irreplaceable. The ultimate fate of Dr. Gourley's library I have been unable to discover.

Dr. Gourley's estate, including the Dollymount property and the monetary worth of investments and other liquid assets, was appraised in 1937 as $500,000. In today's terms it would equate to a sum of about $10 million. Some discord among the three primary legatees arose regarding the disposition of the estate; in the end each received about $100,000.

In 1937 his heirs put up for auction with a minimum price of $40,000 Dr. Gourley's Dollymount estate, acreage and buildings. Because of the severely depressed economic conditions at the time, even that astonishing low price incited no buyers to come forward or bid on the property. Dr. Gourley's nephew William Boyle then stepped forward and bought the entire Dollymount estate at auction for $25,000, presumably buying out the interest of his two siblings.

William Boyle and his family lived at Dollymount from 1937 to 1944. In 1944, at a price of $32,000, he sold the entire estate, save the gatehouse and about an acre and a half of land, to Samuel Spinosa of Totowa, New Jersey. Samuel Spinosa in turn sold the Dollymount mansion for an undisclosed sum two years later in 1946 to his brother, Charles Spinosa. Interestingly, for the next several years, from 1944 to about 1951, all three families resided on Dollymount property: William Boyle and family lived in the gatehouse; Samuel Spinosa, who held title to the remaining 10 acres of Dollymount land, and his family occupied the apartments atop the garage/carriage house; and Charles Spinosa and family resided in the main Dollymount home.

In 1947 the Spinosa brothers, who were active in real estate, presented to Clifton Building Department initial plans for a 30-home development on the Dollymount property they called "Dollymount Gardens." Some months later they announced that because of the unexpected high costs of providing the proposed housing tract with sewers and water lines, they canceled their development plans for "Dollymount Gardens." However, it is likely that, due to the rapid building boom of post-World War II and the need for providing homes for returning soldiers and their young families, the Spinosa brothers began to divide the Dollymount estate's remaining 10 acres into building lots to be sold to other developers or parties interested in constructing the homes themselves. For the next decade or longer, homes were built on Dr. Gourley's beloved estate, some on Valley Road, but most on both sides of Thomas Street, which almost certainly was originally a dirt path traversing the Dollymount estate from one end to the other, and existed from the very beginning of the estate itself.

In 1955, Nurse Sylvia Noll Bolster purchased Dollymount from Charles Spinosa to start the Dollymount Nursing Home (incorporated in 1956) in Dr. Gourley's former mansion. The Bolster family operated the Dollymount Nursing Home until 1998, a total of 43 years, nearly as long as William B. Gourley himself resided in the home. In establishing the Classical Academy Charter School of Clifton, I and our Board of Trustees leased the soon-to-close Dollymount Nursing Home facility from the Bolster family in 1998, and upon the expiration of the initial four-year lease, the school purchased the facility from them in 2002.

From 1998 to 2018, the Dollymount mansion was home to the Classical Academy. During that period the Classical Academy distinguished itself with many awards for excellence, being designated as only the second New Jersey public charter school to earn the "National Blue-Ribbon School of Excellence" award in 2008. The saga of how I came upon the Dollymount and its hard-won acquisition for the Classical Academy, Passaic County's first public charter school, is fully narrated in Chapters III and IV of this work. Considering the Classical Academy's traditional classical curriculum of Latin and classical literature required for every student, and its record of high student-learning excellence, I feel that Dr. Gourley's spirit happily approved of the use to which I employed his beloved Dollymount. In 2018, two years after my retirement, the school's new leadership decided to sell the Dollymount facility, which it owned fully and mortgage free, for about $1,200,000, and to lease the facilities of a defunct Clifton Catholic school.

It is with heartfelt regret, and a despicable dishonor to the memory of Dr. Gourley that I must report the Dollymount building, once renowned for its beauty and charm, features which it retained during its function both as a nursing home and a public school for a combined total of 62 years, is currently in an advance state of dilapidation and decay. It has been vacant of occupancy for five years, subject to vermin, vandals, and fires. The current owners, who I believe to be a real estate "holding" company of some sort, have done nothing to rehabilitate it.

As of this writing (summer 2022), a visit to Dollymount premises will leave one shocked and disgusted. All windows are covered with plyboard, there are piles of broken concrete and asphalt strewn about, as are other disused items; an abandoned, tireless pickup truck and a large bucket-loader machine occupy the rear property; its circular driveway is marked by large potholes; the acre-and-a-half property is egregiously unkempt. It bears all the signs that whoever now owns Dollymount is planning its demolition. A sorrowful and indeed lamentable end to this most magnificent of buildings, once the beloved home to a truly remarkable and eminent man, and one of the most illustrious individuals ever to have resided in Clifton, New Jersey. I beseech Clifton municipal authorities to take some action to save and restore this irreplaceable and historic 132-year old Clifton treasure before it is too late to do so.

A Romantic Legend

Why did William B. Gourley select the name "Dollymount" for his cherished estate? The suffix "mount" is obvious because of its elevated topographical feature, but what or who was "Dolly"? In the many newspaper accounts of Dr. Gourley and his Dollymount residence, no clue is provided as to the origin of the name. Could it be named for a beloved family member or ancestor? Perhaps. Perhaps the name "Dollymount" appears in a literary work of an author whom Dr. Gourley esteemed, thus accounting for the name's origin. Then again around Dublin, Ireland, the name "Dollymount" appears as a well-known resort on the north coast of Dublin Bay. In that same area, there is a popular Dollymount horse racetrack and even a Dollymount golf club. That Dr. Gourley's Dollymount is certainly not on or close to the sea, and there is nothing in his life with which I have become familiar to suggest an interest in golf or horses, I deem these as inspirational sources for naming his estate implausible.

This brings us to an evaluation of the long-circulating legend or rumor that William B. Gourley in his youth fell in love with a young girl in Ireland, a girl named Dolly whom he intended to marry after she immigrated to America, as the deeply-in-love young couple joyously planned. Tragically, she died in Ireland before she could join the young man she loved and who had returned to America. William grieved, the legend says, for a lifetime his lost love, never marrying, but ever steadfast and loyal to her memory which he preserved in naming his beloved residence in her honor, "Dollymount."

There are three considerations which may lend some credence to the romantic legend of a lost love. First, William's return trip to his family home in Ireland. We know from the historic record that after arriving in America at age 11, William B. Gourley returned to Ireland as he became a young teenager. The duration of his stay is uncertain, but he enrolled in school, supporting the assumption he remained for several years, perhaps as many as five years, before returning to Paterson and soon commencing his "reading the law" apprenticeship. A year after Dr. Gourley's death, William H. Belcher, writing in the "Looking Backwards in Paterson" section of *The Paterson Morning Call* (May 4, 1936), penned an article titled *"Some Reflections of Dr. William B. Gourley,"* in which the following statement is included:

> A little later young Gourley went back to Ireland and remained there quite a long time, going to a fine school presided over by the proverbial Irish schoolmaster. He told me once that though he was denied a college education, he considered this time with vacation and study together the crucial and determinative part of his life.

Could or did this "crucial and determinative part of his life" also include the experiences of a first love, which for many is the most intense and unforgettable of all romantic passions, and emotionally quite indelible even for a lifetime?

The second consideration is the stained-glass window depicting as its central focus the face of a young golden-haired girl. Of the many stained-glass windows William B. Gourley commissioned and had installed in Dollymount, all were, as reported, of classical mythology themes, medieval Europe scenes, religious imagery, or scenes from the works of some of his favorite authors. None, I believe, depicted an image of any contemporary person. This unique stained-glass window was one of the very few that still remained at Dollymount when I and the Classical Academy Charter School occupied the building, so I remember it well. Before the school purchased the Dollymount building, the owners requested that this large stained-glass window be removed and returned to their custody, to which, of course, I agreed. But during the four years while it was in the school, we always referred to the girl depicted, who became strikingly and gorgeously illuminated when the sun shone through the window, as Dolly. This stained-glass window was in what I believe to be Dollymount's main dining room, a deliberate location conceivably so William could gaze upon her beauty and his lost love daily while dining, and in this metaphorical or mystical way, they were always together.

The third consideration was the nature of the man himself. William B. Gourley was a man of profoundly deep sensitivities and "indomitable willpower." He filled his meaningful life with high intellectual pursuits, with the greatest literature ever written, with travel, government and politics, career and professional excellence, good works and noble deeds, all earning the highest estimation from his contemporaries and fellow men; and he enveloped himself within the beauty of his home and large, lovely landscaped property, his "Dolly(mount)."

Did William B. Gourley never marry in order to be faithful to a vow made both to himself and to his lost love's immortal soul, a vow of his eternal love for his Dolly? We may never know with certitude. But unless some contrary documentary evidence which eluded me is produced, or if a William B. Gourley descendant comes forward to offer a different and more convincing explanation for the name "Dollymount," I choose to believe the romantic legend of William B. Gourley's lost love. A love to whom he demonstrated a lifelong fidelity and dedication, a love he made manifest in the name and in the beauty of his Dollymount estate. If indeed a lifelong undying commitment to an unconsummated romantic love is the true source of the name "Dollymount," then it is yet just one more attribute of this truly outstanding man for us to admire.